Your affectionate friend,

J. K. Popham.

VALIANT FOR TRUTH

Memoir and Letters
of
J. K. Popham

by

J. H. GOSDEN

with
Introductory Essay
by J. R. Broome

Gospel Standard Trust Publications

1990

7 Brackendale Grove,
Harpenden,
Herts. AL5 3EL
England

© Gospel Standard Trust 1990
ISBN 0 903556 88 X

Typeset by: Palm Print Services Ltd.

Printed by: Redwood Press Limited,
Melksham, Wiltshire

FOREWORD

It is a cause of real pleasure to us that the life of J. K. Popham is being re-published. In many ways he was a remarkable man, not least in the success God gave to his Christ exalting ministry - and this during the long period of over half a century.

Mr. John Broome, in his introductory essay, has shown that reading Mr. Popham's life is not just an academic exercise. It has a vital relevance to things today.

We hope that young people will find the book profitable and helpful and that those, young and old, to whom he is only a name may realise how vital were the things he stood for. "Valiant for Truth" summarises J. K. Popham's life and witness.

B. A. Ramsbottom
Editor,
"The Gospel Standard"

July, 1990

PREFACE

I have been entreated by my dear friend, John Broome, to provide a Preface to this account of the life of my late pastor, Mr. J. K. Popham, and he will not let me say "Nay". I feel I have no qualifications whatever, except that I am, undeniably, the sole remaining deacon in office at "Galeed", Brighton, prior to his death, and further, almost the last of his congregation as it then existed.

That he was revered, loved and feared, by us all, is certainly true, in varying degrees perhaps according to individual ages, but there was about him that nobility of presence which true grace always confers upon a human being, which commands respect, and can never be imitated.

Mr. Popham was very much a Victorian, and believed in class distinctions, and possibly at times found it difficult to unbend. Consequently, he would be quite out of touch with the present trend, and the concept of "the age of the common man" would have been quite abhorrent to him. This could explain past and present misunderstandings. Like all born in the past century, we accepted this attitude without offence. Today, it could arouse much resentment. However, he was a man made truly great by God. His work and memory is still appreciated, and honoured by all touched by the sacred Flame.

H. P. Banfield
Deacon
"Galeed", Brighton

July 1990

INTRODUCTORY ESSAY
by
J. R. Broome

INTRODUCTORY ESSAY

This reprint of the life of J.K. Popham, written by 'his own son in the faith,' J.H. Gosden is not an exercise in reviving an interest in the past history of the Gospel Standard Denomination. It has a deeper import than that. Writing in 1928 at the age of 81, Mr. Popham said, "The Lord is good, but the ministry among us is in a serious condition; my own is. The text, 'And the glory of the Lord went up from the midst of the city and stood upon the mountain which is on the east side of the city' (Ezekiel 11.23), is a solemn word, and to me it appears to be now having a fulfilment with respect to our denomination and the people of God in the land."

What would he have felt 62 years later in 1990, if he could have been spared to view the present scene. But the present scene, he saw coming. He was not without an understanding of its cause. In the same letter he wrote, "Is this state of things Fatherly chastisement, or for some evil thing among us? This is one of my burdens. My own case is far from satisfactory. The text, 'They shall bring forth fruit in old age,' is to me a solemnly trying word as I view my barrenness. John 15 tells me how I can be fruitful, but the union and the abiding in Christ are the vital points. I desire a living not a mechanical union to the true Vine."

This reprint therefore has a purpose as it speaks in the words of Scripture recalling the past manifestations of the Lord in our midst, "Remember therefore *from whence* thou art fallen." (Rev.2.5). None can read the life of this man of God, and stalwart defender of the truth, without being made solemnly aware of the glory that has departed (1 Sam.4.22), and the divine judgment hanging over us. "Repent and do the first works; or else I will come unto thee quickly, and will remove thy candlestick out of his place, except thou repent." (Rev.2.5)

For 67 years from 1870 - 1937 the voice and pen of J.K. Popham were powerful in our denomination, and, "He being dead *yet* speaketh." (Heb.11.4). He was sent of God, brought in from outside, always looking to "the Rock from whence he was hewn," (Isa.51.1), to be a leader in difficult times of solemn declension, vital separation and bitter controversy. He combined the gracious qualities of John Bunyan's two characters, Mr. Valiant-for-Truth and Mr. Standfast, and when he came to his end (17th June 1937) could say with Mr.

Standfast, "I see myself now at the end of my journey, my toilsome days are ended. I am now going to see that Head that was crowned with thorns, and that Face that was spit upon, for me." The weapons of his warfare were excellent. "Great-Heart to Mr. Valiant-for-Truth, 'Let me see thy sword;' so he showed it to him. When he had taken it in his hand and looked thereon for a while, he said, 'Ha! it is a right Jerusalem blade.' (Isa.2.3)." The Lord's servant had "a right Jerusalem blade," in his ministry and writings and he used it lovingly and affectionately in the defence of the Truth and the preaching of the Gospel. Writing in 1934 he said, "Occasionally Solomon's bed is before me and the duty of the men around it, and their swords. Woe is me that I am not valiant." (Song of Sol. 3.7,8). In that same year he wrote regarding the denomination, "The absence of God from us is but little felt, or if and where felt, not much confessed. We as a poor body much need His gracious return. It may be His will to give me rest before *the crisis comes, which I believe is coming.*"

The Centenary Meetings of the *Gospel Standard* Magazine held in London in August 1935 raised his hopes "that the remnant might yet be revived, and some of the younger people see the Lord's returning glory, as we who are near the end of our pilgrimage may not see. Oh it will be wonderful to see the power and glory of God among us. The degeneration which I see is most painful; our young people do not know it. What changes I have witnessed! What divine goodness I have been the recipient of." Regarding his own church, Galeed, Brighton over which he was Pastor for 55 years (1882 - 1937), he wrote towards the end of his life, "Galeed is not today what it was some years ago, and I am very troubled about it." Commenting on Mr. Popham's end, Mr. J.H. Gosden said, "He left the ship of the Church not in a storm, but in a treacherous calm."

Today his warnings sound out across the years with a prophetic ring. Preaching at Galeed in 1915 he said, "We are in a day of great charity, as we talk, of universal love, when that long exploded but revived and persistent error of putting sincerity in the place of truth, is thought much of. If a man be but sincere in anything he professes, then he is right: that is the charity of the day. But the Word of God is strict. 'I am the Way.' If you are right you will have to bear the shame of the cross.... If you are going to heaven you must leave Egypt. If the Lord unchurches churches, as *I believe He will many,* can any poor children of His escape that judgment? Yes. How can they be accounted worthy? Only in one way in the Person, blood and righteousness of Jesus Christ. Pray, that God may account us worthy to escape the judgment that is coming on Zion generally. When the most fine gold shall be quite dim (Lam.4.1,2), when the outward bulwarks in divine doctrine shall be disregarded, pray that we may escape that judgment."

Seventy-five years have passed since that sermon was preached in 1915, two World Wars have been fought and we now live in the Nuclear Age. Gospel Standard Churches have been unchurched throughout the country and "the outward bulwarks in divine doctrine are being disregarded." Universal charity of which he spoke is prevalent in the nation. Every effort is made to smooth over differences and blend truth and error. But our great leaders William Gadsby, J.C. Philpot, J.K. Popham and others stood firm for separation, and as Valiant-for-Truth, wielded "a right Jerusalem blade."

This biography reveals James Kidwell Popham in 1875 (at the early age of 28) taking up his pen to resist error. The error was Arminianism, the Free-Will of the Sankey and Moody campaign, which had come in its tour of Britain to Liverpool, where he was at that time Pastor of the Strict Baptist chapel. In his own Arminian days as a Congregationalist he had raised his hand against God and in bitter enmity exclaimed regarding Election, "If the God you speak of is the God of Heaven, I neither want to know Him nor to be where He is." He says of this, "I have many scars on my heart, but the largest and deepest is that which the above terrible speech made; it was the expression of the unbridled passion of my alienated nature." Under deep conviction for this sin, the Lord blessed him with the word, "All manner of sin and blasphemy shall be forgiven unto men," (Matt.12.31) and followed it with the words, "Go and pray." J.K. Popham says, "I prayed, I know I did." Later under the ministry of Mr. de Fraine, the Pastor of the Strict Baptist chapel at Lutterworth, Free Grace was powerfully opened up to his soul in a sermon preached at Nottingham from Romans 5.2. He was baptised by Mr. de Fraine on 5th July 1868 and received into the Lutterworth Strict Baptist Church, and shortly afterwards was blessed with the full and complete pardon of all his sins through the application of the words, "Forasmuch as ye know that ye were not redeemed with corruptible things as silver and gold...., but with the precious blood of Christ, as of a lamb without blemish and

xiii

without spot." (1 Peter 1.18,19). "Thus," he says, "I learned the doctrines of grace; for they were, as I afterwards found, implicit in my experience."[1] This divine teaching armed the Lord's servant, to pen his first tract, entitled, *Moody and Sankey's Errors versus the Scriptures of Truth*. J.H. Gosden says of him as a controversialist, "He was no trifler, no unprincipled combatant, no mere rancourous faultfinder, no idle, carping critic, but was moved with a jealousy for the honour of God and with the highest of purpose to defend His truth."[2] This first pamphlet ran through thirteen editions including one in Dutch. It brought him many friends, some in Holland, who felt his analysis of the ministry of these "evangelists" was correct.

He quotes D.L. Moody as saying to his congregations "Christ has purchased them, if only they will give themselves to Him; He put away their sins nearly 2000 years ago, but they may yet die in them through unbelief."[3] In his pamphlet he exposed the errors of Universal Redemption and Free-Will and says, "Every religious movement must be judged more by its doctrines than by what we usually see paraded - results."[4] He asked, "Where in all Mr. Moody's preaching do we find any of the doctrine of eternal election?" He had with him in this contest an ally, Dr. John Kennedy (1819 - 1884) of Dingwall, a Scots minister, author of *The Days of the Fathers in Ross-shire*, who wrote a powerful pamphlet entitled *Hyper-Evangelism*, condemning Moody's practice and teaching. Deeply revealing and of significance however was the attitude of C.H. Spurgeon. I.H. Murray in his paperback *The Forgotten Spurgeon* (B.O.T. 1966) says, "It is impossible for us to agree with Spurgeon in putting Moody down on the Calvinistic side."[5]

C.H. Spurgeon proceeded in his "lack of serious concern about incipient doctrinal defects"[6] to preach on behalf of D.L. Moody and invite him to preach at the Metropolitan Tabernacle.[7] When J.K. Popham and Dr. Kennedy wrote against Moody and Sankey in 1875, C.H. Spurgeon leapt to their defence and said, "We are happy to have our friends here in London because somehow or other they manage to get the popular ear. Our brethren have got a grip of the masses, and they preach the Gospel."[8] What Gospel did they preach? And where did Spurgeon stand? In his pamphlet J.K. Popham wrote, "One of the sad features of this movement is that it is approved and followed by so many ministers. Where is the deep experimental religion of our Puritan Fathers and ministers.... to permit to pass unchallenged and with impunity such gigantic errors which strike at the glory of God and the root of true religion.... It is almost amusing to see how very quietly these 'Reverend' gentlemen sit at the feet of this great Revivalist to be lectured.... and yet there is a more serious view to be taken of the matter. Does not their support of Moody and Sankey stamp their characters? Does it not prove that, with respect to them, 'Truth is fallen in the street?'" "Fundamental errors," said J.K. Popham, "preached and sung, cannot produce a true christian." For his pains J.K. Popham was called an "unregenerate blasphemer" and was equally labelled a Hyper-Calvinist, as he had been long before.

Describing Moody & Sankey and their followers he wrote, "By the galvanizing apparatus these men are using, they succeed in evoking 'mere emotion,' and this is called conversion and these galvanized, but dead souls, are then called Christians. Oh horrible profanity! A shocking caricature of a true Christian of God's living army." (Ezekiel 37.10) What a vast gulf existed between J.K. Popham and C.H. Spurgeon in their view of the Moody and Sankey revival! Who was true to the Scriptures of Truth? J.K. Popham and Dr. John Kennedy were the ones who had "a right Jerusalem blade" and were the victors in this contest with error. Mr. Popham's and Dr. Kennedy's writings on the Sankey and Moody revival are reviewed in the *Gospel Standard* for 1875, pages 211 - 223, where some of the worst excesses of D. L. Moody are quoted such as, "It is just as easy to lay hold of Christ for salvation as it is to put the hand to the pocket to see that one's watch is safe." Mr. Popham proceeded in the same year to approach this error with a positive declaration of the doctrines of grace, publishing the substance of two sermons preached to his own people at Liverpool under the title *Imperishable Grace.*[9] This work is included in the present volume.

In 1878 Mr. Popham published a small work, *Thoughts on Regeneration.* Of it he wrote, "I have been induced to publish the following for two reasons. First because regeneration is the root of all true religion - natural religion with all its attractions, erroneous preaching with all its eloquence, with all its power, can never give life to a dead soul. My second reason, is that among the blind followers, of perhaps, still more blind leaders, there may be some of the 'blind people who have eyes.' (Isa.43.8).... To them I would be useful." It is clear in this work that he was still answering the errors of the Sankey and Moody Revival and counteracting its effects, by demonstrating exactly what it was to be "born again of the Spirit," thus exposing the dangerous easy-believism of the Revival.

Writing first of the *necessity* of regeneration, he says, "It is first of all to be found in the Eternal God. It is necessary because God willed it.... The new birth is necessary because God has decreed it." Of the *cause* of regeneration he writes, "The Father's kindness and love are the eternal moving cause, the person of Christ the meritorious cause, the Spirit the immediate all-powerful cause." Speaking of the *nature* of regeneration he says, "It is a mighty change; a passing from death to life, from darkness to light.... In this work God is found of them that sought Him not.... It is not the repairing of old nature, but the creation of the hidden man of the heart." Speaking of Free-Will teaching he says, "They say that the Holy Ghost will save them, if they will allow Him. Imagine a grain of sand saying to the hurricane that lashed the sea into foam and uprooted trees, I have permitted you to turn me over." J.K. Popham was a firm believer in the doctrine of the effectual call. Writing of the *evidences* of regeneration he speaks of its fruits in faith, in the knowledge of God, His Holiness and His Law, living desires, prevailing prayer, love to the Lord, His Truth and His people, a knowledge of forgiveness and a good hope through grace. Somewhat different was this from the Sankey and Moody Revival Free-Will teaching which centred regeneration around a decision for Christ, whilst stating that nothing of a spiritual nature was necessarily felt at the time of the decision. Dr. Kennedy of Dingwall quoted Moody as saying, "Why raise up your sins again to think of and to confess them, for were they not disposed of nearly 2000 years ago? Just believe this and go home and sing and dance." Dr. Kennedy commented, "No man can say that Jesus is the Lord but by the Holy Ghost." (1 Cor.12.3)

In 1886 in a pamphlet entitled *Divine Sovereignty*, J.K. Popham wrote on the subject of the relationship between divine sovereignty and man's responsibility. It is a subject which stands as a dividing line today between Gospel Standard Churches and modern Reformed Baptists and Presbyterian Churches which have developed in this country in the last 20 to 30 years. J.K. Popham took a position identical to William Gadsby and J.C. Philpot. He maintained from Scripture that it was every man's duty according to the Law written in our hearts, "to reverence the Divine Majesty with an implicit belief and perfect doing of whatever He has revealed to be believed and to be done. (i) Has He revealed the invisible things of Himself in creation? It is our duty to believe and embrace that revelation and glorify Him with thankfulness. (Romans 1.20,21). (ii) The written record of God in the Bible has left man with a solemn responsibility as to how he handles or neglects it. Do we hate instruction and cast His words behind us? (Ps.50.16,17). We are responsible. (iii) And when He brings His First Begotten into the world it is the highest wickedness to mock and despise Him. It is equal wickedness not to reverence, worship and honour the Son. (Matt.12.31)."[10] But as J.K. Popham says, "This honouring of Christ as God is quite apart from, does not involve, a saving knowledge of Him."[11] "In this outward honouring of Him all are responsible wherever the Gospel has been preached. (Matt.11.21-24, John 15.22,23). Here in accepting the divine revelation in creation, the written word and the divine revelation of the eternal Son of God is our duty and our responsibility, and our breach of duty renders our punishment necessary. But whether that punishment be inflicted on the guilty person himself or on a Surety provided for him by God, this depends upon divine sovereignty."[12]

He denied the enigma as enunciated by L. Berkhof, "If it be objected that we cannot fully harmonise the indiscriminate and sincere offers of salvation on condition of faith and repentance with the doctrine of particular atonement, *this may be admitted,* with the distinct understanding that the truth of a doctrine does not depend on our ability to harmonise it with every other doctrine of Scripture."[13] J.K. Popham wrote, "It has been said that divine sovereignty merges with man's responsibility in some way; whereas the truth is that the latter is determined by the former which stands infinitely above it and alone. God's sovereignty and man's responsibility are two different subjects dwelling in beings infinitely separate.... Sovereignty is an essential attribute in God, responsibility in man grows out of an obligation imposed on him by God. If one should be found who thinks that these two may be merged into one it may be permitted me to remind him of the Lord's silencing address to Job...." (Job 38.4-12; 42.5-6).[14]

J.K. Popham did not accept that the Lord had laid on all fallen men and women a duty savingly to believe in Him. He did not accept that ministers could sincerely offer salvation to all men and women, while knowing that Christ's redeeming work was particular solely to the elect. The two Scriptures, "I pray not for the world," (John 17.9) and "Go ye into all the world and *preach* the gospel," (Mark 16.15) were not in conflict, but were encompassed within the sacred harmony of, "Father I *will* that they also whom thou hast given Me be with Me where I am." (John 17.24). The preaching and the atonement could never outstrip the sacred will of Christ in election. Such had been the error of Richard Baxter, Andrew Fuller and others. An atonement which was neither particular nor universal resulting from a false concept of man's responsibility, was denied by J.K. Popham. Man was responsible for the great sin of unbelief but he could not be held responsible for rejecting "a well-meant offer" of salvation, which God had never made, on condition of a faith which God had no intention of giving him, "For by grace (that is sovereign grace) are ye saved through faith; and that not of yourselves, it is the gift of God" (Eph.2.8). That offer to all indiscriminately was insincere, since the gift of faith was dependent on God's sovereign grace in election. It was denied by Joseph Hussey (1659-1726) in *God's Operations of Grace but no Offers of Grace*, by Dr. Gill in his *Body of Divinity* (1769), by William Rushton of Liverpool in his *Defence of Particular Redemption* (1831), also by William Gadsby and William Huntington in their writings and ministry. J.K. Popham reiterating the truth in his treatise on *Divine Sovereignty* supported the three Articles of Faith which had completed the Gospel Standard Societies Articles at the time of the formation of the Gospel Standard Poor Relief Society in 1877. Such support was vital in the face of the error of Sankey and Moody.

Thirty years later in 1906, J.K. Popham, by then Editor of the *Gospel Standard*, found himself faced on a denominational level with this same controversy, God's sovereignty versus man's responsibility and how should ministers address the unconverted. While controversy may appear essentially unprofitable, yet it has the effect of making truth shine more clearly against the dark backcloth of error. This was true in 1906 and is equally true now eighty-four years later; these subjects are still an area of debate and misconception. The Gospel Standard denomination is said by some not to preach the Gospel because its ministers do not offer Christ indiscriminately to the unconverted. Accusations are made that Gospel Standard ministers preach only to the elect. J. K. Popham published a small treatise in 1906 entitled *Preaching the Gospel* . He followed this two years later in the January 1908 *Gospel Standard* with an *Address to the Unconverted*. This address and the former treatise were reprinted as a booklet in 1908. These publications are important doctrinal statements of the denomination's position and have remained so ever since.

J.K. Popham writes, "There are some truths which are not yet fully cleared up to the church in the present age. But speaking according to light granted, it can hardly be denied that it is every man's duty to believe what God declares in His Word, both in Law and Gospel - the record He has given of His Son as well as His testimony of man's fall and death by sin - not withstanding he is 'without strength' to believe either. To believe God is His due, and necessary to worship Him as God. 'He that believeth not God hath made Him a liar; because he believeth not the record that God gave of His Son.' (1 John 5.10) It is unbelief of this record that is man's great sin and condemnation, wherever the light of the Gospel is given (John 3.18,19). The heart of man by nature is locked up in unbelief of the Saviour and of his need of Him. This is Paul's assertion, 'The natural man receiveth not the things of the Spirit of God: for they are foolishness unto Him: neither can he know them, because they are spiritually discerned.' (1 Cor.2.14) To tell all his hearers of God's revelation to and concerning them; to affirm that it is their duty to believe that revelation, to reject it their sin; to show them the sin of unbelief, is unquestionably the most solemn and ever binding duty of an anointed minister. This, however, does not involve preaching 'duty faith' but has a right effect. If accompanied by the Holy Spirit it makes a wound that only Christ can heal; it convinces of unbelief; makes men sensibly lost, perishing sinners and all such the Son of Man came to seek and to save. 'I came not to call the righteous but sinners to repentance.' (Mark 2.17)[15] ... Until a sinner is wounded the Gospel cannot be received by means of exhortations to 'repent and believe.' When a minister has clearly laid down the fall and utter ruin of men he is freely to preach the whole Gospel, and make use of the exhortations addressed to the convinced and wounded according to Scripture and grace given him. It is this preaching that God has ever honoured and not exhortations addressed immediately and nakedly to the dead... To call upon unconvinced sinners to repent and turn to God, many of whom in their own esteem may be believers already is to call 'the righteous' whom Christ came not to call 'and the ninety and nine just persons who need no repentance...'"[16]

He further stated that, "Because man had not in his first estate the spiritual life given him in Christ, it is not his duty by the law of his creation spiritually and savingly to repent and believe." [17] "Simply to exhort men in a state of nature to believe in or turn to God or to call upon them savingly to repent, believe and receive Christ, *is not to preach the Gospel to them.*"[18]

The reply of J.K. Popham was that those who accused Gospel Standard ministers of not "preaching the gospel" were themselves guilty of this very error since the indiscriminate offer of Christ is not *preaching* the Gospel. Christ's command to "Go into all the world and preach the Gospel" entailed preaching "the whole counsel of God," "Preach the Word" was not synonymous with "a well-meant offer of Christ" to the ungodly. In re-stating this truth regarding the preaching of the gospel, J.K. Popham was following in the footsteps of John Gill, William Huntington, William Gadsby (Works Vol.1), John Kershaw (See 'Autobiography', Gospel Tidings 1986. P.317-320 on his visit to Scotland), John Warburton ('Mercies of a Covenant God' P.2.), J. C. Philpot, John McKenzie, William Tiptaft and many more ministers of the Gospel Standard Churches who for nearly two centuries have preached in this way, and on account of it have been designated Hyper-Calvinists, and at other times have been accused of being Antinomians, both of which epithets they reject.

In 1907 J. K. Popham produced a small pamphlet entitled *The New Theology versus the Scriptures of Truth.* This was an answer to R. J. Campbell, a well-known minister of the period, who caused considerable contention in "Christian circles" with his denial of the Inspiration of Scripture, the fall of mankind, the virgin birth of the Lord Jesus Christ and His vicarious atonement, and preached a heresy that man's "inner consciousness is God, making man and God to be one." Mr. Popham described his teaching as blasphemy. His pamphlet had a circulation of 28,000 and was translated into Dutch. It was composed entirely of Scripture verses. Today in so called "Christian circles" such blasphemy still rears its ugly head. Church of England leaders have in recent years denied the virgin birth and the resurrection. Closely following on the enthronement of such a bishop, York Minster, the scene of the enthronement was struck by lightning and set alight, causing Editors of national newspapers to speculate on a manifestation of divine judgment against such blasphemy.

In 1930 J.K. Popham wrote against the Universal Redemption and Free-Will teaching of the Keswick Convention. He quoted Dr. Scroggie in his address, "The Gospel of Recoverability" as saying, "Christ is the Redeemer of the whole world and we are living in a redeemed world. Every man, woman and child in the world is redeemed." His response to this error was, "A redemption which leaves some of the redeemed in the power of the slave-master is not redemption. It is an unmitigable blot on the character of God."[19] Dr. Scroggie went on to speak of faith and say, "The difference between secular belief and religious belief is not in the faculty of faith but in its object; in one case it is directed to what we call secular objects and in the other case to religious objects. Faith is a human faculty, a natural endowment and it is universal." J.K. Popham replied to this, "What was true while Adam was upright, is untrue in view of the Fall... the 'flesh', the natural man, cannot receive the things of the Spirit. It is terribly true now that 'All men have not faith.' (2 Thess.3.2) If any sinner of mankind is to have access to God it must be in the exercise of a different faith from that which he lost... In affirming that faith is a human faculty, Dr, Scroggie flatly contradicts the Word of God. He is verbally in error - the Holy Ghost, the infallible Teacher says to the whole Church of God, 'For by grace are ye saved through faith; and that not of yourselves, it is the gift of God.'"[20]

As the situation deteriorated among the Gospel Standard Churches, with many churches in the denomination not fully holding to the Articles of Faith, in 1934 a Northern minister, Mr. Frederick Foster of Patricroft, proposed a resolution in his Church which was agreed, re-stating their "adherence to Gospel Standard principles and practices as distinct and separate from another element that has a more general appeal." This resolution was sent to Mr. Popham who submitted it to ministers and deacons in the Gospel Standard denomination and it was eventually published in the *Gospel Standard* over the signatures of those approving of the re-affirmation.[21] The effect of this move was to bring into the open those churches, ministers and deacons, who stood in undisputed loyalty to the position of Gadsby, Kershaw, Warburton, Philpot and those who followed them like Joseph Hatton. While some churches, ministers and deacons stood separate from this re-affirmation, the majority were bound more firmly together by an action which caused J. K. Popham much concern, *but which time has since vindicated,* as having "strengthened the things that remained which were ready to perish." Even in his great age at 87, he had the strength and wisdom given him to make this major decision, to raise the issue of the vital necessity of separation. He came under much criticism, but he was right in the move he made. Such a winnowing time came to the churches following the 18th Century Revival, under the ministry of William Huntington and William Gadsby. J.K. Popham did not shy from the same need of winnowing in 1934.

Our present need is for a return of the power of the Holy Spirit in the same degree which attended the ministry of J. K. Popham. His ministry was balanced in doctrine and experience. It was Christ exalting. It laid the sinner low. When applied by the Holy Spirit its fruit, in the hearts of his hearers, was manifested in godly discernment, judgment and understanding. Our Gospel Standard Churches were blessed in having two such eminent ministers and theologians as J. C. Philpot and J. K. Popham. "They being dead yet speak." Their writings (still in print) are much valued in Holland, Scotland, the United States and Australia. May this able contender for the faith, James Kidwell Popham, remain as much appreciated for his writings and ministry as he was in his own lifetime.

J. R. Broome
July, 1990

REFERENCES

1. J.H. Gosden, *Memoir & Letters of J.K. Popham*,1938, p.10.

2. Ibid., p.229.

3. J.K. Popham, *Sankey & Moody*,1875, preface.

4. Ibid.

5. I.H. Murray, *The Forgotten Spurgeon*, Banner of Truth 1966, pp.178-9.

6. Ibid., p.182.

7. A. Dallimore, *Spurgeon*,1985, p.166.

8. Ibid., p.165.

9. J.H. Gosden, *Memoir & Letters of J.K. Popham*, p.291.

10. J.K. Popham, *Divine Sovereignty*, pp.16-17.

11. Ibid., p.17.

12. Ibid., p.17.

13. L. Berkhof, *Systematic Theology*, Banner of Truth, 1959, p.445.

14. J.K. Popham, *Divine Sovereignty*, pp.6-7.

15. J.K. Popham, *Articles of Faith & Preaching to the Unconverted* pp.8-9.

16. Ibid., p.9.

17. Ibid., p.7.

18. Ibid., p.6.

19. J.K. Popham, *Keswick Teaching* , p.3.

20. Ibid., pp.12-13.

21. J.H. Gosden, *Memoir & Letters of J.K. Popham*, p.232.

MEMOIR AND LETTERS

OF

JAMES KIDWELL POPHAM.

CONTENTS.

MEMOIR AND LETTERS

OF

JAMES KIDWELL POPHAM.

CHAPTER ONE.

" Then shall thy light rise in obscurity."—Isa. lviii. 10.

1847—1869. Birth at Lancaster—removal to Nottingham—his
mother's conversion—Mission work—a sight of divine holiness—
legality—counselled to pray—preaches at Lubenham—Clipston—Mr.
de Fraine—A. J. Baxter—doctrine of grace—baptism.

ETERNITY alone will fully reveal the far-reaching consequences
hanging upon God's sovereign disposition of an obscure event
which occurred at 51 Penny Street, Lancaster, on 20th
December, 1847. The premises are now a branch of the
District Bank, but there ninety years ago was born to Mr.
and Mrs. James Popham a second son, James. His mother's
former name was Rebecca Scarborough; his father being a
pipe-maker by trade. The intervening ninety years have already
manifested somewhat considerable of the wonder-working
goodness of the God of all grace, as unfolding His eternal
purposes of love and salvation, in the long life and through
the unctuous gracious ministry of the honoured subject of
this little sketch. It is more than probable that thousands of
the saints of the Most High God have truly blessed Him who
fixed that birth and Who, while the son was yet a youth,
effected the miracle of his new birth; then, in pursuance of
divine decrees, set him apart for the solemn office of the
gospel ministry. Very many " souls for his hire " and " seals
to his ministry " were his favoured portion.

In 1850, when James was barely three years old, Mr. and
Mrs. Popham removed to Nottingham, where on 9th August
of the next year was born their son Henry (pastor-emeritus

A

of Grove Road Strict Baptist chapel, Eastbourne). He and
Charles, born in Nottingham in 1861 and still resident there,
are the only survivors of the numerous family.

Of the atmosphere in which he was brought up, our dear
friend gave this description,—" Worldly but moral; irreli-
gious; theatre-going, etc." But about the year 1863 his
mother became the subject of what was termed " a remarkable conversion "; and from remarks made by our friend in
later days it would appear to have been a genuine saving
work of the Holy Ghost; after her death her copy of Hart's
hymn-book was marked in places indicative of a penitent
heart, which confirmed the son in his hope of his mother's
salvation. While deeply interested in the performance of a
" play " at the Royal Theatre, Nottingham, she suddenly fell
under powerful convictions of sin, fearing she would drop
into hell before being able to escape from the building.
From that time the reformation in her life was most marked,
and with her children she commenced to attend religious
services held at a Mission Room in Leen Side, Nottingham.
Of his own state at this early period, our friend many years
later wrote:—

"Last Monday early the goodness of God to me during
the past years was passing before my mind, when this Scripture so fell on my heart as to surprise me: ' I will bless the
Lord who hath given me counsel ' (Ps. xvi. 7). I have two
kinds of thoughts about those years, particularly about my
profession of religion, and as a minister. The first kind is
so distressing, when I see how I have lived, how short I have
come, how selfish, half-hearted, unthankful, and unholy I
have been, that it is difficult for me to raise my face to
look up to God. It is a black thing I look back upon. But on
the other hand, I get by occasions such views of His mercies
and forbearance and kindness, as I had last week, that I
cannot forbear trying to thank Him. I would crucify my
natural disposition in speaking about it, and I would bless
Him for giving me counsel that arrested me in my down-
ward course, and turned my heart to Himself. Naturally I
never should have had any sort of religion; I was too intensely worldly to pick up religion, or look at it. I did not
want it, but it came to me. I can say with Rutherford, ' I

did not love God, but He would love me, and I could not refuse to be loved.'"

Strange to say, the person who kept this Mission Room was named Dr. Popham, but no relation to our beloved friend. He engaged young James with an older man, a Mr. Ash, to travel the surrounding villages two days weekly and to visit the Nottingham market on market days, with a Bible-stall Caravan. Also James, who would now be nearly seventeen, was engaged occasionally to give addresses at the Leen Side and at another Mission Hall also opened by Dr. Popham in High Cross Street.

"Some difficulty" arose between Dr. Popham and James, and not knowing where to go, being unacquainted with any body of professors who held the truth in its purity, he "fled to the Congregationalists as the most respectable body of dissenters, as it then appeared" to him; joining himself with a Mr. Hodgson who had opened a Mission Room in Colwick Street, Nottingham. Here he formed an acquaintance with several elderly people, to one of whom—a Mr. Dakin—he became much attached. An introduction to Dr. Paton, principal of the Congregational Institute, resulted in James becoming a student and attending lectures in theology. It is gratifying to have in his own words an account of the vital change which was produced in his soul toward the end of 1864, at the age of seventeen:

"It is now (1912) nearly forty-eight years since God first counselled me in respect of eternity. Noah was warned of God and prepared an ark; and in 1864, when not quite seventeen years of age, I was warned of my danger; it pleased the Holy Ghost to lay eternal things with weight on my heart. My Arminian heart turned me to Arminian teaching, and to working—and I worked indeed to please God, to make myself fit to appear before Him. But He disallowed and stopped this course. On a never-to-be-forgotten day, as I was walking along a road, the word, 'Blessed are the pure in heart, for they shall see God' (Matt. v. 8), was borne in upon my heart with an amazing power and a penetrating light. The view of divine holiness then given me filled me with consternation and alarm, and I stood still at that spot near the market in Nottingham and inly

said, ' Where that God is, I shall never be.'* It laid fast
hold of me, for in that awesome sight of divine holiness I
saw the uncleanness of my heart; then His divine justice
flashed into my conscience, and I saw my sins; the sorrows
of death and the pains of hell took powerful hold on me.
I tried to keep the law, as who would not, being ignorant
of the gospel ? I was miserable, tried to get happiness but
failed, and grew constantly worse. I flew to more strenuous
working, but my soul was filled with a sense of the nature of
God, and His fire burned up all my works. Thus my meat
and drink were my futile efforts, unavailing tears, black
failures, and shameful defeats. *From that time I was called
out of the world.* I had been plagued from a child with
occasional thoughts of God, had had bitter feelings towards
Him,—the thought of Him spoiled my pleasures and hindered
me in many things. I had previously been determined to
have my own way—what a change! I now found a power
on me I did not understand, and thought it was for my
destruction; but it prevented me from walking as I had
walked. I had no religion and wanted none, but there was
a hand on me. I wandered about a stranger upon earth,
and had no God to go to. In this state some parts of the
Bible were entered into: those that spoke of God's holiness
terrified me and made my heart ' meditate terror '. Sights
of God's justice, how they kill a sinner! sights of His holiness, how they terrify a person! No promises to behave
better, no prayers, proved a shelter for my soul. One day
when passing the gaol at Nottingham, I saw a prisoner
handcuffed entering, and the sight deeply affected me. I
thought, it might have been me; and my heart was for the
first time in my life softened before God. I was quite
unable to restrain my feelings, and at the meal table my
father noticing my emotion asked me the cause, and in my
simplicity I told him. He not understanding, was furious,
and said, ' You bear my name and dare to compare yourself
with a criminal ? I forbid you ever to mention religion again
in my presence.' "

* He frequently referred to this memorable day. In a sermon he
preached on May 23rd, 1937, only three weeks before his blessed death,
he mentioned it. See *Gospel Standard*, 1937, page 327.

We have heard our dear friend say that not until after his mother's death did he again name religion to his father. Of these trying early experiences, he made the following retrospective observations:—

"When young and brought into concern about my soul, I had to leave, literally in some respects, everything I valued in this world; and I entered somewhat into that Scripture, 'If a man hate not his father and mother . . . he cannot be My disciple' (Lu. xiv. 26). If we are concerned about our souls we must not expect to bring the world with us. In so far as we follow the world, our backs will be on God. When He sends the terrors of the law into the conscience, we may leave the world, but that will not bring us really out. But when He sends the attraction of His love to draw us, we say, 'We must leave it all for Him.' There was one thing I could not give up; it was the last thing I had to relinquish. It came to this—one day there was a mighty struggle in my heart, and I knew not what to do. Then it was as if God's voice sounded in my conscience, '*This or Christ—not both.*' Ah, we shall find the world will have to go. We may think it hard, but what a mercy for sinful nature to get blow on blow! When God kills it, it is His kindness; when He lets a man nourish it, it is His anger. What would have become of me if He had left me alone? Everyone who gets solemn dealings from Him which seem severe to be borne, gets that for which he will have to thank God. I cannot bless Him enough for His severe dealings; He knew what my heart was and what I meant to do and to be, for I had formed plans for the future, and had some particular aims. But the Lord came in front of all, and *I hope to bless Him through eternity for it.* From that day I have had a thirst for God. He does not let me drink of the foul waters my nature wants, but gives me of the pure river of the water of life, as He says, 'I will pour water upon him that is thirsty, and floods upon the dry ground.' Now I am getting old, and what shall I say? That Scripture that used to hang about my mind before I knew the Lord comfortably, I have realized to be true: 'There is no man that hath left father or mother . . . for My sake and the gospel's, but he shall in this life receive an hundredfold

. . . and in the world to come life everlasting.' That is, he shall have everything he needs,—friends, companions, kind things in providence, a hope of glory, and the prospect of eternal blessedness."

The Arminianism of fallen nature is not easily slain. Like many more of the Lord's dear people, Mr. Popham had suffered with the rising up in his mind of enmity against divine sovereignty. His own words are:—

"About this time one spoke to me of ' election', and instantly my Arminian nature rose up in its haughty scorn and bitter enmity, and I exclaimed, ' If the God you speak of is the God of heaven, I neither want to know Him nor to be where He is.' I have many scars on my heart, but the largest and deepest is that which the above terrible speech made; it was the expression of the unbridled passion of my alienated nature. It has always appeared, and still appears to me to be the most conspicuous manifestation of divine patience that I was not at once sent into outer darkness where there is weeping and wailing and gnashing of teeth. But though not thus cut off by God, He filled me with His terrors. To pray was more than I dare attempt; was for weeks without the courage to bend my knees, though really praying all the time. I was envying the cattle I saw grazing, and was saying, ' If mine were ordinary sins I might hope,' when God, who is rich in mercy, pitied me and He sent from above that wondrous word, ' All manner of sin and blasphemy shall be forgiven unto men' (Matt. xii. 31). A sweet gleam of hope filled me, and set me praying once more. The unction and power accompanying that word I hope never to forget or give up. ' *Go and pray*'—that was the counsel to me with it; and I prayed, I *know* I did."

At this juncture an event occurred, so trifling as to be hardly noticeable, yet so important in its consequences as to lead to an entire alteration in the whole course of his life. In the inscrutable wisdom and according to the gracious purpose of the eternal God, the young student was diverted from the intended college training; and those who have been favoured to witness the sequel must surely exclaim, " Who teacheth like Him ? " Thousands will thank God that instead of being left to depend upon mere human scholarship, our beloved friend was taken in hand by the Holy Spirit, that infallible " Teacher of Righteousness " (Joel ii. 23, margin), by Whom he was endued with power from on high for the sacred work of the ministry and frequently richly anointed in the discharge thereof, being ordained of Christ Himself (John xv. 16). On a particular evening he set out from his father's house to visit a certain friend, but on reaching a particular corner he obeyed a sudden impulse to turn to another friend's house in the opposite direction. Here he met a gentleman attached to the Congregational Institute, who invited young James Popham to preach the next Lord's Day at Lubenham, as the resident students who usually supplied there were on vacation. Objections that he was not a preacher, had no thought of preaching, etc., were of no avail; and he yielded to pressure and went. Quite recently (in 1936), ruminating on the past and the way he had come, our dear friend, thinking of that word, " Thou art the Guide of my youth," said to the Lord, " Didst Thou guide me then in my youth, to turn to the left hand and not to the right ? " Momentous issues hung on that casual alteration.

Often has he related that, his first, preaching engagement—his anxious train ride on Saturday evening to Kibworth—his cold reception by the ' squire '—his solitary supper and breakfast, his lonely walk to the chapel—his text, Song v. 16 (which, as he has said, amazed him to think he could have taken; but " I just felt Christ was very precious and spoke as I felt ")—the approval of the butcher and his wife, Mr. and Mrs. Morton (upon whose orchard the little chapel was built)—his glad exchange of host from the ' squire ' to the village tradesman, the warm mutual union between him and the godly couple lasting till their death. After the service, good Mrs. Morton said, " Don't go to college, they will spoil you."

With the exception of the two friends mentioned, it appears that the preaching on that day was unacceptable to the Lubenham congregation, and it does not appear that he ever again preached there. Our dear friend was reproached with Hyper-Calvinism—an honourable distinction early conferred and indicative of the discriminating character of his testimony. This was not only a crown of honour for the young

minister, it was also one step in the wonder-working of his
Lord and Master, whose purpose of leading His servant to
the sphere of his future labours amongst the Strict Baptists
was beginning to be evolved. A fortnight later Mr. Popham
received an invitation to preach at Clipston, a village about
four miles south of Lubenham. Mr. Morton had recom-
mended him to two friends, John and Job Carvell, who with
a few friends met for worship in an upper room erected over
a stable at the rear of Mr. John Carvell's home, "Calvin
House." It had been arranged for a number of Strict
Baptist friends from Lutterworth to attend the service; thus
came Mr. Popham's first introduction to the denomination
he faithfully served for so many years. Mr. and Mrs.
Morton shewed him much kindness, and during an illness of
eleven weeks nursed and entertained him with great liberality.

About this time Mr. Popham became acquainted with the
ministry of Mr. Baxter, then of Zion chapel, Nottingham,
and Mr. de Fraine, both of whom were instrumental in
leading him into a clearer understanding of the truth, as he
bore testimony:—

"By the mouth of His servant, de Fraine of Lutterworth,
God counselled me and instructed me in the doctrines of free
grace. Whereas I was trying to stand on works, which never
afforded me standing room, He shewed me the standing of a
sinner, when good, was in *grace*. Dear room in Thurland
Street, Nottingham, where I heard Mr. de Fraine! His text
was Rom. v. 2: 'By whom also we have access by faith into
this grace wherein we stand, and rejoice in hope of the glory
of God.' Never can I forget or give up the life, light, and
power accompanying that sermon. It was God's counsel in
my soul to seek free grace. In that room, too, I heard Mr.
Searle quote two lines of Hart:

> 'Sinners are high in His esteem,
> And sinners highly value Him.'

It was a revelation of God to me, for I was a sinner called
to repentance, and was sure that where the God of infinite
justice was I could never be. Good John Adams, later my
friend, gave out the hymns. Lady Lucy Smith and her
husband were regular, unobtrusive hearers."

Mr. de Fraine* became a spiritual nurse to our friend, instructing him in the truth, expounding to him the way of God more perfectly (Acts xviii. 26). While attending the chapel at Lutterworth under the ministry of Mr. de Fraine, a lady one day asked Mr. Popham if he believed in baptism. He said it was in the Word of God, and if any wished to walk in it, let them do so. "But," said she, "have you ever asked the Lord to shew it to you?" From that time he had to notice the ordinance, and had no rest until he was enabled to walk in it. Having related his spiritual experience before the church on the 5th July, 1868, he was baptized by Mr. de Fraine (the pastor) and received a member of the church worshipping at Lutterworth, on the 6th September, 1868.

Not all at once did our friend learn the truth; here a little, there a little, line upon line. The following is a relation from his own lips of the deep exercises of those days:—

"I began to thirst after what I possessed not. The Spirit of God dropped certain hints on my mind and shed rays of light in my understanding, whereby I was instructed that there was a righteousness to be had, a Saviour for lost sinners. I used to be like this: 'O that He were mine!' And once when I got a hint of the virtue of the blood of Christ, I knelt down and said, (which was unwise,) 'I will never rise till that blood cleanses me.' But God accepts the faith, and takes no notice of the rest. We please God whenever we believe for five minutes that the blood of Christ can cure our souls. At one time two verses of Hart's were a great help to me:

* Mr. de Fraine died February 19th, 1882, and was buried at Lutterworth by Mr. Popham. He had been for some time somewhat enfeebled in mind, and unable to preach. On one occasion in his study conversing with Mr. Popham, he rose and said, "I must now go home," insisting that he was not at home. Being a powerful man, Mr. Popham wondered how he could manage him. So he said, "You have often felt the Lord Jesus Christ with you in this room, have you not?" To which the aged pastor said, "Why, yes, I have!" And he commenced to rehearse many former blessings, and quite forgot the aberration.

A tablet to his memory bears the inscription:—

In affectionate remembrance of Richard de Fraine who after a long and faithful pastorate in this place commencing in 1839, entered into rest February 19th, 1882, aged 79 years. In his preaching he constantly exalted a precious Christ, and laid the sinner low. The Lord gave him many seals to his ministry and souls for his hire, both in this neighbourhood and others which he visited.

' O for a glance of heavenly day,
To take this stubborn stone away:
To thaw with beams of love divine
This heart, this frozen heart of mine!

' But something yet can do the deed,
And that dear something much I need;
Thy Spirit can from dross refine,
And move and melt this heart of mine.'

And it appeared to me about the biggest wonder that could
happen that my heart could be so affected. No churchman
used his prayer-book as I used those two verses for many
days. A hungry man, if he gets an idea where food is to be
had, will struggle to be at it. So did I seek after God.
What a God He is! I thought if I could reach that Redeemer, all my desires would be satisfied; that, once supplied,
all I prayed for would be granted. But not getting at once
the mercies I sought, my soul fainted in me. The old wound
was again opened, and I lost my sweet hope. I went to my
room one night with a fearful sense of despair. As I locked
my door I felt my heart moved to pray, and soon found a
peculiar liberty in confessing my sin and all my sins. How I
justified God should He carry out His severest sentence! While
I was thus engaged, Paul's word concerning the mercy of
God to himself fell on my soul with power, life, and light:
' But I obtained mercy because I did it ignorantly in unbelief ' (I Tim. i. 13). By the power of that marvellous word
my soul was filled with a gracious energy in prayer for the
same mercy. Soon it came; it seemed almost immediately, I
could not quite tell. But the mercy, the full pardon of my
sin, of *all* my sins, was conveyed by the word of Peter:
' Forasmuch as ye know that ye were not redeemed with
corruptible things as silver and gold . . . , but with the
precious blood of Christ, as of a lamb without blemish and
without spot.' My conscience was filled with peace and comfort, and as I laid my head on my pillow that night, I said,
' Now it would be as easy for me to die as it is for me to
put my head on this pillow.' Thus I learned the doctrines
of grace; for they were, as I afterwards found, implicit in
my experience. If I die as I pray and believe I shall die,

hoping and believing in that precious blood, I shall go to heaven in that sea of the Saviour's infinite merits. I bless God that ever He laid His hand on me and gave me counsel of that inward, spiritual kind."

CHAPTER TWO.

" Be ye clean that bear the vessels of the Lord."

1869—1871. Exercised about ministry—Clipston—Walgrave—Coventry—his marriage—removal to Wigston—preaches in Dorsetshire—opposed, but owned of God—family afflictions and providential trials—the Spirit of Adoption.

ALTHOUGH he had given addresses and taken several services, Mr. Popham appears not yet to have considered himself a minister, and had no great exercise and but little understanding of the solemn matter, until his blessed deliverance from guilt. This is his own relation of the commencement of his particular exercises as to preaching:—

"Just before I had that blessed full forgiveness of all my sins, I got, as I believe, the first word about preaching. I was in perplexing circumstances; my health was so failing that for six months it was thought I could not live, and not being among the Lord's people, as now, no thought of preaching had ever laid hold of me. But on a certain day it pleased the Lord to say this to me, ' Depart ye, depart ye, go ye out from thence, touch not the unclean thing: go ye out of the midst of her; be ye clean, that bear the vessels of the Lord. For ye shall not go out with haste, nor go by flight: for the Lord will go before you, and the God of Israel will be your rereward ' (Isa. lii. 11, 12). It persuaded me that I should have to preach; and I think I was imprudent that day, for I told the friends at Lutterworth that I was satisfied about it; and they had for some time believed it to be the case. The good minister kindly received my testimony as to the Lord's work in me, and the call He gave me to preach."

Though not formally " sent out " to preach by Lutterworth church, he frequently preached there; thus his ministry was sanctioned by them. One of the earliest places at which Mr. Popham preached was in the Strict Baptist chapel, Walgrave, a village in Northamptonshire eight miles southeast of Clipston. Mr. T. Knight, an old member of the cause still living there, distinctly remembers the young minister driving through the village in a " four-wheeler " on his way to the chapel. Quite recently, also, a godly friend related how on the 11th April, 1869, she, as a girl in her teens and in great soul distress, heard Mr. Popham (then 21 years of age) preach at Coventry Strict Baptist chapel, in the morning from Ps. xxxviii. 9, and in the evening from Jer. xxxii. 27. She recalls the weight and solemnity of his ministry at that early period when he had but recently been brought into a measure of gospel liberty. He preached at Coventry in 1936, and was very gratified to find yet remaining a godly remnant there.

Mr. Popham seems to have preached more or less regularly at Clipston for about two years, occupying rooms at Job Carvell's house (where Miss Carvell still resides, and remembers Mr. Popham coming to Clipston when she was a girl). On the 30th November, 1869, while still at Clipston, Mr. Popham, then in his twenty-second year, was married at St. Luke's Church, Nottingham, to Harriett Adcock, of Salford Street. She proved a help-meet indeed, for forty-seven years prayerfully sharing in his joys and sorrows: and a tender, prudent mother to their children. Shortly after his marriage they removed (early in 1870) to Wigston Magna,* Leicestershire, where Mr. Popham laboured regularly in the ministry for about three years, although he never accepted the invitation to the pastorate there. He occupied for a time a cottage next to one where lived Mrs. Wilson, niece of the late Mr. Levesley, and who still resides there.

---

* Wigston chapel was built by a Mr. Levesley who had previously held services in his own house, then in a barn. The chapel was opened by Mr. de Fraine in 1859; a church being formed in 1860.

She well remembers Mr. Popham, and his removing later to a larger house in the village. Two children were born at Wigston: a daughter, Mary (Mrs. Whittome), and a son, Kidwell.

An interesting acquaintance with some Dorsetshire people commenced at this period, resulting in firm and long-standing friendship with several godly persons, and his preaching among them occasionally, until dispersed through death and other circumstances:—

" In 1869 I was invited to preach at Langton, Dorsetshire. It was quite three weeks before I could feel my mind settled to go. In my perplexity I thought I would ask Mr. de Fraine's advice, but was stopped by the word, ' Cursed be the man that trusteth in man, and maketh flesh his arm, and whose heart departeth from the Lord. For he shall be like the heath in the desert,' etc. (Jer. xvii. 5, 6). I saw that the thought of consulting Mr. de Fraine had been a hindrance to all spiritual exercise and prayer, and made me correspond exactly to the barren heath in the desert. On the next day I was enabled to confess my sin and to give myself to prayer for direction; and in the afternoon this word laid hold of me as an answer: ' If thou draw out thy soul to the hungry and satisfy the afflicted soul, then shall thy light rise in obscurity, and thy darkness shall be as the noon day: and the Lord shall guide thee continually, and satisfy thy soul in drought, and make fat thy bones; and thou shalt be like a watered garden, and like a spring of water, whose waters fail not' (Isa. lviii. 10—12). Instantly I felt it was God's word bidding me to go to Langton; and not only so, but confirming my whole ministry. Those promises have always appeared to me almost too great to receive, and have been a source of much exercise, that they may be fulfilled. [And how abundantly they *have* been! J. H. G.] My first visit there was in February, 1870, and my first sermon was made a message of deliverance to one woman [Mrs. Hooper], who was brought into blessed liberty. She had been going about to hear and crying out in great distress; and came to hear me as a stranger."

On this visit Mr. Popham preached frequently at Langton and other places in the neighbourhood. The word made a

great stir; partly through the marked change in Mrs.
Hooper, partly by the discrimination of the teaching, and
partly through one poor man who had joined himself to the
meetings, and was first in great trouble, then in a strange
state of rejoicing. After saying several solemn things, and
that none but those Langton people were right, he was taken
to the asylum, and there died during Mr. Popham's visit.
His illness and death were then attributed to the effect of
Mr. Popham's sermon on *Election* at Swanage; and much
bitterness was shewn and open disturbance made. Persons
would openly call out after Mr. Popham, "Who killed Mr.
—— ? " His text at Langton was Eph. vi. 23: "Peace be
to the brethren, and love with faith, from God the Father
and the Lord Jesus Christ." His first text at Swanage was
Jer. x. 23: "O Lord, I know that the way of man is not in
himself: it is not in man that walketh to direct his steps."
The trials he met on this visit adversely affected his health,
never robust. Two letters from one of the Langton friends
are here appended:—

Dear Mr. P.,—. . . People are still busy talking about
us all. Mrs. Bower told me that Mrs. S. had spoken most
bitterly and told her Sunday class that if any of them dared
hold such doctrines as you preached she would have nothing
to do with them. The last report is that you caused the
death of the man who died at Langton last Sunday. . . . I
want to feel more and more of the spirit of that prayer,
"Plead Thou my cause," but find it impossible left to myself
to walk rightly in a path where the flesh is crucified at every
step. . . . Two lines of a hymn you gave out last Monday
include all,

"Thorny is this wilderness; the Lord will have it so."

We miss you very much; it was a support to have you in
the place, but I am glad for your own sake you are not here,
and fear your health suffered from all the trouble. If the
Lord should bring you back we shall be very thankful, and
meanwhile I trust He will give power to the faithful word
that has been spoken, cause it to take root and bear fruit.
The adversaries without are nothing to the mighty enemies
within the heart of man which will rise up and fight against

the Lord unless subdued by divine grace. . . . I should think the reproach that is now cast on us all will keep the *respectable* C. away, which will be a mercy! The report about your preaching at Worth originated in B.'s carrying back from Langton all sorts of false statements. On all sides it is nothing but, " Report, say they, and we will report it." Mrs. B. told me people had come to her cottage and said the most absurd things, and she had " quite to preach to them contending for the truth "! . . .

Trusting that the Lord will be with you wherever you go, giving you peace within, so that you may not " fear the reproach of man nor be afraid of their revilings."

Yours affectionately for the truth's sake,
Swanage.   A. BRODIE.
16th March, 1870.

My dear Mr. Popham,—. . . We are both so grieved to hear of your being so unwell, but not surprised, for you went through so much here. . . . There have been many kind enquiries after you from the people since you left. Last Sunday week at Langton we were all very dejected and felt much the loss of the ministry. I am sorry to say that S. still continues his self-righteous ministrations Sunday evenings. James Lauder seemed very much cast down and could not say a word; his mother heard him say he would have to sit at home and read his Bible. She, poor woman, misses you sadly, feels she could live in an alms-house if she could only hear the gospel preached. W. Brown asks very warmly after you; also Timothy. I think they are all—except R. B. —out of conceit with themselves and their religion; which is a very good thing, for " there is that scattereth and yet increaseth." It is an unspeakable mercy that the Lord should scatter and pull down false experiences, carnal hopes, and empty notions only in the head; if He will only give us a little increase in true spiritual knowledge, which will humble poor sinners, making them feel how utterly lost, ruined, and undone they are; and will exalt the blessed Lord of life and glory, giving Him in their experience " a Name which is above every name ". I hope I felt just a touch of His mercy last Saturday when in much affliction of body and soul—no word came, but I had a sweet blessed sense of God's mercy compassing me about, which made me feel that the " sufferings of this present time are not worthy to be compared with the glory which shall follow "; and my heart was melted and broken down, feeling willing to " follow the Lamb whithersoever He goeth ".

> " If on my face, for Thy dear Name,
>   Shame and reproaches be,
> All hail reproach and welcome shame!
>   If Thou remember me."

What a mercy it is that the Lord should think upon the poor and needy, should remember us in our low estate, should have mercy upon His afflicted people, and that He should cause them to know and trust in His Name, finding it at times a strong tower.

You said in your letter you hoped I might feel a little of the " Blessing of the Lord which maketh rich," etc., so I desire to make my boast in Him and speak well of His Name. And truly I have nothing else to boast of, for I am " carnal, sold under sin ".

Have you seen Mr. de Fraine yet, and what does he say about poor Eli Bower ? I saw Mrs. H. the other day, and she showed me a letter from her son Charles, in which he said, " I feel sure poor Eli is only removed from the harassing persecutions of Swanage to be for ever in glory. The revelations of God were more than his poor heart could contain. God's mercy is past man's finding out, and it was manifested in Eli's case. What a target for Satan's bowmen his poor soul would have been—how they would have taken pleasure in persecuting one so weak in mind; but now he is out of their reach. God shewed him more than ever he told, I believe, for he was so sweet on some things." I asked Mrs. H. if she had told her son *all* about Eli's end, the reproach he brought upon the truth, etc. She said that she had had no heart to write more than just that Eli had gone mad and died in the asylum; so of course Charles wrote his letter with former impressions strong in his mind, and I must say they are just what I felt till the poor man seemed to lose his reason and said such strange things. This is a deep mystery, but I find the Lord's people here, Kezia Tomes, Mrs. Hixson and others, cannot give up his first testimony as he spoke of it *at the time* the Lord was blessing his soul; it seemed indeed a sweet and true experience. K. asks so much for you, hoped you heard " none of the wicked things people said about you!" I told her you did, and " were in nothing terrified by your adversaries ". Poor people! how afraid they all are of the cross, for themselves and for others, and what a strange thing they will think the fiery trial of true faith which must come sooner or later if they belong to the Lord.

Mrs. B. says the malice of people against you was so great that if they could they would have brought you before a court of justice. It is still very trying here in many ways; people staring as much as ever and making remarks. I believe Mr. —— would say anything against us, and our mother's illness is put down to " our unnatural conduct ". Poor thing, there is no doubt that the separation in religion does try her deeply, and so it does us. For many months and years past I have sorrowed much on her account, and especially this winter as I have seen her growing weaker every day. But after all, this is only natural feeling which must be crucified, the sorrow of the world which worketh death. Oh, how I long at times to be able to cast this burden more upon the Lord and ask Him to undertake for me. At times He mercifully does uphold and sustain my weary soul, and then I can leave creatures, and bless the Lord that ever He gave me a desire for Himself and His great salvation.

. . . I hope you are comfortable in your new house and in every way at Wigston, and remain,

Yours affectionately for the truth's sake,

Swanage.   A. BRODIE.

March 30th, 1870.

An account of his second visit to Langton, Dorset, and another peculiar trial in connection therewith is here given in his own words:—

" My visits to Langton were repeated yearly for several years, and in August the following year, 1871, my visit was marked by peculiar trial and blessing. I was to baptize two persons [Mrs. Hooper and Mr. W. Brown] in the open sea at Swanage Bay. On the day before the baptism I was

B

sent for to return home at once if I wished to see my child alive [now Mrs. Whittome of Croydon], whom I had left very ill, and I was preparing to go. Then a feeling was given me that I must not leave the work of the Lord, the word spoken of Levi coming to my mind: 'Who said unto his father and to his mother, I have not seen him; neither did he acknowledge his brethren, *nor knew his own children:* for they have observed Thy Word, and kept Thy covenant' (Deut. xxxiii. 9). With this came real power to commit my child and circumstances and all things to Him. On the following morning early, my mind was completely taken from my circumstances and a view given me of the glory of God in the ordinance of baptism, from Matt. iii. 16, 17: 'And Jesus, when He was baptized, went up straightway out of the water: and, lo, the heavens were opened unto Him, and He saw the Spirit of God descending like a dove, and lighting upon Him: and lo a voice from heaven, saying, This is My beloved Son, in Whom I am well pleased.' I saw the Father acknowledging the Son as He came up out of the water, and the Spirit descending upon Him; which filled me with a sense of His glory and love revealed in that ordinance. I had felt a love to it when I was myself baptized, but not as I did then. The fear of baptizing in the open sea, lest I should be carried off my feet, was quite taken away; and my mind continued calm during the service; I felt the presence of Christ with us. But there were some who were much stirred up and afterwards manifested their enmity."

The Mr. Brown baptized by Mr. Popham, conducted the services at Langton by prayer when there was no minister, and continued to do so till his death. He was evidently a very gracious character. In 1873 a person who had been under concern, was brought to a gracious point in her soul's experience through Mr. Popham's preaching at Langton, and was later baptized by Mr. Knill. Thus God owned His servant, while the adversaries of truth were silenced.*

* An interesting account appears in the *Gospel Standard*, 1908, page 110, of the lady in whose house the meetings at Langton were held, and who while staying at Lutterworth in 1869 first invited Mr. Popham to preach there. She died at Brighton in 1907. Her end was peace.

Also in the *Gospel Standard* for 1907 an account (page 15) of Kezia Tomes, and (page 531) of Margaret Bower who died in the Lord at Swanage in 1906, to whom Mr. Popham's ministry had been made a real blessing.

As previously observed, Mr. Popham never saw his way to accept the actual pastorate at Wigston Magna Strict Baptist chapel, although he preached there regularly until his removal in 1874 to Liverpool. At a meeting held December 8th, 1872, a unanimous resolution was passed by the church to invite him to the office. To this the following is his reply:—

Dear Friends,—When I received your invitation to the pastorate of this church, I felt it to be a most solemn and weighty matter, requiring much prayerful consideration, and now after seeking unto God for His direction, and en-deavouring to weigh all the circumstances of the case, I feel unable to accept your invitation. During the time that I have laboured among you as a supply, I have painfully felt the want of that blessing of the Lord upon my poor labours which is needful to encourage me to hope that it is the Lord's will I should settle among you as your pastor. I would therefore propose that I continue this year, 1873, as your supply, to watch the hand of the Lord to see whether He will be pleased to make manifest that He has sent me. This I think is better than my hastily accepting the pastorate, and after a time, not finding the blessing of the Lord with us, having in grief to resign it.

There is one question, my dear brethren, I wish to ask you: Do you hold the principle of Strict Communion? Your answer will greatly affect my mind in considering the accept-ance or refusal of the pastorate should you ever again be led to offer it.

And now, brethren, I commend you to God, and to the Word of His grace, which is able to build you up and to give you an inheritance among all them which are sanctified.

Yours affectionately in the Lord,

Wigston.   JAMES KIDWELL POPHAM.
7th January, 1873.

Thus weightily did the solemn work of the ministry rest upon the heart of the twenty-five-year-old preacher, already owned of God in many instances. It was indeed to him an inexpressibly serious matter to stand up before the people and be as God's mouth.

In the early days of his married life, our dear friend was

often much tried in providence, and the gracious instruction
he received in those trials became a means of deep spiritual
understanding, yielding to his ministry additional savour,
and fitting him to truly sympathise with and encourage the
tried people of God. A note of his own concerning this
will be of interest:—

" I was at this time walking in a great trial. At times I
felt sin powerfully working, often prevailing; was under
God's solemn providences, in poverty and in debt, and sorely
tempted by Satan. My first (and then only) child being
afflicted for twelve months, constantly needing the doctor,
brought me into great straits, my debts were growing, and
in this deep temporal distress I greatly feared becoming a
reproach to the Name of the Lord.* I left home one Saturday to go into Staffordshire to preach—I left no money in
the house, and had not enough to take me to the end of my
journey except by waiting on Birmingham platform till quite
late for a cheap train. Never I think and hope shall I
forget that time. I often thought I could not live through
the trial, that ' affliction would not rise up a second time '
(Nahum i. 9), for there would be nothing left for it to do.
I would walk down the back streets and fear to meet
anyone. But one day, in the depth of my misery, did free
mercy come. In my room how sweetly did Ps. xxxii. 7
sound in my heart—heard as it was above the waterfloods
which were then surrounding and pouring in upon me:
' Thou art my hidingplace; Thou shalt preserve me from
trouble: Thou shalt compass me about with songs of deliverance.' I was so wounded and distressed I could only answer,
' Lord, Thou canst not preserve me *from* it, for I am *in it
already.*' But He shewed me that wherever I had a wound
He would put a song of deliverance. How did my faith
then see deliverances wherever trouble was! Where was

---

* The doctor one day pronounced the child almost past recovery but
said, "There is one more remedy. I would like to try but it is very
expensive, £1 a bottle." The dear father had not the means to procure
this, but in his distress thereabout, the word (Matt. vi. 32) was given
him; and also in reading Matt. viii. he received faith to believe, as the
centurion, that no disease could stand before the omnipotent God: He
had only to speak the word. That need was then supplied and the child
recovered.

misery there I saw mercy would surely come. Where difficulties were, there I believed deliverances would be commanded; that He would turn every sigh and every want into
a song. O that was a good word to me! And I would add,
He fulfilled His Word in His great goodness. But for
some time longer my debt remained; and a remark that my
dear friend and pastor, Mr. de Fraine, had dropped too
unguardedly, was like a sword in my bones: 'You can only
honour God as long as you pay your way.' But then the
Lord gave me the blessed Spirit of adoption in Matthew vi.
32: 'For your heavenly Father knoweth that ye have need
of all these things.' As He spoke that word, 'Your heavenly
Father,' I was enabled to respond and call Him my Father.
O the sacredness of that room where I received that double
word, 'Heavenly Father'—'all these things.' It raised me
above all my trials for the time, even while I was in them,
and took away my every care. I bade my poor suffering
wife (our second child was about to be born) no longer to
fear, for I knew all our needs would be supplied. Soon
afterwards I was called to bury a dear friend, and after the
funeral I was asked to go to the house. On the point of
leaving, I was requested to remain while the will was read,
and to my utter astonishment I found there was a legacy
of £50 for me,—exactly the needed sum. O may I never
forget the walk, or rather run, home to tell my wife of
God's goodness and faithfulness; how my heart did swell—
how unable I was to speak—what sweet tears I shed—what
humility filled my soul as I viewed the goodness of my God,
my heavenly Father, in this His kind unthought-of way of
delivering me! I then thought I had all that was to come
out of that promise; but I have since found that a promise
is not exhausted when the need is supplied for which it was
first given. The far-reaching of that one has, through the
faithfulness of the Lord, continued to supply me abundantly
in temporal things to this day. If £50,000 were now given
me I doubt if it would be half as sweet—if sweet at all—as
that precious legacy which enabled me to pay my debt and
thus removed all then present existing fear of reproaching
God's most holy Name.

" O how base am I! How often do I fear that my ways,

which must so provoke the eyes of His glory, will move Him
to turn in His most solemn dealings to be my enemy and
fight against me. What room there is in my case for mercy!
. : . It is written, 'No man liveth to himself.' I desire not
to keep and live through that to myself, though something
in me says, 'Don't relate it.'"

Proof of the blessed reality of this rich blessing and its
enduring character came to light in a sermon preached many
years later, in which reference is made to this memorable
period:—

"But there comes a time, O it is a blessed time! when
they can say, 'Abba, Father!' The apostle Paul says, 'Because ye are sons, God hath sent forth the Spirit of His
Son into your hearts, crying, Abba, Father!' Well, that is
an amazing day. The day that in His mercy came to me
is often before me now-a-days. I was in great trouble, full
of fear, full of evil; and God came to me, and made me
know He was my heavenly Father, and I called Him my
Father. That occurred now 45 years ago, and in these later
days of my life I find in my soul that Spirit that almost
daily takes me to Him, and I am enabled to call Him my
Father. It is a great thing to have a Father in heaven; it
means much to you, if you see Him in this relationship to
yourself."—*Published Sermons, No. 110.*

CHAPTER THREE.

" Not for filthy lucre but of a ready mind."

1871—1877. Preaches at Liverpool—accepts pastorate there—his first publications—Moody and Sankey—Thoughts on Regeneration—Imperishable grace.

AFTER regularly serving the church at Wigston Magna for several years, Mr. Popham was invited early in 1871 to preach at Shaw Street Strict Baptist chapel, Liverpool. On his first visit there his ministry appears to have been so acceptable to the people, that on the 1st May in the same year the church resolved to invite him to supply again as soon as convenient. In August the church at Liverpool passed a resolution " That Mr. Gadsby be respectfully requested to place Mr. J. K. Popham's name (for supplying different churches) on the *Gospel Standard* wrapper."* On the 7th July, 1873, a requisition was promoted, signed by 22 members of the church at Shaw Street chapel inviting Mr. Popham to supply their pulpit for the first three months of 1874 with a view to his becoming their pastor, if approved by the majority of the church at the expiration of that period. The covering letter and Mr. Popham's reply are here subjoined:—

To Mr. J. K. Popham, Wigston Magna.

My dear Brother in the bonds of the everlasting covenant,—Grace, mercy and peace be with you. Herewith I forward you the requisition. You will perceive that no one has signed the paper against your coming—you may consider all the members have signed and are favourable, except five. I am sorry that C. has been led away. R. is the chief cause. I am satisfied he has made himself manifest: he has been keeping back books and monies belonging to a Society in which he had been Secretary, in consequence of which I expect on Thursday next at the church meeting he will be separated. I fear he is one that will be numbered amongst those who sow discord among the brethren. We have visited him, but he cannot give a satisfactory account of his con-

---

* This was prior to the magazine being vested in trustees. Mr. J. Gadsby, being then the sole owner and publisher, exercised his absolute right to insert or remove names from the list of approved ministers.

duct. Since I heard of it my earnest prayer has been,
" Hold Thou me up, and I shall be safe." What a mercy to
be kept! I was very sorry to see the account of your wife
and children. I do hope things are more favourable with
you by this time. O it is sweet work to be resigned under
the Lord's afflicting hand. May it be thus with you, my
brother.

Do let me know your mind as soon as you can relative to
the requisition, and the Lord direct you aright in the matter,
is my earnest prayer. I would have come to Rochdale if I
could have made it convenient, but find I cannot. Give my
Christian regards to Mrs. Kershaw and say that I received
her kind note and will write her shortly.

That there may be no disappointment or misunderstanding
I think it best to state what I think the church will be able
to allow you should the Lord direct you to come among us;
that is, during the three months, 40s. per week and your
board and lodging; and in the event of the church giving
you a call, £2 per week will be as much as I think they can
afford you.

Please excuse this hasty line, as the friends have now
arrived to dine with me. The Lord be with you and bless
you both in body and soul, and especially direct you in this
all-important matter, is the soul's sincere desire of your
faithful and affectionate friend and brother,

    Brook Vale, Waterloo.   JAMES KNIGHT.
      29th August, 1873.

It will be seen that the prospect afforded little by way of
this world's goods; £2 weekly with a family of two! But
the man of God had weightier concerns uppermost; the
unspeakably awful and yet blessed work of the ministry, of
being an " ambassador for Christ ", sunk into comparative
insignificance the considerations of " filthy lucre ", as the
brief letter accepting the invitation shews:—

To the church of Jesus Christ meeting for divine worship in
Shaw St. Particular Baptist chapel, Liverpool. Grace,
mercy and peace, from God our Father and Jesus Christ
our Lord.

Dear Brethren and Sisters,—Having, I hope, prayerfully
considered the invitation you have given me to supply your

pulpit for the first three months of next year, I have decided, I hope in the fear and by the direction of the Lord, to accept it. Deeply sensible that I am not sufficient of myself for the very solemn and important work of the ministry, I do pray that I may continually find that my sufficiency is of God, and if the will of the Lord that I should come to labour amongst you, may He condescend to be with me, to make me as His mouth to your souls.

Now, brethren, I beseech you for the Lord Jesus Christ's sake and for the love of the Spirit, that ye strive together with me in your prayers to God for me, that I may come among you in the fulness of the blessing of the gospel of Christ—that your hearts might be comforted, being knit together in love and brought unto all riches of the full assurance of understanding to the acknowledgment of the mystery of God and of the Father and of Christ, in Whom are hid all the treasures of wisdom and knowledge (Col. ii. 2; Rom. xv. 30); and also that others may be gathered unto Him beside those that are gathered.

I am, dear brethren and sisters,

Your Friend and Servant in the Lord,

Wigston.   J. K. POPHAM.

29th October, 1873.

Note from minute book of Shaw Street church, dated 30th October, 1873.—The deacons reported that brother J. K. Popham, with much fear and trembling, had consented to accept the invitation of the church to supply for the months of January, February, March, 1874.

An interesting letter by Mr. de Fraine is here inserted, as shedding light upon the conditions at Wigston and Lutterworth at that period:—

To Mr. J. K. Popham.

My dear Friend,—I was pleased to receive your very kind note of the 9th. As to myself, my health is much better, as well as I may expect at my time of life; but old de Fraine is no better, nor do I expect he will be until the " earthly house of this tabernacle be dissolved ". When the old house is down, all the leprosy will go with it; what a mercy to have an eternal freedom from it!

I do not wonder you are much tried about your position, for it would be a bad sign if you were not. May the "afterwards" bring you the "peaceable fruit of righteousness". Your father Abraham went out, not knowing whither he went, but the Lord went before him and he found the way (though trying) was right. We must (whether we like it or not) walk by faith not by sight, and the desire of our heart is:

"Choose Thou the way, but still lead on."

I am mercifully enabled to struggle on; very often cast down, but not destroyed; always bearing about in the body the dying of the Lord Jesus. "As dying and behold we live!" Christ liveth in us, the Hope of glory.

I hear nothing from Wigston about vital religion, only what James G. tells me. He tells me they are in a very low way. When were they otherwise? Mrs. Popham I saw for a minute at Wigston station; she said, "We are in a very bad way indeed here, Mr. de Fraine." I had no time to ask questions, but I thought, Is this all the fruit of dear Popham's three years' labours? If so, things cannot be worse at Liverpool, anyhow.

I fear Mrs. M.'s zeal lacks a living spring. We both know that Ezekiel's wheels without the Spirit of the living God in them would only be a piece of splendid useless machinery. But "the Lord knoweth them that are His". I expect to baptize B. of W. next Lord's Day week. Our financial account was £11 less this year than last, and yet I was enabled to tell them we did not owe one farthing. You know last year was one of affliction and expense to me, but bless the Lord here I am and I trust I can say, both safe and sound. "Trust in the Lord and do good; so shalt thou dwell in the land, and verily thou shalt be fed."

Mrs. de Fraine is as usual and unites with me in Christian love.   Yours in the truth,

Lutterworth.   1874.   R. DE FRAINE.

On the 2nd March, 1874—a month before the expiration of the period fixed for probation, the church sent the following requisition and letter to Mr. Popham:—

To Mr. J. K. Popham.

Dear Brother in the bonds of the everlasting love of God,—
We had our special church meeting on Monday evening,
when the subject of your being invited to take the pastoral
charge of the church of God worshipping at Shaw Street,
Liverpool, was considered, and under the feeling of a solemn
desire for the glory of God, the welfare of immortal souls,
and the divine blessing to be attendant upon your ministrations according to His gracious will, the *almost* unanimous
desire of the church was that you should be requested to do
so. We enclose you the resolution of the church passed at
the meeting, to which is attached a list of the names of the
members, from which you will gather our unanimity as a
church on the subject.

May the Lord in an especial manner lead and guide you
in this matter, and may we all live to prove by the result the
work to be of God and not of man, and to His great and
holy Name, as is meet, shall be all the praise and all the
glory, for He is worthy.

Yours in the faith of the gospel of Christ,

JAMES KNIGHT } *Deacons.*
JAMES WILTON

P.S.—A resolution was also passed fixing the salary at
£2 per week.

THE REQUISITION.

To J. K. Popham, our beloved brother in the Lord and
   minister of Jesus Christ, grace unto you and peace be
   multiplied.

The following resolution was passed at a special church
meeting held 2nd March, 1874, in the hope that it is the
will of the Lord for you to take the oversight of His people
here and become the stated pastor of the church; testimony
having been given that the Word of the Lord by your
ministration has been blessed to the hearts of the people.

It was resolved, that a requisition be sent to Mr. Popham
under a prayerful desire for the leading of the Lord in the
matter, requesting him to take the pastoral care of this
church.

[There follow the signatures of 23 for, and 3 neutral.]

The letter accepting this invitation is here inserted:—

To the church of Jesus Christ worshipping in Shaw St. Chapel, Liverpool. Grace be unto you and peace from God our Father and the Lord Jesus Christ.

Dear Brethren and Sisters in the Lord,—I received by the hands of your deacons your invitation to become the pastor over you in the Lord, and have endeavoured to wait upon the chief Shepherd and Bishop of our souls to ask direction and counsel at His mouth, that I might return you an answer according to His holy will. And now in humble dependence upon Him for all I need for and in the great and solemn undertaking, I do accept your invitation.

The words of the apostle Paul have been much upon my mind while considering this matter, and in the spirit of them I desire to come among you,—" For we preach not ourselves, but Christ Jesus the Lord; and ourselves your servants for Jesus' sake " (II Cor. iv. 5).

The Lord permitting and enabling, I shall commence my labours among you on the 17th May next ensuing. " Brethren, pray for us."

    I am, dear brethren and sisters,
       Your humble faithful servant,

Crown St., Liverpool.   J. K. POPHAM.
16th March, 1874.

We cannot forbear noting the significant observation in this letter: " I desire to come among you in the spirit of the words, ' We preach not ourselves, but Christ Jesus the Lord; and ourselves your servants for Jesus' sake ' (II Cor. iv. 5)." What is miscalled " experimental " preaching our dear friend eschewed: he emphatically did not preach *himself*. Anecdotal sermonizing he knew to be profitless. But in accord with an unusually rich experience in his own soul of God's solemn teaching and leading, he preached Christ Jesus, the Saviour of the lost, the Friend of sinners. That he was so signally owned of his Lord and Master is a reply to the many adversaries he encountered throughout his long ministry. At Liverpool he profited through painful experiences of affliction and persecution, and many of his hearers derived benefit in consequence.

Mr. de Fraine, his old pastor, " accepted with pleasure " the invitation to conduct a " recognition service ", expressing his " personal interest in the welfare of Mr. Popham ". Services were held on the 17th May, 1874, Mr. de Fraine preaching morning and evening, " publicly recognizing our brother Popham as pastor of this church." Mr. Popham preached in the afternoon, his text being Ps. xc. 1: " Lord, Thou hast been our dwelling place in all generations." A note of this in the church minute book adds, " It was firmly believed that the dear Lord was present in the manifestation of His grace and power, commending the word to the hearts of the people." The tone of this sounds vastly different from the flattering " fraternal recognitions " so popular in certain quarters.

As our dear friend became more known, his solemn weighty ministry gained him entrance into many pulpits, and frequently invitations had to be declined. His health even at that early period was precarious, necessitating several extended absences from the pulpit.

In 1875 the Moody and Sankey American Revivalists came to Scotland and parts of England, visiting Liverpool. Mr. Popham felt impelled to combat their errors in a pamphlet— a vigorous and eminently Scriptural exposure—which ran into thirteen editions within a few months, including a Dutch translation. His preface to the first edition expresses his diffidence, and he tells us that he would gladly have remained silent had any other person in Liverpool come forward to rebut the heresies. He says:—

" I prayed the Lord to slay this Goliath of Free-will (which makes the decree of God the Father, the merit of God the Son, and the teachings of God the Holy Ghost, hang upon itself for their efficacy,) with the stone of divine truth, even though slung by a hand which, in itself, is feeble and unsteady."

This pamphlet, together with three others (by Dr. Kennedy, Mr. Hemington, and Mr. Leigh) on the same subject, was reveiwed in the *Gospel Standard*, 1875, page 211. Mr. Popham's publication spread remarkably and was much approved by the godly. To this may be traced his acquaintance and subsequent firm friendship with several godly

Dutch people, with whom he carried on a very rich spiritual correspondence for many years.* When, in 1877 and again in May, 1881, he was compelled to rest for some weeks from preaching owing to illness, he visited Holland, to their and his own great pleasure and profit. But the strictures on Moody and Sankey received abuse as well as praise, the pamphlet was angrily torn to shreds and thrown out of trains and burnt, and its author scornfully termed an "unregenerate blasphemer".

In the same year (1875), Mr. Popham also published two sermons from Gal. v. 4, entitled "Imperishable Grace", wherein he discourses very clearly on "the nature of grace in a three-fold aspect: as it is seen in God the Father, as it is manifested by God's eternal Son, and as it is applied by the Holy Eternal Spirit". He informs us that the sermons were the outcome of "solemn exercise of mind" and that "our contention for the doctrines of grace is no empty war of words, but a contention for eternal truths. We believe that these doctrines, as revealed and applied, are the life, comfort, and hope of God's dear children; for they are the glorious outcome of the everlasting love of God's heart, of the gracious thoughts of His mind, and of the determinations of His will". This publication was also very cordially reviewed in the *Gospel Standard*, 1875 (p. 264). In the same periodical (Nov., 1875) appears a letter from Mr. Popham pointing out the seriousness of an error in Sears' sermon on justifying faith, asking this unanswerable question, "If the justifying act of believing alone unites to the Lamb, what becomes of the eternal union between Christ and the Church?" These productions of Mr. Popham's pen manifest him, even at this early stage of his ministry, as being well equipped for the defence of the gospel and therein the rebutting of error: "I felt necessity laid upon me, as one who hopes he has obtained mercy to be faithful, to withstand them, doing so 'as of the ability God has given'." (*Preface to "Moody and Sankey"*).

An increasing warmth of attachment between pastor and people, and their appreciation of his ministry, was expressed

* A letter from one of these Dutch friends appears in the *Gospel Standard*, 1938, pages 205—209.

early in his pastorate at Liverpool by an addition to his
stipend, which though small was conveyed to him in most
affectionate terms, unmistakably revealing the influence of
his ministry.

To Mr. J. K. Popham.

My dear brother in that family whose Father fills a throne,
even the throne of glory,—I have sincere pleasure, my
brother, as a servant of the church over which the Lord has
made you overseer, in communicating to you that at its last
meeting there was a resolution arrived at (passed by the
unanimous voice of the church,) making a small addition to
your present income. You will, my dear brother, although
the amount is small, believe me when I say that the offering
is accompanied with true sincerity and the outcome of kindly
feelings towards you; for there is not to be a forgetting to
minister of our carnal things to those who minister to us in
spiritual things.   But with all things, my dear brother,
there is the one thing needful, viz., the blessing of the Lord.
This does indeed make rich, and there is no sorrow with it.
My prayer is earnestly before the Lord that you may be
abundantly blessed, so that in coming before the Lord's poor
people you may have that gracious experience of the good
man who out of the good treasure of his heart was enabled
to bring it forth under the mighty influence of God the
Holy Ghost, who alone can take of the untold and exhaustless treasures of a precious Christ and reveal them to poor
worms; consonant with the saying of the glorious Redeemer,
" Even so, Father, for so it seemed good in Thy sight."

This He does from time to time, and bless His holy Name
He will, so that they—His children—may be kept alive in
the midst of famine. The Lord grant you His holy anoint-
ings in the blessed work, spare you to labour and bless you
in the labour, so that you may see the fruits thereof, even
the power of God, through the foolishness of preaching, converting sinners and comforting His saints. Here is a blessed
reward; may it be realized according to the will of Him who
has created all things for His own glory; consequent upon
which poor sinners receive the benefit.

Yours in the indissoluble bond of the love of God through
a precious Christ,   J. WILTON.

Fazakerly.   7th Feb., 1876.

The lifting of the veil and the privilege of a momentary
glance into the intense soul exercise of this " painful minister " is afforded by a valuable scrap of writing\ entitled:

" 1876. A MEDITATION AT THE YEAR'S END.

" How soon will this year be gone for ever! And yet in
its sins and guilt it will be lived over again,—intensely, hor-
ribly, everlastingly lived over again by those for whom no
surety is found. How great, then, unspeakably great, is the
mercy of finding a hiding-place from the storm of wrath
due to the guilt of the evil thoughts, the loathsome workings,
the idle words, the unbelief, pride, worldliness, hardness and
rebellion of one's fallen nature, in the dear sacred wounds,
the dolorous sufferings, and the infinite merits of the Son
of God.   J. K. P."

Superficial trifling in the pulpit is not likely to issue from
meditations such as these!

The following two short letters relating to ministerial
engagements reveal somewhat the trial of ill-health with
which Mr. Popham contended, and shew a graciously exercised state as the result; they contrast strikingly with some
stereotyped formal invitations and acceptances of the present
degenerate days:—

To Mr. John Ashworth, [minister at Heywood (Jireh chapel),
     afterwards at Evington, Leicester.]

My dear Friend,—I am sorry to have kept you waiting so
long for a reply to your kind note of February 27th. My
apology must be ill health. For some time past I have been
suffering from much exhaustion both physical and nervous,
and have found myself quite unable for writing. In regard
to my coming to Heywood, I can only say that if the Lord
is pleased to strengthen me, I shall be pleased to serve His
people there in the gospel some week evening in June.
Earlier I could not come, as D.V. I leave home next week
for Holland for a change and rest; what the doctor says are
the only likely means to do me good. . . . May a kind and

gracious God grant us to feel our times are in His hands, and also enable us to commit our way and ourselves unto Him, in well doing.

A spark of divine life and a grain of living faith in the soul are worth more than a world, but how often is the former languishing and the latter ready to give up! Then we prove that "no man can keep alive his own soul"; and that faith, both in its being and actings, is the gift of God. The right path is and ever has been a rough one, but it leads to a "city of habitation".

   · With Christian love and best wishes,

                  Yours faithfully,   J. K. POPHAM.

6 Jasmine St., Everton, Liverpool.

9th March, 1877.

To Mr. J. Ashworth.

My dear Friend in the Truth,—. . . As you know, I have been away from home for a time for my health. . . . I now therefore hasten to say that if an evening in June would suit you, I would like to come on from Bolton. . . Through the goodness of the Lord the change was very beneficial to me and I am now, though not very strong or robust, able to go on preaching.

"What are these, and whence came they?" Tribulation of some sort and to some extent we must have if we are sons and not bastards. How often have I felt the verse you quote in your letter:

      "Bastards may escape the rod," etc.

What an amazing escape it will be to escape a richly deserved curse and hell, and O what a wonder to find and enter a freely-given heaven! . . .

With Christian love,   Yours very truly,

Liverpool.   J. K. POPHAM.

3rd May, 1877.

C

CHAPTER FOUR.

" Whether it be right in the sight of God, . . . judge ye."

1877—1881. Visits Holland—opposed by Dr. Christie—Revelation of the Eternal Son of God—pastoral care—inward declension— recovery and healing.

REFERENCE has already been made to Mr. Popham's introduction to Holland. How cordially he was received and the esteem in which he was held by the godly Dutch friends, together with the spiritual character of the friendships, is seen in a letter received by him shortly after his return to Liverpool after a visit to Holland in 1877:—

My dear Mr. Popham,—It is almost impossible to believe that it is already more than two weeks since you left us. It is as if it were only last week that we went with you to Rotterdam and saw the last glimpse of you on the boat. You can comprehend that our thoughts were with you all the time, and I was not at rest before I knew you could be at Liverpool. Mrs. Viveen has told you all about it, how strange it was in the house after your departure; we only comfort each other with speaking together of you as often as we meet. I was very sorry on hearing of your bad journey, but I think the seeing again of your dear wife and children, the glad welcome of your friends, and the powerful assistance you graciously received from the Lord on the following Sabbath, fully made you soon forget the fatigues of the journey.

Last Friday I had again the pleasure and honour of translating your letter; my friend came to me soon after dinner, for although she understands nearly all, she does not yet quite trust herself. I likewise received from her hands the beautiful hymnbook you sent for me, and for which I thank you very, very much. I think I shall never forget the pleasant and blessed days I enjoyed while you were with us. I liked so very much to hear you speaking with Mrs. Viveen on the things of God, and often thought how good the Lord was to me to bring me so much in company with His dear children, and how unworthy I was of it. I believe sometimes that it did me good, for I had, as I never saw before, much opening and clearness in the ways and Word of the Lord. It was sometimes with me as with the two disciples, when He opened the Scriptures to them; their hearts were burning within them. Often I was constrained to say, "This is an everlasting covenant ordered in all things and sure; in this is all my salvation and all my desire." But I know mine is a deceitful heart above all others, that I think I should deceive myself, deceive others, and likewise if it were possible I should even deceive the Lord Jesus. O if I but possessed truth and uprightness! Sometimes it is as if I cannot bring my heart enough to the Lord, to have it searched and tried by Him, and to have discovered every false ground. Should you think it is prescribing to the Lord to ask Him for a real sense and feeling of sin and to see myself utterly lost without Christ? I should like to see in Him as much and as great preciousness as His people do, and to give Him all the honour and love He is so worthy of, methinks.

Last week I had especially great need and much desire to know the Lord Jesus as my Saviour, and to have peace with God. I plead His promise that "All power is given unto Him in heaven and in earth", that He is able to do what is impossible in my eyes, that before Him there could be no real obstacle, that all mountains should be flatted and all valleys exalted before Him, that neither my sins, nor my bad, wicked, hard heart, could prevent Him from making His dwelling within me, if such were His pleasure. O then I sometimes hope deliverance is at hand, and I think of that word that came to my heart a fortnight ago, "Open ye to me the gates of righteousness." But soon after, when I see within myself, it seems it can never be, and a voice seems to say, "You have had many of those times you have wished and prayed, and yet it remains the same." Then I have nothing to answer and it seems again utterly hopeless; for I feel there are no reasons within me why the Lord should hear. I have nothing to move Him or to make myself acceptable to Him; and if the Lord does not incline His ear and hear the voice of my prayer, it is but right; but what then will become of me?

This morning I thought of that word, "Therefore now I will look unto the Lord, I will wait for the God of my

salvation. My God will hear me." O might it be so! May
the Lord give grace and stretch forth His mighty arm to
save and deliver me. . . .

May the Lord bless you abundantly and be with you and
yours. How glad should I be to know I belonged to His
people!

May I ask you to present my kindest love to your wife
and friends. Believe me,

Yours affectionately,   D. COPYN.

Utrecht. 22nd April, 1877.

This seeking soul, whose desires are so fervently expressed,
was soon taken ill and died. Before her end she was in
great distress, and Mr. Popham visiting Utrecht again in
1881, went to see her. She quoted to him Rom. viii. 3, 4:
" For what the law could not do, in that it was weak through
the flesh, God sending His own Son in the likeness of sinful
flesh, and for sin, condemned sin in the flesh," etc.; and
added with much vehemence, " *That is what I want*." And
before her death she realized the fulness of her desire.

Among his opponents at Liverpool was a Dr. Christie, an
ardent distributor of tracts " which, as my manner is, I distributed among the people of your dark synagogue, for
where should I look for patients all covered over with wounds
and bruises and putrefying sores more than in an hospital,
especially an avowed hospital of incurables ? " This vituper-
ation was evidently aroused by Mr. Popham's distinctive
teaching. In a 48 pp. pamphlet, " A Reply to a Strict Baptist Minister," published in 1880, Mr. Popham is held forth
as " having libelled the dead, assailed the Church of God,
God Himself, and what could the devil, the prince of darkness, do more ? " This individual, though evangelically
orthodox, was evidently one who knew nothing of the
gracious exercises of a living soul, being filled apparently
with just that presumptuous confidence which marks the
dead professor. Here is his scornful reference to the tender
fear of a humbled sinner: " You and your followers say you
are justified in quaking in your shoes all your life in your
comfortable little Strict Baptist chapel in Shaw Street, and
drag one Moses into your quaking company, and us also if

you could. . . . To be in the light and joy of Zion leaves you no room for humility, it is presumption with you, 'a beggar poor at mercy's door,' as ye phrase it." Our dear friend, God's servant, might well have bound his adversary's book as a crown to himself (Job xxxi. 36). It certainly was an honour to have been a target for the enmity of such a hater of vital godliness. Dr. Christie was seized with paralysis while preaching in a barn at Ash House, Broad Green, Liverpool. He died November 4th, 1892. Whether Mr. Popham publicly noticed this abusive critic is not clear; probably he did not. The best reply was the use the Holy Spirit made of the Shaw Street pastor in His vineyard.

Whilst at Liverpool, our dear friend received that especial revelation of the Eternal Son of God which made him ever after so jealous of Christ's highest glory, and for his contention against the denial of which he suffered so much bitter reproach from a section of Strict Baptists. The following references to this blessing will be of interest:—

"I have often reflected upon a sad thing, that is, to hear men who profess to believe in the doctrines of grace, to believe in the Sonship of the Lord Jesus, speak of that doctrine as if it were scarcely worth creating any trouble about; as if, though we profess to believe it, we need not talk about it, and certainly not contend about it, so as to make trouble anywhere. The reflection I have made is this: Could any man who has received the doctrine of Christ by divine revelation, and seen and felt the glory of that, speak so lightly of it? More than fifty years ago (in 1876-7) I got a sudden overthrow. I had implicitly, as I judge, received the doctrine of Christ into my understanding. I got a temptation, and I lost everything concerning that doctrine; I found I had never had it, it had been on my tongue but it had never been in my heart by divine revelation. After many months of exercise and sorrow—known only to myself at that time—it pleased God the Holy Ghost to say this in my heart: 'No man hath seen God at any time; the only begotten Son, which is in the bosom of the Father, He hath declared Him' (John i. 18). Then that was in my heart; it has never been out since. I have not half loved it, I do not half love it, alas for me! but I have never esteemed it a light doctrine since that day, I have not been permitted to let it go. . . ." (*Address at "Gospel Standard" Annual Meeting*, 1925).

"On that, to us, sacred spot we stood and, undisturbed by the traffic around us, worshipped Christ as the true, only-begotten, essential Son, of the Father's own substance. . . . If we are asked not to speak at all nor teach this doctrine, we must say, 'Whether it be right in the sight of God to hearken to you more than unto God, judge ye' (Acts iv. 18, 19). While we can use tongue and pen, we will, by God's gracious help, contend earnestly for the faith which was once for all delivered to us in the Word of God, and revealed in our soul" (*Gospel Standard*, 1926).

The following remarkable letter, written to a young person seeking the Lord, and who died in the faith two years later, aged twenty, manifests Mr. Popham's loving energy and gracious ability for tender yet faithful dealing with en-quiring souls; to present whom "perfect in Christ Jesus" was ever his fervent desire and labour:—

My dear ——,—While wondering how to spend the day on which so many thoughtlessly celebrate the birth of our blessed Lord, it occurred to me that perhaps I could not better spend some part of it than in writing to one in whose heart I have often prayed He might be formed the Hope of glory. All true Christians desire to have Christ *in their hearts*. Paul was not able to rest until He was again formed in the Galatians (ch. iv. 19). The Holy Ghost begets in the heart living desires after Jesus, He enables the hungry soul to "follow on to know the Lord", He makes everything else empty, void, and waste to the soul, He breathes that prayer, "Say unto my soul, I am thy salvation." This prayer, Spirit-wrought, never wholly dies away; it is tried, discouraged, damaged by sin, weakened by guilt, and faint by reason of delay, but its Author again and again revives and strengthens it. Satan blows up the wretched unbelief of our hearts till we are ready to conclude that it is useless to continue praying, for the Lord will never hear; then the Spirit presses our needs upon us so that we *must* cry, even though it be only in sighs: "Hear me, and attend unto me; for I mourn in my complaint, and make a noise" (Ps. lv. 2).

The soul's many, many needs, and the sweet suitableness and fulness of Christ, together with the Spirit's secret promptings, forming a happy junction in us, keep us alive in prayer. Little helps, secret encouragements derived from some Scripture resting on the mind, something dropped from the pulpit, and from comfortable feelings in prayer, make us feel we will never give up until the needed and desired good comes. Then guilt rolls over the soul and rests upon the conscience, hardness of heart, distracting fears of being deceived, the inward workings of sin and the suggestions of Satan, that cruel devil, greatly depress and discourage. We then begin to fear we were presumptuous in our earnest pleadings produced by the encouragements above mentioned, we fear we shall never find the Pearl of great price.

But all these changes keep the soul alive, render more and more unsatisfying all earthly good. The fear of presumption forces the soul to cry to be well searched and delivered from every false way; and the tormenting fear of never obtaining that which is so needful, (and, in the desire, so precious,) makes the soul violent. That we may have no false ground, the Lord makes the soul sink in deep mire where there is no standing, and that Jesus may be all in all the Spirit again and again discovers the hidden evils of a fallen nature. While this is being done the soul thinks every fresh discovery of indwelling sin and feeling of sinking into the mire, is a token of divine displeasure. But when again the fulness, mercy, compassion, and power of Christ are seen a little by faith, there is a sweet encouragement felt. All this spiritual labour results in the formation of Christ in the heart the Hope of glory.

I have run on a long way before acknowledging your letter. I was very pleased to read it. I have read it over and over, and each time have felt satisfied that you were under divine teaching. The Lord will not break the bruised reed, and the smoking flax shall He not quench; He shall send forth judgment unto truth (Isa. xlii. 3). It is a mercy for you to fear taking too much encouragement, this will keep you from taking what does not belong to you, it will make you *look well to the nature and source of any comfort* that may be offered you. By this godly fear you will depart from evil and from the snares of death. "The way of life is above to the wise, that he may depart from hell beneath" (Pr. xv. 24). Spiritual honesty makes its possessor fear deceptive comfort as much as any other snare. But it is very difficult to walk in this uprightneess and not, at the same time, refuse to be comforted. I feel thankful to perceive that you were made afraid of presuming, and yet enabled to receive what I believe is your own. "The kingdom of God cometh not by observation" (Luke xvii. 20). You will find many sweet influences upon your mind unaccompanied by a word. Your heart will be drawn after Christ, your affections will be heaven-ward, earthly things will appear in their proper light—"unsubstantial stuff", sin will be hateful and dreaded, you will pray for salvation from it. You will from time to time have such an insight into your fallen nature as will make you cry to God for help and flee to Christ for refuge. Not your own but His righteousness will you seek to be clothed in.

Now all these teachings and influences may be resting upon you without any distinct Scripture. Yet, though unaccompanied by the Word, if enabled to search the Word you will find them all *confirmed* by it. This will teach you that the kingdom of God is not in word only, but in power. Many boast of Scriptures coming to them, in whom we perceive but little, if any, fruit of divine teaching and power.

When it may please the Lord to speak on your heart a word suitable to your case, you will thank Him for it; it will sweetly instruct you, help and confirm you. But when you are feeling the want of that good word, pray to be enabled to observe very narrowly all the motions of your heart. And while you will perceive many motions which will bring sorrow and shame, you will, as under divine teaching, find others which "go upward round about" as did the Lord's House (Ezek. xli. 7). This will instruct you in the difference between flesh and spirit, between the old man and the new (Song vi. 13).

When the Lord is "getting to Himself a glorious Name" He will not allow the soul to "make an experience". But we ought to be very careful in our intercourse with young Christians lest we "strike the dying dead". However, you will suffer no real damage by the fear the remark induced and which still lives in you. All the work is the Lord's: "Thou, Lord, wilt ordain peace for us; for Thou also hast wrought all our works in us" (Is. xxvi. 12). Despise not the day of small things; if the Lord "gives you your life for a prey" and delivers you from the sword and from the enemies of whom you are afraid (Jer. xxxix. 17, 18), you will require an eternity to praise Him for His rich undeserved mercy.

I have not seen the book you name, consequently am not able to speak fully to the case you mention. But if there are no qualifying remarks made upon it, I should say it is a little unguarded. How to distinguish between false and real religion is a very large and important question. May the Lord enable me, not darkening counsel by words without knowledge, in simplicity to shew some of the main distinctions. To begin, then, with the case you quote. The person had convictions of sin. This is very likely, as no doubt thousands have who are not born again. These convictions are only *natural*. Natural conscience in some is tender, and generally such persons become what is called *religious*. Religion is with them a necessity. But in these cases, so far as I have observed them, the trouble is more about the *loss* of the birthright than the *sin* of first despising and then selling it. In other words, the conscience seems to say, "You have sinned, you will sink to hell." The trouble is more about hell than sin, more about the consequence to the sinner than the dishonour to God, against whom sin is committed. *Natural* convictions usually constrain those who are under them to betake themselves to religion to soothe and ease them, and they soon succeed in healing their hurt (Isa. l. 11).

Spiritual convictions make a person know that all religion but that which God works is worthless. When Cain's conscience smote him, it was because of his punishment and the fear of being slain; but when secured by the Lord from that danger he went and builded a city (Gen. iv. 17). But when the Lord smote Saul of Tarsus and he became blind and had to be led by others, he inquired, "Lord, what wilt Thou have me to do?" and he obtained no relief until the Lord sent a direct message to him. When Samuel convinced king Saul

of disobedience he fell under it in a way, but thought more
of being degraded before the elders of the people than of
being a rebel against God (I Sam. xv. 30). But when David
was divinely convinced of his sin he fasted and went in and
lay all night upon the earth; and the elders of his house
arose and went to him to raise him up from the earth; but
he would not, neither did he eat bread with them (II Sam.
xii. 16, 17; Zech. xii. 12—14).

Natural convictions are like light in a man which the
Lord says is darkness (Matt. vi. 23); spiritual convictions
bring the soul into felt darkness and the shadow of death.
The former are *general*, and cause a person to look more
especially, and with awful self-pity, upon himself; the latter
reveal both the miserable state of the sinner and a holy sin-
hating God; and when he feels self-pity he hates himself for
it, while the other has no perception of the sin. True
conviction is lasting and constantly deepens, and the more
mercy is manifested the more the sinner hates himself.
Fleshly conviction is quickly removed by the various reme-
dies which are applied, and the deceived one breaks out into
a liberty and a confidence nowhere found in the Word of
God. The former is never permitted to lose a sense of his
sinfulness and weakness; the latter, having no supplies of
life and light from heaven, moves on smoothly in the light
of his own fire until he lies down in utter darkness (Isa. l.
10, 11). Spiritual convictions convince not only of sin but
of the necessity of the Lord saving the soul; they not only
make a person know himself to be a sinner, but a *lost* sinner,
lost beyond all creature help and remedy, and that if ever
he is saved it must be first and last of God.

I believe natural convictions never sink as deep, never
penetrate as far as this in all its branches, as *total* blindness,
entire corruption, *absolute* weakness and folly, *entire* want
of will as well as of power; and these are not passing
thoughts but more or less *abiding, humbling, abasing* convictions. While natural convictions compel a person to take
up a religion, spiritual convictions make their subject
afraid of *touching*, much less taking up, religion; and while
the one is soon *satisfied* with his religion (Isa. lviii. 2), the
other is only more and more stripped of everything, and is

again and again brought in guilty before God (Lev. xiii. 44, 45).

These, my dear young friend, are some of the distinctions between natural and spiritual convictions. I hope you may find something in them to set your mind at rest on this important point, if it please the Lord. With regard to the person E. H. speaks of as feeling some sweetness in divine things, I would remark that it is no new or uncommon thing. The stony-ground hearer lives still (Mat. xiii. 20). But please observe that there had been no plough driven through the stony place, no breaking of the fallow ground, consequently there was no *affliction* in which to receive the word (I Thess. i. 6). Having some natural convictions, a *general* notion of salvation, of heaven, would at once, without searching of heart, be received with joy; but the word that brings reproof, compunction, that lays in the dust, that brings with it a yoke and a daily cross of self-denial and other things, is unknown to such persons. . . .

I must hasten to say a word upon your next question. The Scripture you ask me about is I Cor. xii. 3. The passage teaches that we cannot spiritually call Jesus Lord, but by the Holy Ghost whose covenant work it is to glorify Christ. Every believing look a poor sinner casts toward Jesus, every spiritual view he has of His Person and work, every new beauty that the soul sees in Him, every sweet time of pleading His Name and merits wherein boldness and freedom are felt, the soul has by the almighty influence of the eternal Spirit (John xvi. 14). And when the needy and undone soul is enabled to say, " *My* Lord, and *my* God," it is by the sweet persuasive power of the Spirit. I know well your feelings of inability to plead that dear Name, and also the softening of your heart so that you were enabled to plead for mercy through Him. Go on, and prize every such feeling, and, as enabled, follow after Him, who, though He may seem to turn away from you, will eventually tell you all His Name and open His heart of love and mercy.

I am thankful that your mother and sister are now acquainted in some measure with your feelings; embrace every opening there may be to communicate to them how you

fare, it will be a great comfort to them and, in the end, a
mutual benefit. . . .

Never fear to ask any question you may desire; it is no
trouble. My only fear is that I may fail to give you the
satisfaction you require. However, I will assist you according to the ability God giveth. . . .

Yours very sincerely to serve in the gospel,
6 Jasmine St., Liverpool.   J. K. POPHAM.
25th December, 1877.

The discrimination evident in the above weighty letter,
written so early in his career, characterized Mr. Popham's
preaching from the first to the last, and is just that vital
distinction between the precious and the vile (Jer. xv. 19),
which was the deep secret reason for his separation and
insistence on separation throughout his long ministerial and
denominational life,—a cause of much hatred on the part of
nominal professors and superficial preachers, but of deep
attachment in the case of those who were truly taught of
God.

A third contribution of no mean order our friend made to
the treasury of spiritual religious literature, by publishing
in 1878 a small treatise, *Thoughts on Regeneration*. The
theme is treated with an earnestness and downrightness
evidencing the author's sense of its vast importance, which
he thus expresses:—

" I have been induced to publish the following ' Thoughts
on Regeneration ' for two reasons: First, because regeneration is the root of all true religion in the soul. If this be
wanting, all else is of no value. Whatever profession of
religion may be made, whatever knowledge may be possessed,
whatever good works may be performed, all will leave a man
a natural man, dead in trespasses and sin, if the new birth
be wanting. Nothing can rise above its own nature. Being
spiritually dead, man cannot work himself into a Christian,
cannot raise himself into divine life. He may cover himself
with virtue, wrap himself up in a robe of self-righteousness,
yet he is only a natural, carnal, spiritually-dead creature.
He cannot invest himself with another nature. . . . Galvanism may produce a shock and evoke a movement, but there
it stops; it cannot infuse life into a corpse. So, natural

religion, with all its attractions, erroneous preaching, with all its eloquence, with all its power, can never give life to a dead soul. . . . My second reason is, that among the blind followers of, perhaps, still more blind leaders, there may be some of the ' blind people who have eyes ' (Isa. xliii. 8), who, being ' ruled with force and cruelty ' and ' scattered ', are wandering through all the mountains and upon every hill, with none to search or seek after them (Ezek. xxxiv. 4—6). These are ' lost, driven away, broken, and sick '; if they eat at all, they must eat of pastures ' trodden down '; if they drink, it is of ' fouled waters '. Now for these, if it should please the Good Shepherd to direct this little book to them, I write. To them I would be useful " (*Introduction to* " *Thoughts on Regeneration* ").

What tender care and faithfulness breathes through these preliminary utterances! Thus ministerially visiting the sick, seeking the lost, " drawing out his soul to the hungry and satisfying the afflicted soul," our dear friend's light was beginning to " rise in obscurity ". He became useful, through God's grace, to many souls in Liverpool and other places, to an extent that the Great Day alone will reveal. Bitter trials, persecution, disappointment, and affliction he endured, but the Lord stood by him. " Thoughts on Regeneration " was favourably reviewed in the *Gospel Standard*, 1878. Making all allowance for natural temperament, there is no comparison between the social, gossipy, popular sort of minister and the labourer who has a purpose to fulfil. To this purpose the following letter alludes:—

To Mr. J. Ashworth.

My dear Brother in the Lord,—. . . I am glad to hear that your prayer meeting is well attended. It is a good sign. I think the late Mr. Tiptaft said the prayer meeting was the gauge of the church. It has often cheered me much more than an increase in the Sunday congregation, and if I perceive a slackness in the prayer meeting, my mind is soon sensible of some gloomy feelings about the people.

It gives me pleasure to find that you approve of my little publication [his *Thoughts on Regeneration*]. To live a lazy life is my dread, and many have been my petitions against

it. "Occupy till I come," is a word I would wish ever to
be mindful of. 'Tis but a little one can do, but this has
been a comfort, "If there be first a willing mind, it is
accepted, according to that a man hath, and not according
to that he hath not."

I hope you find the Lord with you both in your own soul
and in preaching. The first is of the first importance, for
without it, in some measure and at some times, preaching
must be dead profitless work. To preach in a warm living
manner there must be some tasting, handling and feeling
of the Word of Life. But why do I presume to write thus
to you? You know so much more about these solemn and
weighty matters than I do. Excuse it; out of the abundance
of feeling in my heart about preaching, its awful weight and
solemn nature, I have penned these few words. The Lord
help each of us and make us good ministers of Jesus Christ.

With Christian love to yourself and Mrs. Ashworth.

Yours very truly,

Liverpool.   J. K. POPHAM.
May 13th, 1878.

To the same.   December 5th, 1879.

My dear Friend,—. . . My thoughts were not the Lord's,
for on my return I was taken ill, and have remained an
invalid ever since. One Sunday was a dumb one: I was
confined to my bed, but last Sunday by riding to chapel I
was able to speak for about half an hour each service. In
how many ways does the Lord try His people! The mercy
is not to escape the cross, but to be bettered by it. For
the most part I have been low in mind during this affliction,
indeed much of the affliction consists in prostration of the
nervous system; and Satan is well skilled in playing on weak
nerves. Just in the worst the seventh hymn was helpful,
specially verse 4:

> "When sore afflictions on me lie,
>   He is (though I am blind)
> Too wise to be mistaken, yea,
>   Too good to be unkind."

. . . You kindly hope I am favoured with many tokens in
my ministry, of the " good will of Him that dwelt in the

bush ". My dear friend, one of my greatest trials is my barrenness in the ministry. I dare not say I am quite left, but O to my sense of things I am so poor, empty and sapless! How is it with you? Do you find your people searched, humbled, broken, comforted, lifted up, and built up under you? And are there any deliverances wrought, any clear conversions?

What a loss has the Church sustained in the death of dear Covell! Without exception, in my judgment, the most living, solemn, weighty preacher in our connexion. What life there was in his simple unlettered utterances! He has gone. Our mercy is the Lord liveth. . . .   J. K. POPHAM.

53 York Terrace,
    Everton, Liverpool.

Not only could Mr. Popham be a " Boanerges " to the stiff-necked, but also a " son of consolation " to afflicted, broken-hearted sinners; as the ensuing letter shews:—

Dear Friend,—I hope that you may be enabled to believe for yourself Heb. xii. 6. I say *enabled*, for I well know how impossible it is in time of affliction without the Spirit. The Lord loves His people too well to let them alone; but how hard to regard divine chastisement as the " privilege of a saint "; the part, or the portion, of a son. But so it is, and the comfort of it the Lord will give in His own time. The " third part " is the Lord's portion, and that part He will bring through the fire. There He will refine them; there He will try them. O heavy painful work! specially when, as in refining silver, the dross first rises and appears; when the depravity and defilement of our fallen hearts are seen and felt. But He who sitteth as a refiner and purifier of silver not only sees the dross, but also knows what silver there is in the sons of Levi.

But this is not all. In the fire they *shall*—from necessity by divine teaching—" call upon My Name." How unspeakably great is the mercy of being a praying person! There are none such by nature. Then, further, there is a most gracious promise—" and I will hear them "; which means, I will answer them. As we read, " I will hear the heavens, and they shall hear the earth, and the earth shall hear the corn and the wine and the oil." This most merciful promise the Lord makes good in drawing near and saying, "Fear not;" in staying the feeble mind upon Himself, even in the dark; in reviving hope, in giving some assurance of a good issue, in working sweet resignation to His holy sovereign will. O blessed answer! answer of which my dear friend is not, I hope, ignorant.

There is yet another word: "I will say, It is My people." Blessed comforting recognition! Where now are all the cruel suggestions of the father of lies? Where the thousand misgivings of an unbelieving heart? Who could have expected such a resting-place in the fire? "Certainly," said the Lord, in another case, "I will be with thee." And here, in the fire, the purifying fire, which has destroyed many hopes, burnt up much wood, hay and stubble, and has left only a naked, needy soul, the Lord comes and says, "Thou art Mine. I will bring thee *through* this fire." What an effectual work is this! It enriches most abundantly the person who is favoured to receive it.

The same blessed enriching work the Spirit describes under another figure. The Lord promises the Church her vineyards from the valley of Achor; from the valley of trouble comes peace; out of the wilderness the vineyards grow. Who would go to the wilderness, to the valley of Achor—that gloomy vale—to look for a vineyard? But trouble, conflicts, divine chastisements, painful discoveries of our deep depravity by the Spirit, greatly enrich the soul in godly fear, in living desires to know, love, and be found in Christ; in earnest prayer, in cleaving to the Lord with purpose of heart, in deep feelings of nothingness in self, and in high esteem of Christ and all He has for *poor* persons, and in a full enjoyment of heavenly things. And when the last word comes, "It is My people," back then flies the response, "The Lord is my God." Not earlier could the confidence be found to say so great a thing; now it cannot be restrained. Better wait till the Lord says that before we say this. I do hope, my dear friend, that you may find a quiet resting-place in Jesus, and be favoured to feel that

> "It is the Lord, whose matchless skill
> Can from afflictions raise

> Matter eternity to fill
> With ever-growing praise."

My pen has run on rapidly. I hope you may find some help and comfort from the word upon which I have hurriedly written a few hints. I beg you will not think of answering this; no, not by the scratch of a pen, while you are weak. It is not worth an answer; it is but the utterance of a few thoughts which perhaps you may find somewhat suitable to your present case.

I remain, yours very truly in hope of eternal life,
Liverpool.   J. K. POPHAM.
March 14th, 1879.

A further insight into the gracious pastor's tender heart is given us in an obituary from his pen of a member of his church, Mrs. Brabbins, published in the *Gospel Standard*, January, 1880, from which the following is an extract:—

" Before her departure she had one more fiery dart to receive in her soul—a dart more fiery and dreadful than any she had received before. One day, as she was thinking of Christ, Satan suddenly and powerfully injected the thought and the words, ' Say you don't want Him; let Him go.' And though, as she told me, she put her hand to her mouth and prevented the utterance of the words, yet both the thought and the words were distinctly perceived and felt within, and got a strong hold. Then the adversary turned accuser with such fury that she was plunged into the most dreadful state of grief and dismay. ' Ah!' said the accuser, ' you are an apostate; over you the second death will have power.' Never shall I forget the expression of grief and anguish that was settled on her poor wan face, nor the cry with which she met me as I entered her room: ' O! I did not say it! I did not say it!' I felt it was kinder to leave her, and go and try to pray for her; and the Lord was pleased to grant a spirit of prayer for a tempted suffering saint. The evening of that day being our prayer-meeting, I felt constrained and encouraged by Mat. xviii. 19, 20, and particularly by Acts xii. 5, 17, to mention our sister's case and ask the friends to pray for her. During the whole of that night, until three o'clock in the morning, I was unable to sleep, and could

D

do nothing but lay the poor tempted one's trouble before
the Lord. As early as was prudent the next day I went to
the sick chamber; but what a change! It was no longer a
'house of mourning', for Jesus had come, the 'accuser of
the brethren' was cast down, and the dear saint was once
more as a 'hind let loose'. Mrs. B.'s account of her deliverance was, in substance, as follows: 'About three o'clock
this morning the Lord's words to Martha (John xi. 25, 26)
came to me, and to the question, "Believest thou this?" I
felt enabled to reply, "Yea, Lord; I believe that Thou art
the Christ, the Son of God, which should come into the
world." Then light began to break in upon me, and I
pleaded with the Lord. I told Him that I *did want Him;*
that I believed in Him and loved Him. Then I felt the
power of God increasing in me, and the temptation break;
and the Lord sent that word: "Blessed and holy is he that
hath part in the first resurrection; on such the second death
hath no power." O what glory I saw in Christ! He is the
Son of God. I do believe in Him. I shall be with Him.
But O! that dreadful thought! I can never forget it.' Truly
the Lord had made the storm a calm, so that the waves,
which had lifted up themselves, were still. . . . Down to the
last the dear saint suffered much pain. . . . At length the
summons came; and after a long and chequered pilgrimage,
our sister fell asleep in Jesus, and went beyond the cruel
archer's reach, and left for ever the sad, grievous, and
grieving companionship of a body of sin and death.—'The
memory of the just is blessed.'—J. K. POPHAM."

The bitterest enemies of our late beloved friend would find
it difficult to produce a livelier example of loving pastoral
care than the above. Eminently he was a man of God,
through grace; diligent, faithful, tender. The obituaries of
two other choice saints, members of the church at Shaw
Street who died during Mr. Popham's pastorate, appear in
the *Gospel Standard*, 1881. They, too, shew the pastor's
same tender appreciation of and love to the work of God's
grace in the heart. Of one, Charles Pooley—a poor man,
but a choice character, who died March 12th, 1881, aged 34;
"dear Pooley" his pastor affectionately calls him—Mr.
Popham said:

"The Lord has again seen fit in the exercise of His sovereign pleasure to take away in the midst of his days one of
the favourites of heaven. We feel we can ill spare him; he
was a tender, humble, praying soul; but we desire to say
before Him on whose shoulders the government of the
Church rests, 'Thy will be done.'"

The obituary of Charles Pooley recalls one interesting
episode in the ministry of the worthy minister of Shaw
Street, Liverpool, which is here given in his own words:—

"One Lord's Day morning I had particular liberty in
preaching from John xv. 15, and said in concluding, 'I
shall resume the subject in the evening.' This was my intention until four o'clock, when all was taken from my mind,
and I began to be in great trouble and exercise about the
evening service, until that word came to me: 'Bring my soul
out of prison, that I may praise Thy Name' (Ps. cxlii. 7).
That was my text in the evening, and I felt more authority
in preaching than even in the morning, and was sure the
Lord was working in the hearts of some of the people.
Then, foolishly, I expected to hear the next morning of the
Lord's work by means of that sermon; but I heard nothing
that day, nor the next, nor during the first month, nor the
second month. But at the end of the third month, I went
to visit some of the people, and as I was at the house of one
member, she said, 'Have you heard about Lizzie Crispin?'
I said, 'No, I have not; what about her?' 'Well,' she said,
'she has been in great trouble, and the Lord blessed her
under that sermon you preached from, "Bring my soul out
of prison."' From there I went to another house, where
the person began telling me of the trouble and exercise she
had been in, and that the Lord had come and delivered her
under that same sermon. Then I went to good Charles
Pooley. He had gone out, but his wife whom I had not met
before, asked me to come in. She began telling me of her
trouble, and said that one Lord's Day morning her husband
came home from chapel and said to her: 'You are to go this
evening; I will stay and look after the children.' But she
said she would not. 'Yes,' he said, 'you go this evening.'
'No,' she said, 'I will not go there again; Mr. Popham only
strips and wounds me.' But her husband insisted on her

going, and the Lord blessed her with a clear deliverance. So three times that day I heard of the Lord's blessing the word preached on that occasion. They were godly people, Mr. and Mrs. Pooley. Mrs. Pooley was persuaded they would be the caretakers of the chapel, although we had almost settled with another couple to come; and her faith was so strong that she said, 'If they come, they will have to go back again; we are going there.' And so it was, and I suppose no chapel could have been better kept. It held 750 persons, and they scrubbed a piece of the floor every week. Then there was good old Mr. Lacey. When going to chapel he was assaulted by the enemy thus: 'You have been going to chapel a long time?' 'Yes,' he said. 'And you never get anything, do you?' 'No,' he said. 'Then give up going.' And the temptation so far prevailed that he turned back again towards home; but the suggestion came that he had better try and go once more. So again he started walking towards the chapel; but the enemy again thrusting at him, he again turned back. Then these words came, 'Who can tell?' and a third time he turned and ran, and was just in time for the service. My text was, 'The Lord is good unto them that wait for Him, to the soul that seeketh Him' (Lam. iii. 25). And the Lord gave him a clear and blessed deliverance. Oh, the Lord did work by me in those days!

"I was in great trouble and in a very low depressed state, and one day threw myself on the couch and said, 'I shall rise no more.' Then at that moment the Lord appeared and delivered me with the words, 'Happy is he that hath the God of Jacob for his help, whose hope is in the Lord his God: which made heaven and earth, the sea and all that therein is: which keepeth truth for ever' (Ps. cxlvi. 5, 6). At that word, 'keepeth truth,' all that the Lord had done for me in the past came to mind, and I said, 'Thou wilt keep this word, Lord; Thou wilt do that; Thou wilt do all that Thou hast spoken to me of.' The next day Lacey came to see me, and I told him what had happened, and how the Lord had delivered me. He said, 'When did that happen?' When I told him, he said, 'Well, that was just the time I left off praying for you!'

"On two occasions I told the people I must resign and

leave them, as the Lord was not working by my ministry. They would not have it, but I said to my wife, ' I will go away; the Lord does not speak by me.' But one day after the service, two men stayed behind and said, ' Can we come and see you during the week ? ' A time was arranged, and they came; then a woman also came; and all three told how the Lord had spoken to them by my ministry during the time in which I was saying He was not doing anything by me. Then I said to my wife, ' I have been like a servant discontented with his master's service, and his master would not let him go. Now I am going to unpack my boxes.' "

The other obituary appeared (*Gospel Standard*, 1881, p. 61) under the title, " Choice Fragments." It related to Mrs. Jacques, a personal acquaintance and a hearer of William Huntington. She was greatly blessed in her latter days, and her last attendance at Shaw Street chapel was a time of special favour. She died on November 8th, 1880, aged eighty-two. Referring to a letter written by her in her early days, and to her expressions of faith in her last moments, Mr. Popham said, " The desires which thus lived in our friend's heart fifty-three years ago, continued to live and move there until her death, when they rose to a blessed, full, eternal realization." What a solemn sacred pleasure the godly pastor takes in the good finish of the saint whose " death is precious in the sight of the Lord " (Ps. cxvi. 15).

Of Mrs. Jacques' three daughters, one died but a few months after her mother. Mr. Popham, who was convalescing in Utrecht at the time, wrote the following letters, the first to the dying sister and the second to the two who were bereaved:—

To Miss E. Jacques.

My dear Friend,—You have often been in my mind since I left home, and I have several times thought of writing to you, but have not done as I wished. But hearing from Mrs. Popham that you are not so well, I feel I must attempt a few lines.

Your poor body groans under the weight of affliction, the fruit of sin original and actual; the end will be, sooner or later, death. But O what an unspeakable favour you have

in the possession of a good hope through grace—a fruit this
of the life and death of our blessed Lord and the end everlasting peace and bliss with God. When the Lord bends
our hearts and makes our ears obedient in affliction, and
then grants glimpses of His eternal love in Christ, how easy
is the cross! Otherwise how hard, yea, intolerable it is! To
the tempest-tossed, God has given a most comforting promise. O what an end will He make of all the trials, sorrows, pains, sins, fears, and enemies, earthly and devilish, in
His own time! And then what an eternity opens out for
the redeemed—redeemed by price (what a price!) and by
power. Touches and glimpses are what we get here below,
for the most part. " They shall be holpen with a little
help," enough and none to spare. A moving of the Spirit of
life, a gleam of hope, a pouring of the heart out before a
prayer-giving, a prayer-hearing, and a prayer-answering
God: then darkness, deadness; no felt nearness to Him whom
the soul loveth, are among the things which make up the
life,—the real life of a vessel of mercy. Should the God of
infinite mercy put a speedy end to these changes in your soul
by taking you to Himself, what an advantage you will have
over those left behind! Well, His time is best and His
way is best; only our self-sufficient, proud, ease-loving
hearts do not allow these truths.

May the Lord be your all-sufficient Friend, be nigh to help,
strengthen faith, and either banish or sweeten care, and
" from the affliction take the curse ". Dear friend, it is not
in anger.

I hope that your sisters are better and that they may be
preserved in a measure of health. Please give them my
Christian love. I know that you will be pleased to hear that
I am feeling better for the change and rest, and I have thus
far much enjoyed the society of the few godly people I have
met in this place.

Do not trouble yourself to think of answering this by a
word. I shall hope to hear of you through Mrs. Popham.

With Christian love,   I remain, etc.,

Utrecht. May 10th, 1881.   J. K. POPHAM.

To The Misses Jacques.

My dear afflicted Friends,—I cannot express the feeling of sorrow and sympathy I have for you in this time of distress. Yesterday afternoon I received the sad intelligence of your sister's departure. I feel I cannot say much beyond expressing my fervent hope and prayer that you both may be so supported and feel so divinely assured of the love, wisdom and goodness of God, that your souls may say, "It is well." It is well with your departed sister. She has left for ever a sin-polluted body and a troublesome, sorrowful path. O what a weight of trouble, what piercing sorrow has she left! It is well with her now, for she is in the blissful presence of Him whom, as I have often witnessed, she sought with many tears, and whose absence was her greatest grief. O how inconceivable is her ever-swelling joy; her delightful uninterrupted gaze upon the Lamb and all His full-assembled glories! How her overflowing gratitude and admiration will ceaselessly flow to Him who loved her and washed her in His own blood! The crown is His; and with infinite pleasure will her ransomed spirit cast it down at His ever-adorable feet, singing the glad, the glorious song, "Worthy the Lamb," etc. Oh! as one writes one could wish to be in such a wondrously glorious place, to walk the shining streets, to drink at the ever-flowing, overflowing, pleasure-giving Fountain of living waters. It is well with your dear sister now, for all her wishes, best wishes, all her sighs and prayers, are answered and fulfilled to the full. No more will she go out of the Lord's blessed presence.

And, dear friends, it is no less *well*, though far less *happy*, with you. It is well in this trial, for an ever-gracious God, a tender Father has done it. Infinite goodness and wisdom and faithfulness are in this great affliction. Oh, may the eternal Spirit say to your souls, "It is well." Well *now* though not comfortable. Well, because the God of all grace will manage for you, because an Almighty God will strengthen and keep you, and because a promise-performing God will bring you through all to Himself. May He work sweetest submission to His will. Our vile nature can do nothing but rebel; may grace reign.

I feel much being away at this time; but this no doubt

is well. An all-sufficient God is near. Accept my warmest, deepest sympathy and Christian love. At the earliest moment on my return I shall see you.

Believe me, dear friends,

Your affectionate friend in the Lord,

Utrecht.   May 16th, 1881.   J. K. POPHAM.

The bereaved sister wrote, " At the time dear E. died, our dear and valued minister, Mr. Popham, was at Utrecht, but he wrote us a blessed letter, indited, we are sure, by the Lord, and speaking assuredly of the safety and blessed happiness she was enjoying, released from a suffering body and all her troubles. . . . Mr. Popham's ministry, visits, and prayers, she much prized."

Many were our friend's trials at Liverpool, but until the Lord's time for him to move, no attempt on His servant's part shall succeed. He has told how on one occasion he was so full of bitter sorrow and trouble that he determined to run away from it all, and Jonah-like actually travelled into Leicestershire to secure a house into which to move with his family. But he had to return without accomplishing his design. No one but himself knew at that time the solemn inner workings of his heart, until many years later he related them to the Lord's honour. From this narration the following is a note:

" After a time I was in God's providence and by His good Spirit guided to the pastorate of the church at Liverpool, where I remained some years, and was permitted to see some evident fruit of my labours. I there fell into a very cold, backsliding state inwardly, walking in a formal way to the services of God's House, even at length saying of His service, ' What a weariness is it!' and of His Table, ' It is polluted, and the fruit thereof is contemptible' (Mal. i. 12, 13). I became so proud and independent that I said (inwardly) of the Bible, ' I do not want to look at it; I know all that is there.' After a time the Lord made me aware of the terrible distance that had grown up between Himself and my soul, and He brought my sad state home to me by sharp rebukes in my conscience and a heavy trial in the church. He sent this word, ' Ephraim, strangers have devoured his strength, and he knoweth it not; yea, gray hairs are here and there upon him, yet he knoweth not' (Hosea vii. 9). Then I had an overwhelming sense of His reproofs; for they came in upon my soul for some weeks together, till I thought there would be no end of them. No sweet words of comfort then, nothing but reproof and rebuke. Outwardly I suffered wrong, but was left to speak in my own spirit to one whom I felt had taken a wrong course. [One who had appeared to be his friend turned bitterly against him, and did all he could to injure him; and smarting under the injustice, he felt a revengeful spirit working.] When I tried to pray, I felt the Lord stand aloof, His ear was closed. Passages in Jeremiah and Micah were with me: 'O My people, what have I done unto thee? and wherein have I wearied thee? testify against Me.' 'Hast thou not procured this unto thyself, in that thou hast forsaken the Lord, when He led thee by the way?' 'Is Israel a servant? is he a home-born slave? why is he spoiled?' And I fell under them: 'I am guilty, Lord.' At length He sent me this dream:—[He awoke one night in great distress having dreamed he had murdered a man; it was to him a relief to find it only a dream, and he again fell asleep, and dreamed again the same dream. This so distressed him that he resolved to keep awake, but in spite of himself he again slept, and a third time dreamed he had committed murder. His distress was great, and he said, 'Lord, what is it?' Then it was the Lord brought to his mind the words, 'Whoso hateth his brother is a murderer,' and he saw that he had committed murder in his heart by hating one who had risen up against him and injured him. A voice within urged him to go and confess: 'Therefore if thou bring thy gift to the altar, and there rememberest that thy brother hath aught against thee; leave there thy gift before the altar, and go thy way; first be reconciled to thy brother, and then come and offer thy gift.' He continues:]

"Then I sinned terribly, as I hope you will never sin. I said inwardly, 'I never will. Lord, it is too bad of Thee to tell me to do this. He has injured me, I have not injured him. I will not go.' And oh what a state I was in all that day, fighting against the Lord! Time after time I went to my room to try to pray; but each time it was, 'Go thy way; first be reconciled to thy brother.' The Lord stood aloof; yet I said I would not go, and fought against the Lord, until late in the day there came a change. The Lord expostulated thus: 'I forgave thee all that debt.' This was repeated with such emphasis, 'ALL THAT DEBT,' that I was quite overcome, and I went to my room and asked the Lord if He would *allow* me to go, after my baseness. He did not repel me then, but allowed me to pray. At the first opportunity the next day I went to see this man, and told him that God had commanded me to come and be reconciled to him; that He had taught me that my anger with him because of his injuring me was murder. He received me coldly and took it that I acknowledged myself wrong in everything, evidently not seeing his own fault; but that did not matter to me, he forgave me. Then the Lord forgave me also, and delivered me from my dreadful backsliding. After this, the church wanted me to deal with this man; but I said, 'No'; however, eventually we had to withdraw from him."

Thus the Lord healed the wounded spirit of His servant, giving him a sense of His divine approval, restoring peace to his soul. Then he experienced the fulfilment of Joel ii. 25, which he so frequently quoted in the course of his ministry: "I will restore to you the years that the locust hath eaten, the cankerworm, the palmer-worm, and the cater-pillar, My great army which I sent among you."

These heavy trials produced nervous exhaustion so severe that for a time he could not even endure the sound of his children. Then again the Lord hid His face, which was a sore affliction; but he was restored and delivered by the words of Ps. cxlvi. 5, 6. The last words, "Which keepeth truth for ever," shone in his heart with double lustre, and God's unfailing faithfulness through all the past and His promise concerning the future, brought him quite up and healed both body and soul. Thus did the Lord graciously counsel and instruct His dear servant.

CHAPTER FIVE.

" I will help thee."

" THE way in which my name was brought before the deacons of the church at Galeed was as follows:—I had two friends at Wigston Magna, near Leicester, Mr. and Mrs. Levesley, who, through a grandson, living at Brighton, became acquainted with Mr. and Mrs. Marshall [a deacon at Galeed]. Mrs. Levesley was taken ill, and word of her illness came to me; a strong impulse came on me to write to her, and, though I knew nothing of the state of her mind at the time, the Lord guided my pen to write suitably and usefully to her. After the letter was read, Mr. Levesley remarked to his dying wife that he thought Mr. and Mrs. Marshall might like to see it. The letter was sent to them. It was approved, and Mr. Marshall took it to the next deacons' meeting at Galeed and read it. The result was that an invitation was sent me to supply for two Lord's Days, June 12th and 19th, 1881. After a fiery trial [before-mentioned, page 57], out of which the Lord graciously delivered me, and made some further use of me, I had no desire to leave Liverpool. But, a year or more before I saw Brighton, though after I received the invitation to supply, a fear—a feeling—that my ministry at Liverpool was drying up had taken possession of me. Later, I learned that the most gracious members, some of them my children in the faith, were troubled with the feeling that the Lord was about to remove me. But, while they had grace to say, ' The will of the Lord be done,' I fell under the power of the tempter, who was permitted to make me believe I was not called to preach. The sufferings of many months during which I lived under that piercing temptation, can only be entered into by one who has passed through the same. Hundreds of times I sought the Lord in secret and used to say, ' Forgive me for having preached, and do open an honourable way out of the ministry for me.' While thus suffering, the time drew near for fulfilling my engagement

at Brighton, and I used to say, ' O if I could get out of that
engagement!' When I made the engagement I had heard a
good report of the church there, and wished to go. I dare
not ask to be released from it, though earnestly wishing it.
Thus I came. On the morning of June 12th, I was arrested
by the clock striking ten. In weakness and fear, and crushed
by sorrow, I said, ' Lord, one hour more and the people
expect me; I cannot go like this, and I *will* not.' In infinite
mercy and compassion He immediately spoke to me. He
said, ' I will help thee.' I knew the voice, felt the power
of it, and falling on my knees, I adoringly said, ' Lord, I
believe it.' Now, though physically weak, I longed to go to
the pulpit. Often since then I have said, ' If I am in my
right place, I was put in it that morning.' Oh, blessed day!
Rather, blessed be God, who so graciously delivered a poor
captive from the mighty, lion-like enemy and oppressor!

" At this time, and for many months previously, and afterwards, the church at Galeed was much exercised concerning
a pastor. Past experience made them afraid. There was no
minister in their mind, yet they could not rest in a pastorless
state. In private and at the prayer-meetings, the pressing
need was one of the burdens which they sought to cast on
the Lord. At one prayer-meeting a member said, ' Lord,
what are we to do? the stream of supplies is dried up.'
There was then no change, either in the number or character
of the supplies. The prayer was the urgent desire for a
pastor. On another occasion, at the close of a week-evening
service, the same subject was the burden of a conversation
among several of the members, when one of them said, ' I
believe, if we are to have a pastor, it will be as if the Lord
dropped a man down from heaven, of whom we now know
nothing.' This was said months before my first visit. Thus
it seems that the Lord was preparing the people to *receive*
a pastor, not, in an important sense, to *choose* one; while I
was being reduced to ashes regarding my ministry, by a fiery
temptation, and most unlikely to be the appointed one. Less
likely, if not impossible, would it appear that the months of
sorrow, sighing, groaning, and all but despair of having
received a heavenly call to preach, could be a preparation for
such a position as awaited me.

"As stated above, I was very mercifully delivered an hour before the first service at Galeed. From that hour to the end of my visit—two Lord's Days and two week evenings— the Lord much indulged me with His gracious presence. And the persuasion of some of the people that the answer was given to their prayer, was strong. By the questions, quite prudent and proper, which the deacons asked me about Liverpool, I perceived the trend of their thoughts. As the Lord was now with me, my memory of His gracious dealings with me was lively, and I only named them, resolving not to say one word about my temptation and my fears that I must leave Liverpool. Thus the first engagement was fulfilled. But it soon became evident that God was working in the people; and I could not put away from me the exercise that came on me day by day. One of the members, whose name shall go down to the end of the church's existence, Charity Trowers, while hearing the first sermon, heard also the word, 'Arise, anoint him; for this is he.' She believed at that moment she should live to see me the pastor. On the evening after the matter was settled, Mrs. Marshall went from the church-meeting to Charity's dying-bed with the intelligence, and a few hours afterwards she died in the Lord.

"Yet another step must be mentioned. To the request of the deacons, after the first Lord's Day of my visit, for some help in the following year, I was obliged to say I could not come. After a considerable pause, one of them said, 'I believe you will come next year.' In a remarkable way the prediction was fulfilled. It occurred thus: The people at Trowbridge had for a long time desired their deacons to call a church-meeting for the purpose of asking me to the pastorate, but I never felt able to consent to their deacons' request. Tired of waiting, another minister was invited, and shortly took up the work, and that released me for two Lord's Days, which were then given to Brighton. The concern about Brighton deepened on both sides.

"Here perhaps I ought, even at the risk of being wearisome, to relate a remarkable circumstance which powerfully influenced both the deacons and myself. In August, 1881, the way was made for a visit to Brighton for a week-evening service. Before leaving Liverpool for Shepherd's Bush, to spend the night with my friend, Mr. Glover, on my way to Brighton, I was indulged with access to the Lord, and in committing my way to Him I found myself saying to Him, 'Lord, do not allow me to speak at Brighton of my fear about Liverpool, unless there be a lawful opening.' At Shepherd's Bush I found Mr. Combridge (a deacon at Galeed) and his wife were there, finishing their holiday. Mr. Combridge said to me, 'Whenever I pray for and about you, I have an impression that you are not satisfied about your position at Liverpool.' He assured me he had not heard of the matter from anyone. I remembered my prayer of the previous day,—a 'lawful opening'. Then I told the case. The following day Mr. Marshall (another deacon) used the same terms to me; and on the Friday of the same week, a third deacon, Edward Stenning, said the same. To each of us separately, and jointly, it was remarkable and solemn, since neither had spoken to the other of his impression. When in secret before the Lord about this singular circumstance, He most graciously said to me, 'Do not interpretations belong to God?' Then I was assured that He was in the matter, and would in His time make it known. Thus things went on until December in this eventful year (1881), and a month before the church formally invited me to become the pastor. About October, in reply to a question put to me by the deacons of the church at West Street, Croydon, 'Are you free to remove from Liverpool?' I said, 'Free to remove, but not free to come to Croydon.' So I thought I should hear no more from that church."

In November, Mr. Popham received from a friend, a member of the church at West Street, Croydon, an unofficial suggestion as to his becoming the pastor there. His reply is here inserted as shewing the gracious caution with which he was enabled to deal with the delicate and important matter:

My dear Friend,—Will you kindly thank Mrs. Poller for her unexpected and undesired acknowledgment of my little services? I only wish that when her time and yours, dear friend, and mine, comes to be laid in the grave, we may be "well laid" there.

That part of your letter which I am attempting now to

answer, I desire to answer in the fear of God. My first thought was to write and say an absolute " No "; but after a little reflection I felt I must not do that. You refer to some remarks I made with respect to the fears I have about Liverpool. Perhaps I am to blame for making them; but you will remember we were speaking of the generally low state of the churches, and my observations were more illustrative than anything else. They were not made in a particular way, and as growing out of a conversation as to my position here.

Nevertheless, I afterwards thought how strange, though few and general they might seem, and that you might suspect me of putting out feelers. But of that impropriety I am clean, and I had no inducement to such a thing, since I am not free to move towards you. But now as the matter has gone so far in your mind, I feel that perhaps I ought to just indicate to you my present position.

I am unsettled here; not through unkindness shewn me, but the withholding of divine power from the preaching. This has been my trial for more than or about a year. In June last I went to Brighton for the first time. As the result of my visit something has been said to me by the deacons—not officially—which may or may not lead to something further. At the present moment the deacons are not pledged to me nor I to them; but both they and myself feel that there are those leadings in the matter which lay it imperatively upon us to try to spread it before God.

More I cannot say to you, for more has not been done; less I think I ought not to say, because I know not yet what the will of God may be. I know not yet that He intends me to leave this place and the few dear souls whom I have espoused to Christ. If He does, I have felt sufficient power at Brighton to make me wish that might be the spot; but at times I have had grace enough to fall down before God and say, " Anywhere, Lord, so that I am made a blessing."

I shall be glad if you will regard this letter as strictly confidential. I remain, . . .

53 York Terrace,   J. K. POPHAM.
   Everton, Liverpool.
     November 14th, 1881.

Two very choice "Meditations", written at this anxious time, are preserved; and as revealing the innermost workings of his soul, are here appended. They are saturated with spirituality and breathe an atmosphere of deep devotion and humble submission to the will of God.

"November 23rd, 1881.—A MEDITATION. A PRAYER.

"Oh to have one's heart more undividedly taken up by Him who is so inconceivably fair and so divinely full of all that is both desirable and needful! What vanities fill my mind; with what trifles am I taken up! Lord, in mercy draw me, then I will run. Reveal, O eternal Spirit, reveal to me the matchless beauties, the all-sufficient grace, the exhaustless fulness of the Saviour, that I may feel and then confess to Thee, 'My heart is fixed, O God, my heart is fixed.' Subdue, O subdue my many and strong sins; subdue me under Thee and unto Thee. O Lord, let me, most graciously permit me to find my all in Thee.—J. K. P."

"December, 1881.—A MEDITATION.

"The last moments of this (to me) eventful year are rapidly running out. A review of the year discovers many contrary things, and begets many singularly mingled feelings. As I look back upon myself—a weak, sinful worm— what cause do I see for shame, confusion, repentance, and mourning before God! I have been unthankful for mercies, insensible of countless favours, fretful under the much-needed rod of discipline, and most unbelieving at the smallest appearance of trial.

"Though engaged in the ministry, the affairs of this life, especially the cares of a young family, have too much engrossed my attention. In my ministry, how remiss and cold have I been! with an unmoved heart have I often read the sacred page; with what formality have I prayed; how small, therefore, has been my profit by the one and success in the other! Though my conscience does not charge me with handling, in my public ministry, the Word of God deceitfully, yet how little lasting good has been wrought by my many preachings. And why? Ah! I have, alas! sowed but little in tears, therefore no deliverance has been wrought in the earth. How might I enlarge the heavy indictment against myself! Pride, self-will, self-pity, and backslidings of heart, fill and foul every page of the year's record. Therefore,

> " Not a gleam of hope for me,
> But in sad Gethsemane."

" But as, on the other hand, I am enabled to look back upon the Lord's dealings with me, I am lost in wonder. Mercy, power, faithfulness, and tender compassion meet my view on all sides. A sin-forgiving God has cheered, and a faithful God has sustained me. O Lord, Thou hast borne with all my ill manners, rebuked my conscience for evil, and delivered me out of trouble. My wants have been greater this year than during other years [there were now five children], and the supplies from Thy good hand have been abundant. What shall I say unto Thee, Thou preserver of of my life? Honour, power, and glory be to Thee, Father, Son, and Holy Ghost. Let, O Lord, my heart be soft with contrition; fill me with self-loathing, animate me with hope, fire me with zeal, enlarge me in knowledge, melt me with love, and greatly increase me in faith that I may walk by it. O Lord, let my heart be sincere, make it upright in Thy statutes, and stedfast in Thy ways. Prosper me greatly in spiritual things during the year which will soon dawn upon the world. Thou, O Lord, knowest my great perplexity in respect to my future. Order my footsteps by Thy Word. Leave me not. Do not allow me to be influenced either this or that way by carnal motives. Though by-ends and selfish motives will mix themselves in my deliberations, let them not influence my decision. Bless my feeble labours; make them more abundant and increase their usefulness. Bless my dear wife with more health, if consistent with Thy will. But above all, sanctify her affliction to both her own and my soul. Bless, O Lord, our five precious children; preserve them in health if for their good; make a way for them in Thy holy providence. O Lord, graciously make them partakers of the heavenly calling and heirs of the grace of life. Abundantly bless, most gracious Lord, Father, Son, and Spirit, dear Zion with peace and prosperity. Lord, spare and bless England.

E

"Hear, O Lord, a sinful worm, and when Thou hearest, forgive, for the sake of Jesus. Amen.

10.45 p.m., December 31st, 1881."

Unexpectedly, early in January, 1882, Mr. Popham received an official invitation to supply at West Street, Croydon, on probation. The invitation and the reply are subjoined.

Invitation from Croydon.

My dear Friend,—At our church meeting held on Monday evening, January 2nd, it was decided by the church, with the exception of three only, that we, the deacons, should write to invite you to supply for us for three months with a view to your taking the oversight of us as pastor.

This decision may appear to be hasty, but in reality it is not so. From the time of the death of our late beloved pastor, Mr. Covell, with some of us there has been a constant crying to the Lord that if it was His will we might have another pastor to go in and out before us, who should feed us with knowledge and understanding. From the time you supplied for us in August, 1880, you were laid upon the minds of some of the friends, but more especially your visit in October last, when the weight and savour which attended your ministry amongst us created an earnest wrestling spirit of prayer to the Lord in many, both of the church and godly of the congregation, that if it could be in accordance with the Lord's will you might be brought amongst us; but we have felt some hesitation lest we should hurt the minds of those over whom you are now placed, and lay ourselves open to the charge of trying to entice you away.

The matter was, however, named at our previous meeting in December, when it was left to stand over for a month that each of the friends might seek the Lord's guidance and direction in so weighty and important a decision. This we believe has been done, and we also believe it has been done with a sincere desire that the Lord's will may be done as regards ourselves as well as you.

We therefore lay the request before you, begging you to give it your earnest and prayerful consideration, and may the Lord Himself, who is the Head of the Church, so direct your mind to that decision that shall be most for His honour and glory and the good of His church and people.

As early an answer as can be consistent with your duly considering the matter will greatly relieve our minds. And now, dear friend, we desire to commit you into the hands of the Lord, who has fixed the bounds of our habitation and in whose hands are all circumstances and events.

We remain, dear friend, on behalf of the church at Providence chapel, Croydon,

THOS. WONHAM
J. B. RIDLEY   } *Deacons.*
Croydon. January 9th, 1882.   RICHD. LANDON

Mr. Popham's acknowledgment.   Jan. 11th, 1882.

My dear Friend in the Lord,—Though you had in the kindest and most prudent manner expressed your own feeling and that of some of your friends towards me, I was totally unprepared for the invitation the church has, through its deacons, sent me. It was, therefore, received with what I may truly describe as a shock of surprise.

I am merely acknowledging the receipt of your invitation. Oh, that the Lord may condescend to communicate to me His will in this important matter! I do feel poor and needy —poor in spiritual wisdom, needy in respect of counsel. An unworthier, viler sinner never received grace than I, nor did ever a more unlikely, unworthy person receive part in that ministry Christ has given to the Church. Sometimes I can see neither grace nor ministry received from God.

Just now, however, I trust my heart is tender and my soul humble before Him with whom we have to do. My desire is to spread your letter before the Lord under the influence of that word, "Walk before Me, and be thou perfect."

I am deeply grieved to hear of your domestic trouble. The Lord help you, dear friend, and grant that support you so greatly need. I hope that ere this there is some mitigation of the affliction. With Christian love and sympathy,

Yours sincerely in the truth,

53 York Terrace,   J. K. POPHAM.
Everton, Liverpool.

In February, 1882, came the official invitation from Galeed,
Brighton, to supply for three months on probation with a
view to the pastorate. The remarkably gracious terms in
which this invitation and the reply were couched are observable.

To Mr. J. K. Popham, minister of the Baptist chapel, Shaw
    Street, Liverpool.

Dear Friend,—From the preliminary note sent last evening
you will be in a measure prepared for our communication
to-day. The step we have taken we sincerely hope has been
done in the fear of the Lord, with a single eye to His glory,
and not without deep exercise of mind and much prayer to
Him to be led and guided aright in such a solemn and
weighty matter. For years past we have been waiting upon
the Lord with a prayerful hope that He would send us an
under-shepherd agreeable to His promise: " I will give you
pastors according to Mine heart, which shall feed you with
knowledge and understanding." And though at times almost
ready to faint, yet we could not quite give up our hope that
the Lord would graciously grant us this favour.

From your first visit in June last, many of us had an
inward persuasion the Lord would remove you from Liverpool to Brighton. This conviction has been greatly strengthened by each subsequent visit, and more especially confirmed on the last occasion. And though you came among
us " in weakness and in fear and in much trembling ", your
preaching was " in demonstration of the Spirit and of
power ", attended with unction, savour, and weight, having
an abiding effect upon our souls. To the truth of this
many can testify.

Thus viewing the effect of your ministry, accompanied
with our constant exercises, as the Lord's leadings towards
us, and believing you felt a solemn sacredness upon your
spirit, with much life, power, and peace in your soul in
preaching, we were constrained to call the church together
last week to consider the propriety of inviting you. This
met with a warm response and a oneness of feeling. Then
notice was given of a special church meeting which was
held last evening, and a very peaceful one it was, well
attended, and not one dissenting vote.

We now feel we can as a church heartily and cordially, in love and affection, invite you to supply the pulpit at Galeed for three months consecutively with a view to the pastorate. May the Lord graciously perfect that which concerneth us, smile upon and bless you with sweet peace, reveal His mind and will to you, and fulfil His promise: "I will instruct thee and teach thee in the way which thou shalt go; I will guide thee with Mine eye." This is the earnest and prayerful desire of

Yours very sincerely in Christian love and on behalf of the church,

EDWARD STENNING,
D. T. COMBRIDGE,
Brighton.   JOHN MARSHALL,
February 9th, 1882.   WILLIAM AKEHURST.

Of his keen exercises in reference to these two simultaneous requests (from Croydon and Brighton), Mr. Popham wrote:

"From that day until March, I lived days and nights never-to-be-forgotten by me. Croydon, dear Mr. Covell's church—he was most kind and encouraging to me in the early days of my ministry and on my going to Liverpool—rich; my desire to educate well my young family; its contiguity to London, the obliquely-obtained medical opinion that in the event of leaving Liverpool no more suitable place than Croydon could be found for my wife, who was then not strong; all these considerations took hold of me. But on two occasions, when seeking divine guidance, the Lord very distinctly and mercifully and powerfully said to me, 'Ye are not your own.' Oh, how humbly did I pray that He would not permit me to act as if I were my own! He then took possession of me in my movements. His will was my choice, if He would but make known that will to me. But after this I did what no servant ought to do, I dictated to my best Master and Friend, and told Him I would not budge an inch to the right hand or to the left till I got the most distinct word He could speak to me. I warn my friends never to dictate to their Lord, never tell Him how to guide them. It cost me sore trouble for two months. For the moment He did not disallow it in my conscience, but let me wear myself out by night and day exercises. I turned from

everything He had already done in the matter, and set my
face on having that one word; till He graciously counselled
me. Yes, He counselled me; and I *was* in trouble for this
thing. He said, 'Thine ears shall hear a word behind thee,
saying, This is the way, walk ye in it, when ye turn to the
right hand, and when ye turn to the left' (Isa. xxx. 21).
The scales fell from off my eyes and I saw that I had
behaved as a servant ought not. My dictation was gone, and
I fell before Him, begging He would guide me as it pleased
Him. And He did not allow me to walk in the dark, or
decide in the dark. No, He was kind and gracious, though
I was base to Him. At this very important juncture, I was
under engagements to speak at Croydon on the Wednesday
evening, March 22nd, and at Brighton on the Friday of the
same week. My spirit was made tender and watchful. At
Croydon [Text: I Thess. i. 6], I had liberty as on some
former occasions, but nothing more. At Galeed [Text:
John i. 14], I had not spoken long before my soul was *filled*
with the peculiar love which I believe a pastor has to the
people over whom the Lord places him; and when I sat down
in the pulpit, I said in my heart, 'This is the place.' Thus
I was settled. After the people had left, one of the deacons
said to me, 'I almost told the people you are our pastor.' I
said, 'But you have no authority.' He replied, 'I *know* you
are our pastor, for I have such a hold of you in prayer; I
know you are.' The above is a very brief account of my
entrance into and becoming the pastor of the church at
Galeed."

Accordingly, Mr. Popham wrote to the church at Galeed,
accepting their invitation to supply on probation for three
months, commencing October 1st, 1882, in the following
terms:—

To the church of God meeting for divine worship at Galeed
        chapel, Brighton.

Dear Friends in the Lord,—Since I received the unanimous
invitation you sent me through your deacons to preach among
you for three months with a view to taking the oversight
of you in the Lord, I have anxiously, and I trust earnestly,
at times, sought to know the Lord's mind in the matter.

While I dare not at once without prayer and consideration, say " No ", I was equally afraid of hurriedly uttering, " Yes." Often all my heart has been fully expressed by the psalmist in his short prayer, " Show me Thy way."

Perhaps as I now feel a hope the Lord has heard prayer, given me some light upon my path, and enabled me to decide what to do, it will be well if I give you a brief outline of the way by which I have been brought to that decision. When in God's holy providence, I came to speak among you for the first time in June last, I came in a great conflict and many fears. For many months previously I had feared the Lord was not using me in this place as He formerly had; this withdrawal of His blessing from my ministry caused me much trouble and many fears; it also brought a solemn exercise about my call to speak in the Lord's Name. When I reached Brighton I was in great distress of mind, and continued so until ten o'clock on the Lord's Day morning. At that time I said, " Lord, I cannot go without Thee;" and in my heart I felt the words, " and I will not." Almost immediately the Lord answered me, " I will help thee;" and with such singular power did He answer me in those words that I at once said, " I believe it, Lord." At once my bond-age, fear, and distress fled, and my whole soul was engaged in adoring, with grateful tears, the God of all grace and power. Some of you will, I doubt not, remember that first visit. I trust it is not presumptuous in me to say the Lord helped me beyond what I could have thought. How good I felt the Lord during my stay in Brighton! What sweet peace I enjoyed when alone with God! How broken and tender He, in much mercy, made my heart!

I quickly perceived, dear friends, that the Lord had made the word effectual amongst you, and that by means of it a place was made for me in your hearts. Perceiving this, I decided, as in God's sight, not to say one word about my trial with respect to Liverpool. And your deacons will be able to testify that I most studiously avoided uttering any-thing by which they could even suppose, much less judge and conclude, that I often wondered and asked the Lord whether it was His will to remove me.

Shortly after my first visit, things were so ordered that I

had to come to Brighton again for a few days, and then to my utter astonishment, three of your deacons separately and without any knowledge of each other's impressions or intentions, told me that they had an impression that I was not satisfied with respect to my position at Liverpool. I then felt I could not keep silent, but must tell them, each as he spoke to me, the naked truth. This brought much exercise of mind, many inquiries whether the Lord had a meaning in this.

Just before this, to me, solemn circumstance, I was one day entreating the Lord to shew me His mind respecting me and my. position in this place, and I felt that He answered me and fixed my mind for a time by bringing this word, "Do not interpretations belong unto God?" This word produced a peace and a waiting spirit, for I felt that, poor and worthless though I am, the great and ever-gracious God looked upon me, and would in His time make straight that which was crooked. About this time also I twice felt the word, "Ye are not your own." "Then don't let me act as if I were, Lord," was my petition. What sweet peace the word brought, and what satisfaction! How glad I felt to be clay, how anxious my soul was not to move one step any way without Him whose I then believed I was and Whom I desired to serve.

And when I came to supply for you in January, my soul was made attentive to what God might say and do; and though I spoke amongst you in bodily as well as spiritual weakness, yet I felt peace both in and out of the pulpit. But though all these things had taken place, I was not quite prepared to receive your cordial and unanimous invitation. No, dear friends, I am for the most part so pressed down with a sense of my own ignorance and unfitness to speak in God's great and glorious Name, and frequently am unable to make out my call to preach, that I am kept from thinking myself fit and able to stand in any pulpit. Your letter, then, did humble and break my heart. Almost immediately I said, "Now, Lord, I will not move without a most direct word;" but afterwards I had to ask forgiveness for seeking to dictate to the Lord as to *how* He should direct me. One morning He condescended to bless me by speaking in Ps. xxxii. 8,

" I will instruct thee, and teach thee in the way which thou
shalt go; I will guide thee with Mine eye." Oh, what comfortable persuasion the word brought that I should get well
through my perplexities and exercises, and what a sweet
humble willingness was again wrought to go in the Lord's
way and not my own!

Soon after this I was very earnest early one morning in
seeking a distinct word from the Lord, when I was, in a
manner, stopped by the word, " And thine ears shall hear a
word behind thee, saying, This is the way, walk ye in it,
when ye turn to the right hand, and when ye turn to the
left." I at once saw I had been wrong in trying to bargain
with the Lord, and that He would not allow it. Oh, how
earnest I now was in begging His forgiveness, and, then, in
asking for an attentive, obedient ear, that I might listen to
past providences, experience, and divine leadings. But again
in a week or two I fell into the old way of begging and
almost saying I *must* have what I wanted—guidance in *my*
way, and again did the Lord in infinite mercy answer me by
this Scripture, " We walk by faith, not by sight." How good
I feel the Lord was to again check my wayward spirit and
put me right before Him. For if we are not right with
Him we cannot rightly consider or act in any matter in
which His glory and His people's good are concerned.

And now, dear friends, you may be asking, " Where did
all these things point? What interpretation has God given
to your exercises previous to your first visit here and to your
blessing when here? What has the ' voice behind ' said ? "
To these questions I must reply,—and I would reply in the
tender fear of God—All these things do, in my mind, point
to Brighton. And I now, therefore, in reply to your
invitation, write to say that, though I feel the vilest, poorest,
unworthiest of sinners, and the feeblest of all who speak in
the Lord's Name, I do feel I must accept it. Neither
lightly nor hurriedly have I come to this solemn point, nor
has a want of proper affection for my friends here [at
Liverpool] brought me to it; but so far as I can at the
present moment see and interpret the Lord's dealings with
me in bringing me amongst you and working in such a
singular manner, this appears to be the right way. Oh, may

we live to prove it to be so! I trust I may be given to you through your prayers, as Paul says to Philemon; should it be so, it must turn out well. In much weakness, and fear, and trembling, I came to you as a supply, both at first and at each subsequent visit, and so I must come again, if spared and permitted to labour statedly amongst you.

As I am anxious to leave my dear friends here in as comfortable a state as possible with respect to supplies, I feel I cannot get away before the end of September. If, then, I am spared and permitted, I will commence my labours in your pulpit for three consecutive months on October 1st of this year. Oh, may the good will of Him that dwelt in the bush rest upon us in this solemn and important step!

With much love in the Lord, I remain, dear brethren,

Yours affectionately to serve in the gospel of Christ,

Liverpool. April 10th, 1882.   J. K. Popham.

It has often been observed that whatever is definitely of God will be positively opposed by the devil. The coming to Brighton, and indeed the whole of Mr. Popham's ministry, was combated not merely by the keen inward temptations he mentioned, but by a few evilly-disposed persons. He had suffered at Liverpool from certain individuals; and the enemy forestalled him at Brighton. One case deserves recording as manifesting the tender care of the Lord over His dear servant, and the grace given to him to walk discreetly and in the tender fear of God; exemplifying the faithfulness of the Lord to His promise, " Them that honour Me, I will honour." Shortly before Mr. Popham's first preaching engagement at Brighton, a certain busy-body maliciously repeated a false report concerning him to a deacon of a chapel in Sussex where Mr. Popham was to preach in the week between his Brighton engagements. The deacon was much perturbed and declared he would not permit him to enter the pulpit until some explanation was given. This, however, was not done; although the deacon and Mr. Popham spent the morning together, nothing was said about the matter, and Mr. Popham duly fulfilled the engagement. A week later Mr. Popham was again preaching at Galeed, and

was the guest of a brother of the deacon before referred to.
The next morning his host said to him, "My brother wishes
to ask you some questions." The brother (the deacon before
mentioned, being on a visit to Brighton) replied, "I do not;
I *did*, but now I have heard you pray and preach, and am
satisfied." Recalling the incident many years later, Mr.
Popham said:—

"This was a humbling mercy, and has more than once
been a guide. If the Lord then took, and on some remarkable occasions has since taken, such care of my worthless
name, need I be anxious to defend it? Oh! it is good to be
made to know that our defence is of God! Besides, what has
my heart muttered against Him? and how unprofitable has
been my life, how vile I am! Troubles sent of God are made
mercies when sanctified. The chastening is severe, we tremble for fear of the Lord and the glory of His majesty in it,
but when confession, self-loathing, and pardon are the fruits,
God is glorified and He says, 'It is enough.' 'He that
feareth God shall come forth' of all his afflictions."

It is saddening to observe that on one occasion a report
was circulated by a jealous individual that Mr. Popham
knew neither law nor gospel; but the sequel is pleasant and
interesting. It was his first visit to Trowbridge, June 24th,
1881; and the malicious report had gone there before him,
but he knew nothing of it. His text that day—evidently
selected by God for His dear servant, for in the circumstances the Scriptures contained none so appropriate—was
Rom. v. 20: "Moreover, the law entered that the offence
might abound; but where sin abounded, grace did much more
abound." Thus does the devil outwit himself and confound
his own agents in their endeavour to calumniate the character and discount the testimony of the Lord's own sent servants, especially those whom He makes eminently useful in
His vineyard.

Considering that Mr. Popham was now only about thirty-
four years of age, there was an unusual gravity, wisdom, and
depth of discernment about his ministry. Studying to shew
himself approved unto God, he was enabled rightly to divide
the Word of truth. To one who, having felt this, wrote to

him, he replied in what seems to be a pattern of remarkably judicious encouragement:—

Dear unknown Friend,—. . . You speak of my last sermon at C. as rooting up all your religion, and you say, "How can I tell if I have one vital spark?" I think as I read on I can discover one spark, not to be despised: You were not *offended* with what rooted you up so entirely. Notwithstanding your exercises, your trouble, you would rather the rooting up went on, you would choose to be still more searched, than have a root whose tree and fruit God would dry up and curse, than be in a refuge of lies.

My own judgment is that hypocrites know not this spirit. Jesus said, "Blessed is he whosoever shall not be offended in Me." How many were offended in Him in His Word by which their sins, the thoughts of their hearts, were made manifest. No falling under the discerning Word, but an indignant exclaiming, "Are we blind also?"

Not so the child of God. When he reads or hears of many whose carcases fell in the wilderness, he says, "I, too, may likewise fall." When any case of apostasy is named, he feels how easy it would be for him to fall in the same way. When the ministry searches, then every mark of the hypocrite, every feature of the reprobate, the honest God-fearing man takes to himself, while every word that is in his favour he puts away, fearing to take what doesn't belong to him; but all this is in his favour, and turns to his good and the establishment of his soul in the end. If the hypocrite can sigh and groan, it is only when he has some object to gain, but he cannot sigh and groan when God binds him. "Will he delight himself in the Almighty? Will he always call upon God?" I venture to say if any were offended on the occasion I am now referring to, they were not the children of God, but persons who did not wish to be disturbed in their false peace and hopes. Did not the enemy envy you the encouragement you received on the previous Lord's Day? Yes, and therefore he endeavoured to especially distress you by things which really you may see in the Lord's light are in your favour.

I hope you may be favoured from time to time both in hearing the word and also in secret.

Wishing you much of the Lord's presence and blessing,

I remain, Yours in hope,

53 York Terrace,   J. K. POPHAM.
  Everton, Liverpool.
    June 23rd, 1882.

There were born at Liverpool two daughters, Gertrude (Mrs. Walters) and Alice (Miss Popham has been for many years a member of Galeed church, Brighton), and a second son, Edgar.

It may here be convenient to record the texts from which Mr. Popham preached at Brighton before commencing his pastorate there,—a period of vast importance to himself and to the church at Galeed:—

1881.—June 12th: *morning*, Luke xvii. 20; *evening*, Song i. 4. Against this date is a note appended by the dear man which reads: " My first visit, never-to-be-forgotten! O blessed day for my soul! Also on this day I was anointed for my future pastorate here."

Monday, June 13th: Song i. 4.

Sunday, June 19th: *morning and evening*, Jeremiah xiv. 8.

Monday, June 20th: Phil. iii. 16.

Friday, August 19th: Ps. lxxi. 1.

Wednesday, October 19th: I John iv. 19.

1882.—Sunday, January 22nd: *morning*, Jonah ii. 7. (This sermon was published in *The Sower* for May, 1882.) *Evening*, Genesis xvii. 1.

Monday, January 23rd: Isaiah xlii. 4.

Sunday, January 29th: *morning and evening*, Ps. cxix. 94.

Monday, January 30th: John iii. 6.

Friday, March 24th: John i. 14. (The occasion referred to above, when the deacons said they were persuaded he would be their pastor.)

Sunday, July 30th: *morning*, Ps. xxxviii. 9; *evening*, Heb. vii. 24, 25.

Monday, July 31st: Ps. lxxii. 17.

Mr. Popham preached his last sermon as pastor of Shaw Street, Liverpool, on Monday, September 25th, 1882, from the text, "This poor man cried, and the Lord heard him, and saved him out of all his troubles" (Ps. xxxiv. 6). He commenced at Galeed on probation on October 1st, with the text, "And Jacob asked Him, and said, Tell me, I pray Thee, Thy name. And He said, Wherefore is it that thou dost ask after My name? And He blessed him there. And Jacob called the name of the place Peniel: for I have seen God face to face, and my life is preserved" (Gen. xxxii. 29, 30).

FAREWELL DESIRES AND RESOLUTION PASSED BY THE CHURCH AT SHAW STREET, ON HIS LEAVING LIVERPOOL, SEPT., 1882.

THAT we as a church under the circumstances in which we are placed by the resignation of our dear pastor, desire in the first place to seek grace at the hands of the Lord to be rightly guided and directed in all things, and in this matter in an especial manner. We would desire to express and record to and concerning our dear brother (Mr. Popham) our sincere and unfeigned affection for himself as a faithful minister of the Lord Jesus Christ, and that in his removal he goes forth with our heart-felt prayers that God may be with him to direct and guide him in all his ways, that he may be abundantly blessed by the Spirit of God as a Spirit of revelation in his own soul, blessed in the declaration of the gospel of our Lord Jesus Christ and made greatly useful to the Lord's dear people whenever and wherever he may be called to stand up in the holy Name of the Lord; and we would say according to the precious Word of truth, "The Lord hear thee in the day of trouble, the Name of the God of Jacob defend thee, send thee help from the sanctuary, and strengthen thee out of Zion." Amen.

CHAPTER SIX.

" Do not interpretations belong unto God? "

1882—1886.   Acceptance of Galeed pastorate—Address—publishes
Divine Sovereignty—pastoral care.

BEFORE the expiry of the period of probation, the Lord so
moved in the hearts of the deacons at Galeed, independently
of each other, and in some of the members, that in December
the church was gathered together and called Mr. Popham
immediately to the pastoral charge. His statement to the
church accepting this solemn position in which he was so
signally owned and blessed of God and which he was to hold
until death, was as follows:—

ADDRESS TO THE CHURCH AT GALEED, BRIGHTON, ON ACCEPTING
THE INVITATION TO BECOME THEIR PASTOR, FRIDAY EVENING,
DECEMBER 15TH, 1882.

I do a great deal feel the very solemn position that I now
occupy before you, dear friends. I feel glad of the privilege
of meeting you instead of writing to you. It is often easier
to speak than to write about an important matter, and perhaps I shall be able to say a little more than I could write.
Perhaps it will be as well for me, if you will allow me, to go
back in this matter as far as the commencement. You remember it is now about a year-and-a-half since I first came
to preach here as a supply. As many of you now know, I
had been about a year previous in a great deal of exercise
as to whether it was God's will for me to remain at Liverpool or not. For a few months the exercise had grown much,
and had been taken advantage of by Satan to sorely tempt
and try me about my call to preach, and that as God was
not sensibly present with me as formerly at Liverpool, I was
therefore not called to preach at all. And I used to say,
" Lord, do forgive me for having preached at all, and open
an honourable way out." About that time the trial had come

to its height, and I felt it impossible to go on any longer, and the fact of coming to a fresh place increased my trial. I said, "My old friends here can bear with me;" but the thought of coming to a strange place did increase my trial. When I came into Brighton it was with the feeling that I could not preach. That feeling grew to its height at ten o'clock on Sunday morning, when I leaned against a chair and said, "O Lord, I can't go like this," and in my heart I said, "I will not go." There was a sort of determination in my mind not to preach any more in that state. And then the Lord spoke that word on my mind: "I will help thee." I dropped down on my knees and said, "O Lord, I believe it." Then the Lord drew near and communed with me as He had not done for many months. The whole thing was changed. Instead of feeling as I had done, that I could not preach, instead of wishing for an honourable way out, I wished for the time to come to get into the pulpit. I suppose I need not say anything about that visit, June, 1881. It is, I believe, still fresh on some of your hearts. I love to think of God's goodness to me at that time. I said afterwards, if I never came to Brighton again, I would try to praise God all my life for His goodness to me during that visit. It established me greatly, and made clear to me for the time my call to preach. You know how afterwards I came to preach to you occasionally. Once or twice I had this feeling, "Lord, if there is nothing but what is ordinary in this matter, do not let there be anything but ordinary feelings between the people and myself." And you know how in a particular way our friends, Marshall, Combridge, and Stenning, each without any knowledge of what the other had said, spoke to me on three several occasions about their personal impression that I was not settled at Liverpool. I had not uttered a word to them, for as soon as I could see there was any feeling in the minds of your deacons, (who, to their honour I would say it, said nothing but what was right,) I resolved not to hint to any creature that I was in any exercise, but to keep it solemnly before God; so that when Liverpool was named, I never uttered a syllable of my exercise, but used to put before them the goodness of God to me in the past at Liverpool, and the cases in which He had been pleased to make use of me. But then I may say this, I could not keep it so in secret. I was obliged often to go before God about it, because it so pressed upon my spirit, and there was no getting away from it. I was willing to spend my days at Liverpool, and I did not want to leave it. I never left Liverpool to supply any pulpit out of it with a desire to leave it. The comfort that has been to me since, I could not tell you, and I cannot praise God enough for making me loyal and sincere in my feelings to the handful of people I had there. When the people at Croydon invited me to go there, it increased my difficulties. It made me understand that the Lord was kind to me in one word that He spoke after one of my visits here: " Do not interpretations belong to God ? " And I thought that I had a time to wait, but that the Lord would in His own time make it plain. One day the Lord brought me right down to be willing either to remain at Liverpool, or to go to Croydon, or if anything grew out of the matter at Brighton, to go there. I was like a weaned child. I was weaned from my self-will and could make a full surrender of body, soul, and spirit, and everything, and was enabled to look to God for direction. It was a very sweet time to my soul.

When your invitation came, dear friends, it became my heart's desire that the Lord would manifest His will towards me. At the first I tried to bargain with the Lord that I would not leave, nor decide to remain, without He gave me a distinct word on the matter. But after a time, one night as I was pleading with the Lord on these grounds, I was stopped with this Scripture: " And thine ears shall hear a voice behind thee, saying, This is the way, walk ye in it, when ye turn to the right hand, and when ye turn to the left." I said, " Lord, what is the voice ? " In a moment, as if in answer, the whole of the circumstance connected with my coming here, the blessing of the Lord on my soul and on the word that I was enabled to preach, came to my mind, and seemed rather sweetly to say, " That is the voice." And it was that, with another word, that constrained me to accept your invitation. The other word was given me when I was supplying at Gower Street. I was before the Lord early one morning, saying, " Do, Lord, let me have it out; do tell me

F

what to do!" I was getting back on the old ground, wanting
a distinct word, and this came: "We walk by faith, and not
by sight;" and the old Scripture, Isa. xxx. 21. Well, very
soon afterwards, I accepted your invitation to supply this
pulpit for three months on probation. I felt on Monday
evening, when you sent me so unanimous an invitation to
become your pastor, that it would be affectation for me to
keep you longer for a reply. I can say that the matter, as
far as I can find out, has been settled by God in my soul.
He knows how I feel my weakness and insufficiency for the
ministry, and since I have been here these two and a half
months, He only knows what I have gone through in the
way of exercise. I have sometimes been as weak as a child
in my feelings, and have said, "I cannot preach, I cannot
cannot stand before the people!"

Last week, when the exercise was exceedingly severe, and I
was saying, "If the people ask me, I dare not come, I cannot
stand before them; I am so weak," the Lord graciously
dropped these two Scriptures on my spirit: "We have this
treasure in earthen vessels," etc., and, "That your faith should
not stand in the wisdom of men, but in the power of God"
(II Cor. iv. 7; I Cor. ii. 5). They were very seasonable and
precious to me, and enabled me to be content to be a weak
foolish creature, if God would but glorify Himself thereby.
I have also had some feeling from this Scripture: "We
preach not ourselves, but Christ Jesus the Lord; and our
selves your servants for Jesus' sake" (II Cor. iv. 5). And
many times, when I have been before the Lord about this
matter, I have found these words sweetly following me—I
do not say they have dropped with that power and unction I
like to feel, but they have been whispered quietly on my
soul: "Certainly I will be with thee" (Ex. iii. 12); and oh,
the help it has been!

On Monday morning early, when I was having the matter
before me and praying that you might be guided rightly at
your meeting in the evening, the whole circumstance of
Cornelius sending for Peter (Acts x.) and the word the Spirit
spoke to Peter when the three men sought him, "Arise,
therefore, and get thee down and go with them, doubting
nothing, for I have sent them," came upon my mind, and I

felt immediately that God had settled it as far as I was concerned, and I had a certain persuasion as to how you would be led if that came from the Lord. And when, after the meeting, the invitation was brought to me by your deacons, although I was silent that evening as to what answer I should give, it dropped with such sweetness upon my spirit, that if I had been there before you in the chapel, I could have said what I am now about to say: "That in much fear and trembling, but I hope in the fear of God, I accept your invitation." I do not do it in self-sufficiency. I shall need a great deal of forbearance from you, for I feel there never was a more unworthy person standing up in God's Name. I am often tried about my call to preach, and perhaps in the position I now occupy amongst you, it would be as well for me to speak to you a few minutes about it.

I believe all God's servants have a special call to preach, a holy anointing; and it has been a severe trial to me, because I did not begin to preach as most of our ministers do. Many of them are brought up amongst the people of God, and after they are brought to a knowledge of the truth they are baptized, the exercise of the ministry comes on them, and they go out to preach. Mine was not at all like that. I was a bitter enemy to God's truth, was not a believer in the doctrines of truth, and if I have the life of God in my soul, it was put there before I knew there was such a people as the elect people of God, excepting that the doctrine of election aroused my indignation, and I used to point with scorn at the place where it was preached. The recollection of it has been bitter to me many times since. After I had had some concern about my soul, as is often the case where there is a young man professing religion, with some small gift for preaching, I was pushed forward to become a preacher. I had a false peace for a time, though I was not altogether at ease, and I gave up all my prospects in life, and accepted a mere pittance to subsist upon, and became a Scripture reader, visiting poor people in the dirtiest part of a large town. While engaged in that work, the Lord graciously laid His hand upon my soul a second time, convinced me powerfully of the truth, made the ixth of Romans

like a maul upon my head, laid my pride in the dust, and
made me feel as a worm before Him.

What I passed through for many long months while so
exercised about my state, and enduring a dreadful conflict
about election, I could not tell you; but as often as I tried
to get away from that doctrine, so often did the Lord
solemnly convince me it was true, and at times gave me such
a sight of His glory as brought me into the dust. My mind
had been so long and severely exercised as to reduce my
bodily strength, and I was an invalid for many months in
the house of a friend with whom I had become acquainted
just before. Towards the end of my visit, when I was in-
tending to return to business, as I was one day reading
my Bible in my room, I came to this word: "Depart ye,
depart ye, go ye out from thence," etc. (Isa. lii. 11). In a
moment, a most solemn and weighty conviction entered into
my soul that I was to preach the gospel. I had before
spoken a good deal about condemnation, and now came the
conviction that I should have to preach the gospel. I began
to recover, and was brought into connection with God's
people. A constraint was laid upon me to preach when asked
to do so. At one time this word was given me, when sorely
exercised: "Feed my lambs" (John xxi. 15). At another:
"Go through, go through the gates," etc. (Isa. lxii. 10). At
another time I had a great deal of feeling from these words:
"If thou draw out thy soul to the hungry," etc. (Isa. lviii.
10).

After a time I became exercised about baptism, and was
baptized by Mr. de Fraine, who said, "Your preaching is
before God and your conscience, but as you have joined us,
you must come and preach before the church;" and though I
was never formally sanctioned by them, I think I had their
sanction by preaching for them scores of times afterwards.
My exercise has often been severe in this way, that I have
not come into the ministry as others do, and I say, "Lord,
if I have come in the wrong way, let me go out." Breaking
stones has often appeared easier to me than preaching
without the Lord. I know a little of what Paul said: "My
preaching was not with enticing words," etc. (I Cor. ii. 4).

I hope the Lord will be graciously pleased to seal with His

approbation what I have felt to be a very solemn matter, the accepting the pastoral office in this church. What I have, what I am, body, soul, and spirit, I have felt before the Lord, and now say to you, " I give to you." I have felt what I believe every man ought to feel before taking a church,—a pastor's heart for this church. I hope the Lord will give me grace and humility to preach, and behave myself as I ought to behave in the Church of God. I know in a degree the solemn position I occupy, and how many have their eyes on the servant of God, but I believe my strength lies in being a fool, because when I can do nothing without the Lord, that makes me pray. I do humbly hope, and believe too at times, that what I have done is of God; and that we may go on together in peace and union is my soul's desire. I hope the Lord may sanction all that has been done, and would fall into His hands as a servant of Jesus Christ. If the Lord will do one thing I shall be glad— quicken poor sinners and hasten the number of His elect. Huntington says, " It is sweet to be a father, as well as a nurse." I would be a nurse to you in your spirits by bearing meat to you from time to time, and a father also by souls being quickened into divine life through my ministry. I thank you for permitting me to see you instead of writing. I hope the Lord will lay me a good deal on your hearts. If you do not pray about your hearing, you will suffer. No prayer, no praise. Praise does not depend upon prayer, but God has connected them.

The following Lord's Day, Mr. Popham spoke in the morning to the congregation concerning his pastorate. The address is here given in full, for although it contains much repetition of what was said to the church, there are interest- ing, instructive, and profitable points of a wider application. Moreover, having in view his natural temperament and the fact that although his own experience was " woven into " his ministry, he very seldom spoke in the first person of his exercises, the simplicity and transparency of this discourse are remarkable, evidencing his sense of the weighty charge laid upon him and the gracious dependence with which the Lord enabled him to enter upon the same—two character- istics marking the whole course of his pastorate at Brighton.

SERMON PREACHED BY MR. POPHAM AT GALEED CHAPEL,
BRIGHTON, ON SUNDAY MORNING, DECEMBER 17TH, 1882,
NEAR THE CLOSE OF HIS THREE MONTHS' PROBATION, AND
UPON HIS ACCEPTANCE OF THE PASTORATE.

"But we have this treasure in earthen vessels, that the excellency of the power may be of God, and not of us."—II Cor.
iv. 7.

It may be right that I should this morning go out of my
ordinary course, and speak a little about the circumstances
that are present, no doubt, to all of you, as well as to myself.
Since I have been engaged in speaking in God's Name, I
have always had rather a strong feeling against speaking
much about myself. I have not felt it was the right thing to
do. But as the circumstances under which we are met this
morning are not ordinary, but far from it, I think it may be
right that I should speak a little about my ministry and
myself in connection with this place. I do know this in
measure—what it is to stand up before God's people, and
before you here, in weakness, and in fear, and in much
trembling; and you all know this, that my speech and my
preaching has not been with enticing words of man's wisdom
(to that I make no pretension). What I desire is, that it
may be "in demonstration of the Spirit and of power".

I have been speaking amongst you now for two-and-a-half
months under circumstances which have been necessarily
trying to the mind. One thing I desire to thank God for,—I
have felt from the first Lord's Day in October until now no
bondage in the position I have occupied, and in sincerity I
can say this (and God knows I speak the truth before Him),
that I have not once been left to lay myself out in order to
gain your approval; and that is a mercy for me. I have
not visited the members of the church, and now my lips are
free to give you the reason for it. I felt it better not to do
so. It has been a matter of conscience before God with me
that, whatever acceptance I might have amongst you should
be purely from the pulpit, and not from friendly visits to
your houses. When I first came, I said, "Now, Lord, I will
not go to their houses during the time of probation."
Excepting for the deacons, and a few friends who are not
members, I felt it better to stand before you in the pulpit,

and in no other way; and the satisfaction I feel in my conscience is not small.

When I came, I determined not to know anything among you save Jesus Christ, and Him crucified. In some small measure, God has granted me my heart's desire in that respect. What a satisfaction we feel when God is pleased to make us sincere! You know I have made no reference whatever to the circumstances in which we have been placed to each other. I thought it better not to do so. We are but poor creatures at the best, and if the minister were to lay himself out, and speak a great deal of what he felt, the devil might make an evil use of it.

My dear friends, I never wanted to leave Liverpool, that God knows. Well, when I came to preach to you the first time in 1881, it was in great trial and exercise of mind. The trial that had been on my mind a year or two before I came to you the first time, was whether God had intended me to remain at Liverpool or not; and that exercise, coupled with other circumstances well known to my friends there, issued in a solemn fear that God had never called me to preach the gospel; and in that state of trial I came to preach to you the first time, with the feeling still on my mind that, if it were possible honourably to be relieved of the engagement, I should feel thankful. Then when, on the first Sunday morning, after an almost sleepless night, and distress that increased hourly until about ten o'clock, when I leaned against a chair and said, " Lord, I cannot go like this, and I will not go,"—and if God had not given me a word, I do not think I could have come; but with power He dropped this on my spirit: " I will help thee." The power was so remarkable that immediately I fell down on my knees and said, " Lord, I believe it." I felt the chain broken; my mind was greatly enlarged, and for half an hour I enjoyed communion with the Lord in secret. Then I began to feel what was utterly contrary to my feelings up to that moment—a desire for eleven o'clock to come, to get into the pulpit.

About that visit I do not think I need say anything. It is still present in the hearts of some of you. For myself, I may say, from that moment to the end of my visit, I had more or less of God's sensible presence with me, both in the

pulpit and in private. That was the turning of my captivity.
I had been, in my feelings, a poor broken vessel, with not
an atom of spiritual treasure; but now I was like a bottle
wanting vent. Then, my friends, what I felt in my heart
to you as a people I never told anyone, for when a hint was
thrown out by your deacons respecting my position at Liverpool, I studiously refrained from giving the slightest hint
that I was in the least exercised about my standing there.
I laid before them everything God had done by me there as
well as I could. I have a satisfaction in remembering it,
and thank God that He enabled me, so as not to lay myself
open to a charge by your deacons that I was saying, " Here
I am, if you want me."

When the broadest hint was uttered, I said this: " If I am
to come to Brighton, God must both level mountains and
exalt valleys, for between me and Brighton there are both."
When the invitation from the church came at the beginning
of this year, oh what a broken thing I was! How my heart
flowed down in humility and tenderness before Him! I said,
" Lord, I am not fit to have a place amongst Thy people as
a hearer, and yet some of Thy people at Brighton, and some
at Croydon, want me to go in and out before them." What
a mercy to have such feelings in such black dreadful
hearts,—hearts black with sin. Nothing but the grace of
God can bring a sinner down in humility before God under
circumstances that are likely to puff him up with pride.
The effect, under God's mercy, has been, and is this morning
still upon my spirit—I can hardly speak before God or
before you because of His mercy—it has so broken me, so
humbled me, that I can only say, " Is this the manner of
man, O Lord ? " Then, when I think of what you need,
when I think of your precious souls, and of how the Lord
has been with you in the past, and then think of my own
ministry and of my weakness, fear, and trembling, I am
ready to say, " I cannot hold on."

A few days ago this was my feeling: " If they ask me, I
cannot come." I was so tried with my weakness and emptiness, till the Lord gave me a most seasonable relief from the
verse which I have read to you as a text, but which I am not
really preaching from: " But we have this treasure in earthen

vessels, that the excellency of the power may be of God, and not of us." The effect was, I was willing to be a fool, to be weak, to go on tremblingly, to be nothing, if God might thereby be glorified. When your invitation came to me at first—having had before that an invitation from the church at Croydon, and being in perplexity to know what to do—I said, "Lord, I will not move a step without a distinct word from Thee telling me what to do." I went on in that way for two months, day and night, for I had but little sleep. One morning, I was early entreating the Lord to give me what I wanted, when I was stopped with this Scripture: "And thine ears shall hear a voice behind thee, saying, This is the way, walk ye in it, when ye turn to the right hand, and when ye turn to the left." In a moment I saw I had been committing an error in dictating to the Lord how He should guide me, and God gave me grace to repent of my sin. "O Lord," I said, "what is the voice?" Then, in reply, all the circumstances connected with my coming here came before me, and something seemed to say, "That is the voice." But, Gideon-like, I wanted it reversed. So I began again: "O Lord, do tell me what to do, do tell me which place to go to, Brighton or Croydon, or whether to remain at Liverpool." Twice, in an especial manner, this came to me: "Ye are not your own," and I was brought to submission to God's will. I was willing to remain at Liverpool, to go to Brighton, or to Croydon; the only leaning in my spirit I could discover was towards remaining at Liverpool. Twice I said, "I will remain here," when immediately I felt bondage and confusion of spirit; and I said to a friend, "If I am to remain here, I shall not decide in this spirit." Then in March, when I was supplying at Gower Street, I said one morning, "Lord, do tell me what to do, that I may relieve the minds of the people at Brighton, Croydon, and Liverpool." I was again urging the old request: "Give me the distinct word I have been wanting." And then the Lord kindly stopped me with that Scripture: "We walk by faith, not by sight;" and then followed what had been spoken to me before: "And thine ears shall hear a voice behind thee," etc. In measure it was then settled in my soul—I say in measure, because I was not then able to decide.

I then went to Croydon to supply, and had not a bad time in the pulpit; but I watched my spirit narrowly, and found I lacked one thing. On the Friday evening I came here, and while opening my mind to you respecting my exercise, I felt freedom, and a spirit of affection for you, so that while at Croydon I had not an atom of liberty to speak about the matter, at Brighton I had; and I left this place with this feeling, " This is the place." It was settled in my soul, and I was able to say, " Lord, I am willing to preach to Thy people in this place." And so far the Lord was pleased to settle it then. I have now no small exercise; it has never been wholly taken away from me. Here I am before God, and before you. You have asked me to come. I said before the church on Friday evening, and I now say it publicly before you all: " I will come." But oh, what solemn feeling I have in my soul about it!

Last Monday morning, very early, when trying to carry it before God, hoping you might receive divine guidance at your meeting in the evening, and asking the Lord if I had made a mistake to shew me, and though it was so near a decision to break it if it was contrary to His will, I felt the circumstance of Cornelius sending for Peter, and the word the Spirit spoke to Peter when the three men sought him: " Arise therefore, and get thee down, and go with them, doubting nothing; for I have sent them," dropped down with such unction that I felt I knew what you would say to me, and if it had been prudent, I could have said to you at the close of your meeting on Monday evening what I now have said. I am brought to accept your invitation; yet I do feel my insufficiency. Earthen vessels only have value from the treasure they contain. Earthen vessels are very liable to be broken at the wheel, and I am very often broken in my feelings.

Since the Lord sent me forth to preach the gospel, what fears I have had about my call to preach! I believe the Lord gives every servant of His a special inward call to preach the gospel. When the Lord gave me this call I was laid aside, and had been for three months, with sickness brought on chiefly through exercise of mind. I was not thinking about the ministry at that time, and I might just tell you, I was then among the Arminians, I did not know the people of God. As I was recovering, and expecting shortly to return to my business, the Lord one day dropped this Scripture: "Depart ye, depart ye, go ye out from thence, touch no unclean thing; go ye out of the midst of her; be ye clean, that bear the vessels of the Lord. For ye shall not go out with haste, nor go by flight: for the Lord will go before you; and the God of Israel will be your rereward" (Isa. lii. 11, 12). I dropped down immediately with the most solemn and mighty conviction on my spirit, wrought there by the word and, as I hope, by the Spirit of the Word in it, that I should have to preach the gospel. How I sank under the feeling of my great insufficiency to do it! but if the Lord has sent me to preach the gospel, I date my inward call to that time in 1867. I was then young and exceedingly inexperienced, as I now feel myself to be. No man can believe I am called to preach from what I say, unless the Lord convey unction with the words; but if He witness with the ministry in your hearts, you will not doubt it.

At another time, when sorely tried about my preaching, and begging of God to forgive me if I had run unsent, that word settled it for the time: "If thou draw out thy soul to the hungry, and satisfy the afflicted soul; then shall thy light rise in obscurity, and thy darkness be as the noonday" (Isa. lviii. 10). The exercise at that time was occasioned by my receiving an invitation to go to a certain place to preach, which brought on much perplexity, not knowing how to act. I decided to go to Lutterworth, to lay the matter before my late dear pastor, Mr. de Fraine, for I thought he would know what direction to give me. I arranged to start the next morning. As I was retiring to rest that night, this word dropped on my mind: "Cursed be the man that trusteth in man, and that maketh flesh his arm, and whose heart departeth from the Lord." Instantly I knew my sin, confessed it, and cried, "Lord, do forgive me. I will not go to Mr. de Fraine." The next morning He gave me grace to search my Bible, and wait on Him for direction. I opened on this Scripture: "If thou draw out thy soul to the hungry," etc., and in a moment it was as if the Lord said, "That is the direction." And I know it was, because the

Lord delivered a poor soul under my ministry during that
visit.

Now, my friends, I come amongst you in exactly the same
weakness and trembling I have ever felt about preaching.
I say often in secret before God: " I cannot preach; Lord,
help me." I do not covet a pulpit. I have looked at a
labouring man sometimes and inly said, " How easy his work
is compared with what I feel in my conscience about preaching!" To stand before the living God, and living and dead
souls, and speak to them in the Name of the Lord, is most
solemn.

I have felt from the first a strong affection for you as a
people professing to fear God. During my first visit, I once
used the word " brethren ", and I did wish I had not used it;
I was afraid people would think I meant something by it. I
have felt you laid a good deal on my mind in prayer, and I
believe at times I have been enabled to beg hard of God to
bless your souls, you who are His people, and do you good;
and those of you who do not fear Him, to give you grace.
What a mercy if God would make me a blessing to those of
you who are dead in sin! When I look at this people, and
then at myself, I am ready to say, " What can one who is so
young in the way say to those who are older in godliness
than I am in natural years ? " But then, when God has been
pleased to bless my ministry, that word has quieted me:
" Say not, I am a child; for thou shalt go to all that I shall
send thee, and whatsoever I command thee thou shalt speak."

On another occasion, when I was deeply exercised about
preaching, asking the Lord that I might be ill rather than
to go into the pulpit if unsent, this came: " Who made man's
mouth ? " When God speaks, it produces a willingness to do
and be what He would have you. We are made sensible
that He wants none of us, yet He has been pleased so to
order it that He will work by means, so that it is not presumption to say, " Lord, take me, make use of me, for Thine
honour and glory." The Lord means that we should feel
our weakness, that the excellency of the power may be of
God, and not of us. If I were able to come up to my own
standard of a gospel minister, how little room should I leave
for God! But when He makes me feel that I have neither

dew nor unction for the pulpit, and then He communicates life and sweetness to the people, where is the excellency ? In the Lord. All the value the earthen vessel possesses it has from the treasure it contains, and the excellency of the power in the ministry is of God, and not of us.

What a wonderful thing a gospel ministry is! "How then shall they call on Him in Whom they have not believed ? and how shall they believe in Him of Whom they have not heard ? and how shall they hear without a preacher ? And how shall they preach except they be sent ? as it is written, How beautiful are the feet of them that preach the gospel of peace, and bring glad tidings of good things!" How often have I gone fearing this Scripture: "They shall not profit this people at all, saith the Lord, for I have not sent them." I have said, "Do not, Lord, thus speak concerning me." Some time ago, the snare was sweetly broken in this way. I was sorely tried, and tempted to believe the Lord never meant me to preach. "Well," I said, "I don't want to preach if the Lord does not want me. If Thou, Lord, hast done with me, do make an honourable way out. I would rather listen than speak; it is a constant exercise to speak." Oh, the solemn pleasure, the holy sweetness, in speaking in God's Name, in trying to speak well of Him! My dear friends, I greatly need your prayers and your forbearance. I want you, as the Lord may help you, to constantly hold me up in prayer. I shall need a deal of forbearance, and I know I shall have to bear with some things in you. I shall have to cut very close, and if you are left to backslide and wander from God, if God is with me in the ministry, He will meet you in it with rebukes: "Show My people their transgressions, and the house of Jacob their sins." That is done in the preaching, though the Lord only can work effectually by it. I have proved in my own case the utter valuelessness of false religion. If the Lord put the heavenly treasure into us, if He puts the treasure of His Word into our souls, we shall hold on; but we shall not get to heaven without difficulties and tribulation. If I may not be able to call on some of you so often as you require, you must bear with me. If I am to preach profitably to you, I shall not be able to spend six days of the week visiting; I shall have to try and wait on God in secret. If I am always giving out and never taking in, I shall soon be reduced to bankruptcy. I must have some time in my room, not for what the world calls studying, but for waiting on God with prayer and reading. I have often had a barren time in preaching, and had solemnly to confess that I had been indolent before entering the pulpit, and have felt guilt, then pity for my hearers, and sorrow for my prayerlessness. I do hope God will grant me grace so to walk amongst you that I may bear holding up to the light. I do not want to speak one thing in the pulpit, and walk another out of it. I would fain prove what is that good, and acceptable, and perfect will of God. I am glad that the Lord has not left me to come in a spirit of self-confidence and sufficiency: " Who is sufficient for these things ? "

May the Lord's rich mercy be upon us, may He surround us with mercy, compass us with favour as with a shield. May the convoy of His love go before us, and the copious manna of divine favour fall around our wandering camp day by day. The Lord grant you who fear God grace to pray hard, to wait on Himself, to do that which is pleasing in His sight. And those of you who do not fear Him, who have not divine life, I feel about you, and cry to Him to quicken you into divine life, so that when many who are advanced in life are laid low, there may still be a generation to call Him blessed in this place. Some of us have families; we need wisdom to bring them up. You will bear with me for taking up the time in speaking about myself. I am glad I have been able to do so. I think it is right, so that we may have a good understanding in the matter. May the Lord in rich mercy bless you and do you good, and grant you all needed grace for time and eternity. Amen.

Although the Lord's dear servant came to Brighton under such gracious exercises and favourable auspices, and had left behind a number of godly souls in Liverpool, whose good will and prayers followed him, and notwithstanding the clear evidences of the Lord's approbation upon his course, it seems that his fears and questionings about the ministry still hung about his mind from time to time. But about two years later, in 1884, he received a very decisive and gracious deliverance. Of this he later said:—

"The Lord sent a word which went far to remove the fears I still had at times that I was not called to preach. I remember with pain my intense unwillingness, which arose partly from my natural disposition. (No one knows what it costs me to be in the eye of the public.) I used to say, "Why give me such a disposition, if I am to preach?" and this aversion gave great advantage to the temptation that I was not called of God to the office. But one day I was reading in the vith Isaiah, when I came to that wonderful condescension of the Almighty, who commands the army of heaven and the inhabitants of the earth, whose servants all creatures are—I came to that condescending request, 'Whom shall I send? and who will go for us?' And I hope never to forget the awful sense of the majesty of God that filled my soul; and with it I said, 'Here am I, send me.' *I covered my face, and worshipped; I know not how long.* What willingness I then felt to preach as long as the Lord should give me strength! My intense aversion to it was gone. I had been helped against the temptation before, but the effect of this word was more abiding than any previous help."

Never robust and not sparing himself in the work of the Lord, it is rather to be wondered at that Mr. Popham had not more illnesses than in fact he did; for his labours were abundant. In 1885 he was absent for some weeks and visited Utrecht once again. Apparently the change did not benefit as hoped, for soon after returning he wrote, "I am sorry I cannot say much beyond a continued mental fatigue. Dr. E. says I returned too soon, but I desire to feel the Lord's good hand." Soon after we find him offering as evidence of his being "quite well" the fact that "the writing of this letter has not fatigued me". Addressed to an exercised person who felt unfit and unworthy to join the church, it contains eminently practical and spiritual advice in such a case, and is here inserted:—

My dear Friend,—Your letter, written within and without with lamentation and mourning and woe, came last evening.

And what shall I say about it? Why it has the features, the voice, the diseases, and the complaints common to Zion's children! Yes, and the issue will be the "garment of praise for the spirit of heaviness". Now, for peace you have great bitterness, your faith cannot find Him whom your soul loves, and though free-born the enemy serves himself of you. Your old complaint, of which the glory of God shining in the face of Jesus Christ had so sweetly cured you, has, now that glory no longer shines upon you, begun to manifest itself again. Now you can say with Job, "By the great force of my disease is my garment (of praise) changed; it bindeth me about as the collar of my coat;" and with the psalmist, "There is no soundness in my flesh because of Thine anger, neither is there any rest in my bones because of my sin. For mine iniquities are gone over mine head; as an heavy burden they are too heavy for me." This burden will cause you to bow down; your felt darkness will make you feel that you only stumble at every step, that you are not in the way of understanding; now is the hour and power of the adversary, the accuser; how restless your heart will be, how it will meditate terror, how would you hide in the dust if you could; for all things look upside down! For all this there is one remedy,—the Fountain opened for sin and uncleanness—the Spirit's ever blessed witness—the unchanging love of the Father. You want the Lord to bid this affliction drive you home to anchor on His grace. This blessed remedy would once more remove the great force of your disease—infidelity, and take away all fear and dismay. But the Lord knows best when to apply that precious everlasting gospel. And here is the fight of faith at this particular time,—to press through the confusing crowd, to struggle hard and call aloud on the great Physician. Mr. L.'s was good advice: "Venture in the dark." What you know not now, you will know hereafter.

You anticipate that I may point out to you what the Lord has done for others—well, and so might I do with very good reason and grounds. "Awake, awake, put on strength, O arm of the Lord; awake, as in the ancient days, in the generations of old. Art thou not it that hath cut Rahab, and wounded the dragon? Art thou not it which hath dried the sea, the waters of the great deep; that hath made the depths of the sea a way for the ransomed to pass over?" Read Isa. li. Why? Because the remedy you need and are seeking is there, and because "Whatsoever things were written aforetime were written for our learning, that we through patience and comfort of the Scriptures might have hope." And remember, my friend, that grace is *free*. . . . How that wretched legality lurks in you, as in all others; it works evil in us and obscures the glory of God, under the deceiving garb of humility. But He will destroy the face of this covering with the glorious beams of His love and goodness. Are you five hundred pence deep? He will frankly, freely forgive you all. After all this trouble, folly, sin, darkness, lack of faith and love, how sweet will be restoring grace! "He restoreth my soul." Venture on Him, and venture forth on the ocean of His free love; a venturing faith He will never disown. All unbidden, Esther ventured in and found favour. Poor soul, you will find the Lord more gracious than your heart has ever yet thought. Your sin is ever before you (O it is a sickening sight!) but who can prize the salvation which is in Christ Jesus with eternal glory but those whose sins are as a cloud, a thick cloud? God's glory is great in salvation. Wherein? "And I will cleanse them from all their iniquity whereby they have sinned against me; and I will pardon all their iniquities whereby they have sinned, and whereby they have transgressed against Me. And it shall be to Me a name of joy, a praise and an honour before all the nations of the earth which shall hear all the good that I will do unto them," etc.

You make a mistake in supposing I cannot understand your trial about speaking before the people. I can. I have gone through it. The Lord will help you. But you seem to think your letter will give me such a shake about you that I may not think you a fit and proper person to join the church. I more than suspect that if all such poor lame, tried, and tempted souls (who, through all, are at times enabled to take the prey, and whose diseases are healed) were either, being members, turned out, or seeking to join churches were forbidden, there would be no churches of Jesus Christ. No. You must be joined to Jesus Christ the living Vine as

G

a poor wild olive—a dry tree—a sinful worm—and you must
join the number of the disciples as one whose fruit is alone
found from that ever-blessed compassionate Saviour. The
good Lord bless you with a waiting spirit of faith.

Thank you for G.'s letter. It is indeed encouraging to me
to believe I have some here to whom my poor ministry is
acceptable and useful. . . . Accept best wishes and Christian
love.   Yours in hope of eternal life,
6 Beaconsfield Villas,   J. K. POPHAM.
    Brighton.   1886.

Writing in 1886, after recovering from an illness and
absence of three weeks, he discloses in a letter to a friend his
very intimate self-acquaintance and the gracious spiritual
profit through " being exercised thereby ":—

"How good I found the way of ' sorrow for a night ', and
now this *day!* especially after feeling the bitterness of the
sorrow! Grace came to my aid, power was given to bend
my neck to have the yoke put on. Again I have found the
easiest way to bear trial is to be enabled to submit to it.
I have blessed the *dear, kind, gracious hand* that has laid on
me a gentle (for such it has been) blood-softened rod. It is
for my good, my humbling, to caution me, and to teach me
to make God my Refuge, and to rest in the atonement of
Jesus Christ. I have said, ' Turn away my reproach which
I fear,' and I believe it will for ever be turned away by that
sacred crimson flood which flows from a dying Saviour's
veins."

Referring to a treatise on " Divine Sovereignty " which he
had published at this time, and for which a second edition
was asked,* he writes:—

" I hope if I am spared to reprint it, the approving smile
of God will rest upon it; I am now favoured with just
enough religion to feel after *that* in all things. Oh, that my
heart were more gracious and tender, that I could fear God
and love and pray more; that I had more grace, light, life,
and power in my soul!"

---

* Of this weighty discourse there were printed in all five editions, the
last being issued as recently as January, 1938, by the Sovereign Grace
Union.

An interesting view of his tender heart and the wise pastoral care he took over his flock, is given in a letter to one exercised concerning Strict Communion:—

My dear Friend in the Lord,—. . . I fear my last letter to you must have been obscurely and clumsily expressed to have conveyed to your mind the impression that, feeling as you do, you ought not to be a member of the church. No such impression was intended by me. I felt, and still feel, that the distinction in your mind which is so painful a reality to you, does not really exist. A second wrong impression I fear I have created: you gather that I judge you to be left by the Lord "a tool in Satan's hands". Do forgive me for penning any word which will bear such an interpretation, and kindly regard it as not written. What I wanted to say was that Satan, jealous of God's gracious visits to you, and hating both Him and you for His sake, sought to destroy your peace by what is, in my judgment, a distinction where no difference exists. Between the Lord permitting Satan to tempt us and leaving us tools in his hands, there is, happily, an immense difference. Bear with one word more from me on this, to you, so painful a matter. I cannot but feel for you greatly. I am not hurt, not disappointed. I have great comfort in you. God has made you tender in His fear; you will eat the fruit of this affliction. Out of this eater will come forth meat; out of this strong sweetness. But I must entreat you to do nothing hastily. Let the matter remain as it is till the Lord shall speak. I cannot forbear saying that there appears to me to be in your mind in connection with signing Article 15, a very strained interpretation—a meaning which you are not required to say it carries. You are a Strict Baptist. That it is Scriptural to baptize before administering the Lord's Supper you own and feel. I see no more really in the article, though there is more in your mind. Let us, then, take the point which is in your mind. Suppose a few of God's people, not Baptists, feel it right to partake of the Lord's Supper; Article 15 says they do not partake according to the Scripture mode, but it does not impute sin, as that word is ordinarily used. I do not see that you say less than this. You

regard the views of such Christians as unscriptural; you
could not join with them in their practice. I know of no
Strict Baptist who, while fully maintaining the only Scripture mode, would deny that the Lord may very graciously
accept the love of such persons, and their faith, as fixed in
the atonement of Christ, in His dear Son. For wise purposes the Lord has not powerfully led some of His choicest
saints into the blessed ordinance of baptism, as witness the
godly Scotch Reformers and their people, the English Inde-
pendents, and later, Huntington and his followers. I do not
imagine it was ever intended to say that these were rejected
in that way of theirs in regard to the ordinance of the Lord's
Supper, though we (yourself among us, I apprehend) cannot
allow that their mode was the Scriptural one. I need say no
more. You are in good gracious hands—the Spirit will shew
you the right way I doubt not. When I said it would be
your mercy to drop the matter, I did not intend to convey
either that the matter was small to you, or that you could of
yourself let it go. The Lord alone can settle your mind.
But as you cannot drop it, so may you be divinely kept from
taking a hasty step. That you will remain in the visible
Church I entertain no doubt. It is a most painful trial to
you, and I feel deeply for you, and more, my spirit shares
it with you. I desire to weep with those who weep. Wait
on the Lord who now for a season hides His face. Through
many dangers He has already brought you, out of many
troubles He has delivered you; after long delays He has,
in days past, heard you. Will He now forsake you? No.
He is faithful. "There hath no temptation taken you but
such as is common to man; but God is faithful, who will with
the temptation make a way to escape that ye may be able
to bear it." Wait on Him then, and beg for grace to wait
until He shall all explain. His light will open up the narrow
path to you; His power will make you to walk in it; and
you will yet have the high praises of God in your mouth.
The Lord bless you, my dear afflicted friend. If by any
uncouth expression I have given you pain, or darkened
counsel by words without knowledge, forgive me, and kindly
believe my intention is in the right direction.

May you soon be convalescent and able to join God's

people in worship, and sing praises for a double mercy—one to your body and one to your soul.

Accept our united love and sympathy.

I remain,

Yours very truly in hope of eternal life,

Brighton. Oct. 2nd, 1886. J. K. POPHAM.

CHAPTER SEVEN.

" The people shall dwell alone."

1886—1895. Death of his mother—abundant labours blessed— separation imperative—son of consolation—visit to Highlands—a profitable affliction.

IN December, 1886, our beloved friend was called upon to suffer a very heavy bereavement in the death of his mother; " the greatest sorrow " he had hitherto known. The change which came to her in 1863, while her son was but a lad, has already been related; but as the tremendous concerns of eternity weighed heavily upon the son in his watching for souls, he sought for very clear work in those for whom he had most regard. Hence, though—as he has told us—he had a hope his mother was truly a child of God (her copy of Hart's hymns was found to be much marked in those places expressive of penitence for sin and the redeeming work of Christ), he anxiously awaited news of her last days. A letter referring to this will be of interest, as shewing his tender filial affection for his parent, his godly jealousy, and his sympathy with one similarly bereaved:—

My dear Friend,—It is most kind of you to write in the midst of your own sorrow; thank you so much for your letter. I must go on to-morrow night, otherwise I cannot reach my home until about mid-day on Thursday.

I feel utterly broken at times and know not how to stand up. God is right; my lips have not charged Him with foolishness, but O what my heart feels! How awful and terrible is His majesty; how unsearchable are His judgments and His ways past finding out! Who can stand before so holy a Lord God? It is unspeakably solemn and awful to have to do with Him. I would hold my peace, but fearfulness hath taken hold upon me. Once to-day, for a minute, as I sat alone, I felt some soft approach to the Eternal God, through the rent veil of the Saviour's humanity. But for the most part I tremble beneath His awfulness—the great and dreadful God. This suffices to keep rebellion down, but I want soft, humble, godly submission. This evening a kind friend called to condole, but I found much hardness and rebellion under the ordinary religious talk. I long to see my brother to know all I can about our dear mother's end. I imagine he has some hope. And O, I cannot tell you how something in me catches at such a word as, "He that is not against us is for us." But I will not burden you with my sorrow. I feel it is the greatest I have known.

Now indeed my sympathy with you is true sympathy. I feel *with* you, as well as *for* you. But it is well I cannot stay with you. I cannot speak. I can write these lines, but speaking is so hard. How shall I do to-morrow night? yet I feel the Lord's work is so the first, I dare not go away from it.

The Lord will return to you, dear friend, and may He help you to pray for me. Ask that a "standard-bearer" may not faint.

Excuse this paper—when I saw yours I remembered my neglect, but I think my *heart* is in deepest mourning over a loved parent whose voice and welcome to my old home I shall never again hear.

With reciprocated, deepest sympathy and love,
　　　　　　Yours in "many waters",
Brighton. Dec. 14th, 1886.　　　　　　　J. K. POPHAM.

There are no recorded details of it, but we think we can warrantably infer that our dear friend obtained help of God in this sore bereavement, for the next evening he preached at

Galeed from Job xxxvii. 23: " Touching the Almighty, we
cannot find Him out; He is excellent in power, and in
judgment, and in plenty of justice; He will not afflict." It
is obvious that the Word of God to which he had recourse
in his trials, was made in and through him a living power,—
his ministry was in the truest sense " experimental ". His
dignified utterances would at times be so solemnly weighty,
that the chapel seemed charged with an awesome atmosphere.
There was no attempt at outside effect: theatrical oratory, so
popular and so delusive, he strictly avoided.

On March 2nd, 1887, Mr. Popham preached remarkably
from Isa. xxix. 24: " They also that erred in spirit shall
come to understanding, and they that murmured shall learn
doctrine." The hidden secret of that sermon is revealed in a
letter, in which, after naming a simple but trying domestic
difficulty, he writes:—

" What ignorant things we are in reality! ' We are of
yesterday, and know nothing.' I am glad of that word, ' If
any of you lack wisdom, let him ask of God,' etc. One says:

' My soul through many changes goes,
    His love no variation knows.'

" But all real good comes in and by trial, as you know.
My recent trial has been a good thing for me; I have felt
established, and the people, without knowing the matter, have
received the benefit. How satisfied I feel to have it so. I
can *almost* say, ' Lay on any burden that will be for my
good, the people's benefit, and Thy glory.' But I am a faint-
hearted thing, and can bear but little, nothing indeed but as
sustained."

In addition to his pastoral labours, Mr. Popham preached
very frequently in many pulpits,* and visited the north twice
annually during his early days at Brighton. There were
severe trials, of which he seldom spoke except to a few
intimate friends, as well as many mercies. Several of the
Galeed members turned against him, and discontinued attending the services. Concerning two of these, whose cases were
a very acute trial to the dear pastor, while he was deeply
exercised before the Lord concerning them, he heard the

---

* There is a record of 182 pulpits in which he preached.

direction, " Of some have compassion, making a difference "
(Jude 22). One of these backsliders was graciously restored,
while the other came to his end apparently impenitent.
These solemn matters weighed heavily, and lent an even
deeper tone to his already discriminating ministry. There
were good days, too, in the best sense of the term. There
are still living those who know, for instance, the significance
of a note against October 7th, 1888: Text, Ps. cxix. 133,
" A memorable time "; then follow the names of six persons
who received special blessing under the sermon that morning. Such entries may not be numerous, but the gospel net,
though small-meshed, caught choice fry,—Mr. Popham's was
a ministry not calculated to hasten into presumptuous confidence.

Many labours and severe trials—not unmingled with frequent evidences of God's gracious approbation of His dear
servant, brought his health low, and in 1891 he was taken
suddenly ill while travelling to Redhill, on July 7th, to
preach at Shaw's Corner that evening. Of this seven-weeks'
illness he gave the following account:—

" My illness did not find me in a bad place; I had had
several special revivings just before, but there was nothing
particular in the first week, till on Tuesday, July 14th, the
Lord came. I had found the bottom—that I deserved the
affliction for my sins. When ice was brought to me, I felt,
' They gave Him vinegar to drink.' Feeling so weak, I was
on the point of falling into self-pity at being reduced so low
as to need to be fed. Then my most merciful, pitiful,
glorious Redeemer came near and spoke to me. If anyone
had told me the Lord would have come in the way He did,
I could hardly have believed it. He spoke these words,
' Blessed is he that considereth the poor: the Lord will
deliver him in time of trouble. The Lord will strengthen
him on the bed of languishing. Thou wilt make all his bed
in his sickness ' (Ps. xli. 1—3). I said, ' Lord, I have
never done it, I have not had the opportunity; mine has been
receiving.' I took the word literally. Then He shewed me
He had seen every desire and cry I had put up for His poor;
that I had considered them in my heart, and He accepted
it, and would be with me in trouble; and I could hardly bear

it, and wept as He spoke to me. He talked with me and made me believe His astonishing words, shewed me His Person, and poured in His everlasting love. Then I began to confess my sins, my utter unworthiness; told Him I was not fit for Him to look on and love; not worth all the trouble He was taking with me. But the more I confessed, the more He seemed determined not to notice what I said. Day after day I lay in unutterable peace. I tried to bring up my sins and press them upon His notice; and when I had done this for two or three days, one morning in particular being pained at my sins and unkindness to Him, I said, when I had laid all before Him, 'Lord, canst Thou be kind to me after all this?' And O how He made me hear His voice in Isa. xliv. 22! 'I have blotted out as a thick cloud thy transgressions, and as a cloud thy sins: return unto Me, for I have redeemed thee.' I felt He would not let me go on in that way of confessing. I saw the atonement was a bed long enough for me to lie on, and His righteousness a covering broad enough to cover me. He did indeed make my bed in my sickness, and suffered nothing to interrupt me for a whole week. For the time I was able to lay down my ministry, and had no trouble about it. The chief passages in which He revealed Himself to me were, Ps. lxxv. 2: 'When I shall receive the congregation I will judge uprightly,' and following verses, and Ps. xli. 1—3 above-mentioned, and verse 12: 'Thou settest me before Thy face for ever.'

"I want to lift up this ever-glorious God-man. I did ask Him—and felt He accepted my prayer—that if He raised me up again, He would grant me a fresh horn of oil, to go forth and preach Him. I also felt He gave me an answer to prayer in my illness, concerning delirium; for I had asked Him to preserve me from saying anything that would stumble His people, if that should befall me. He led me into the subject of the mortification of sin, to feel that in His presence the body of sin was subdued as if it were dead. I was bathed in peace, and thought of spending an eternity with Him. Many verses of Hart's came up:

'Dearly we're bought, highly esteemed,
Redeemed, with Jesus' blood redeemed.'

How little I know of Him! I am ashamed and confounded at my base sins; yet the Lord will love me."

After seven weeks' absence, the loved pastor again preached in his dear Galeed pulpit on August 23rd, his text being Ps. lxxx. 2: "Before Ephraim and Benjamin and Manasseh stir up Thy strength, and come and save us." A note against this says, "After a severe, but not wholly unprofitable illness. J. K. P."

This illness left him apprehensive about the future, having many ministerial commitments; but his God brought him through and enabled him to bear testimony that His strength was "made perfect" in His servant's weakness:—

"June 12th, 1892.—I had many fears and great conflict about my engagements to preach, and often thought I should break down in body, that I had made the engagements after the flesh, and one stroke would lay me by. These things I laid before the Lord over and over for weeks, not knowing if He would answer or what He would say to me. Now I feel He has of late helped me with more strength in body than I have had for some time, and also has helped me in spirit and given peace in my soul; so that after speaking I have felt, 'For this child I prayed.' I could never have thought He would answer me so abundantly.

"Some time ago I was in much trouble because I felt I had so little grace, (I was not left to think I had none, but so very little,) and the Lord dropped in this word, 'According to the word that I covenanted with you when ye came out of Egypt, so My Spirit remaineth among you: fear ye not' (Hag. ii. 5). And the other day, when full of fear lest I should be left to barrenness in the ministry, that word came again with some little efficacy and authority. What a mercy not to be *left!* 'If Thou shouldst leave us, we must fall.' I have thought of the dealings of God with me at times were such as would cut me off from His people; not much like one who is 'a companion of all them that fear Him'; not much like 'lifting up my head with joy among the sons of God'. I have thought,

'Yea, more—with His own hand He seemed
Intent to aggravate my woe.'

But let a little gracious operation of His Spirit begin to flow again, as the sap from the root, and spring returns, the leaves appear, the tender buds and blossoms are formed. It is the empty, dark, barren, afflicted person, with no religion, that is a fit subject for Jesus Christ. How much better it is to be naught, that Christ may be all—the sum and substance of religion!"

While such exercises were being wrought in his soul, the cause at Galeed was reaping the benefit; and pastor and people were drawn closer together through their mutual afflictions as a means. A most interesting glimpse of this is given by the drawing aside of the veil in a letter (he seldom spoke of himself, directly, from the pulpit) written to an intimate friend at this time:—

". . . Now about dear old Galeed. . . . Mr. M. and family return, all being well, to-morrow. Dear old S. lingers in very great suffering, but wonderfully helped to bear all with patience—is as full of divine goodness as his frail body can well bear. Last evening he said, 'Not a wave of trouble rolls across my peaceful breast. My last days are my best days. I love the brethren with pure heart fervently.' His daughter, Mrs. B., is very ill and suffering. E. H. looks better and was in her place in chapel last night. Mrs. L. has got a deliverance and is in a wealthy place. Mrs. C. appears to be in better health. Mr. C. said last evening, 'The Lord has been with you this evening.' This, for him, as you know, is much. Mr. B. discovered more liveliness than usual. . . . The congregation was thin last evening, and at first it so depressed me that I was exceedingly troubled and filled with confusion. But soon after I began to speak, I found an influence falling on my heart, and enlargement, unction, love, authority, filled my soul. (II Cor. iv. 6: 'God who commanded the light to shine out of darkness, hath shined in our hearts,' etc., was the text.) The light the Spirit casts on the Person of Christ in His humiliation, occupied all the evening. There was a remarkable stillness in the chapel. How short was the hour which at the commencement looked almost an interminable period! My thoughts ran to you and I wished that you might be per-

mitted to gaze upon His wondrous face and feel His love
more than ever. . . ."

Throughout his long ministerial life Mr. Popham's vital
soul-exercise, through the gracious work of the Holy Ghost,
necessitated the maintenance of separation from everything
in religion of a general superficial character. This brought
him much reproach and no little difficulty; but his God
honoured him. That this was not a bigoted, haughty separ-
atism—as has been maliciously suggested—was known to his
gracious and more intimate friends and colleagues. A discovery of this inward spiritual root of outward separation is
made in the following incident. He was persuaded on one
occasion to join in a combined prayer-meeting held in the
town by various protestant ministers; and he even shortened
the regular prayer-meeting at Galeed for this purpose. His
impressions were as follows:—

" They suggested our giving up our prayer-meeting as Mr.
H. did, but if I had required special justification for *not*
doing so, it was furnished me at the Town Hall. A hot
political speech by Mr. L., after he had scolded Mr. H. for
having introduced politics; then *talk, called prayer. Not one
word of confession of sin in any I heard save H.'s* [a member
at Galeed]. *We must walk alone.*"

It is hoped that this extract may reveal the true secret
(known long to some), and will convince his enemies that his
separation was not the ' proud aloofness ' for which they have
censured him. Whilst stedfastly resisting compromise with
error of spirit, practice, or doctrine, he was ever ready to
recognize and cherish the least evidence of spiritual life
wherever perceptible, and was skilled out of personal spiritual
experience to recommend the gospel of Christ to troubled
consciences. The following is typical of his early efforts in
this direction, written to one whose painful sense of sin
almost prevailed to hinder attendance on the means of grace:

Poor dear Friend,—Is the gospel for good, whole, and
altogether believing people ? Or is it not rather, yea, much
more, for bad, sick, plagued, unbelieving, dead, polluted
souls ? Have you not some such case as is set forth in the
words *dead, leprous, lost, weak, enemies, unclean?* You must
go to chapel for Christ's sake, for your own sake. He will

take it more amiss if you stay away because His and your
enemies tell you, than anything you may do in the way of
venturing in the darkness of your unbelief and confusion.
Would you like *Him* to tell you to stay away? If not, if
such a word would grieve you even now, how will He take
it at your hands if you agree with your own heart against
Him? GO. Your sympathizing friend,

Brighton. ? 1892. J. K. POPHAM.

Having faced the most momentous of all questions in his
own soul, and received satisfaction respecting it, his presentation of the truth in most discriminating form was tempered
with a tenderness which involved no concessions of doctrine.
Accredited ministers and others have complained as to the
doctrinal nature of his ministry, whereas they desired *experimental* preaching. Such are apparently able at will to draw
from their hearers tears of sympathy with themselves (" None
so troubled as they!"). Mr. Popham's ministry, coming out
of vital personal experience in the secret of his own soul
before God, led his hearers to CHRIST, set HIM before the
fainting souls of the sin-troubled, tempted, and afflicted—a
vast difference! In the truest sense was his ministry " experimental "—not merely talking about experiences, but
preaching the doctrines as experimentally learned in the
school of Christ. Better were it for the churches that such
a ministry were oftener sought and given by the Lord. Of
a finely-calculated, dry, scholastic theological production, he
once said to us—a remark pregnant with vital significance—
" There is nothing there for a broken-hearted sinner." On
the other hand, of his secret experimental entrance into the
deepest doctrines, an example is here furnished:—

" I have of late such a sense of the Lord's felt pity and
sympathy poured into my trouble, I have felt it almost more
than I could bear. I was favoured with a greater sense of
the suffering humanity of the Lord Jesus than ever before.
It began on Tuesday with the feeling that there is access for
all that come to God by Him; and I sensibly felt it was
unbelief holding me back and stopping prayer. Power was
given to bring my sins and trouble to Him. Then I had a
discovery of His path, the agony of His heart, when ' He
offered up strong crying and tears ' and wrestled in agony

for our sakes; and that He knew my path, everything in it,
and was touched with the feeling of it. This continued
several days, till Saturday, when I feared the sacred power
was withdrawing. But it returned again with these lines:—

> ' See here an endless ocean flows
> Of never-failing grace;
> Behold a dying Saviour's veins
> The sacred flood increase! '

I was overwhelmed with His pity and sympathy for me in
my trouble. I spoke on Lord's Day from Heb. ii. 17:
' Wherefore in all things it behoved Him to be made like
unto His brethren, that He might be a merciful and faithful
High Priest,' etc."

The Priesthood of Christ was a favourite theme with him,
for he knew experimentally the value of His offering, mediation, and intercession; he was acquainted with His love and
mercy, and had received some divine impressions of the glory
of His divine Person. Paul (II Cor. i. 3, 4) could bless the
Lord, even the Father of our Lord Jesus Christ, the Father
of mercies, and the God of all comfort, Who comforted him
in all his tribulation that he might be able to comfort those
who were in any trouble with the comfort wherewith he
himself was comforted of God, for as the sufferings of Christ
abounded in him, so his consolation abounded by Christ. The
following memorandum sheds a light on similar tuition in
the pastor of Galeed:—

" In much sorrow and exercise of mind on Saturday night,
July 22nd, 1893, at Croydon, under deep searchings of heart
and sense of guilt in many things, I found Ps. cxxx. 7 a
most gracious word: ' Let Israel hope in the Lord: for with
the Lord there is mercy, and with Him is plenteous redemption.' It raised up faith which held me in prayer and supplications and confessions; it told me where to go, to whom
I must look for redemption, even plenteous redemption. On
the following morning, very early, Isa. lvii. 15 was made
spirit and life, power and comfort in my heart: ' For thus
saith the High and Lofty One, whose Name is holy; I dwell
. . . with him also that is of a contrite and humble spirit,'
etc. It furnished me with food for my soul and also matter
for the pulpit. Now it seemed as if light came from all

parts of the Scripture. I could read nowhere without finding sweet light and heavenly comfort. In the afternoon of
this good day, Ps. xvii. 15 was made my own in a particular
manner and was my evening's text: ' As for me, I will behold
Thy face in righteousness: I shall be satisfied, when I awake,
with Thy likeness.' Never before was I more assured of a
good issue of all my trials, sin, and this mortal life. I saw
by faith the well-pleased face of God in Christ, and the
endless satisfaction my soul would enjoy in the possession
of His glorious likeness. Oh, if one might only *live* under
the smile of God! But this I ever find: I must come into
some trial to be ' emptied from vessel to vessel ' to make
way and room for the Lord's most merciful return to my
sinful weary soul. How unspeakably gracious of His divine
Majesty to come when one is in some self-procured trouble,
to speak words of mercy, favour, and comfort, to smile on a
chastened aching heart! I find He has a wonderful way of
drawing forth faith into a prevailing act upon Himself—by
a smile, a touch, a word. Unbelief, which one vainly com-
bats and chides, cannot stand against the persuading power
thus communicated. Circumstances which, like fierce winds,
drive one, lose their disturbing, distressing power, and a
quiet rest is felt; one enters into the word, ' Rest in the Lord,
and wait patiently for Him.'—J. K. P."

Notwithstanding much favour from his Lord, he was continually brought into fresh exercise, and humbling grace
was manifested in his tenderness towards seeking souls. He
said about this time, " I find much fear on my spirit. A low
place becomes me. Oh, if I may but receive some heavenly
communications! A humble broken spirit seems to me this
morning of more value than thousands of gold and silver."
In that tender exercised frame he was able to " nurse " the
seeking soul, entering into their path, but without setting
them down short of Christ. An example of this is in the
following letter, written at this time:—

My dear Friend,—The Word of God looks most kindly
upon all who *seek, cry, follow on,* and *wait.* It employs the
above terms to set forth the labour, pain, intenseness, and
continuance of poor people who cannot rest short of a saving
knowledge of the Son of God. " Seek ye first " is one of

the sweet promises the Lord of glory left for all who, quickened and taught by His good Spirit, should be in pain, fear,
and confusion, feeling their desperate condition by sin and
the law. How such seek relief! What cries they send up to
heaven for mercy! How they seek life to deliver them from
their dreadful death, pardon to ease their burdened consciences, and love to dissolve their frozen hearts. To such
seekers the ever-enduring Word of God is that they shall
find. Oh what a great blessing a *case* is! That which
troubles us brings us where we alone can find relief. And a
gracious God in His own time will say to every seeker, "Be
it unto thee even as thou wilt."

You will find many changes. By them God's people live.
I trust you may find such power upon you as will keep you
well exercised, burdened and anxious, that nothing short of
a revelation of Christ will bring rest and peace to you.
Even your *sense* of ignorance will thus be a real blessing
and help to you. If you were "wise in your own conceit"
you would not seek divine teaching. No "Spirit of wisdom
and revelation in the knowledge of Christ" would you then
seek. "Unto us which believe Christ is the wisdom of God
and the power of God." Oh, then what a mercy it is to
need such a Christ, to have a grain of vital faith in His
Person and atonement! The Lord shew Himself very
gracious to you. With every good wish,

Yours very truly,

Brighton. ? 1893.   J. K. POPHAM.

His hearers profited from his Spirit-enriched ministry, yet
his own views, especially at times, of the preaching were
low indeed. The following note will strike a chord in the
heart of a few tried and honoured servants of the Most
High:—

"I am more depressed and tried than I can tell at my
unprofitable ministry, and often wonder how the Lord bears
with me; am often weary of myself and even of the sound
of my own voice; yet I feel, 'Woe is me if I preach not the
gospel.'"

In this year (1893) Mr. Popham preached, on the occasion
of the death of a godly person, a remarkable sermon from

MR. POPHAM AT FIFTY.

Ps. xxxvii. 37, which he was persuaded to publish, under the title, "The Perfect Man and his God." The discourse is a beautiful combination of discrimination and tender encouragement, calculated to search the soul, to detect sin, and to reveal grace. Of this publication he wrote:—

"The sermon is selling well, but that is not the only nor the most important thing. Oh, if the Lord would bless the reading of it in various places! I have posted one to my dear boy."

Scripture says, "A man's gift maketh room for him." Mr. Popham's engagements increased abundantly; but he was careful not to force his own way, viewing the importance of the Holy Spirit's work in disposing *where* and *when* as well as *what*, he was to preach. Writing to one who gave him a *carte-blanche*, he discreetly said:—

"By waiting for my friends to invite me, I avoid the danger of going at any time when not wanted. All through my ministerial life this has been my practice; partly, it may be, from natural backwardness, but chiefly, I hope, from the fear of moving before the Lord, going to any place unsent. Many doors has He opened for me; I think I speak the truth when I say none have been opened by myself. . . . Yesterday I had three services. Oh, I wish I may never forget the Lord's kindness to me each time; and though I feel the reaction to-day, while speaking last evening I felt no more fatigue than I often do with one service in the day. How easy is His divine yoke! how light His sweet burden!"

It is well known that our dear friend was much attached to the godly remnant in Scotland, but before his first acquaintance with them, his experience while on holiday in Perthshire in 1894 yielded little spiritual satisfaction. A letter written while there displays the "vexing of his righteous soul" (as Lot) "with the filthy conversation of the wicked"; and reveals the trend of his mind Godward:—

"Indolence has conquered me; moreover, I am continually either to one spot or another to gaze on ever-new beauty, and I seem to be unable to drink in enough of the health-giving air. I wish I could give as good an account of my soul as I can of my health; but alas! I cannot. Spiritually I faint and languish. Death, formality, and sad profanity

H

surround us. There is religion which, if consistent, one would in a natural sense be glad to see; for it is good for man to pay homage to his Creator. But to witness, as we did last evening, men and women playing cards, hear a clergyman sing a song, and in five minutes after see the same persons joining in singing a hymn and kneeling in prayer, was too awful and sad. I said to the mother, 'I go in to prayers—so called—no more.' Yet I felt, and now feel, glad my soul revolted with sadness for men and grief for the dishonour done to the Lord's holy Name. I could say, 'O my soul, come not thou into their secret; mine honour, be not thou united to their assemblies.' Now I soon turn my face homeward, and shall have nothing to say to my friends of any new and sweet views I have had of the fair face of the Lord Jesus. One good walk and talk I had with Mr. P. . . . Oh, if I were more godly and bold, I might say something for Him who has, I hope, begun to shew me His greatness! At Dunkeld I intensely longed to speak after a young minister had wickedly played and trifled with his congregation by reading his essay on angels. How I have thought of godly Rutherford since being in his dearly-loved Scotland. How often he said wrath was coming on the land. *It is now upon it* in the form of 'strong delusions'. What will the people do in the end thereof? (Jer. v. 31.) We met two men on Monday in the train who I think fear God. How they lamented the awful preaching throughout the land! What unfeigned delight they shewed in hearing Mr. P. talk! I only dropped an odd word, but on leaving the train one offered me his hand—working hand. . . ."— J. K. P."

It is perhaps not a little significant that his text on returning to his own pulpit (July 15th, 1894) was: "Hungry and thirsty, their soul fainted in them," etc. (Ps. cvii. 5, 6). And most probably his hearers reaped the benefit of those weeks of painful famine.

Early in 1895, sickness overtook him and several of his family, keeping him out of the pulpit for three weeks. Of this heavy trial and its profitable fruit, the dear man wrote a valuable memorandum, part of which has survived and is here reproduced:—

A Memorandum.

"*Feb.* 24*th*, 1895. I will, by the Lord's gracious help, put down a few words relative to His solemn dispensation with me recently and now. Truly He has come into my house as a whirlwind.

" For some days before the affliction came, I found working in my heart many strong affections and desires after the Lord. I longed to be godly. On Wednesday the 13th inst. I was much struck by Eccles. vii., and found faith mixing with verses 2 and 3 particularly; also the viiith chapter, 6th verse, of the same book; and in the evening of that day preached from the word, ' Because to every purpose there is time and judgment, therefore the misery of man is great upon him.' On the following day I was so unwell I was obliged to go to bed, but had no special exercise of mind. The following day, Friday the 15th, dear Mrs. Combridge entered into her eternal rest; and feeling that I was needed I went out, though at great risk, and saw my dear bereaved friend, Mr. Combridge. I was pressed in spirit also to visit two sick people, members of the congregation, and then went to the prayer-meeting. On Saturday, the 16th inst., I was very unwell, and dull and flat in spirit, and depressed with the feeling that my child Gertrude was becoming seriously ill. In the evening I felt some sweetness in meditating upon Eccles. vii. 1, specially as the wonderful word, ' For we are members of His body, of His flesh, and of His bones,' came into my mind. I rose on Sunday morning feeling ill, and went to chapel quite unaware of the state I was in. I spoke with much difficulty and in pain, yet with some sweetness, to myself, from Eccles. vii. 1. In the afternoon I became worse, and it was evident I should not be able to go to chapel in the evening. My Gertrude was now very ill, also Mary and Edgar failed, and my wife perfectly helpless with an attack of eczema which covered her whole body. But Gertrude was specially on my mind as the one before whom was long and serious illness; and what was most painful to me was I could not raise a cry in my heart for her mortal life, but I felt a living and, what seemed to me, a mighty cry for her precious soul. This cry was with

me through a sleepless and painful night. When the doctor
on the following morning pronounced the children and
myself ill with influenza, my heart sank as lead. I looked on
my dear wife very ill, and now there were also four other
invalids, two of whom, Mary and Gertrude, were already in
high fever. Now commenced four awful days. May four
such days never again fall to my lot! Job made the mistake
of concluding that God was finding occasions against him,
but I committed the sin of high treason in seeking to find
occasions against God. My heart sought pleas against His
wisdom, justice, and mercy. Judas sought an opportunity to
betray his Master; I endeavoured to quarrel with my God,
Saviour, Friend, and only Refuge. O fallen wretch! There
was not only no prayer in me, but I appeared to lack a
desire to pray. I thought indeed I did well to be angry.
Thoughts of extreme hardness and rebellion filled my heart.
Anger rested in my foolish bosom. This grievous state of
mind continued with much strength for four days. A little
there was of intermission, once or twice, and wonderful it
was to me to perceive during those moments—all too brief—
a party in my heart speaking for God, that did not believe,
would not listen to the hard, bitter and cruel things my
depraved nature so proudly uttered against His divine
Majesty, did not consent to the thief who came only to rob
and kill me, and take all glory, wisdom, sovereignty, and
lovingkindness from God in my eyes." [*remainder missing.*]

Here is another glimpse into the inner secret of the
gracious fortitude with which the dear pastor and parent
endured, laboured, and prevailed:—

A MEMORANDUM.

" *Nov.* 21*st* 1895. Joshua i. 5: 'There shall not any man
be able to stand before thee all the days of thy life: as I was
with Moses, so I will be with thee: I will not fail thee, nor
forsake thee.' This great word, too big for me, was, notwithstanding, most sweet, living, and powerful in my heart this
morning. It has made me look for many things. I could
not take it in, yet it would come in. I found it within me.
O that I may prove it to have been really made over to me!"
On January 26th, 1896, the honoured pastor of Mayfield,

Mr. E. Page,* died, and on Lord's Day, February 2nd, Mr. Popham preached in his pulpit from Rev. xiv. 13: ". . . Blessed are the dead which die in the Lord," etc. This commenced a close connection with the Mayfield cause, and thereafter the Brighton pastor preached at Mayfield one Monday evening monthly, and presided at their church meetings until 1918, when the present gracious pastor was appointed. Mr. Popham continued to preach at the annual services in May, the last time being on May 13th, 1936, when his text was Luke xv. 1, 2. His services at Mayfield were highly esteemed, and he was by God's grace very useful during a critical period of the church's life.

For many years he had rendered a similar service for the Shaw's Corner cause, at Redhill, preaching there one Tuesday evening monthly until the present esteemed pastor was instated in 1918. His last sermon at Shaw's Corner was on an occasional visit, November 24th, 1936, from Acts x. 36. His labours were truly abundant, the Lord honoured him and "helped him marvellously" (II Chron. xxvi. 15). Ever ready to assist where he felt there was a right aim, he was anxiously watchful for the manifested fruit,—the work of the Holy Ghost. To one who had commenced to hold services in a town where there was no regular sound preaching, he sent this wise word concerning the dissatisfaction of some:—

" The circumstances of your little meeting are very solemn; men love darkness rather than light. In every place it is so, but if in any neighbourhood the truth is preached and not applied to people with power, their enmity is brought to light. Thus Christ preached brings to light the thoughts of many hearts (Lu. ii. 35). There is a rejecting by men of the Word of Truth—God's pure Truth. . . . Still, the ser-

---

* *Note of Eli Page's last days:*—When visited by Mr. P. during his last illness, Mr. Page said on Mr. Popham's leaving him, " Goodbye, brother. Farewell, brother. I can say all is well. I am like one going on a long journey; all is ready packed. I have not the clear inshining, but I know it is all right. Oh, there is not a thing between the Lord and me. Perfectly justified! The truths I have preached will do to die by."

As he drew near the end, he said four times, " Jesus only, Jesus only, Jesus only, Jesus only. Tell Mr. Popham he is not to exalt the creature but Jesus only." The last words he was heard to utter were, " Exalt Him." He fell asleep Jan. 26th, 1896.

vices may be useful to you, your family, and a few others. Ploughing on the rock is hard and profitless work; but we cannot tell what the Lord may accomplish. If one person is in any spiritual way blest, all the labour will be well repaid. It is no light matter to me to have persons under my ministry in whom are appearances of some gracious disposition. Oh, if I may teach them right things and be an instrument for good to them! If I am, it is most likely my preaching will more wound than anything else for a time. God turns man to destruction, and then says, ' Return, ye children of men.' Do you find a spirit of prayer poured out upon you for the meeting ? "

To this place Mr. Popham went preaching one Thursday a month for many years, and God did work marvellously in several particular cases.

CHAPTER EIGHT.

" Do the work of an evangelist."

1895—1904. Family trials—tempted concerning ministry—fiftieth birthday, recognition at Galeed—pastoral joys and griefs—sanctified affliction—recovery and abundant labours—three months' silence—no idle shepherd—knitting of heart between him and the flock. " Of some have compassion, making a difference."—Resumption of preaching.

SAYS John Bunyan:

" The Christian man is seldom long at ease,
When one trouble's o'er another doth him seize."

Among the various afflictions, sorrows and domestic trials which befell our dear friend, his eldest son had gone under trying circumstances to South Africa. The foolish raid of Jameson (December, 1895) which led on to the great South African Boer war, naturally affected the father's loving sensitive heart. The subjoined extract from a letter written to a godly friend relating to political affairs provides an interesting interlude, and shews that even in this sphere the divine supremacy of the King of grace—to the godly a source of solace in every distress—is not forgotten by him:—

" . . . O may we hear the voice of the Lord in this dispensation, and watch His hand! . . . I am much impressed with the serious condition and position of matters relating to our dear though deeply guilty empire. . . . But the government is upon the shoulders of Him who reigns ' expecting till all His enemies be made His footstool '. The impropriety and the unwisdom of the German Emperor, the madness of Jameson, the turbulent passions of ungodly, self-seeking men, are only so many agents in the mighty skilful hands of the Lord Jesus, to whom is committed all rule, authority, and judgment."

How little do hearers realize what may be transpiring in the innermost soul recesses of the minister in the pulpit! What great cause there is for the godly to hold up the pastor's hands by prayer! Toward the close of 1896, Mr. Popham again came under temptation and trial with regard to his ministry, an account of which and his deliverance, with the profitable result to the church, is here given in his own words:—

" I had been walking mournfully under a sense of my poor preaching, often laying it before the Lord. Gradually it seemed that Satan was allowed to work upon what at first was a right feeling and exercise, and in his subtilty to assail and almost overthrow my faith in my call to preach. The questioning on this point became at times so severe that it was painful and difficult for me to enter a pulpit. More than once I contemplated calling the church together to tell them my fears and that I could not continue.* But I was kept from taking a step which would have been yielding altogether to the tempter. My friend, Mr. Marshall, who knew my case, said, ' If you are wrong in it, what becomes of us ? we are all in the same boat!' But I was assailed

---

* At a regular church meeting about this time Mr. Popham did actually name his fears to the people, telling them he could not preach; but in returning home he was so reproved by the words, "As when a standard-bearer fainteth," that he vowed he would never again reveal to the people his feelings, however greatly he might be tried.

night and day with little intermission, and nothing anyone could say gave any relief, till the Lord spoke. One day in March, 1897, when on my knees in my study, these words settled the matter: ' Do the work of an evangelist, make full proof of thy ministry ' (II Tim. iv. 5). So He answered the groanings that could not be uttered, and delivered me out of the hand of the cruel one."

Our dear friend has often told us of how the above delivering word also strengthened him to go about here and there preaching in various places, in addition to his pastorate at Brighton. Frequently he asked the Lord not to let his dear friends at Galeed, who were his chief care, suffer on account of his weariness in consequence of so much preaching elsewhere in the week. And it must be acknowledged by many that his ministry at Brighton was fuller and richer than anywhere else, although the Spirit used him in many cases in other parts. We have several times heard him remark, speaking of a service somewhere away from Brighton, " I think I could have said more at home;" meaning that he felt the capacity of his own regular hearers would have received a fuller treatment of the subject. The correspondence between the pulpit and the pew, between the hunger, felt need, the urgent prayers of the hearers, and the fruitfulness of the ministry is no less real because so little perceived. Besides which, all the usefulness in other places with which God honoured him could not make him to others exactly what he was alone to his flock at Galeed,—a tender undershepherd. In 1897 he wrote: " I cannot tell the fear which presses on my heart of being left with only outward comfort in the cause. Perhaps no poor minister in our connection has more peace, love, and union than I have here among my friends. But how I have felt that this mercy may be turned into a snare by one so vile."

The occasion of attaining his fiftieth birthday (1897) was marked by his affectionate church and congregation, on which occasion they presented their beloved minister with a clock, a purse of money, and a loving address. It will be of interest to give the latter in full:—

Address presented to Mr. J. K. Popham on his Fiftieth
Birthday, December 20th, 1897.

Dearly Beloved Pastor, whom we love in the truth and for
the truth's sake,—Grace be with you, mercy, and peace,
from God the Father and from the Lord Jesus Christ, the
Son of the Father in truth and love.

In presenting this Address to you on your fiftieth birthday, we ask your acceptance of the accompanying timepiece,
and a purse containing £97 9s. 6d., as a tribute of loving
friendship and grateful appreciation of fifteen years' ministerial labour, and we desire to do it in the fear of the Lord.
Our object is known to Him Who is the searcher of all
hearts; we have no wish to flatter you, but to manifest to
yourself and others our love and esteem for you, more especially as an honoured servant of God, whom He hath separated for the work of the ministry; and we are exhorted by
the apostle " to esteem such very highly in love for their
work's sake ".

We sincerely trust that you may yet be long spared to go
in and out amongst us, preaching the unsearchable riches of
Christ, under the sweet and unctuous anointing of the Holy
Ghost, and be made instrumental in the awakening, quickening, and converting of many poor sinners who are as yet
dead in trespasses and sins, and also in comforting, building up, and establishing the poor and afflicted of the Lord's
flock, in the blessed truths of the everlasting gospel. And
may you live to see the fruits of your labour, and have
many seals to your ministry, and souls for your hire.

And in conclusion, we desire to thank the dear Lord for
placing you over us as an under-shepherd, and also for that
bond of love and union that has existed and still continues
between us, trusting it " may know no change, save only to
increase ".

May the Lord bless thee, and keep thee; the Lord make
His face shine upon thee, and give thee peace.

In the name of the church and congregation,

We are, dear Pastor, affectionately yours,

B. Beal ⎫
J. Marshall ⎬ Deacons.
D. T. Combridge ⎪
A. S. Hampton ⎭

The gracious humble sincerity evident in this message and the fervent spirit running through it, must have greatly cheered the heart of the tried and exercised labourer, as being a token of divine favour to himself and to the church over which he was placed in the Lord.

We have already seen that it was no mere negligence, but due to a conscientious discharge of secret labour for the pulpit, that Mr. Popham probably visited his people less frequently than some ministers. His pastoral visits, however, were marked with much judiciousness; especially he sought to find clear evidences of the genuine work of the Spirit, and watched with tender solicitude the development of the work of grace in his hearers. He was no creeper into houses (II Tim. iii. 6). The following are examples:—

"Mrs. S. is ill and most anxious. Like many others, she knows the truth of grace and yet wants to have a bit of her own—all the while repudiating self. O how legal we all are! I hope there is some good thing in her."

One member, being somewhat disaffected, had absented himself, causing the pastor considerable anxiety. Mr. Popham called on him and, forestalling any possible resentment, pleasantly said, "When sheep stray, is it not the shepherd's duty to seek them?" The member was quite disarmed, and what might easily have led to a breach ended in reconciliation.

To a distressed seeker whom he could not visit, he wrote:

Dear Friend,—. . . It was a pleasure to me to see your distressful anxiety, and I hope the issue will be a saving knowledge of the Son of God. According to the Scriptures, it is a blessing to be chastened out of God's law, to be taught what sin is, what its desert is, what its power and condemnation; for such chastening and teaching end in rest when the pit is digged for the wicked. Therefore, though the sight and feeling of sin be so bitter, so sinking; though it is so awful to feel the heavy hand of God upon us; though by the work of the law we come to understand that all we have done or can do is to treasure up wrath against the day of wrath, and also by the same work of the law upon our guilty consciences we can only feel wrath and enmity, yet the issue must be good—even a manifestation of the love, blood and righteousness of the Lord Jesus.

Do not you now and again cast a wishful eye upon the atonement? How you wish you were interested in it! Yes; and no one with knowledge and authority has yet told you you are *not* interested in that glorious and sufficient work of Jesus Christ. The Scriptures have not said so. Neither has the Spirit. Oh then wait, look, beg as well as you can under sin, guilt and fear. The Lord's gracious word is, " All that the Father giveth Me shall come to Me; and him that cometh to Me I will in no wise cast out." . . .

Yours very truly,   J. K. P.

Mr. Vine, the dearly-loved pastor for many years of The Dicker, Sussex, died on December 8th, 1896, on which occasion Mr. Popham preached from Rev. xxi. 4: " And God shall wipe away all tears from their eyes." He visited The Dicker occasionally from before his coming to Brighton as pastor, latterly preaching at their special services in September, the last occasion he preached there being March 5th, 1936, when his text was Eph. iii. 8. In the burial-ground attached to this time-honoured sanctuary, which has recently celebrated its centenary, besides the various pastors, Cowper, Drake, Vine, Botten and Hickman, there rests also the body of Eli Ashdown, the beloved pastor of Zoar, London, whose native place is in the neighbourhood and who elected to be interred here.

At Rotherfield, on May 19th, 1897, he preached from I Tim. iv. 16: " Take heed unto thyself and unto the doctrine," etc., it being the occasion of the settlement of Mr. Dickens as pastor over the church there. He became very attached to this good minister, who occasionally occupied Galeed pulpit in the minister's absence. During the long and severe illness terminating his life, Mr. Dickens was frequently visited on our return journey from Maidstone; on one occasion accompanied by Mr. Popham. An indelible impression is left on the heart of the survivor of that visit and of the lively conversation between the two veterans; also of the sober smile of deepest satisfaction which lit Mr. Popham's face when Mr. Dickens warmly said, " *Your* Christ is *my* Christ!" What a sacred union is that which exists between the saints of the Most High! It fell to Mr. Popham's lot to officiate at Mr. Dickens' funeral in 1922.*

An affecting time to many was May 22nd, 1898, when Mr. Popham preached at Galeed from II Sam. xiv. 14: "For we must needs die," etc., occasioned by the somewhat sudden death of Gabriel Tucker, aged eighteen (son of the present aged deacon at Galeed), and who had been the subject of a remarkable conversion.

Another death and victory in the same year is thus recorded: "June 12th, 1898. The death and good end of S. B., who for many years was a seeker and at last a finder." The text on that occasion was Luke xv. 10: "Likewise, I say unto you, there is joy in the presence of the angels of God over one sinner that repenteth."

One of those deep hidden griefs peculiar to the faithful minister, comes to light in a note: "Poor H. proved a thorough hypocrite and heretic (II Peter ii. 2)." This was some years after the individual concerned was baptized with another, of which occasion Mr. P. had said, "A good time; I felt a free spirit and love in my soul." The case is reminiscent of Philip and Simon (Acts viii.), and as Philip met by divine appointment and was made useful to the eunuch, so Galeed's pastor received comfort in others whom he baptized and who "endured unto the end".

In November and December, 1899, Mr. Popham was laid aside for some weeks, during which he was much blest in his soul. He addressed the following letter to his dear people relating his exercises:—

To my Church and Congregation.   Dec. 1st, 1899.

My dear Friends,—Being sufficiently recovered to leave my bed, but with no hope of being permitted to meet with you and fill my place next Lord's Day, I feel my mind moved to send you a few words. I know you will have no preacher, for it was my wish that, in case Mr. Newton, who was asked, could not come, you should meet to seek the face of God, who has laid on us His hand, to seek that I may, if it please Him, be allowed to be with you on the 10th of this month, and to seek that profit may come to us—to me, to you—by means of this trial.

* For a brief account of Mr. D., see *Gospel Standard*, 1922, page 193.

I would like, if strength and wisdom be given me to do it, to tell you a little of the Lord's dealings with me during my illness. For the first few days I was in a suffering state of body, and a very dark, prayerless, self-pitying state of soul. On Sunday, the 19th *ult.*, I was made sensible of this sad condition, and tried to ask the Lord to come to me; but a legal heart told me He—that holy God—could only come to one in such a state as I was in with furious rebukes. But during that day the words, "Herein is love, not that we loved God, but that He loved us, and sent His Son to be the propitiation for our sins " (I John iv. 10), fell on my mind, and caused me to see how the Lord could come even to me. Then I found this prayer in my heart: "O Lord, come to me *for love's sake.*" This prayer was strengthened into a mighty cry by Jer. iii. 1 and Hosea iii. 1 falling on my heart, and blowing like a heavenly wind over my soul: "They say, If a man put away his wife, and she go from him and become another man's, shall he return unto her again ? shall not that land be greatly polluted ? but thou hast played the harlot with many lovers; yet return again to Me, saith the Lord." "Then said the Lord unto me, Go yet, love a woman beloved of her friend, yet an adulteress, according to the love of the Lord toward the children of Israel, who look to other gods, and love flagons of wine." Oh, what I saw in free eternal love! "*According to the love of the Lord to Israel.*" But as yet the Lord stood aloof from my sore; only I could, I *could* ask Him to come for love's sake.

Thus I continued till Tuesday at noon. My bodily suffering was severe; I thought at times no man's brain could long keep its balance under such terrific pain. In this state at mid-day on Tuesday I could only ask the Lord to preserve my senses. I pitied myself. I was ready indeed to "slip with my feet" under this suffering. But while I was thus forlorn, helpless, and wretched, the Lord came. In a moment He took me in the Spirit's power to Gethsemane. I saw by faith the holy, harmless, undefiled Son of God and Man in His agony. It was permitted me to see His bruised soul, His willing hand taking the cup which His Father gave Him. It was given me to see *Immanuel* there, "*God with us;*" and I cried out, "God with *me!*" That gloomy garden was to me full of light, the light of eternal love, eternal justice, in their fulness, power, and glory. I now loved Him and hated myself, loathed my sins, which I saw brought Him to that sad, that low, that grieved, that agonized state. Thence in spirit and faith I was permitted to follow the lowly injured Sufferer to the judgment hall. I saw Him falsely accused, yet silent: " But Jesus held His peace." And why? Because, though " He had done no violence, neither was guile found in His mouth," yet He stood in the place of those—of guilty, unworthy me—who, having broken the law, could only be dumb. His silence was vicarious.

Then I was taken with the patient, meek, lowly, silent Sufferer to the cross. Wondrous cross! Divine wrath, awful curse, His Father's face hidden, His holy soul smitten, bruised, His heart broken, His strength dried up like a potsherd, His tongue cleaving to His jaws, His soul brought into the dust of death (Ps. xxii. 15). And I was sweetly forced to believe all was done, suffered, and endured for me. How I wept, mourned over my sins, over my bruised, injured, dying Lord! I could only say, " O, it is pleasant to lie in this pain and look on inconceivable pain, vicarious; love and pity, omnipotent!" The Lord had come. Love—His own uncaused love—had brought Him. I was ready to live, to suffer, to die. But though I asked not for it, if He had said, " Now you may come home," I would gladly have closed my eyes on self, sin, and time.

December 2nd, Saturday.—I could go no further yesterday; my strength failed. And now I will add to the above only one or two brief reflections:—

First, What a blow to a legal prayer-hindering spirit is a faith's view of the free love of God! Such a view will pull prayer through the hell of felt sin, and make the trembling sinner bold in asking for love's sake—the love of God in Christ.

Second, What a cure for sin is a revelation of Christ! " Christ crucified " is more than death, hell, and every evil. As the saving knowledge of Him falls on the soul by the Holy Ghost, the soul knows within itself that it is healed of the plague. Submission to God's holy will, godly sorrow for sin, falling unreservedly into His good hand, confidence of a good issue finally from all afflictions, love to the Lord and His people, fear, meekness, tenderness, heavenly-mindedness, —all flow as sweet and divine effects of "Christ in you, the Hope of glory".

Third, The way to heaven is heavy to flesh and blood, which cannot inherit the kingdom of God; but it is right, straight, and pleasant to living faith. One forgets his own pain in gazing on the agony of a dear, injured Saviour; self-pity thus becomes a hateful sin.

My beloved friends, "Farewell; be perfect, be of good comfort, be of one mind, live in peace, and the God of love and peace shall be with you" (II Cor. xiii. 11). I must attempt no more. Pray for me. I hope it may please the Lord that I may be among you to-morrow week.

May every good be with those of you who are quickened and taught by the Spirit, and may that divine Spirit be given to those who are dead in trespasses and sins. So prays,

Your affectionate Pastor,

J. K. POPHAM.

He was again enabled to meet at Galeed with his friends on December 10th, and it can be truly said that he came up among them at that time "in the fulness of the blessing of the gospel of Christ". The substance of the address he then delivered appeared in the *Gospel Standard*, 1938, page 215. It was a time of favour to many.

During the first eight months of 1900 his labours were excessive, and he was much helped and owned of God; but his strength was overtaxed, and at the end of September he was again silenced, this time for three months. An entry reads:—

"*September 30th*, 1900. Acts xx. 32: 'And now, brethren, I commend you to God, and to the Word of His grace,' etc. The last time I preached before a painful and delicate operation was performed on my throat, and a sorrowful silence of three months."

A week later he wrote the following memorandum:—

"*October 7th*, 1900. Luke ii. 49: 'Wist ye not that I must be about My Father's business?' Many years ago, when my dear wife was very ill, and my leaving home seemed improper, unnatural, and yet I had an engagement to preach at Trowbridge, I kneeled down early in the morning to ask the Lord to shew me what I ought to do. While thus engaged the above passage came to my mind very distinctly and with gracious power. I immediately objected that it belonged to the Head, the Lord Jesus. But it was most mercifully made out to me that what belongs to the Head flows down to the body. This was wonderful to me, and exceedingly humbled me. Also it made my course, my duty clear. Committing my afflicted wife to the Lord's most merciful and sufficient care, I went about His business who now appeared to me in the condescending and lovely character of Father—even *my* Father in Jesus Christ. To-day the reading of the same word much affects me. How different now are my circumstances! Now I cannot preach; may not for three months. Last Monday morning, very early, after an almost sleepless night, spent in reviewing and mourning an unprofitable life, I was much favoured in prayer, and with power to commit all that was dear to me into the Lord's good hands. My ministry, too, which I received from Him, I resigned to Him, and with much quietness went to London for an operation on my throat. It was wonderful to me that I should walk so quietly, without a fear for body or soul, into the operating room. The blood of the everlasting covenant sustained me. But to-day my silent days have a pain in them that is keen. Yet the Lord does not seem displeased with me that I thus mourn. For I think it is not rebellion. Is this feeling of sorrow attended with submission to Thy will, O Lord? Let me not be indifferent and unsorrowful for the serious circumstance of my long silence. Yet cause me to count it an honour to have become so weak in Thy service. Deeply sanctify the affliction to me, for Christ's sake. Amen.—J. K. P."

Letters to friends and to his people at Galeed shew the man of God in the Refiner's fire. Extracts are here given:

45 *Devonshire Street, London. October 4th,* 1900.—I want to tell my friends of the Lord's most gracious dealing with me this week. He has made His goodness pass before me. Before I left home, I felt powerfully enabled to commit

GALEED, BRIGHTON.

GALEED, BRIGHTON.

everything that is dear to me in this world to Him, and make
a full and free surrender of all to Him. I felt I could place
in His hands my ministry, which I was then persuaded I had
received from Him, to keep for me for a time, or to withhold altogether if that were most for His glory. I was very
quiet on my way up, and when I walked into the room for
the operation, I did so without fear. The " blood of the
everlasting covenant " sustained me; it was peace. I fell into
God's good hand. By prayer I put the hand of the surgeon
into the Lord's hand, as the instrument was put down my
throat. It was wonderful to me, the sharp pain was made
bearable. I still feel the Lord is not far from me. This
affliction now has no anger in it; I see no frown of God in
my painful silence. My weeks of anguish, black as night
and the shadow of death, are turned into the morning of His
favour. I seem like those who feared exceedingly and said,
" What manner of man is this, that even the winds and the
sea obey Him ? " I enjoy reading. Preston on " The Vanity
of the Creature " I have much felt. He tells me what I
believe, that my unevenness arises from my lack of persuasion
of God's all-sufficiency; that I therefore run to creatures.
Prayer is given. I go on confessing; and at the end the
blood of Christ appears to me to answer all, meet all. " All
manner of sin," etc. Isaiah xliv. 22 (" I have blotted out,"
etc.) is nearly always in my mind as I confess my sins. In
the night I mention sin after sin to the Lord, and that sweet
word answers all. O my friends, those dear to God, wait
with me at this Fountain. We are crippled by what defiles
us; but the Fountain is opened for sin and uncleanness.

[To the people at Galeed.] *October, 1900.*—Taken from
you for a season as to my preaching, I am with you in spirit
and affection; you are in my prayers day and night. We
are as a people in affliction. The Lord has something to say
to us, to teach us, to shew us in and by means of this trial,
I hope. It would be one of the darkest and most threatening judgments if we were without exercise in this laying me
aside for a time. It would look much as if we were the
" fool brayed in a mortar among wheat with a pestle ", if no
voice came to our consciences in it. But, blessed be God, I
know some of you are, with myself, exercised toward God in

I

respect of our present case. Though in and by means of affliction the Lord may have something to reprove in us, some fault to find with us—I know He has with *me*—yet this is in mercy, from love, and that we may be "partakers of His holiness". "As many as I love, I rebuke and chasten: be zealous therefore, and repent." And what a gracious word follows! "Behold, I stand at the door, and knock: if any man hear My voice, and open the door, I will come in to him, and sup with him, and he with Me" (Rev. iii. 19, 20). . . . The Lord says, "Thou shalt consider in thine heart"—solemnly, seriously consider whose work this chastening is. . . . It is because He is thy Father, and thou art His son (Deut. viii. 5). When this truth is opened by the Spirit, what humility it works! what acceptance of His will in the trying dispensation! Well, this train of thought is good to me just now. I now feel enabled to *endure* what I before bore of necessity. I feel it is not sent in anger. My heart does not now despise this solemn providence, nor on the other hand does it faint under it. I have done both. I am searched, and many hidden things are brought to light. I am reproved, and my ear is mercifully opened to discipline; and confession of my iniquity is the effect. "Only acknowledge thine iniquity" is the Lord's word; and obedience is wrought in my poor heart.

Do not be over-anxious to obtain preaching. That might be a feasting where the Lord calls for a *fast*, and so would be disobedience and not receiving His chastening. Through rich mercy the operation is successful, so far as can be judged. The Lord very graciously brought me through the painful ordeal. He has supported, and now is supporting my mind by "the blood of the everlasting covenant".

> Ah! "Who of mercy needs despair,
> Since I have mercy found!"

I am a wonder to myself this week. I who am such a wanderer, who have such a runaway heart, can through rich grace say, "My heart is fixed, O God, my heart is fixed; I will sing and give praise." . . . The Lord help you to pray without ceasing. Such Spirit-given prayer as brought Peter out of prison can bring me forth out of this sore affliction more godly, and to be more useful among you.

A Memorandum.

October 17th. 1900.—I felt Jer. xxxiii. 20—26 fall on my heart. I believed and felt that the Lord had made a covenant with me to be my God when He first pardoned my sins, and that He had several times most mercifully renewed it in my soul's experience. This quieted my mind in my present heavy trial of three months' silence from preaching owing to my throat affection. "Who am I, O Lord God, and what is my house, that Thou hast brought me hitherto?" Here is all my desire,—all my salvation. Nothing greater can the love and wisdom of God effect in regard to a sinful creature than to take him up into a new covenant relation and put his sins away. Bless the Lord, O my soul, for a part and lot in this great effect of everlasting love and infinite wisdom.—J. K. P.

[To a Friend.] *October 27th.*—. . . I long for my home and my friends, long to " see the Lord's power and glory so as I have seen Him in the sanctuary ". . . . Sometimes a fear falls on my spirit—though I feel there is no anger in this affliction, yet I fear the Lord has put me aside permanently. I know He is righteous in all His ways and holy in all His works, yet when this fear is on me it weakens and pains and perplexes me beyond expression. I *would* not even in such an event murmur, but O what power I should need to say from the heart, "Thy will be done"! . . . *I am persuaded that the Lord only needs instruments because He has decreed to need and use them.* I would wait on and for Him.

He was no "*idle* shepherd," though perhaps some were unwisely apt to make of him an *idol,* for which both they and he suffered. Viewing the possibility of his voice being permanently silenced, he wrote: "Yes, I think if my activity to preach is to cease—has ceased—I shall get a typewriter. I feel ashamed of my tiredness and the wretched scribble I now write; my fingers refuse to work." His diligent concern for the good of his flock, however, moved his heart to dictate and forced his tired fingers to pen the following weighty letter which was read at Galeed on October 21st, 1900:—

My beloved Friends,—My absence from you becomes more painful as it continues, and I deeply feel to-day my need of a powerful influence from the Holy Ghost to enable me to quietly and graciously submit. The dispensation is heavy, sad, and mysterious. I did not more need the gracious word with which I first entered our chapel than I need it now. *Then* the Lord spoke to me with power, saying, " I will help thee." *Now* I need the same divine help. Then it was help to speak amongst you; now it is help to bear submissively the sorrowful silence imposed on me, help to wait on God, to humble myself under His mighty hand, help to stand upon my watch and set me upon the tower—" fenced place," margin—and watch " to see what He will say unto me, and what I shall answer when I am reproved ". And this divine help we all need in several particulars at this time.

1st. We need the Spirit's gracious help or power to sincerely and freely confess our sins. Confession of his transgressions appears to have been something special to the psalmist at one time. In the 32nd Psalm he seems to have reached the blessedness of forgiveness of sin and the justification of his person, through severe conflict. A heavy dispensation of God was upon him. " For day and night Thy hand was heavy upon me; my moisture is turned into the drought of summer. Selah;" and for a time he appears to have been surprised, confounded, almost as one stupefied; and he was silent, silent as to any sensible, comfortable, clear approach in prayer to the Lord. The poor man roared all the day long. He felt the strong, heavy, afflicting, withering hand of God upon him, and was bewildered; he reeled to and fro, and staggered like a drunken man, and soon reached his wits' end. This was a sore experience, a woeful, bitter plight. All his moisture was gone. By this we may understand the sensible decay of all liveliness in the soul. What child of God does not know this sad experience in some measure? Truly, if the Lord shuts the heavens, we dry up, wither, and die as to all *comfortable* feeling, believing, hoping, loving, and walking in His fear. " A man can receive nothing, except it be given him from heaven."

But this experience may be attended with much confusion, hardness, and blind wonderment as to why it has befallen us. For a time there may be no heavenly instruction, no pointing out of any particular matter for which the Lord has entered upon a controversy with us. Hence we may roar by reason of the disquietness of our hearts, and not perceive why that disquietness has been sent. "Who can understand his errors?" None, none, till the Spirit of knowledge shines on them. In this blindness 'we may soon fall to thinking we have the heaviest of all loads, are the most hardly dealt with. It was not when he was in the solemn, the awfully solemn, self-discovering light of the divine presence that Job said, "My soul is weary of my life; I will leave my complaint upon myself; I will speak in the bitterness of my soul. I will say unto God, Do not condemn me; show me wherefore Thou contendest with me. Is it good unto Thee that Thou shouldest despise the work of Thine hands, and shine upon the counsel of the wicked?" No. Nor do we think our strokes the heaviest when we are under the Spirit's light and teaching. But on the contrary we, like Job, thus think and speak when we are in the dark. Much, very much that we may at one time think is right in our experience, we at another, a later, a more gracious time, discover was only ignorance, vanity, and death.

But when the Lord draws near to us to judgment, to cause us to judge ourselves,—which is to be chastened that we should not be condemned with the world, then we join with Job in spirit and in speech,—"Behold, I am vile; what shall I answer Thee? I will lay mine hand upon my mouth. Once have I spoken, but I will not answer; yea, twice; but I will proceed no further." Thus we see that the knowledge of self, in a case of affliction, and confession of sin, proceeds from divine teaching.

This, then, is an important point, and I would call your very serious attention to it. The good Lord help us to confess our sins. Go with me again to Ps. xxxii. We there see that after his silence and his roaring, and while in his withered condition, a change comes over him. He says, "I acknowledged my sin unto Thee, and mine iniquity have I not hid. I said, I will confess my transgressions unto the Lord; and Thou forgavest the iniquity of my sin. Selah." Here is a mighty change; a most acceptable change. The man of God had again wrought in him a free spirit, a spirit of *free, full, sincere* confession. So could he do, as the Lord in another and a later case called upon His people to do:

"Only acknowledge thine iniquity." Go on, my dear friends, in this divinely appointed way of confession of sin. The Lord will have every Spirit-discovered sin acknowledged and forsaken. "He that covereth his sins shall not prosper; but whoso confesseth and forsaketh them shall have mercy" (Prov. xxviii. 13). "If we confess our sins, He is faithful and just to forgive us our sins, and to cleanse us from all unrighteousness" (I John i. 9). Until the Holy Ghost removes it, what a bar is a self-justifying spirit! How right to such a spirit it seems to be angry, because some pleasant, sheltering gourd is killed by a worm!

Has the Lord discovered to any of us any particular thing, any sin, in connection with this our present, painful dispensation? O if He has, let us go forth unto Him without the camp, bearing our reproach, *confessing that sin.* May He help us in this. Turn to that remarkable, that godly prayer of Solomon at the dedication of the temple of the Lord. Look at it particularly; see the cases, the afflictions, the famine, the defeats, the captivities, the plagues Solomon anticipates, and what is the remedy he in each case sets forth? Summed up, they all come to this: "Yet if they, shall bethink themselves in the land whither they were carried captives, and repent and make supplication unto Thee in the land of them that carried them captives, saying, We have sinned, and have done perversely, we have committed wickedness; and so return unto Thee with all their heart and with all their soul in the land of their enemies which led them away captive, and pray unto Thee toward their land, which Thou gavest unto their fathers, the city which Thou hast chosen, and the house which I have built for Thy Name; then hear Thou their prayer and their supplication in heaven Thy dwelling-place, and maintain their cause; and forgive Thy people that have sinned against Thee, and all their transgressions wherein they have transgressed against Thee, and give them compassion before them who carried them captive, that they may have compassion on them. For they be Thy people and Thine inheritance, which Thou broughtest forth out of Egypt from the midst of the furnace of iron: that Thine eyes may be open unto the supplication of Thy servant, and unto the supplication of Thy people Israel, to

hearken unto them in all that they call for unto Thee"
(I Kings viii. 47—52). So may the Holy Ghost help us to
walk in all our afflictions.

In the second place, and inseparably connected with confession, as shown in the above verses, is the prayer of faith.
What power from heaven must come on sensibly guilty people
to cause them to believingly pray for forgiveness! But He
who by John says, "If we confess our sins," will surely give
power to believe that "He is faithful and just to forgive us
our sins, and to cleanse us from all unrighteousness." A
faith's view of the atonement imparts power, strengthens the
soul's cry, causing it to come to God believing that "He is,
and that He is a Rewarder of them that diligently seek
Him." "The blood of Jesus Christ His Son cleanseth us from
all sin." O what an "ALL" it is in some of our cases!
"Five hundred pence." Sins against light in our consciences;
sins against checks, admonitions, warnings; sins against
manifested mercy, love, and pardon; neglect of the gracious
knocks, according to Rev. iii. 20, "Behold, I stand at the
door and knock: if any man hear My voice, and open the
door, I will come in to him, and will sup with him, and he
with Me;" neglect which nothing but the wicked commission
of, would have made some of us believe possible to us—Song
v. 3—all, all these sins we need full and free forgiveness of.
And who but the Lord, who has this forgiveness to bestow,
can help our souls, so enfeebled by guilt, to wait on Him for
it ? But nothing else, nothing less, will restore the soul.
The still waters—"waters of quietness," margin—of eternal
justification, brought again from under the threshold of the
house, alone can restore the soul. These waters heal and
make afresh to live everything they flow to. Christ appearing again to one under a cloud in a day of rain, a day of
trouble, is as a morning without clouds, as the clear shining
of the sun after rain. He makes all things new. He puts
another aspect on what before was a frowning providence.
Forgiveness takes the sting out of the rod, blunts the keen
edge of the sword which may be upon the house. O guilty
soul, the Lord help you, powerfully help you, to wait on Him
for this. Make known all your requests. Beggars are
welcome. He receiveth sinners. Once you knew this; per-

haps you have often known it. Try again. Is the heart
faint through fear? The blood of Christ can strengthen
your heart, fortify it against despair and the devil.

Thirdly, we need help, divine help, to deny self, take up
our cross, and follow the Lord. A cross is a cross. It proves
to us how weak, how unwilling, how unbelieving we are.
So, at least, I have found myself under a cross. Shifting
about will never make a cross more tolerable. It is tolerable
only as graciously taken up. Much of the galling weight of
an affliction lies in our unwillingness to take it up. Two
things make the soul willing to take up the cross which the
Lord has sent. 1st. An instruction given by the Holy Ghost
that it is needful. "If need be" is the word by Peter. Is
thy pride to be let out? Is thy soul to be more deeply, truly
humbled? Is thy mind to be more separated from time
things and more set on things above? Manifold temptations
shall come. The devil may be let loose to tempt, allure, and
deceive thee in some things. Peter was too strong; Satan's
sieve lets out that self-strength. A scar, on which men could
look, which Peter should never lose sight of, brought him
down, made him willing to go halting. Paul had a thorn in
the flesh, the messenger of Satan to buffet him, lest he should
be exalted above measure. Thus he took pleasure in infirmities, took up his cross.

2ndly. The communication of heavenly grace from Christ's
fulness. O as grace is received from that ever full, ever-
flowing Fountain, the receiver can do all things, bear all
things, believe all things. "Thou therefore, my son, be
strong in the grace that is in Christ Jesus." What follows?
Why this: "Thou, therefore, endure hardness as a good
soldier of Jesus Christ." The obedience of faith in taking up
the cross is better than sacrifice. "Hath the Lord as great
delight in burnt offerings and sacrifices as in obeying the
voice of the Lord? Behold, to obey is better than sacrifice,
and to hearken than the fat of rams" (I Sam. xv. 22). But
how does our nature set up its desires and claims! "Behold,
now, this city is near to flee unto, and it is a little one. O
let me escape thither (is it not a little one?), and my soul
shall live." It is bitter and killing to the "old man" to
have no certain dwelling-place; and for faith to go on in

patient pilgrimage there must be continual communications
of power. There is much lacking in our faith—in mine—
which only Jesus, the gracious, omnipotent Author of it can
supply. And must we not say that self-denial is one thing
which it lacks? How little, for example, have we ever
denied our own wisdom and view of things. To prove Philip,
Jesus said, looking on a "great company" of hungry people,
"Whence shall we buy bread that these men may eat?" Ah,
creature wisdom can supply no answer. Have not some of
you been put to it as to how provision for the way was to
be made? But when some vision of faith has been granted
you, the answer has been in your hearts, "The Lord will
provide; it shall be seen in the mount. Get behind me,
reason, wisdom of the flesh, for you do not savour of the
things that be of God." So have trials been taken up,
chastening has been endured, the back of pride has, as it
were, been broken, and God has been sanctified in our hearts.
Well may we prize such a favour. It is an inward victory
of grace. It is the blessed effect of the atonement. It is
the work of the Holy Ghost. It is the fulfilment of the
new covenant promise, "Fear thou not, for I am with thee;
be not dismayed, for I am thy God; I will strengthen thee,
yea, I will help thee; yea, I will uphold thee with the
right hand of My righteousness. Behold, all they that were
incensed against thee shall be ashamed and confounded; they
shall be as nothing; and they that strive with thee shall
perish." Thus, though self-denial is hard, painful, and impossible to us, and though all our natural feelings and
desires and designs work against it, we prove that the Lord
is mightier than all; yes, and mightier *in* us, as John says,
"Ye are of God, little children, and have overcome them;
because greater is He that is in you than he that is in the
world." Ah, and in this most gracious working of the Spirit
in the heart, the substance of Paul's words is known, "For
which cause we faint not; but though our outward man
perish, yet the inward man is renewed day by day. For our
light affliction, which is but for a moment, worketh for us
a far more exceeding and eternal weight of glory; while we
look not at the things which are seen, but at the things
which are not seen; for the things which are seen are tem-

poral, but the things which are not seen are eternal." Unseen things, the invisible God in His kindness in Jesus Christ, nourish faith, and faith takes up the appointed cross, wars a good warfare, and thus goes on till the end. But O there are many interruptions, many defeats, falls, and wounds. Nor should we ever rise again but for the everlasting love of God and the covenant of grace which is ordered in all things and sure, and is administered by the Holy Ghost. "I will help thee" will stand thee in good stead, poor, tried, chastened child of God, who art now gazing with dismay at an almost untouched cross, untouched, I mean, by the hand of faith; though thou mayest be groaning under its galling weight, and be saying, "I shall fall under it, and be crushed by it." The Lord has laid help upon One that is mighty, and He will send help from the sanctuary and strengthen thee out of Zion.

There is yet a fourth point I desire to draw your attention to. The Lord must help us to commit our way and interests to Him, and leave the issue of all with Him. For this to become an important point to us we must needs be brought into close places, go forth with our souls continually in our hand, and not know what is going to befal us, but see danger and death around us. It was no easy journey for Paul when he went bound to Jerusalem, not knowing the things which would befal him there, "save that the Holy Ghost witnesseth in every city that bonds and afflictions abide me." Nor would it have been possible for him to go forth in the spirit and way he did, but for the almighty power of God in him. Hence, in that power he said, "But none of these things move me, neither count I my life dear unto myself, so that I might finish my course with joy, and the ministry which I have received of the Lord Jesus, to testify the gospel of the grace of God." And, my dear friends, has not the blessed Spirit set an end before some of us, even the salvation of our souls, union with God, and everlasting glory in His presence? To reach all that our souls have seen at times in God in Christ has made us feel bold and ready to follow the Lamb whithersoever He goeth. Our poor, fallen, weak nature shrinks and refuses, but faith is strengthened by the right hand of God's righteousness; a sight of Him who is

invisible imparts enduring vigour, gracious resolution: " I
will trust and not be afraid;" or if fear is strong enough to
move and work in our minds, then faith says, " What time
I am afraid I will trust in Thee." There is a gracious power
imparted at times. In that power the soul commits itself
and all its interests to the Lord. " In Thee, O Lord, do I
put my trust: let me never be put to confusion." " Into
Thine hand I commit my spirit: Thou hast redeemed me, O
Lord God of truth." O it is sweet living when we can thus
live. It is a dying to the flesh and living to God. " I die
daily," was Paul's rich experience. But nature dies hard and
very slowly. Self-interest is a strong life in us. It is first
and last and all till the mighty power of God comes into the
heart to dethrone it and give it a wound which shall never
be healed. Much confusion falls upon us, within us, without
us, before we give in and cease trying to manage our own
things, selves, and ways. But how truly blessed is the
sacred touch on the soul, the kind look, the heavenly attraction by which self-management is, for a time at least, broken
up, and we without reservation commit all to God. So I
have been permitted to find it lately. I can bear sweet
testimony that it is a good way, a safe way, a quiet way.
And yet not an indifferent, careless way. My dear friends,
what the Lord says is true: " Cast thy burden upon the Lord,
and He shall sustain thee: He shall never suffer the righteous to be moved." May He impart to us power to obey
the word and enrich our soul's experience of the sweet promise. It is in this way we prove He cares for us, prove that
He is mightier than the waves of the sea, that He keeps
the mind in perfect peace when it is stayed on Him; that
when He giveth quietness none can give trouble. Some
of you have found that when this divine help has been given,
and by it you have committed all to the Lord, it has been
like turning the shadow of death into the morning. It has
been the most wonderful stilling of the noise of the mighty
waves of trouble, the strong and dreadful fears of your dis-
tracted minds. The government of all is on the shoulders
of our Immanuel. He numbers the very hairs of our heads.
He changes the times and the seasons. And so it is vain for
us to rise up early and sit up late, and eat the bread of

sorrows. He who is the "most upright" does weigh the
path of the just. It is therefore good, it is heavenly wisdom
to wait on Him and for Him in the way of His judgments,
to follow the gracious course David took in a great strait:
"Let me fall now into the hand of the Lord; for very great
are His mercies." This is my desire in this solemn dispensation both for you all and for myself personally. We know
not what an hour may bring forth. But, if we are blessed
with it, we shall find wisdom is a defence. It will point out
the only safe way. "Let us come boldly to the throne of
grace, that we may obtain mercy and find grace to help in
time of need." The help is promised, promised by "God
that cannot lie", by "Jesus Christ, the same yesterday, and
to-day, and for ever".

Farewell, my beloved friends. "Consider the work of God;
for who can make that straight which He hath made
crooked? In the day of prosperity be joyful, but in the day
of adversity consider: God also hath set the one over against
the other, to the end that man should find nothing after
Him." . . .   J. K. P.
  Chippenham, Wilts.
   October 14th, 1900.

The vital secret of his ministerial success was in his
obtaining access to God in his secret meditations and in the
midst of the various trials with which it pleased his divine
Master to exercise him. In this way his own personal religion, his preaching, and the varied cases of the people were
woven together: "Knit together in love" is Paul's word (Col.
ii. 2, 19; iii. 14). A sacred harmony existed between pastor
and people, and the value placed upon Mr. Popham's
ministry is illustrated at this time of trial by the gracious
exercises of many of his hearers, as the following valuable
letter witnesses:—

My dear Pastor,—. . . Being told you may be visited by
letter, and not wanting to be absent, I will venture a few
lines. From what I gather, you can still say, "The Lord is
good." What a mercy to do this in an affliction that touches
the thing dearer to you than life! I know what the cutting
off of your ministry for a time is to me; it must be heavier
for you. I hope I may say I have tried to beg for you, that

the enemy may be kept at a distance, and that the affliction in the end may " turn to the furtherance of the gospel ". This morning the words, ,

> " Thou highly should'st esteem
> The cross that's sent to purge thy pride,
> And make thee more like Him,"

fell on my spirit with a little sense of the mercy it is to possess anything worth putting into the furnace. The pain of this affliction makes me shudder; may you have grace and strength to endure. I cannot tell you the weight of this word to me, " Instead of a girdle, a rent." I was persuaded that you were to be laid aside. The cry followed, " If that is so, keep me from trying to patch up a girdle; and if Thou hast called for *sackcloth*, keep me from hunting about for *ornaments*." But it is heavy; the Lord has now for some years made use of your ministry to bind me to paths that He had previously put me into, paths that nature would not walk. He has taken some pains to shew me that " flesh and blood cannot inherit the kingdom "; I am rarely without a fresh trial, and again need the stumbling-blocks taken out of the way and fresh instruction sealed home on my spirit. How gracious has the Lord been to make you as His mouth to this end. I cannot look around my own circle, at my children, at my friends, without seeing so much to pray about; and my poverty in prayer staggers me. My own path is contradicted; what am I ; and where am I ? Not in the " Plain of Ease "; but does the furnace yield any gain ? I hope when on your bed if you are able to think of your flock individually, I am not out of it. Certainly of late your furnace has been more than once heated.

> " They who the Lord's correction share
> Find favour in His eyes."

May He give to us the blessed " afterward "—the " peaceable fruit of righteousness ".

With sympathy and real desire for your recovery,

October, 1900.   M. J. P.

When Mr. Popham came to Galeed a few were disaffected and left. This naturally greatly tried the godly pastor; and his exercises before God were heavy. On an occasion when

at the throne of grace concerning the matter, the word in
Jude 22, 23, was made an instruction and a direction to
him: "Of some have compassion, making a difference: and
others save with fear, pulling them out of the fire; hating
even the garment spotted by the flesh." Mr. Popham has
related how some who had left, died apparently without God.
There were others who were brought back. The following
letter (which may now be safely published, seeing each of the
parties is deceased) relates to one such case. The husband
had for years absented himself, but the time of restoration
is approaching. The godly wife who had confided in her
pastor in the bitter sorrow, now expresses the hopes she
entertains; incidentally shedding a ray of light upon the
character of that sacred concord and mutual response which
should flow between the shepherd and the flock. It shews,
too, the wholesome teachableness which instead of endeavour-
ing to "wrap up" in generalities, desires to be probed,
throughly purged, and then healed:—

Very dear and valued Pastor; kind and faithful Friend,—
Your absence and the cause of it tries me this time I think
more than ever before; and that on two grounds. First,
because the fresh trouble which has come between us has
cemented more strongly the esteem and love which has these
many years pervaded my heart for you. Secondly, it grieves
me that you should have to carry our trying case with you.
I feel sure you do carry it, and the assurance is a source
of hopeful consolation to me. In your letter you ask, Shall
I reap of my labours and God be glorified? When I look
back a year and review what has been done, it emboldens
me to reply, Yes, you will. It may be a long time before
the overturning will be thoroughly accomplished, but I believe
the work of restoration has begun, and therefore we must
hope the Lord will finish it. The Word says, "Ye have
need of patience." Who can say what is included in that
word *need*, or what it may mean to either of us?

Since you left, I have felt very tried on many accounts;
one of which is this: In thinking over our visit to you, it is
very apparent to me that neither myself nor my husband
were much under the influence of humbling grace, considering the gravity of the case, and how much it had cost you.

To feel guilty and to confess is better than making excuses and pointing out where we are right and others wrong. When we are *not* walking in the ways of God, we *are* walking in the paths of the destroyer; and therefore we are wrong everywhere. While I saw this, I saw also to my comfort that the Lord must have done much for my husband during the last year, for him to have accepted at your hand the good and faithful letters he had received, and which I believe he really values. So I am constrained to say there is much to be thankful for as well as much to deplore. It is a trembling (not to say dangerous) spot to stand in. May the Lord uphold us in His ways. Believing as I do firmly that my husband is *not* conscience-hardened, I felt from the first intimation of his return to chapel that the straight line of your ministry would either be instrumental in plucking his feet out of snares, or that it would drive him away again; and as soon as this trial came it crossed my mind at once as being a stroke from the Lord's hand to hasten that end. I do hope and believe it is having some good effect in making him take steps to be delivered out of some undesirable things. I want to acknowledge to the honour of God that one of my husband's practices (which tried me above all others next to his absence from the House of God) has been quite discontinued. The ministry has so worked and barred his way that he cannot do as he formerly did; so that I have really some ground to hope you will reap good out of your godly, painful labour. You were led to speak of the very thing, saying what snares hasting to be rich would bring one into. Next morning I asked my husband if he had noticed your remarks. He replied very promptly that he had, and that it had quite settled him to give up all connection with the matter under consideration. . . . Here again I experienced the value of a living ministry, and saw at once how serious a thing it was for one of my husband's temperament to have lived so long without such an influence.

Some of my reflections this week have been to this effect, that we may feel much mortification without any humbling grace. At times I feel sensibly to be two parts: much tried and full of compassion for my husband; but greatly helped inasmuch as I feel persuaded the Lord is at work, doing the

very things I so much desire, though by such painful means.
Dear Hart puts a suitable plea into my mouth:

> " May faith and patience hold us fast
> To our correcting God."

Your last sermon sank into my heart with many reproofs;
your questions were so stirring. . . . Your letter to my
husband is so good, so godly, so compassionate; I cannot
prize it enough or thank you adequately for your kind and
faithful dealing; so different from some others who flatter
and fawn. One of my husband's frequent remarks is that
the precepts are as dear as the promises. True, but do our
feet say the same? I have always thought it was the pre-
ceptive part of your preaching that my husband stumbled at;
he used to say you preached him into bondage. James
Bourne's letters and Gilpin's memoir he called bondaging
books and used to express surprise at my reading them.
These things would make me question within myself, Are we
seeking a liberty in which is no peace of conscience, no
walking with God? I say *we*, because essentially I am also
guilty. But I find my husband's spirit different from what
it formerly was; I mean more chastened. . . .

In writing all this I am inwardly convicted of great faulti-
ness in not having more lifted up my voice against evils
which so weighed on my mind. May the Lord pardon our
sins of commission and omission, and bring the pair of us
to His feet, guilty as we are, with weeping and supplications.
Then I know you will reap your reward, and God will have
all the glory. You are much in my thoughts, with prayerful
desires that your usefulness may be further lengthened out
to us. With real love and sympathy, I remain, my dear
friend and pastor,   Yours truly,   C. L.

Such were the excellent hearers to whom Mr. Popham
ministered. What minister would not covet the like! To
them no mere formal orthodoxy would be acceptable. They
knew what is meant by the oft-used term " a living ministry ". Such they had, substantial, solemn, unctuous. To be
deprived by its suspension even for three months was a
serious matter for them. Many very gracious letters did
the Lord's servant receive while absent from his flock, and,

as has been seen, his affectionate concern for them was expressed in wise, weighty, considered communications.

Early in November, a special prayer-meeting was held at Galeed to unite in supplicating for the recovery of their pastor, and by God's mercy he was enabled to resume his ministry in December, a matter of thanksgiving and rejoicing to the people, and no less to the Lord's dear servant, who, notwithstanding the Lord's goodness to him, felt it a kind of banishment to be away from home and his loved employ in the pulpit. A note of this reads:—

"*December* 30*th*, 1900.—To-day I spoke in the Name of God. It was a trying time in respect of my nervous temperament, but good in respect of the help the Lord mercifully vouchsafed. . . . If now my poor ministry is to be resumed, may it be for the glory of God."

The text on that occasion was Job xxxiv. 9, 10: " . . . Far be it from God that He should do wickedness," etc. Many during the thirty-six years following have thanked God for sparing and enabling His servant to continue in the work of the ministry.

Soon we find him again fully occupied, preaching continually both at Brighton and elsewhere in the week. The weakness in his throat, however, reappeared in the spring of 1902, by which his ministry seemed again threatened, necessitating an entire absence for five weeks from the pulpit and confining his preaching to Galeed for many months. In this trial the word, " But Thou remainest," was made a strength to his mind " filling my desolate and waste places ". The blessing of the Lord attended his ministry in an especial measure at this period, which he gratefully acknowledges:—

"The Lord was with me and put His Word in my mouth, and by it brought into liberty Miss M. Praise the Lord! The blessing of God rested on several sermons I was led to preach from Matt. xiii. 9; and xii. 31, 32. In the first instance to the alarming of a backslider; in the second to the deliverance of that person from the dreadful gloom, bondage and terror she was held in by the temptation that she had committed the unpardonable sin."

K

CHAPTER NINE.

*" I laboured more abundantly than they all: yet not I,
but the grace of God which was with me."*

WHEN in May, 1905, the Editor of the *Gospel Standard*
(Mr. Feazey) died, the trustees of that magazine appointed
Mr. Popham his successor. Although he was constrained
to immediately step into the breach, he did so reluctantly:
" Till I get some assurance, though legally appointed to the
arduous position, I shall not adopt the editorial ' We ' nor
write an Address." Only after much severe exercise and
" gathering assuredly that the Lord had called him to the
most weighty and solemn work ", did he consent to definitely
occupy the vacant chair. Extracts from a letter disclose
somewhat of his exercises and thoughts in this important
matter:—

" . . . My election to the arduous and difficult post of
Editor of the ' G.S.' was a very great surprise to me. I
could not say ' yes ' definitely, as I had no time to ask
counsel and direction of the Lord; and no step is well taken
without seeking guidance. ' If Thy presence go not with
me, carry me not up hence.' Reflection increases my reluc-
tance. But that is not all. Some right steps have had all
the *appearance* of presumption, as when David went out
against Israel's enemy. To my sense it looks much like that
to even think of going beyond the three months. But I
believe my weakness, insufficiency, and nothingness can be
turned to God's glory. Thus I want not to listen to reason's
voice, nor follow the direction of sense. I find myself saying
rather often, as the various and numerous difficulties rise
before me,—' The whole resolves itself into one question—Is
it God's will ? ' The thought, the feeling of my withered,

poor state is so discouraging as to sink me; the view I get now and again of divine sufficiency lifts me up. Thus I live. To be useful is my desire. And if in the way now opened to me the Lord says, 'I have set before thee an open door,' I will go in the strength of *that*. He can help. O in how many cases has He helped me! In what seas, storms, sorrows, deaths has He made His goodness pass before me, His power known in me! I have heard His voice above the noise of many waters, and have seen them flee before Him. Once I saw Him in Ps. cxiv. remarkably. . . . May the Lord give you a heart to pray for me."

His first "Address to our Spiritual Readers" (August, 1905) is a veritable compendium of divinity, and indicates the painstaking manner in which, through grace, he discharged for thirty years this service of love for the denomination. As in the pulpit, so in his editorship he preserved a due proportion of doctrine, experience and practice. "Through good report and evil report" it fell to his lot to "contend earnestly for the faith which was once delivered unto the saints"; this he did with conspicuous ability and gracious unflinching courage, having himself received that doctrine in the Holy Ghost and "as one that had obtained mercy of the Lord to be faithful" (I Cor. vii. 25). In the capacity of Editor of the denominational magazine, he preached the annual sermon each year from 1906 till 1936 (with the exception of 1912, 1916, 1931, and 1934). These were occasions of strengthening to many who assembled, the Lord giving His servant very suitably to address the large and representative gatherings. His "Opening Word" in each January number—the outcome of weeks of exercise and labour before the Lord—bore evidences of a "wise master-builder".

In 1905 godly Mr. Marshall, deacon, died; a very great loss to the church which the pastor deeply felt. This good man was a strength to Mr. Popham from his first settling in the pastorate at Galeed. Mr. Marshall was at one time considerably exercised with a feeling that he himself was intended for the ministry, but fearing presumption, he found it in his heart to petition the Lord that did He not intend him for that solemn work, would He make him useful in visiting His afflicted people? This prayer was

abundantly answered. He never preached, but many could
testify of the exceptional blessing resting upon Mr. Marshall's visits. In this he was found worthy of " double
honour ". Of this godly deacon, a very savoury and interesting notice from Mr. Popham's pen appears in the *Gospel
Standard* of 1906. Of him his pastor said, " Mr. Marshall's
devotion, service, and usefulness as a servant of the church
will never be known in this world. He possessed an unusual
combination of qualities,—the tenderness and sympathy of a
woman, and the strong understanding of a man. These,
crowned with the gift of great grace, made him remarkable
in every situation he filled, and eminently so in the church."
Mr. Marshall's last words were, " Who shall separate us from
the love of Christ ? "

Occasionally after preaching Mr. Popham would reveal to
an intimate friend the fact, if not the details, of some trial
and deliverance which led him to the particular text taken.
On November 7th, 1906, his text was Phil. iv. 6, 7, upon
which he preached a remarkable sermon. Thus he referred
to that occasion:—

" I was entering on trouble, and did not know it till the
next day. This was a wonderful word in my heart, and I
wish that I might often have it working there powerfully.
Well might the Lord say to such an one as I, as in the verse
preceding, ' Let your moderation be known unto all men.'
O what immoderate care, immoderate movings, gaddings,
wanderings, as well as death, carnality, and unbelief one
has! and how one is drawn far from God, then driven in
another direction by violent impressions from gloom and from
the devil, and shut up in the most trying darkness! Now,
says the Spirit, ' Be careful for nothing;' as if He said,
' Take these cares and difficulties, these sins and temptations,
these necessities that are on you, and all that weakness that
makes you fear apostacy and falling by temptation,—take
them all to the Lord by prayer and supplication.' If there is
any way of letting our moderation be known unto all men,
I believe this is it; and this was wrought in me at that time:
' Casting all your care upon Him; for He careth for you.'
This is the narrow path of life; here the child of God finds
himself brought to the atonement of Christ, as I was then.

I shall never forget what I found in that singular power of the Holy Ghost that came upon me at that time, when I felt the Lord was preparing me for some care, and bringing me near His holy Majesty. Says the Spirit by Paul: 'But now in Christ Jesus ye who sometimes were far off are made nigh by the blood of Christ' (Eph. ii. 13), and that nearness gives an open heart, an open mouth, and strengthens faith to go to the Lord with all the things upon us. I had no knowledge of what was before me, but shall never forget the strange, sweet attraction to God I felt on that day, when my whole soul was poured out before Him, and requests for future things were made, and when body and soul and everything connected with me I was moved and taught to commit to Him. O the goodness of God in enabling the soul to cast all its care upon Him, drawing it to Himself. Whatever comes on that, there will be an effect on the heart to keep it in some gracious quietness. I then entered into that word, in the trouble which followed: 'When He giveth quietness, who then can make trouble?' (Job xxxiv. 29.) I have known what it is for an unbelieving heart to gather all my cares up into a bundle and tie them on my back, making me to stagger and reel to and fro. O the times I have been at my wits' end! the gloom and forebodings of unbelief! But we are to know the difference between ourselves left for a time to the enemy and our own glooms, and ourselves when helped by our gracious God. I was brought to feel, 'Thou wilt keep him in perfect peace whose mind is stayed on Thee;' and this continued for a fortnight in a time of great natural anxiety. The peace of God was so powerful in me I felt it put me into a garrison, and for a time He let no soldiers of the devil come to rob me. I was just shut up in His truth and promise, hedged round by His goodness, and kept in peace; and could say, 'I will both lay me down in peace, and sleep; for Thou, Lord, only makest me dwell in safety.' I could not be cast down or miserable. Then it was whispered, 'Without natural affection;' and so I was robbed. But let us enjoy His mercies while we can. I felt this morning requests grew in my spirit. It is good to pray, and I felt to 'give myself to prayer'."

Mr. Popham preached on many special occasions in various

pulpits,—the opening of Bethel chapel, Luton, on November 26th, 1906, being one of these, when his text was Jude 3. A note made by himself against that engagement reads: " Opening of a new chapel. The place packed with people, and some went away not being able to get near the door. Oh that God may be glorified there! "

In his position as Editor of the *Gospel Standard* (the organ of that group of churches identified by their adherence to the specific doctrines enrolled in the Societies' Articles of Faith), Mr. Popham was moved from time to time, to call the people to special prayer. On one such occasion (May, 1906) he suggested meetings for united " confession of sin and prayer for a gracious return of the Lord to us ", carefully disclaiming any usurped authority, " entreating as a brother." His weighty words at such times brought him reproach from certain quarters; for sorrowfully recognizing the declension in the churches, he knew the only true remedy. To a subversive pamphlet, entitled " Loyalty and Revival ", he considered it his duty to reply, which he did in a booklet, " Preaching the Gospel." The attack arose really from an outstanding grievance respecting certain articles of faith held by the *Gospel Standard* denomination, and the implication was that those articles imposed an unscriptural stricture on the preaching of the gospel,—a charge against discrimination still made by Arminians and semi-Arminians; the latter category more difficult to handle than the thorough-going free-willer, because formally more nearly aligned to truth. Mr. Popham's pamphlet was designed to rebut that charge of " gagging " ministers of the gospel, and to throw clearer light upon the intention of the articles in question. The spiritually-discerning were never in doubt as to where vital truth lay, in this camp or that, but the object was to remove for the honest enquirer obstacles founded on misconceptions. So satisfying to the Societies' Committee was the explanation given that at their request the pamphlet (which had been printed privately, the author purposely avoided using his position as editor in this matter) was reprinted in the denominational magazine as voicing their own warm approval. This was done in the December, 1906, issue. That this was no private personal defence, the following excerpt may shew:

" It is not for me to . . . affirm that they were all accurate
theologians, but this I know: they have long lived and yet
live in the hearts of many of the Lord's family; their memory
is loved and honoured, and their names I wish to defend
against the harsh and unjust aspersions. They were, first,
Mr. W. Gadsby, Mr. M'Kenzie, Mr. Philpot; afterwards, in
1878, Mr. Covell, Mr. Hatton, Mr. Hazlerigg, Mr. Hemington, Mr. Mockford, and Mr. Vine—men remarkably owned
of God to the calling of sinners."

The gracious firmness and clear enunciation of the truths
held, together with the evident sincerity of desire to defend
the honour of God and His truth and servants, were commended to all such as were inspired with the same concern.
It, however, as always, provoked to enmity some whose zeal
was not tempered with the sobering knowledge of divine
sovereignty, and who consequently inclined to a thinly-veiled
Arminianism, though professing the doctrines of grace. The
dear man of God could be caustic in criticism, he could be
unyielding as adamant in a controversy involving the integrity of divine truth; but none with a gracious spirit can
fail to appreciate the affectionate nature of his appeals to the
friends of truth and peace, or the sincerity of purpose in his
sternest denunciation of error.

His jealousy for the sacredness of God's House was misunderstood by some. Asked to give his views on a " Mutual
Improvement Class " in connection with a cause of truth, his
reply (December, 1907) evoked some criticism, which he disposed of in a brief explanation in January, 1908, of which
the following is an extract:—

" . . . We desire to emphasize the fact that we used the
word *unclean* with regard to a Mutual Improvement Class
as referring to a distinction made in the Word of God
between what is *set apart for the Lord's own dwelling-place
and worship*, and all other things. What is not ordained for
and consecrated to the Lord is, in Scripture use and meaning, ' common or unclean.' So were the Gentiles until called
(Acts x. 9—16). In no other place does God dwell and
shew His glory as in the Church (Eph. ii. 22; iii. 21). But
we would also lay stress on the truth that there is nothing
unclean (margin, ' common ') of itself (Rom. xiv. 14). Thus

all lawful occupations and [necessary] contact with the world
may be without defilement to our consciences, if 'sanctified
by the Word of God and prayer' (I Tim. iv. 5); and so,
'Unto the pure all things are pure: but unto them that are
defiled and unbelieving is nothing pure; but even their mind
and conscience is defiled' (Titus i. 15). As we stated in our
Answer, the lectures on Protestantism have our warmest
sympathy; we now repeat that statement. Likewise we again
affirm that an individual saint has liberty to do what a
church, as such, is not allowed (I Cor. x. 27—31). Therefore
it does not follow that because a church may not sanction
and adopt a Mutual Improvement Class, it is wrong to
educate our young people in our great doctrines and principles and duties of life. 'Train up a child in the way he
should go' (Prov. xxii. 6). Personally we have long and
deeply deplored the lack of teaching among us; and we
specially wish all God-sent ministers were impressed with a
sense of the need there is that they should be teachers in the
pulpit (Rom. xii. 7). . . . Always keeping in mind the
Scriptural distinction between the Church and *all* else."
—*Gospel Standard*, 1908.

Similarly, his weighty sense of the importance of imparting
sound Scriptural instruction and of eschewing that mere
natural humanistic teaching of the young which is so largely
catered for by the general religious press and pulpit and
Sabbath School, constrained him to deliver the following
warning concerning certain literature submitted to him:—

"The importance of divine truth, as given in the inspired
Scriptures, can never be sufficiently expressed and emphasized; for it sets forth God as He will be known in the
world and in the Church. In the world, for which Christ
does not pray (John xvii. 9): 'And the Egyptians shall
know that I am the Lord, when I stretch forth Mine hand
upon Egypt' (Ex. vii. 5). 'Lord, when Thy hand is lifted
up, they (the wicked) will not see, but they shall see' (Isa.
xxvi. 11). In the Church: The Church is to know 'the manifold wisdom of God, according to the eternal purpose which
He purposed in Christ Jesus our Lord' (Eph. iii. 10, 11).
The knowledge of the Father, and Jesus Christ whom He
sent, is life eternal (John xvii. 3). In these ways God will

make Himself known. But His chief glory is in the Church: 'Unto Him be glory in the Church by Christ Jesus, throughout all ages, world without end. Amen' (Eph. iii. 21). The truth is put within her, beneath her, round about her. Therefore it is incumbent on all her sons and daughters that they, even as Timothy, should know how to behave themselves 'in the House of God, which is the Church of the living God, the pillar and ground of the truth' (I Tim. iii. 15). Here He tabernacles; here He will be sanctified in all that come nigh unto Him, and before all His people He will be glorified. As God is set forth in and by the truth, so He blesses His people by it. The Spirit of truth is given them, that they may be led into it, and know 'that no lie is of the truth' (John xiv. 17; I John ii. 21). They are sanctified by the truth (John xvii. 17). Their girdle for strength is the truth (Eph. vi. 14). All their true liberty is by the truth (John viii. 32). Believing all this, and knowing how liable they are to err, their cry is, 'Lead me in Thy truth.' 'Open Thou mine eyes, that I may behold wondrous things out of Thy law.' 'Give me understanding, that I may live.' It is an unspeakable mercy to be savingly acquainted with the truth by the teaching of the Spirit of truth.

"And it is under a sense of the tremendous importance of divine truth, and also a concern for you as a church of Christ, that I have looked carefully into the book. . . . I have no private views in religion. A published book is not a subject for private conference. It has gone forth; the public have read it, and if any error is in it, it has had its effect, and no *private* pointing out of the error can counteract that effect. I deem it my duty to endeavour to prove my charge that it is an ignorant book and contains spiritual error; a charge I repeat, repeat deliberately as in God's sight, and as realizing the solemnity of my position in doing so. It is a *religious* book. Let not this be lost sight of . . . there is a vein of religion running through the whole; and it is there by intention, not by accident. The young, to whom it is addressed, are generally regarded as religiously inclined, if not fully entitled to the name of Christian. This, again, I beg may be kept in mind; for it has an important bearing upon what I have to say of the book. I do not wish to

make a man an offender for a word; on the contrary, I
would deal tenderly. But when the question is one relating
to God, to the souls of men, then faithfulness is the
most important matter. ' It is required in stewards that a
man be found faithful.' "

Mr. Popham then proceeded to shew the "serious omission " in the book of any teaching concerning the Fall of
man, the necessity of the new birth, and instruction in the
Person and work of the Lord Jesus Christ, and pointed out
the dominant idea of a stock of good things in the readers
themselves; and asked, " Is this Scriptural teaching? All
who know the Bible will emphatically say, No. But it will
be said, ' The book was written for the young.' Even so, but
do the young need anything in religion which the old do not
require? If the ' little children' must have their bread
broken up, it *must be bread*. If they are not able to take
strong meat, they require the ' sincere milk of the Word '.
. . ."

There is every reason to believe that some who were
temporarily offended with Mr. Popham's rigid adherence to
Scripture teaching, and his uncompromising attitude regarding *spiritual* instruction, subsequently saw the necessity of
it, and were glad to own that " faithful are the wounds of a
friend, but the kisses of an enemy are deceitful ". Whenever
this came to his knowledge, it gladdened his heart, and he
was not slow to recognize God's mercy therein. It may
be convenient here to insert a letter written to an enquirer
(not a Strict Baptist) on the subject of Sabbath schools. It
was written towards the close of his days, in 1933, and therefore gives his most mature views on the subject. That he
did not actively oppose or violently condemn all Sabbath
instruction of the young, is well known, and is proved by his
occasional addresses to assembled scholars (such as those able
and weighty lectures to the Zoar, London, Sabbath scholars,
published in 1889). Mention might also be made of his
monthly letters written to the youth of the denomination
through the *Friendly Companion* during his editorship, 1919—
1935.

His occasional especial addresses to the young from the
pulpit, too, were obviously the fruit of much genuine con-

cern for their moral and spiritual welfare. For example, see the sermon published in the *Gospel Standard,* 1916 (p. 197). But there has never been a Sabbath school in connection with Galeed. Yet perhaps in the denomination no cause has been more highly favoured of God; thus sealing His ordained way of teaching, through His own ministers, in their preaching the gospel.

Dear Mr. M.,—. . . In regard to the subject of *baptism* I have written nothing. One of the best works on the subject was written by John Norcott in 1674. Spurgeon republished, and then, in 1911, Farncombes, London.

Sunday Schools. You ask who are the proper persons to teach in them? A precedent question is always before me when the subject is named, viz.: Is the pattern of such a school found in the Word of God? My answer is that the Sabbath School is a delegation of parental duty. But seeing that the S.S. is a national institution, the answer I have to give to your question is that the proper persons to teach are godly men, *men only.* I am painfully aware that this rules out the vast majority of teachers. But if the rulers, the pastors, of churches duly considered the Scriptures in the matter of teaching and teachers, I think they must see the right thing to do in the case, and would at all costs do it. But it is to be feared that the Lord is far from the bodies of professing Christians, and the result is that the traditions of man have supplanted the Word of God.

It is an infinite mercy to be taught of God, to be under that teaching of the Holy Ghost which puts the sinner in the dust until Christ is revealed and true liberty is found, and the sinner is sealed unto the day of redemption. . . .

Yours sincerely,

Brighton. December, 1933. J. K. POPHAM.

A movement was promoted in 1907 with a view to closer communion between the northern and southern churches, and meetings were held in London and Nottingham, at which Mr. Popham preached. The first was on October 4th, 1907, the text being Ps. lxxxv. 5: "Wilt Thou be angry with us for ever? wilt Thou draw out Thine anger to all generations?" A note to this says, "Meeting of northern and southern churches. A solemn day, and we know not the issues. I was sensible of much help—help much needed."

R. J. Campbell, like John Henry Newman, has had many phases to his religious complexion. We remember meeting him in our early youth in a quite respectable nonconformist periodical. But in 1907 he developed his " New Theology ", which after all was neither " his " nor " new ", but old heresies revived. Indefatigable in the interest of the truth, and anxious to help the people of God, " the poor of the flock of Christ who are not able to follow elaborate arguments," Mr. Popham drew up a three-page Scripture compendium —" The New Theology *versus* The Holy Scriptures "— in refutation of the heresies of Mr. Campbell's system, which comprised the denial of the fundamental doctrines of the Fall of mankind, the inspiration of Scripture, and the virgin birth of the Lord Jesus Christ, and His vicarious atonement; and the assumption that man's " inner consciousness " is God,—practically involving the figment of an impersonal God. This short tract is an unanswerable refutation of heresies for which Mr. Popham could find " no softer word than *blasphemy* to adequately describe ". It had a circulation of 28,000. It is not without reason to believe that God's blessing attended this effort at rebutting dangerous doctrines ruinous to the soul.

This year (1907) also saw the twenty-fifth anniversary of the pastor's occupancy of Galeed pulpit, which occasion his friends marked by presenting their minister and friend and loved counsellor with two-hundred guineas and the pastor's devoted wife with forty pounds, accompanied by an address remarkable for originality, fervour of spirit, and graciousness, exemplifying the true gospel harmony existing among them. The address is here subjoined:—

AN ADDRESS TO MR. POPHAM ON THE OCCASION OF THE TWENTY-FIFTH ANNIVERSARY OF HIS BECOMING PASTOR OF GALEED, BRIGHTON.

Beloved Pastor and dear Servant of Christ,—We have in the Sacred Records, concerning the history of the Church in apostolic days, the following Minute: " And when they had come, and had gathered the church together, they rehearsed all that God had done with them."

We have thought, dear sir, that the twenty-fifth anniversary of your coming amongst us (the thirty-ninth of the erection of this building and formation of the church), would be a fitting occasion for us to follow this ancient precedent, and hence our request, to which you have so readily acceded, to set apart this evening for that purpose. Do we not well, have we not great reason, to gather together to rehearse all that God has done with us as a church and people? May the Holy Spirit graciously preside over our meeting, fill our hearts with humble love and gratitude, prompt our utterances, and make our whole aim "the praise of the glory of His grace".

Forty years ago we were some seventy people, men and women erstwhile devoted adherents to the ministry of that man of God of blessed memory, John Grace, after whose decease we withdrew from the place where we had been accustomed to worship, and waited on the Lord as to the course we were in the future to pursue. Seven men amongst us of honest report bore the burden and heat of those trying days. For a while we met in an upper room, which soon became too strait for us. Fervent united prayer was made unto God continually for a more certain dwelling, and at length He graciously indicated the site for a permanent building. The year 1868 saw the foundation laid, and in October of the same year the structure was completed and opened for public worship. Mr. Knill, Mr. Covell, and Mr. Pert all preached on the opening day, and Mr. White was our pastor-elect.

Though with much fear and trembling we started, signs were not wanting that God was with us. But soon trouble came. Within six short months our minister broke a blood vessel; he never preached again, and in less than a year he passed to his eternal rest. His "greatest earthly wish" was realized ere he departed; for so he expressed himself when, in the autumn of 1869, Mr. Godwin formed us into a church. We were then ten in number. Our sad bereavement was keenly felt, and to add to our discomfiture we had a big debt upon our chapel. But, God be thanked, He has declared

"The eyes of the Lord are upon the righteous, and His ear is open to their cry;" and we have verified it over and over again. Through boundless grace He taught us in some humble measure to "make His service our delight", and He "made our wants His care". In temporal matters our funds were equal to our immediate necessities, whilst the pulpit was supplied with gracious heaven-sent ministers, most of whom have now ceased from their labours, but their memory is fragrant still.

Yet there was one request oftentimes preferred before the God of all grace, which "He bore long with" ere He "avenged us". We longed for a settled pastor, a man after God's own heart, to shepherd us; we now know that all this while He was most graciously preparing you, dear sir; so that when, in the month of June, 1881, He sent you for the first time as a stranger amongst us, the hearts and eyes of many were upon you, and some were more than ever exercised concerning the momentous matter, with a growing conviction that in you they beheld "the Lord's anointed".

The manner of your entering in amongst us is still fresh in the memory of some who survive, and as a matter of history is deeply interesting to all. The great trial which preceded your first sermon, together with the Lord's timely appearing with the assuring word, "I will help thee," we never forget. We have a record, too, in your own words to us, on the occasion of your acceptance of the pastorate, how the Lord spoke to you again and again in the midst of your deep exercises on the important subject. At one time you told us it was this: "Thine ears shall hear a word behind thee, saying, This is the way, walk ye in it;" at another, "We walk by faith, not by sight." And again, when you were faltering and pleading your weakness: "We have this treasure in earthen vessels, that the excellency of the power may be of God, and not of us;" and, "That your faith should not stand in the wisdom of men, but in the power of God;" and you had some feeling from this Scripture: "We preach not ourselves, but Christ Jesus the Lord, and ourselves your servants for Jesus' sake."

Thus you came to us, and to-night we are here present to celebrate the twenty-fifth anniversary of your pastorate.

With one heart and voice we salute you, and in the language
of the immortal Bunyan, bid you "Welcome, welcome, good
Evangelist, and may the sight of thy countenance ever bring
to our remembrance thy ancient kindness and unwearied
labouring for our eternal good."

We desire to acknowledge the Lord's great goodness to us,
in bringing you amongst us in His all-wise providence,
placing you over us, and sparing you to minister to us in
word and doctrine for so long a period. With the deepest
gratitude, we humbly present our united thanksgiving to the
Lord of heaven and earth, for His marvellous kindness and
mercy in making your ministry so eminently useful. He has
abundantly fulfilled His word upon which He caused you to
hope, from the first day until now, and we are witnesses, and
God also, that you have not shunned to declare the whole
counsel of God. In our times of distress, sickness, and
bereavement; in our temptations, soul-travail, and all spiritual trouble, we have ever found you affectionately solicitous,
and your prayers and sympathy have been highly prized. In
dark days and national calamities, when God's judgments
have been abroad in the land, you have called us together for
united prayer and humiliation; and when blasphemers have
reared their impudent heads, and lifted up their voices
against God's Anointed, you have not failed from pulpit and
press, to denounce the impiety, and to proclaim with renewed
zeal the sacred doctrines which are most surely believed
among us. For all these things, be it now and always said:
"And they glorified God in me."

We pray that your dear and valuable life may be greatly
prolonged; and that as we have been taught of God to love
one another, so we may, by His grace, endeavour by all
means to keep the unity of the Spirit in the bond of peace.
May He still continue to bless your ministry amongst us;
may many sinners yet be converted unto Him, transgressors
learn His ways, and those who are in bonds be delivered and
brought into the glorious liberty of the children of God.
Thus may He bless you while you live, and when in you and
by you His work of grace is done, may He grant you an
abundant entrance into His everlasting kingdom.

We beg your acceptance of the accompanying cheque for

two hundred guineas as a token of our heartfelt affection
and esteem, and we also desire to ask Mrs. Popham, your
beloved wife, and our sister in the Lord, to accept the
enclosed offering of forty pounds, recognizing as we do in
her a godly help-meet and true yoke-fellow.

"The Lord bless thee and keep thee, the Lord make His
face to shine upon thee, and be gracious unto thee; the Lord
lift up His countenance upon thee, and give thee peace."

And now to God the Father, God the Son, and God the
Holy Ghost, be ascribed glory and wisdom and thanksgiving
and honour and power and might for ever and ever. Amen.

Signed on behalf of the church and congregation,

D. T. COMBRIDGE
A. S. HAMPTON
R. BENTALL   }   Deacons.
B. HUNT

October 16th, 1907.

It may be of interest to give an example of the pastor's
way of welcoming, with due solemnity, new members into
church fellowship. The address given on June 2nd, 1907, at
the reception of three new members:—

"I now have the duty and privilege of giving, in the
name of the church, the right hand of fellowship to the three
friends who recently witnessed a good confession before the
church and then were baptized.

"My dear friends,—I receive you in the name of the
church as members. In the Name of God, whose servant I
hope I am, whose minister God has made me of some use
to you, I receive you into the church. It has been a business
with all of you, as you have told us,—very heavy, very
serious, very solemn. You were taught your sinnership, how
lost you were; and, with different degrees of light and power,
you were each led to cry for mercy; and, in God's time, each
got an answer in different degrees. But the same Lord has
been rich to you all, and now you are brought into fellowship
with us,—a small church of poor people.

"You gave yourselves first to the Lord—the greatest of all
acts that a creature can be made capable of here is to give
himself to the Lord, the Lord who reveals Himself to him
and shews Himself suitable, gracious, full of love, and full of

attractions to such a soul. By the power of the Spirit you gave yourself lost, wretched, miserable, guilty, undone; in that state you gave yourself to Him, and He made good to you that Scripture, 'This Man receiveth sinners, and eateth with them.' What a privilege He bestowed on you then! And now, in His providence and by His grace, you have given yourselves to us who are, as we believe, your brothers and sisters in Him. You have professed to believe the doctrines that we believe and hold, that are preached and held here, and we believe your profession to be honest. You have professed yourselves willing to be subject to the rules that we are subject to and willing to submit yourselves to us as we here are, as we trust, willing to submit ourselves to you in the fear of God. 'Yea,' says the apostle, 'all of you be subject one to another.'

"Now, a church blessed with this spirit is really blessed. What a mercy to have it! What a mercy for us thus to walk together in love begotten of the Spirit, in union begotten of the Spirit, in mutual esteem— 'each esteeming other better than himself.' Now, I trust we shall be made a blessing to you; not only my ministry, but that we, as a people, may be made a blessing to you. Cleave to the friends; as you have opportunity, seek fellowship with them. I trust you will be made a blessing to us, that we shall have your prayers, that we shall have the benefit of your membership with us; and that in all things we may walk together in the Name, in the fear, by the goodness and love and grace of the ever-blessed God. May this be a good time to you. May the Lord Jesus, whose you are and whom you serve, now come, and having granted you your desire of union with us, grant you your further desire—for I am sure you desire it—grant you to feel His presence now, and say to each of you, 'Eat, O friends, and drink abundantly, O beloved.'

"One little word to the whole church: May we this night give thanks to a good God for His tokens of goodness and of His presence amongst us; for surely as we were privileged to hear our friends relate what He had done for them, we must acknowledge—and we did acknowledge, and do, I hope, acknowledge that He has been very good. Your testimonies,

L

I can say to you, were an encouragement to me, for you were enabled to say that God had made my poor ministry as His mouth to you all. Now may His blessed hand rest on us."

To Miss E.—" The Lord be with you and teach and bless you, keep you little in your own esteem, cause you to follow after Him."

To Miss F.—" The Lord bless you, grant you mercy still; for, although you have had much, you need much, and you will to the very end."

To Mr. J. D.—" The Lord bless you and make you still a follower. You have known Him and seen Him. May He now speak to you and be with all of us."

In the Address to the readers of the *Gospel Standard*, January, 1908, the Editor occupies some space in addressing " those who have lived thus far without God in the world, or without distinct knowledge of Him or of themselves, who do not, therefore, realize their danger ". A perusal of that address would in any ingenuous mind dispose of any question as to Mr. Popham's fervent desire for the conversion of souls, and dispel the vile aspersions cast on him that he " never preached to sinners, as such ". He was approached by friends with urgent representations that the wise words might be well circulated further, as he had been again attacked, and it is a touching insight we get into his heart in a note he made on the exercises this suggestion produced:—

" I have been much exercised about the matter of the leaflet, and have left it with the Lord many times, and do still. Though I feel He is with me, it is a trouble. I have seen in my life nothing but sin, everything I have touched I have spoiled; and I have received nothing but divine mercies from the Lord. Yesterday morning, as I was confessing and committing myself to Him, this word was most sweet—it seemed too big to admit: ' Because He is at my right hand, I shall not be moved.' I do not want to say a word, lest I should take that matter out of the Lord's hands."

The pamphlet, entitled " Preaching to the unconverted ", was duly published. But controversy was not the *forte* of our dear friend—though he was no mean controversialist, and faithfulness impelled him to engage in it. Preaching the gospel was emphatically his God-given and loved employment. In 1907 he published a volume of twenty-five sermons, inscribing it to the church and congregation at Galeed, Brighton, " as a token of tender love and a memorial of twenty-five years' service among you in the gospel." In 1909 commenced the monthly publication of a sermon in tract form, continuing till his decease, and now posthumously by his daughter, Miss Popham. These sermons have reached far and wide, and much blessing has attended them.

Mention has been made of Mr. Popham's attachment to some of the godly remnant in Scotland. In 1908 he visited the northern Highlands, and formed friendships with several of the ministers and men of Caithness. By invitation he preached in the Free Presbyterian church at Halkirk on July 5th, from John viii. 36. Quite recently one who was present at that service thirty years ago spoke of the sacred influence pervading it: " If the Son therefore shall make you free, ye shall be free indeed." Truly " Christ and Him crucified " was his theme; he followed Donald Cargill in keeping to the " main things ".

Zoar chapel, Great Alie Street, London, (the scene for twenty-three years of the ministry of good Eli Ashdown, pastor, who died in 1904,) was in 1909 condemned as unsafe. The last sermon preached there was on June 21st, 1909, by Mr. Popham, from Isa. vi. 5. Since the death of Mr. Ashdown, the Brighton pastor had " taken the oversight " of the church and preached one Thursday every month for the friends at Zoar. His warm interest in that cause of truth and his intimate attachment to Mr. Ashdown dated from about 1885, early in the ministers' respective pastorates. There were published in " A Few Historical Links " (a brief history of Zoar printed in 1889) three most excellent Sabbath School addresses given by Mr. Popham to the scholars. Mr. Popham also officiated at Mr. Ashdown's funeral at the Dicker, Sussex, on March 21st, 1904. The Autobiography of Zoar's late pastor, published the same year, has a Preface written in most affectionate terms by Mr. Popham. Against the entry of June 21st, 1909, is a note: " The last service in the dear old chapel, which was built in 1698." And he expressed his wishes for the cause of God there in these pathetic sentences:—

"How many were born and nourished there during the long period of 200 years, the Lord alone knows. But He seems no longer to have need of the place. This is solemn. It may well cause searchings of heart to the remnant who have had to seek another place in which to meet. A familiar landmark is removed. An ancient fold is taken away. The Lord, the Good Shepherd, watch over the sheep in this cloudy and dark day! They have our sympathy. May they have the presence, love, and power of Christ with them in their new meeting-place. Then, though they miss their hoary Zoar, they will find their true Object of worship, hope, confidence, and love; and union with Him will cause them to cleave to each other in Him, and seek His glory."

After meeting for many years in a neighbouring hall, the friends previously occupying Zoar were minded to erect another chapel. On February 3rd, 1922, the opening services were held at the Central Hall, Philpot Street, when Mr. Popham preached; in the afternoon from I Kings viii. 27: "But will God in very deed dwell on the earth?" etc.; and in the evening from Luke xv. 2: "This Man receiveth sinners, and eateth with them." An opening sentence of the afternoon sermon will shew the solemnity of the occasion—it was no light-hearted matter to the preacher:

"It would seem that Solomon had an overwhelming sense of the majesty of God as he was opening this wonderful building, this magnificent temple; as if his eye of faith was directed and carried heavenward, and the eternal God appeared to his faith and he saw Eternal Majesty—Jehovah —as only faith can see Him—the Father, the Son, and the Holy Ghost, one God, Creator of heaven and earth and all that therein is, and the sea and all that is therein. And the contrast was so great between that blessed One and this poor little house—no more now, in his view, perhaps, than a dunghill—and men, sinful men on the earth, polluting it, that he asks this question, 'Can the blessed God, holy, holy, holy, infinitely so,—can this God indeed dwell on the earth? Is there a place on the earth for Him whom the heaven of heavens cannot contain? Is there a spot which is in any way worthy of His holy presence?'"

After discoursing on the various reasons why God will visit the earth and dwell among men individually and in churches, he concluded: "This house (the new chapel) is built for His great Name. High is that courage of faith—God-given faith—that can and does say to the Almighty, 'Do come and fill this house.' And what a wonder it will be to the worshippers if when they meet they are not able to stand because of the glory of God filling the house (I Kings viii. 10, 11); that is, if human nature cannot stand, if pride is broken, if human reason is subjected, if the will is subdued, if the mind is purified, if Christ comes and says, 'Here will I dwell. Here shall be My grace in powerful operations; here shall be My love in sweet experience known; here shall be My atonement in the peace of conscience felt; here shall be My righteousness worn for the sensible justification of these people; and here shall be My presence as a wall of fire separating them from the world and protecting them from all evil.'"

Many churches were represented at those services, and not a few such representatives received sound spiritual instruction that day. The evening sermon was one of those characteristic untrammelled gospel sermons, solemn, searching, but sweetly encouraging to every sensible sinner. Although, with others of the friends, Mr. Popham mourned over the decline, he never lost interest in Zoar, one of his last preachings (away from Brighton) being there, on November 19th, 1936— only seven months before his death—when his text was Isa. xliii. 21: "This people have I formed for Myself," etc. At the close of that service he requested hymn 730 ("All hail the power of Jesus' Name") to be sung, evidently enjoying the substance of it in his own soul. It was a time remembered by many.

CHAPTER. TEN.

" I will sing of mercy and judgment."

1909—1913. Foretastes of heaven—loss of a deacon—Protestantism
and loyalty—bitter family bereavement—contending for the truth—
personally searched—favoured in soul—a slip, a rebuke, and a recovery—reminiscences of former visits.

DURING the years 1908—10, Mr. Popham was very remarkably favoured in his soul and ministry, and frequently—
almost invariably for a time—some mention of heaven would
be included in his sermon; so that his friends were wont to
say among themselves, " Our pastor will, we fear, be either
taken from us, or he will have to come down and preach
differently;" by which they intended not disapproval of the
preaching, but their judgment that he would not be likely to
continue so much treating of heaven if he were to stay on
earth. His editing the magazine, too, during these years
bears a similar impress; and some hearts, now saddened with
their great loss, have yet a sweet and fragrant remembrance
of the ministry of those days, for which they would humbly
bless the great Head of the Church. The annual sermon for
the denominational Societies, preached on April 2nd, 1909,
contains a declaration of the doctrine of Christ based on
John i. 18, embodying a relation of the preacher's own
experimental reception of that vital doctrine for which he
was constrained earnestly to contend. His article, " A Word
for the Present Day," in the *Gospel Standard*, 1909, throbs
with life,—inserts a wholesome, if painful, probe into the
malady in the churches and, skilfully setting forth the
Remedy, concludes with some most practical inferences, which
it had been well for us to have followed.

In addition to the monthly sermons, Mr. Popham published during this year, 1908-9, " The Power of God unto
Salvation " and " The Riches of Assurance ".

On October 11th, 1910, there died at the early age of fifty
years, Mr. B. Hunt, an esteemed deacon of the church. This
was a bitter sorrow to the beloved pastor and a heavy blow
to the church. The next evening Mr. Popham preached a

solemn discourse from Ecc. vii. 14. These painful trials were a means of much stirring of heart and profitable exercise in many members of the church. In reviewing the year, referring to sore trials, Mr. Popham said:—

" Wherever mercy is seen in union with judgment in sweet harmony working, the experimental result is a song composed of them both: ' I will sing of mercy and judgment; unto Thee, O Lord, will I sing ' (Ps. ci. 1). By sending afflictions to us the Lord has, as it were, laid fresh claims on us to be more and more His; for the end of God in dealing with His saints is that He may be more and more glorified in them."

Loyalty to the throne, and Protestantism of a vigorous if not militant type, characterized Mr. Popham's attitude towards politics. On the unexpected death in 1910 of King Edward VII. a special service was held at Galeed on May 20th, when he did not fail to voice his conviction that that event was God's judgment against the nation's sins. A somewhat generous acknowledgment of the deceased monarch's qualifications is followed by the following weighty and sober words:—

" To many who realize the wickedness of this our beloved land, the fear that God has taken away our late king in wrath, is heavy. The nation has not rendered to God according to His mercies. He gave us the blessed Reformation at a great cost—the blood and sufferings of martyrs; and we have taken into our bosom popery, that system that blasphemes the Mediator, and desolates every land where it prevails. Moreover, we have become a nation of Sabbath breakers, disregarding with high disdain the honour, the claims of Him who gave us the day of rest, because He Himself rested from all His works, 1, of creation; 2, of redemption. Not content with this double sin, we now allow that men are Christians who deny the inspiration of the Scriptures, the divinity of the Lord Jesus, His miraculous virgin birth, His vicarious death. Can it be thought that God will not avenge Himself on such a nation as this ? "

Mr. Popham then reminded us of " the binding obligation " (according to I Tim. ii. 1, 2) on all who in the nation and empire make a profession of God's Name, to pray for the successor to the throne, King George V. And when later the Accession Declaration was by Act of Parliament shorn of its powerful significance, Mr. Popham stood out in the following dignified protest:—

"Divine providence is profoundly important—important for eternity. God turns over leaf after leaf of the book of His decrees, and nations and individuals are affected. Man and things decay and fall as leaves touched by the autumn chill. Among the most notable dealings of God with our nation in the past year was the sudden removal from us by death of King Edward VII. His fatherly care for his people, his ceaseless labour for the peace of his wide-spread empire and of the world were cut off as in a moment. Mysterious and inscrutable providence! Its full importance and effects we have not yet fully experienced; but we desire that his royal successor may, on these points, continue in his father's course. But one effect ought to be noticed and deplored by all who love their country and, above that, the God of truth. By an Act of Parliament the present King is relieved from the God-honouring obligation to declare the Mass and the so-called worshipping of the saints to be blasphemous and idolatrous; and in place of that noble declaration and protest he is required to make a meaningless, worthless statement. Thus England is no longer protesting against Rome's chief insult to the ' one Mediator ' whose ' one offering ' perfected for ever them that are sanctified. And now belong to her the sin, guilt, and shame of practically esteeming her God-given, martyr-procured Reformation a thing of nought."

Although, as has been said, he was no blatant zealot, he was certainly not " a dumb dog who could not bark " (Isa. lvi. 10). It is due to say, for the honour of God's grace and His servant's name, that never was he left to bring mere political themes into his sacred position in the pulpit; whenever he touched upon them it was as they affected the cause of Christ and with a deep sense of his imperative duty in his grave responsibility as a watchman on the walls of Zion.

When King George V. died, in 1936, Mr. Popham wrote an appreciation in a letter to the *Friendly Companion*

(March, 1936), which manifests his loyalty notwithstanding his firmness for the Protestant constitution. He concluded that letter by saying, " Let us all say in sincerity and heartiness, GOD BLESS KING EDWARD VIII." Not to dwell upon a painful and shameful subject, we could hope that that prayer might be answered for the Duke of Windsor; should it be so, what deep repentance would the abdicated king manifest!

A very heavy bereavement befell our dear friend, when on January 31st, 1911, his youngest daughter (Mrs. Jackson) died in the Lord. The rich mercy of God to her " brought comfort in the terrible blank. Only One can enable us to accept with submission so grievous a dispensation." So briefly wrote the sorrowing father.* A brief reference to the exercise of his mind during the trial shews it not to have been profitless to his own soul, nor was it void of benefit to his hearers—his ministry was influenced thereby. These are his words:—

" The year (1910-11) was marked by one great sorrow in which the Lord manifested special mercy and answered prayer. I had often asked Him to come into my house, my family, and feared *how* He would come. His coming was sudden. In February my youngest daughter was not well, but nothing serious was apprehended, until on Sunday morning, 27th, before preaching, I was informed by telegram that it was feared her recovery was hopeless. There had been no clear evidence of a gracious work in my child, but under these solemn tidings I found power to bring my overwhelming trouble to the mercy-seat, and to say with Job, ' Will He plead against me with His great power ? No, but He would put strength in me;' which I was helped to speak from in the morning. In the first few days that followed, I was permitted to see the Lord had begun to work and mingle mercy with judgment. This was clearly and blessedly brought to light in the long and severe illness, through more than twelve months, ending in her triumphant death. From

---

* A relation of God's most gracious dealings with his daughter was published in the *Gospel Standard* for December, 1914, together with an account of the blessed death of his dear wife who entered into rest that year.

that time heavy family afflictions have followed one another, but have been softened and sweetened by special love and mercy inscribed upon them all."

We may be pardoned for inserting here a touching letter written by the loving parent when in the midst of this keen domestic sorrow:—

My dear Children,—Many best thanks for your dear and welcome letters, and your share in the beautiful screen. You are all too good to me.

This is the saddest birthday I have ever had, and only God's goodness to our precious one makes it bearable. Now that you are all grown up and my poor life seems of small value, I long to die and be with Christ which is far better. If I may be of any small use to any I would fain live, but my choice would be to depart. God has been amazingly good to me in you all, and in thousands of other things. But time has lost its attractions for me.

I trust you may be long spared to each other and your dear children, and all of you have given you the grace of God. It is eternal life to know Him.

A thousand thanks for your tender love. I prize it more than all else.   Ever your loving Father,

Surrenden Road.   J. K. POPHAM.
December 20th, 1910.

Extremely tender as a father, he hesitated to leave home on a long journey to fulfil a preaching engagement; and was tempted to cancel it to stay with his child. In an agony of soul, his daughter being apparently near death, the Lord brought powerfully into his mind the word, "Wist ye not that I must be about My Father's business?" It seemed so great a word, and he said, "This cannot be for me; it was Christ's word" (Luke ii. 49); when it came forcibly to him, What belongs to the Head belongs to the members; they and He are one.* He then experienced such a sense of his union with the Lord Jesus Christ that he gladly left all to go and preach Him.

Jeremiah lamented, "Woe is me, my mother, that thou hast borne me a man of contention to the whole earth!" (xv. 10.) We have previously observed that controversy was not Mr.

* Twice this Divine instruction was given him; the other occasion being during Mrs. Popham's illness many years previously. See page 128.

Popham's chief element. But he was "set for the defence of the gospel", and therefore felt the attacks made against it, especially—as Christ Himself—by professed friends. Personal abuse he ignored, but with uncompromising persistency he "contended earnestly for the faith which was once delivered to the saints". To an intimate friend he thus wrote while feeling "a multitude of thoughts within him":—

"Though abused, called harsh, narrow-minded, and accused of not caring for the poor, etc., yet the sense given of divine approval far more than counterbalanced all that. . . . My contention is that persons belonging to a denomination holding, in our view, a capital error, . . . cannot divest themselves of their religious character. . . . Persons must go, reputation must go. By God's mercy we, as a denomination, must abide by what is our foundation. . . . Oh that the tender fear of God may more and more move us! Rightly you interpret my desire for liberty from my present position and its awful responsibilities; but just now I would not seek it."

This unflinching attitude was born, not of a pharisaic, self-sufficient spirit, but of a deeply-rooted experience of the truth, with respect both to fallen nature and to the all-sufficient grace of God in Christ crucified. No dead cold logician or unprincipled gladiator could deliver himself of the following self-revelation:—

"*March*, 1911. O the self-indulgence I see through the past years! Looking back, how full of sin, how the flesh has been indulged! Pray against it, and the next moment something comes, and the carnal spirit is moved and indulged. Sin is to be resisted by grace. Paul's aim to win Christ means a laying aside of all other aims, denying self. I wonder God has borne with me—so much indulgence of sin, more than any Christian, almost everyone seems to have more grace than I. And then to be in my office! It would be bad if I were but a private Christian, but it is far worse with me. All I can do is to look *there:*—'If any man sin, we have an Advocate with the Father, Jesus Christ the Righteous.' I feel the humanity of Christ is constantly before me as full of all the provision needed for a sinner.

There is enough to keep us from gadding and wandering.
He will have us tied to Him by His atoning blood, His perfect law-fulfilling righteousness—a justifying robe, and His
fulness of grace and truth. The sense I have of my *ignorance of God* is now the one thing pressing. It swallows up,
so to speak, what I have often suffered from—the sense of
my natural ignorance. I wonder at the goodness of God in
bearing with me. Such great ignorance of God is the cause
of all our idols, all our wandering."

At least one survivor of our departed friend is thankful
that that note has been preserved, that I John ii. 1 stands
good, and that there is given a divine warrant—" Whose
faith follow."

Church troubles which, but for the great mercy of God in
giving to the pastor much skill in handling them, might have
led to disruption, fell upon Galeed in 1911 and 1912. The
details are now in oblivion, but the mercy of God in enabling
the pastor to so wisely handle them and in bringing out
among the people a zeal for God's glory, should not be
disregarded. The following extracts relate to these matters:

" It is most difficult for me in this so awful sorrow to
write. Two things we ought to be most thankful for:
(1) That the matter is brought to light. (2) The blessed,
warm desire for God's honour manifested. Many searchings
of heart has this caused me. Now may I, may we all fall
down in humble confession of sin, and mourn for the dishonour done to Christ, this new wound in the house of His
friends. Oh that such a heart as His should be wounded
anew, so tender a heart, so full of love! Surely this calls
for profoundest prostration, humiliation, supplication and
prayer that the evil may be put away from among us. Who
can tell but that this most gracious, loving, sin-forgiving
Lord Jesus may repent, return, and leave a blessing behind
Him ? And what if my soul, if yours, should get some of
that blessing! ' God be merciful to me a sinner,' suits me
well. . . . Too well I can sympathize with the languor you
speak of. Keeping up is not just now quite easy. . . ."

" . . . My feeling is that our proper course is to keep
silence and, as grace may be given, mourn before the Lord.
It is an evil time, and the prudent will keep silence (Amos

v. 13). This is my counsel to all who speak to me in the matter. My desire is to know if there is *in me or in my present walk* any evil for which the trouble is sent, or if there is evil in the church. Oh that the Lord would show me, or it! Another solemn consideration comes to me at times: this may be a sifting dispensation. Yet again, it may be to mercifully prevent other and worse evils. Often an inexpressibly sad fear seizes me with respect to the effect on me in the near future. We all need wisdom, humility, sorrow, confession, and the ' hope of the gospel ' now, and power to walk in the exhortation, ' In all thy ways acknowledge Him, and He shall direct thy paths.' Also, ' My son, despise not thou the chastening of the Lord; neither be weary of His correction: for whom the Lord loveth He correcteth; even as a father the son in whom he delighteth.' . . . I now desire to commit the whole case to God. The sorrow is bitter; it has disturbed me night and day. . . . My dear J., be not moved by this. Look on Him who has told us that offences must come. Remember Rom. xv. 4: "Whatsoever things were written aforetime were written for our learning,' etc.—O what it is to me at this time—and apply it to the defections, declensions, and evils which came into churches even in apostolic days. This application has taught and comforted me exceedingly in recent months. . . ."

The Lord honoured the God-given wisdom and grace exemplified in the above letters, and we find later the favoured servant of God rejoicing in some new prosperity in the church:—

" . . . The Lord knows just how and when to encourage me. Yes, it *was* a good meeting. The favour of God to us just now is very great. I would fain thank Him for it; and I hope we may render to Him according to His mercy. Not doing so has been one of my life sins: ' Neither were they thankful.' The Lord grant that as a church we may ' walk unto all pleasing '. May He enable me ' so to walk that the ministry be not blamed '. . . . D. is still enjoying the favour of the Lord. . . ."

" These words have been much on my heart of late: ' Though thy beginning was small, yet thy latter end should greatly increase ' (Job viii. 7). I cannot say how many

times I mention them to the Lord. I think I see some
answer of late to those many cries for years I have thought
were not answered. There is more springing up within—
living in the dust, in confession—liberty in the forgiveness
of sins—walking up and down in His Name, in that word,
'Having forgiven you all trespasses.' That Scripture was
spoken on my heart recently and brought sweet intimate
communion with the Lord."

In the course of a sermon on September 7th, 1913.

Text, I John iv. 16.

" 'God is love;' and He lets His love down into the souls
of His people at times, so that they are happy in Him. I
have had such happiness in God this afternoon that I want
to speak of His love. It began a little in the pulpit this
morning when I asked Him to come for love's sake. And I
had this afternoon two such recollections of what He has
done for me that an unusual thing happened—I shed tears
of happiness. I remembered what He did for me in
December, 1899; when, after a good deal of deadness, darkness, distance, and prayerlessness, and feeling if ever He
came it would be in the severest rebukes, *He came in love.*
He made His love then so precious to me that I asked Him
to come for love's sake, and He did. The happiness of that
time came like a flood into my mind this afternoon. I was
glad to read the letter that I wrote to the people at Galeed
at the time; the substance was again in my heart. His love
is very sweet; when we get it, we know it is.

'On such love my soul still ponder.'

It is so free it will not allow our objections. If we say we
are not fit, He will not have it. If we fall down and confess our prayerlessness, our feeling hard and dark and distant, making that an objection, He will not listen to it. He
will listen to the confessions, but not to the conclusions. He
always disallows the conclusions that unbelief builds on truth.
It is true we are sinners, hard, unworthy, unfit to approach
Him; and because we are so vile, we think He will not come.
But O the happiness that is to be had in God! O the brightness,
the greatness, the glory of Christ! When He lets out His

love, nothing can keep us from His footstool or out of His bosom.

"The other recollection was this, and it followed the first one sweetly and swiftly. I remembered with pain my intense unwillingness to preach, my aversion from being in the eye of the public; and how this was overcome on a day when reading the vith of Isaiah, at that condescending request of the Almighty Jehovah: 'Whom shall I send, and who will go for Us?' I thought of His condescension in taking a poor man, unworthy to think or speak of His Name, unworthy to mention His love; and yet He would say, 'Go.'

"Now while I remain here, I want to speak of Him, and say constantly as well as I can, 'God is love.' And I want to leave all, and go to Him. I would like to part with all the joys of sense and just go and bathe in the heavenly seas of love and glory. The love of Christ is impressed on my heart. He is mine, and I am His. If I live to the end of this month, I shall have completed thirty-one years among you; and I wish the Lord would greatly increase your latter end individually, as I pray He may mine; that we who have had small beginnings may be greatly increased. In mentioning these personal things, I would not ask you to look at a sinner, except in so far as it may exalt the grace of God; or at a failing minister, but to see the Hand that has sustained him. The Lord be praised for His infinite kindness to me."

Former favours recalled at a prayer-meeting,
October 17th, 1913.

"I want to say a few words relating to what my heart became rather full of through the singing of the second hymn (158), at the lines,

'While I see divine compassion
Floating in His languid eye.'

"I suddenly was filled with the memory of a blessed vision of the Lord in my soul many years ago. At the time I was suddenly plunged into trouble, and with the trouble was blessed with such a sense of my unworthiness and sinfulness that I began more to mourn over and confess my sins than to think of my trouble. Usually the trouble is the thing that catches the mind, and holds it; but it was not so at this time. My sins were before me, and I began to confess them, to confess that I deserved the trouble, and that if He dealt with me for my backslidings, I should never have anything but trouble. I was engaged deeply in this sweet work of confession—for it is sweet—when in a moment I got such a look from the Lord Jesus, such a sense that *He looked on me with compassion*, that convinced me that He intended good, that He would not leave me to wander, nor abandon me to be overcome by affliction; and all I could do was what I did—commit myself and circumstances into His gracious hand. All this came streaming into my mind as a sweet memory. Lately I have had several recollections of His goodness to me in days past. Things I had forgotten have come back, as if they would say, ' You are going home, going to the God you know. He will take you to be with Himself.' In this way my confidence is strengthened in Him, and I get such happiness in my soul that I can hardly bear it. It has a weight in it, like a bag of wealth, as much as I can carry. I saw the Lord's mighty working in that particular case which came to my mind; first, the sorrow, the wrathfulness that appeared against me, but then the singular providence that came to pass by His hand; and He brought me out, as Israel out of Egypt, with some wealth. That is, I had an increased experience of His goodness. So may God help us to remember His kindness. If the Lord looks on us in a gracious way, it will be like the sun shining in on our souls. The spot in a train where I got that manifestation of His love to me was, as it were, filled with glory; and so was my soul. My whole heart was as full of His goodness as it could hold, and I believed I was going to be in that light that then shone—not in that restricted way as then, but in all that fulness which is in Christ. When I think of it, it makes trials light, as Paul says, ' Our light affliction, which is but for a moment, worketh for us a far more exceeding and eternal weight of glory ' (II Cor. iv. 17). I have had many gleams since then, and many dark days because I have sinned. Who can sin, and not have trouble ? But I believe I am so many years nearer the rest that remains to the people of God, and to myself the worst of all. Let us then lift up our heads, O people of God, for our redemption draweth nigh, and our salvation is nearer than when we believed (Lu. xxi. 28; Rom. xiii. 11)."

While our dear friend was suffering the onslaughts of tongue and press on account of his adherence to our historic denominational position, he was being secretly sustained by such sacred inwrought experiences as noted above. One godly minister who predeceased him said of his opponents, " I have searched their writings, and cannot find in them the Spirit of Christ." It would be difficult for any but the most abandoned and hardened to affirm so of Mr. Popham's writings; they were as unctuous as discriminating, and sweetly impregnated with the Spirit of the gospel. Of one such bitter enemy (a great professor and an editor), a godly minister sadly declared, " I have known him for many years; he can talk of every doctrine and any experience; but I have never seen him a broken-hearted sinner, penitent before the Lord." A solemn observation indeed! One trait in Mr. Popham's religion, through grace, was this unction of repentance, as those who knew him were aware and the following extract will manifest:—

" Last Tuesday (Nov. 8th, 1913) I was mourning and feeling I ought not to be comforted, because of my sins; and as I was in that state, this word sweetly dropped in, ' Blessed are they that mourn, for they shall be comforted.' On Wednesday evening, speaking from that word, I felt I had the presence of the Lord, and this prayer has been with me,

> ' Dear Lord, may I a mourner be
> Over my sins and after Thee.' "

" Great men are not always wise," said Elihu. Yet Job, submitting himself to God, was honoured of Him (xxxii. 9; xlii. 7). It is small wonder that even a man of God should occasionally slip. A divine proverb is, " Surely oppression maketh a wise man mad " (Ecc. vii. 7). Sin must never be extenuated, but grace should be acknowledged. Feeling the sting of a long course of unjust propaganda and bitter enmity, Mr. Popham, once addressing a meeting, yielded to his powers of causticity, making short shrift of a chief

M

unprincipled opponent. The writer's love and esteem for his friend and privileged intimacy with him, prompted him to gently expostulate with him after the close of the meeting. "O John," said Mr. Popham, "I have already had a visitor, before I left the platform;" meaning his conscience. And he manifested such grief and shame at what would generally be considered perfectly permissible banter, that did reveal a tender regard for the honour of God, lest His cause should suffer on account of his invectives. We recall how even Moses' renowned meekness (Num. xii. 3) once failed under the strain of provocation. It is strange that the critics— some otherwise intelligent—cannot distinguish "righteous indignation" from acrimony, faithfulness from querulousness. Tender regard for the truth "as the truth is in Jesus" inspired our friend to contend where those more solicitous of their personal comfort and quiet would preserve a tactful silence, oblivious—wilfully or otherwise—to the fact that in some instances silence means consent or compromise.

In 1913 Mr. Popham was moved to write in the denominational magazine a powerful Review of a tract entitled, "The Rich Man and Lazarus," by E. W. Bullinger, D.D.,* wherein was taught the doctrine of the unconscious sleep of the soul at death. The author being a leading representative of the Trinitarian Bible Society which is considerably supported by the *Gospel Standard* denomination, Mr. Popham was very solicitous lest the false teaching might thus gain some entrance among them, "which, if left alone, would eat as doth a canker into the vitality of our churches". That Mr.

---

* The re-reading of this Review since his death, has vivified three indelible last impressions of my dearly-loved friend. (1) With his dying lips he expressed to me with sweet and solemn satisfaction his *immediate* prospect of being "with Christ which is far better"; and said over and over, "I am so happy!" (2) A few hours before the end, I was favoured to gaze upon his familiar form, all-unconscious to present and "seen things" which are temporal, yet surely not to "unseen and eternal things"; but as I believed and felt, with his soul in lively anticipation of its imminent release. (3) The sacred privilege was granted to view his temporarily vacant clay tabernacle, when the vast mystery and blessed truth was borne in upon the mind, "Absent from the body, present with the Lord." Not unconscious, not sleeping in his soul, but in full possession of expanded powers, beholding and worshipping his God. "Ye are come unto the spirits of just men made perfect" (Heb. xii. 23). His dust, sleeping in Jesus, awaits the blessed resurrection morn. An unutterable deep! no less a blessed reality!—J. H. G.

Popham later (1925—1935) occupied the Presidency of the
Brighton auxiliary of that worthy Society, goes far to reveal
that the incisive analysis and fearless denunciation of Dr.
Bullinger's error was not unacceptable to the management.
The Review is more than a negation of the heresy; it is a
very beautiful and most skilful enunciation of the true
Scripture doctrine of the immortality of the soul, and was
republished in 1914 in separate pamphlet form under title,
" Death an entrance into Life."*

Alternating dark and light—numbers of encouraging addi-
tions to the church, and many losses by death and removal,
marked the course of our friend at Galeed. Grace con-
spicuously shone in some of the especially dark dispensations.
On the loss of one member, the pastor made this entry:—

"Tuesday, December 17th, 1912, while sitting with her
family at tea, my most godly and valued friend, Mrs. P., died.
To her family, to the church at Galeed, to me the pastor, the
loss is most grievous. I desire that good may come to us all,
and glory to God, by this so solemn dispensation, but how
it can be is not apparent. The providence is as dark as the
skies which are pouring seemingly unneeded injurious floods
on the earth. Oh Lord, give me submission to Thy all-wise
will!"

In the obituary notice of this gracious person, there is in
a footnote an interesting reminiscence of Mr. Popham's early
ministry at Brighton:—

" The reading of this reference to my ministry brought a
warm and encouraging remembrance of the Lord's goodness
to me in a distinct answer to prayer. On my way to Brighton to commence my ministry there on Lord's Day, October
1st, 1882, I met good Mr. Row at Edenbridge on the
previous Thursday, September 28th; where I was appointed
to preach in the place of Mr. Hazlerigg. My host said to me
the day before, ' You will have a number of ministers to hear
you to-morrow.' This threw me into a tumult and great
fear, and through the greater part of the night I was dis-
tracted and in bondage. But early in the morning I found a
strong cry in my heart for divine help and for a token for

* Obtainable from Farncombe's, London. 32 pp., price 3d.

good. The token I asked was favour in the eyes of the
ministers, then strangers; some of whom would be my neigh-
bours. The help was given, and with it the token. Among
the ministers present, only one of whom now (1913) remains,
was Mr. Row; and never shall I forget his kindness to me."
This disclosure of sanctified fear and God's goodness to His
servant may well caution those over-bold spirits who—with
far less remarkable gifts and grace than our beloved friend—
boast their fearlessness, and encourage those who painfully
fear bringing a reproach upon the Lord's cause and Word
on account of their timidity in preaching before other ministers. This is very different from the fear of man which
" bringeth a snare ".

CHAPTER ELEVEN.

*" The remnant of Jacob . . . in the midst . . . as dew
from the Lord."*

1914—1919. The Great War—true patriotism—death of his wife—
concern for sons—Press attention—responsibility a counteractive to
flattery—old-fashioned theology—Anniversaries at Hanover—Mr.
Newton's death and funeral—illness of daughter—death of deacon
and members at Galeed—consolation in persecution.

WHEN in 1914 the terrible war-cloud burst over the conti-
nent, and on August 4th our country became involved, Mr.
Popham, strongly patriotic, was deeply moved. Unchecked
by the fear of God, so-called patriotism rose to feverish
height, and many extravagancies were heard and seen. But
Galeed's minister was weighted with the realization of a
primary cause (while not disallowing second causes) of the
catastrophe—God's displeasure with our sin. Moreover, the
hand of the Lord had been for nearly two years heavily upon

His servant in the affliction of his dear wife, who finished her course in triumph on September 26th, 1914.*

His ministry was even more than usually grave and unctuous during this period; though in preaching he seldom made direct reference to his personal sorrows and trials, the influence of deep, solemn, and graciously fruitful exercises was perceived by the godly, and the people were edified. Led up to God by his own exercises of soul, he received divine testimonies whence frequently his texts and his sermons emanated. In a letter to a member he mentions this:—

" . . . God's dealing with me is solemn, but I am often too hard of heart and slow to believe and hear the rod. Only the *wise* man is able to see His Name in His cry to the city (Micah vi. 9). I have seen His wonders in the sickroom and heard a wonderful testimony; it will be terrible if I learn nothing, profit nothing at all. And now added to this, is our national sorrow. The nation is deaf alike to threatening, warning, and fulfilment, so far. What will be the end? Is the Church hearing the voice? Is this war the beginning of Armageddon? "Blessed is he that watcheth," etc. (Rev. xvi. 15). Early this morning that Scripture fell on my heart and moved me to pray to be made and kept watching. So may we be at Galeed."

Rev. xvi. 15 was his text the following Lord's Day. We have no record of the sermon, but it no doubt embodied a clarion-call to watchfulness. The following sentences are culled from a sermon at this period:—

Extract from a Sermon at the commencement of the Great War.

" 'In the day of prosperity be joyful, but in the day of adversity consider' (Ecc. vii. 14). Ah, and we are brought to consider,—Who has sent this? It is crooked, who can straighten it? It is emptying, who can fill, who supply? It is weakening, who can give strength? It wears out, who can give patience to hold on? 'Call upon Me,' says God. Earth is insufficient; friends are feebleness itself; cisterns are all

* An account of Mrs. Popham's blessed death, and of his youngest daughter's, under the title of " Mercy and Judgment " will be found in the *Gospel Standard*, 1914, page 480.

broken. . . . A day of trouble is on the nation. It is present, it is on everyone's tongue, it fills everyone's mind; but
the thing is this: where God's people are concerned, it becomes more than an ordinary trouble, widespreading though
it is. Why, how can it be more than that ? ' Oh,' says the
child of God, ' what have *I* done ? have not I had a share in
the sins which have provoked God ? Is not my nation very
guilty ? Is not the church in the nation very guilty ? Thus
in some way and measure I have to do with the state of
Europe as blackened and like smoke, covered with the soot
of sin.' And so the trouble becomes more to a child of God
than to a man of the world. The latter says, ' So-and-so has
brought this on Europe,' and wishes evil to ' So-and-so'. The
children of God may or may not agree as to the instrument,
and they are taught to pray for their enemies; but they see
more than that. What is that ? SIN. . . . We cannot be
indifferent naturally; may we be concerned spiritually, and
may it be given us unitedly, day and night, to bring the case
before that God we know,—know to be gracious, know to be
a God of love, a God full of compassion, of whom it is said
concerning His dealings with Israel of old, ' He, being full
of compassion, forgave their iniquity, and destroyed them
not: yea, many a time turned He His anger away ' (Ps.
lxxviii. 38). . . . When you come to nations, you can expect
but national repentance; if God should give it, it would be
a great mercy. . . . But may it be given to the saints of God
to make supplications to Him in this day of trouble. As
Englishmen we are interested in our dear country. Pray
that the foot of an enemy may never tread our fair land;
I pray for this daily. May we be enabled to go on praying
and confessing our sins continually, and imploring mercy."

What true patriotism is this! how it contrasts with the
blatant empty show of the mere political zealot! One of his
hearers,—a member of the church at Galeed, whose character
is inscribed in James ii. 5—found prevalence with God on
behalf of Brighton, and was assured in the words of Isa.
xxxvii. 33: "He shall not come into this city, nor shoot an
arrow there." The town had not a single ' air-raid ' throughout the war. Had we but a right perspective, how differently should we estimate relative values! But how priceless

to a community is the benefit of a resident God-fearing remnant! How solemn when a city, a nation, loses all its salt! Sodom might not burn during Lot's residence. The good Lord of His infinite mercy maintain and increase yet in England a godly remnant, and again raise up a powerful, separating, edifying, spiritual ministry.

The gravity of the situation and the momentous issues involved moved him as a faithful watchman to issue a call to united prayer throughout the denomination in the following weighty terms:—

"In times so serious, in circumstances so calamitous and terrible, we feel moved to say a few words with respect to what we, as a people, should do. We cannot be indifferent to the welfare of our dear country. It is the land of our birth, our privileges, our blessings. In our midst God has in infinite condescension placed His Name. He has given us His glorious gospel, bestowed upon us the unspeakable gift of a long line of true ministers, some of them mighty in the Scriptures, clear and powerful in expounding them, and eminently useful in their generation, and destined to be so in the future. England has been a land of Goshen; and dark as our country has become, we doubt not God has still many in it in whose dwellings the true light shines. But this nation, so peculiarly favoured, has deeply revolted from God, and provoked Him to anger with continual sins. Our national sins, our church sins, our family sins, and our personal sins are before Him. We His people have not listened and answered to the warning voice of His servants the Reformers, the Puritans, and the ministers of later date who have spoken in His Name to the people of our land. Many of Owen's words are appropriate to us and our times; we give an instance from one of his posthumous sermons: 'Neither you nor I can tell what to say as to the sins of the nation, of all sorts of persons,—our priests, prophets, princes, people. Nor you nor I can tell what to say unto the deadness and slowness of all sorts of professors—of me and you and of all sorts of professors—to come to such a reformation as may give us faith to plead for an interest in the fining pot, and not in the furnace. I know what the general hopes of men plead and speak. Well, bring forth your

reasons, plead them before God this day if you can, and if
you have anything to plead but sovereign grace and mercy.'
We can use these words as our own. And if God should now
come to search Jerusalem with candles and punish the men
that are settled on their lees, who should stand ? (Zeph. i. 12.)

"Can we then wonder that evil has overtaken us? True,
the war is unjustly forced on us. Against Germany we have
done nothing to cause it. So far we go to battle with clean
hands; we must fight for our national existence. *But we are
not guiltless before God;* against Him we have grievously
sinned, cast His Word behind our back, provoked Him to
anger continually to His face. And so we go behind the
injustice done to us by men, and see the richly-deserved
wrath of God coming down upon us. "Without cause" GOD
was moved against Job, and permitted a four-fold evil to
befall him. And to Job there were as if no Sabeans, no fire,
no Chaldeans, no wind; but only GOD. Shall not we, against
whom God has many things, acknowledge Him the Author of
this present calamity ?

"We believe there are a few in our land who are moved to
pray in secret and mourn with godly sorrow over their own
and the nation's sins; and we are thankful that there have
already been special meetings for humiliation and prayer held
in some of our chapels. But we think it would be pleasing to
God if we, as a denomination, set a time apart for such
meetings. Many instances are given us in Scripture of
God's people in calamities and necessities unitedly waiting on
Him (II Chron. xx. 3, 4; Joel ii. 15; Zeph. ii. 1—3). Be it
ours to follow them. And we venture to suggest the second
week in September as a suitable time for this purpose; and
may the Lord pour upon us a spirit of prayer and true
repentance, and cause our eyes, like Jehoshaphat's, to be
upon Him alone in this day of trouble."

As the war increased and the youth of the land was being
removed, Mr. Popham was much concerned. He said, "One
of the most portentous signs in our present grave position,
the apparent peril of our Empire, (which we do recognize
generally,) is our blindness and unrepentant attitude toward
God. At present there is scarcely any appearance of national
recognition of our position before the Most High God." In

prayer, in preaching, and in his addresses in the *Gospel Standard*, continually he referred to it and kept before the people the need of prayer, confession, and faith. Not but that his ministry was still richly endued with spiritual gospel truth, but the influence of the national trial was felt in a special way from time to time; and the imperative need of the vital dealings of God with the soul was even more than ever insisted upon. Besides, he received in his own soul such encouragements from his God as enabled him to direct his hearers to the one infallible source of relief in the sin-bought distress, and while deploring the widespread devastation and slaughter, and the sin which provoked its permission, he saw a prospect most glorious for the Church of God, when all her enemies should be destroyed and all her sin fully removed.

Domestically the war affected him, for both his sons were engaged in different capacities in connection with the conflict; and it was with a pardonable fatherly pride that he saw his younger son decorated by the king, for devotion and bravery in the field whilst acting as chaplain. But the weight with which spiritual matters bore upon his mind, the state of the Church, and his concern for the glory of God, tempered any disposition to exultation. In secret he constantly sought God's mercy on the sons who had gone forth from the denominational churches; and when by Galeed church there was issued a small book of hymns (chosen by J. R. from Gadsby's Selection) for use on active service, the pastor wrote the following *Foreword* to it:—

"A word of goodwill may be acceptable, with this small hymnbook, to you, noble young men, who have left our churches and congregations to defend the hearths of parents, wives and little ones.

The hymns will be familiar, having been taken from the dear book known from childhood; the sight of them will awaken pleasant memories, while to those of you who fear God, they may be the means of evoking melody in your hearts.

God bless you all—preserve your life, limb, hearing, and sight, and bring you home, that we may hold meetings for thanksgiving.   Yours affectionately,

Brighton. February 22nd, 1918.   J. K. POPHAM.

In April, 1918, Mr. Popham was moved to pen a stimu-
lating though sober message to the young men of the denomination who were serving in His Majesty's forces overseas.
This was read and approved by the church assembled at
Galeed on Thursday, April 25th, and circulated by the
medium of the *Gospel Standard* magazine, of which Mr.
Popham was the editor. The letter read as follows:—

To the Young Men belonging to the *Gospel Standard* denomination who have so nobly gone forth to fight for their
country, the church worshipping at Galeed, Brighton,
sends all good wishes.

Dear Young Friends,—We desire to send you a word
through the magazine belonging to our churches. Our admiration of your courage and self-denial, in leaving home
and all its comforts for the hardships and risks of the battle-
field, and our gratitude to you for so doing, would not be
easily expressed.

But chiefly we desire to let you know we do not forget
you when we get access to the throne of God's heavenly grace
in private, nor in our public worship. You are missed from
our congregations, and we earnestly long for the day when
you will, by God's mercy, take your places there again. In
your present circumstances you are brought face to face with
death. Naturally this may cause some serious reflections
and touch you deeply. But the teaching you have been
accustomed to may have been, to most of you, sufficient to
impress upon you the sacred fact that only the gracious work
of God the Holy Ghost in your hearts can produce in you a
right knowledge of sin and of your ruined state in the law,
and bring forth a prayer for mercy; and also that that
blessed Spirit alone can impart to you the knowledge of
salvation by the remission of your sins (Lu. i. 77). And
that you may be the subjects of that gracious work is our
prayer.

We know there are some among you who fear God, and
some are members of our churches. Into your hearts may the
Lord pour abundant consolation by Jesus Christ, give you
to realize that you dwell in the secret place of the Most
High, and are abiding under the shadow of the Almighty,

and that therefore no plague, no death, can come nigh your dwelling (Ps. xci.).

We pray that the all-protecting hand of God may be the covering of each and all of you in each battle, in each hour of danger.

We, now assembled, send this word to you from our hearts.

(Signed)　On behalf of the church,

J. K. POPHAM, *Pastor.*

Brighton.　April 25th, 1918.

It is observable how extremely careful God's dear servant and faithful minister was to discriminate between the movings of natural fear owing to the dangers with which the young men were surrounded, and that real saving work of the Holy Ghost which produces repentance towards God and faith in the Lord Jesus Christ,—a vitally important distinction. How many thousands were deceived at that time by the false teaching of so-called ministers and others leading them to think that to be saving which was nothing more than natural. In such cases no doubt the circumstances of the war nourished error and gave a great impetus to sentimentality and superstition. Dear Mr. Popham, knowing so well the awful solemnity of eternal things, and the natural liability to catch at any comfort, was enabled to very seriously warn against such deception, while at the same time to sympathize with and encourage those in whom there appeared the least sign of the fear of God.

Occasionally Mr. Popham received attention in the general religious and secular press, sometimes appreciative, sometimes critical. Sir William Robertson Nicoll in the *British Weekly,* May, 1914, gave his readers his impression of Galeed and its pastor, which may be interesting enough to transcribe:

"I have often heard in Brighton of the Strict Baptist chapel called Galeed, ministered to by Mr. Popham, who is, I believe, a leader in his own denomination, and editor of its monthly periodical, the *Gospel Standard*. Galeed Chapel lies rather out of the ordinary beat, and stands among many small houses. It is as plain externally as can be. Internally, also, its appearance is severe. . . . There is room, I should think, for about 600 people. The pulpit is one of an

old pattern, standing over a lower pulpit, from which the
hymns are given out. There was a green-baize door behind
the pulpit, and a stair of three or four steps. When the
service began the chapel was practically full, and the minister descended into the pulpit, looking round him as he came
down. Mr. Popham is an elderly gentleman with silver
hair, a keen intellectual face and a slender figure. . . .
"A deacon gave out the hymn from a very fat hymnal,
Gadsby's selection. The first hymn was full of grammatical
and metrical slips, but it had that touch of beautiful mystic-
ism which suits the heart:

> 'Jesus is Zion's only rest;
> Thrice happy is the man, and blest,
> That into Him believes;
> His six-days' toil is finished then;
> His slavish fear for ever gone;
> By faith in Christ he lives.'

Mr. Popham read a chapter from Isaiah, engaged in prayer,
and then gave out as his text the words, 'When it shall turn
to the Lord the veil shall be taken away' (II Cor. iii. 16).
The sermon was long, nearly an hour, but I never saw any
sermon followed with more devout and concentrated attention. . . .
"Mr. Popham is in his way a great preacher. He uses
not a scrap of notes. For the most part his hand lies on the
page of the open Bible; very rarely he lifts his voice a little,
and with it his hand. But he pursued a long subtle argument without any faltering or any slip, verbal or grammatical. It was a fine discourse, containing a complete system
of theology. Mr. Popham rose to his best when he spoke
of the vicarious sacrifice of Christ. . . ."—W. R. N. in
British Weekly, May 21st, 1914.

If some of his followers were inclined to be elated on their
minister's account, that he should receive occasional notice in
the religious and secular press, his truest friends were at
times apprehensive lest their beloved pastor should be injured
thereby, and they were moved to pray for him, "a man of
like passions with themselves;" so that their gratification was
to find the steadying influence of grace, a sense of the incal-
culable value of souls, the weight of responsibility in his

awful charge, counterbalance any attraction to mere popularity. The following observations were an answer to the intimation of his being referred to in a London Daily Paper:

" It pleases the Lord to keep me low enough in my own eyes to preserve me from being puffed up by the praise of a London newspaper. By the mercy of God to me, it is enough if I am approved of Him and commended to the consciences of His people to whom I minister."

For that humbling and ennobling grace given to their pastor, the godly could never sufficiently extol the God of all grace.

In the vestry at the conclusion of one service, a somewhat popular doctor of divinity in the nonconformist world said to him, " I like your preaching; but your theology is 300 years behind the times!" A criticism the worthy minister valued as an honour, feeling himself unworthy to be placed with the Puritans. On one occasion when asked how he got his sermons, he replied, " Gentlemen, on my knees in this study I obtain from God what I deliver to my people." Such was the man of God, a true labourer in the vineyard of the Lord.

For upwards of fifty years Mr. Popham preached on August Bank Holiday Monday at the anniversary services at Hanover chapel, Tunbridge Wells, the last time being in 1935, when his text was I Tim. ii. 5. Notable gatherings were these! the chapel usually packed to the doors, the atmosphere almost stifling, yet such was the spiritual power sometimes realized that attention was rapt and one could almost literally " hear a pin drop ". Once or twice remarkable hearings were given, notably when the texts were, " Now unto Him that is able to do exceeding abundantly," etc. (Eph. iii. 20, 21), and " . . . It is finished," etc. (John xix. 30). The memory of them is fragrant still.

The occasion in 1914 stands out fresh in the memory of many. It was the day prior to England becoming involved in the great war; consequently fewer than usual travelled with their loved pastor from Brighton to Tunbridge Wells. On the journey, noticing the holiday-makers, Mr. Popham, who was evidently much favoured in soul, said to his Galeed friends, " All people will walk every one in the name of his

god, and *we* will walk in the Name of the Lord *our* God"
(Micah iv. 5). His text that day was Rom. v. 19: "For as
by one man's disobedience many were made sinners, so by
the obedience of One shall many be made righteous." It is
believed that a considerable number of hearers received
special blessing on that occasion.

On November 15th, 1914, the honoured pastor of Hanover,
Mr. J. Newton, entered into eternal rest. Almost his last
utterance was, "He's come!" Intimate friendship subsisted
between the Tunbridge Wells and the Brighton pastors
from 1882, and in 1902 a compact was entered into between
them, that whichever of them survived should bury the other.
Only three days before Mr. N.'s death this agreement was
referred to. Mr. Popham thus wrote: "Pleasant and sweet
was his touching reference to our friendship at our last sight
of each other. An upright, humble, tender, godly man, a
laborious minister and watchful pastor, was my dear friend.
He will be much and seriously missed by the church he so
loved, and by many friends, by none of the latter more than
myself. For again and again he told me how often he had
a spirit of prayer given him for me. Thanks be to God for
such a friend!"

After officiating at the funeral, according to Mr. Newton's
expressed wish, Mr. Popham preached at Hanover chapel
from I Thess. iv. 18: "Wherefore comfort one another with
these words." Mr. Newton himself desired this to be the
text when that occasion arrived. The sermon, which was
heard by a large sorrowing congregation, was published
under the title of "Comfort under Bereavement". The discourse very clearly shews the tender affection in which Mr.
Popham held his late dear friend and brother.*

The year 1915 was one of much trial. Early in the year,
within six months of Mrs. Popham's death, an illness fell
on Miss Popham, which caused him much distress in his
desolate state. He wrote, "I became very troubled and self-
pity came up; but I see now that I was praying all the
time. I had thought of giving up everything—selling the
house by auction—relinquishing the *Gospel Standard*; fearing

---

* Letters from Mr. Newton to Mr. Popham appear in the *Gospel
Standard*, 1938.

God was against me. ' Wilt Thou pursue the dry stubble? Shew me wherefore Thou contendest against me.' One stroke after another. (Natural ties are very strong; though if I should lose her I should rejoice on her account.) In this fearful distress, on Tuesday morning this word came to my mind, ' Unto you that fear My Name shall the Sun of Righteousness arise with healing,' etc., and I could but hope the Lord would arise and cover me and sustain me, whatever came. Then that word, ' If ye endure chastening, God dealeth with you as with sons,' etc."

Of the four deacons in office in 1882, at the commencement of Mr. Popham's pastorate at Galeed, the one remaining, Mr. D. T. Combridge, died September 21st, 1915, at the age of eighty-seven years. This was a sore grief to the pastor and a great loss to the church. Prefacing the highly interesting biography issued by Mrs. Combridge,* Mr. Popham speaks of "two beautiful characteristics" in his late deacon:—

" *Naturally:* in his friendships he was refined, considerate, uniform; and this quality was sanctified and much used in the church. For on retiring from business he addicted himself to the ministry of the saints. This the poor of our people well knew. . . . The Lord alone knows how many ' cups of cold water' His servant gave to His disciples. *Spiritually:* perhaps the most striking feature in him was the fear of God. It was conspicuous in his whole life; in his hesitations and in his movements; in his silences and in his utterances. . . ."

Speaking in a sermon shortly after this trial and church bereavement, in solemn and tender warning, the tried faithful pastor said:—

" I do not want to close my eyes to the bereavements we have recently suffered. I do not want to say, ' O but God is a sovereign; He has a right to do what He will.' I know it, I believe it; but why does He do it? You may say in one case, ' We ought to have expected, we could not do other than expect, that our aged brother should have been removed.' True. But when it comes to another comparatively

* Mrs. Combridge died May 18th, 1938. See *Gospel Standard*, page 258.

young,* then there may be a question. Why does God send
trouble ? On a general ground you may say truly, 'He sends
trouble for sin.' But why does it fall on a particular person ? why on a particular church ? There may be some
error of spirit, if not error of doctrine, which weans the
spirit and affections from Himself; and He may send trouble
for these things to reprove for them, *and to redeem from
them.* Look at these points, my very dear friends. It
becomes me to mention them to you; and God give you wise
ears to receive them, and believing hearts to look into them.
. . . We are in a day of great charity, as we talk; of universal love, when that long-exploded but revived and ever-
persistent error of putting sincerity in the place of truth, is
thought much of. If a man be but sincere in anything he
professes, then he is right: that is the charity of the day.
But the Word of God is strict. 'I am the Way.' . . . If
you are right, you will have to bear the shame of the cross;
if God is with you, you must bear the reproach of Christ.
If you are going to heaven, you must leave Egypt; and this
will mean sorrow and loss and reproach. O brethren, watch
respecting doctrine. . . .

"If the Lord *un*churches churches, as I believe He will
many, can any poor children of His escape that judgment ?
Yes. How can they be accounted worthy ? Only in one
way—the Person, blood, and righteousness of Jesus Christ.
Pray, O dear friends, that God may account *us* worthy to
escape the judgment that is coming on Zion generally. When
the most fine gold shall be quite dim, when her outward
bulwarks in divine doctrine shall be disregarded, pray that
we may escape that judgment."

Note of a conversation on his return from a week's preaching ending at Trowbridge on May 26th, 1916, and preaching
on the 28th at Galeed from Rev. xxi. 7: "He that over-
cometh," etc.:—

"I think I am kept confessing my sins and looking to the
blood of atonement; have been at that business this morning,
and feel to have a broken heart. On Friday I felt overdone
when I reached Trowbridge (after two services at Uffington

* Mr. C. H. Dillistone, a member at Galeed, who died October 21st,
1915.

the previous day). I could not get through such constant preaching if I were not much alone to enable me to meditate and dwell in my thoughts on Christ. The joy set before Him—the river of pleasûres—I hardly like to speak of it so, lest it should be derogatory to His sacred Majesty; but He was a Man in our place, and the Scriptures speak so—the joy set before Him—His Father's smile after His sufferings. I do not want to have to do with other things, nor to judge anyone. . . . I want to live like Him, the meek and lowly Jesus."

[Referring to a particularly cruel persecution.] "I am quiet; it brings home my sins; I keep confessing them, and it is good to be in the dust before the Lord. I find myself praying when awake in the night. I feel a broken heart, which is an acceptable sacrifice. I think of what James Bourne said, 'If I should be charged with robbing the Royal Mail, I should say, O Lord, what is coming next?' I can commit it all to Him; that is just my daily life."

CHAPTER TWELVE.

"Thou shalt guide me with Thy counsel."

1916—1924. His second marriage—exercises—end of the war, thanksgiving—The *Friendly Companion*—rich consolations—false charges refuted—desiring rest but willing to serve—fortieth year of pastorate, presentation.

On September 16th, 1916, Mr. Popham was married to Miss Elizabeth Ashley Keen, of Cambridge, daughter of the late Rev. Charles T. Keen, baptist minister; his friend, the late Mr. J. E. Hazelton, officiating at the ceremony. All who knew the dear man would be well assured that this step was undertaken in the fear of the Lord only after much thought, but it may be for the glory of his God and the

N

shame of some who failed not to use the opportunity to speak
ill of His honoured servant, that to an intimate friend he
named a few of his exercises which are here now recorded:—
    "On June 19th, Ps. xvi. 11 was most solemnly encour-
aging: 'Thou wilt shew me the path of life.' I thanked the
Lord for enabling me to meditate in the night season. Under
the view of Christ's sufferings I felt much sobriety, solemnity,
and humility on my spirit. I prayed not to deny Him if
tested, but to be allowed to 'walk with Him in white'.
Often had I asked this, when I felt to receive Christ, eating
His flesh and drinking His blood; and the blessedness of
knowing anything of that suffering and the joy set before
Christ.

    "About April I became much exercised about continuing
as I am (a widower), having had a strong resolve not to
marry. But I then felt enabled to commit myself wholly
into the Lord's hands to do what He would with me. On
May 4th, I preached at St. Ives, and saw there my friends,
Mr. and Miss W. and Miss K. They had been several
times before at different places to hear me, without any
thought of anything further. Then for the first time the
thought of Miss K. came up in a different way, and I became
much exercised before the Lord. But it seemed like presumption in me to think of it; yet this word would come in,
'I will open before you the two-leaved gates, and the gates
shall not be shut.' Afterwards I found the Lord was working in her too, and the same thought entered her mind for
the first time that evening. The night after, lying awake,
this word was given her: 'From this day will I bless you;'
so powerfully that she got up to kneel down and thank the
Lord for it, not at all knowing what it might refer to, and
not connecting it with that matter. The exercise did not
leave my own mind, and once this word came, 'I will work,
and who shall let it?' On July 6th, preaching at Godman-
chester, all three friends were present but left quickly after
the service to avoid general talking before the train. I left
with Mr. Oldfield to wait at his house for the train, and we
came upon them. When asked in to supper, they hesitated,
but finally all came. I could not see how the thing was
possible for me, but this word came powerfully: 'Said I not

unto thee that if thou wouldest believe thou shouldest see the glory of God?' which almost settled it to me. Just after that I preached at Cambridge and afterwards spoke to Miss K. and said, 'I shall call on you to-morrow.' I asked the Lord for two things: that if it was His will to go on with the matter, I might on that visit feel a union to her religion and also that she might shew some natural feeling. He granted both; but I made no intimation of my thoughts, which rather puzzled her. July 9th, when preaching at Gower Street, she was there. Afterwards with much exercise of prayer, I wrote; and I think if ever a letter was put into the post-box with prayer and exercise of faith, that one was."

Mrs. Popham proved to be a real help-meet, especially in supporting him in his pastoral visitations and in connection with his editorial labours. Her kindly attention to the poor of the flock—often beyond her strength, for she was frail and suffered with spinal weakness—was greatly appreciated.

Grave warning, spiritual instruction, and gracious encouragement marked many of Mr. Popham's prayer-meeting addresses during the war period, some of which were printed in the *Gospel Standard* and were much appreciated, as were also the timely annual New Years' Addresses in that magazine. He issued also in 1915 an earnest protest against the British Government Mission to the pope, also several fervent calls to the denomination to gather together for humiliation and prayer. Truly he laboured in prayer and by word and pen for the good of the churches, and his example was an inspiration to not a few of the godly in those days of stress. A number of young men went out to the war from Galeed, several of whom never more returned. Of those who fell on the battlefield it is believed from their letters that some went thence to heaven. Stirring years were those both for those who went abroad and for those who remained at home " by the stuff "; and the beloved pastor entered very tenderly into the trials and sorrows of the mourners. When at length the relief of the armistice and then the peace declaration came, and the surviving young men returned, a meeting was held at Galeed to give thanks to Almighty God for His great goodness and to humbly seek His mercy and favour. The

sober gladness and gratitude of the dear minister was very
touching to witness.

When in 1919 Mr. Jefferies, the Editor of the *Friendly
Companion* magazine, was taken ill and passed away the
following year, Mr. Popham was asked to "step into the
gap". In doing so he wrote to his young friends, "Your
old and esteemed Editor, Mr. C. Jefferies, is ill, and in a
very feeble state, quite unable to conduct the magazine you
look for month by month. All of you, I am sure, sympathize
with him in this dealing of God with him, and with Mrs.
Jefferies, his sorrowing companion and devoted nurse. They
need sympathy. And you will be glad to hear that the
Lord has been pleased to visit him and bless his soul. It is
truly good to hear of such mercy obtained, and grace to
help in time of need. Many may be encouraged in hearing
this, and may be led to lay up in store many petitions for
the day which will come to them. . . . Having already my
hands quite full of important work, I hesitated to add to it,
. . . but I will do my best, by God's merciful help, to
provide you with some good reading."

His monthly letter to the young—a most valuable feature
of the junior magazine—was greatly appreciated by many, by
some no longer young. Through a friend's generosity there
was published in 1934 a volume of sixty-two of these letters,
classified in subjects; forming a useful addition to the book-
shelves of any youth.*

Mr. Popham continued to conduct the two magazines until
in 1935 increasing infirmities of age, and his approaching
end, impelled him to relinquish.

Frequently in his ministry Mr. Popham would mention
the need of sanctifying grace to make affliction profitable
to the soul; and it was very obvious to those who had discernment that he himself often profited by trading in that
way. When away from home in 1919, after an illness of
some weeks, he wrote:—

"The trial of silence is keen on Lord's days. At times
my heart is Godward, and I have said to Him, 'My soul
followeth hard after Thee.' One night in much pain, I was

---

* This is still obtainable from the publishers.

enabled to say, 'I do take the cup, Lord, and would drink
it.' I felt God had no other such case as mine, yet He
came and blessed me and made me feel sure I should go to
heaven. I long to see you all again and to speak, as enabled,
once more in the Name of the Lord. O that He would visit
us all as a people! Our guilt, fears, weakness, bondage,
sloth, and all evils would then fly as to their dominion."

"I was much exercised and troubled on Monday at not
being able to fulfil engagements all this week, fearing there
was wrath in my being prevented, and was full of trouble
all Monday night. But on Tuesday morning early I found
myself drawn out to the Lord as my God, my Portion, my
living Head, and saying, 'My Father!' My heart went with
that beautiful hymn:

'Immortal honours rest on Jesus' head' (667).

I think it is the most beautiful Gadsby wrote. I felt everything was right, and I was content; and this morning I am
quite happy in the Lord."

At another time of affliction and trial he said, "I was so
blest by the Lord telling me He had chosen me in the
furnace of affliction, that it was many hours before the
furnace came into my thoughts. All I could do was to praise
Him, love Him, and weep and wonder at His kindness to
such a sinner; and when again I noticed the furnace, even
then my soul was happy." In the following remarkable
letter, written about this time, there is again the evidence of
spiritual fruit to his affliction:—

Dear Miss B.,—Almost ever since I received your kind
letter I have been looking for an opportunity to write to you,
but sickness in my family, and sickness and death among my
friends have hitherto prevented. . . . God's people must bear
a cross, and my desire is to have one of the blessed marks
of a Christian,—grace to bear it meekly and to profit by it.
It is even sweet when one can hope that the Lord will purge
one's tin and dross by the afflictions. There is a needs-be I
am persuaded for all the trials, crosses and burdens it pleases
the Lord to exercise us with. Sometimes my wonder is that
the burden is so light. I see such a foundation in my wicked
nature for chastisement; and feel thus,—If I am so barren,

wayward and foolish with a cross and a weight, what should
I be without? Hart's words have been a comfort to me:

> " Know whom the Saviour favours much,
>   Their faults He oft reproves;
> He takes peculiar care of such,
>   And chastens whom He loves."

And a short petition in that precious little book of the late
Mrs. Benson's, " Footsteps of Mercy ": " Never leave off to be
a Reprover in my heart."

Oh that He should, that He will, so to speak, take such
pains with a wayward unbelieving sinner as to correct him,
tell him his faults, reprove him for his sins, and over and
over again condescend to shew him the Way of Life! It is
painful but blessed work. " Is this the manner of man, O
Lord God? Then went king David in and sat before the
Lord, and said, Who am I, O Lord God? " Such feelings
my soul has had at times lately. It is good when afflictions
meeken, humble, chasten, and make tender the spirit:

> " Soften the heart by due degrees,
>   And make the spirit meek."

I am distressed at times by many fears of what may be
in the future for me, but for the last two days David's language has been in my mind, " I was dumb, I opened not my
mouth, because Thou didst it." O that that might more
and more be my feeling: " Wherefore doth a living man
complain, a man for the punishment of his sins? " According
to the Scriptures he is happy whom God correcteth. It is
blessed indeed when we are taught to " hear the rod and
Who hath appointed it ".

Since I last wrote my soul has been visited and favoured.
The day before Christmas day I was in a very sad state
of feeling, and walking up and down my room in much felt
misery, when Phil. iii. 8, 9, came to me with much efficacy
and sweetness. Immediately I was overcome and said, " O
Lord, is all this looking within and misery because I cannot
find any good, an opposition to Christ's righteousness? "
Then an entire going out, so to speak, of wretched sinful
self unto and into the Lord Jesus followed. Oh, how real
and sweet is the rest of the weary soul in incarnate Deity!

"We which have believed do enter into rest." My soul obeyed the invitation, "Come unto Me, all ye that labour and are heavy laden, and I will give you rest." Just before this I had felt Isa. lv. 7 and i. 18 to be very suitable to me who had no marks of grace to shew. How full, sweet, and suitable is the Word of God, how low it comes! I feel now more than ever that my poor soul must again and again come in as needy, naked and undone; not as having a good, large, or deep experience, but as a sensible, wounded, lost sinner, without a raft, plank, or even a straw to hold on to. But how hard this is,

> ". . . to be receiving strength,
> And yet be always weak;"

to possess grace and yet be poor and needy, to possess all things and yet have nothing, to be rich and yet so poor as to beg mercy every hour. Here Christ becomes "more precious than gold, even than the golden wedge of Ophir". Who can describe His glories, especially the glories of redemption!

On the first Sabbath of the month, I went to the ordinance praying for a broken heart, and my petition was, I hope I may say, answered; that was a good word, "Even as the Son of man came not to be ministered unto, but to minister, and to give His life a ransom for many." It is sweet to mourn for Him, to see Him weltering in blood, agonizing in death, groaning under the hidings of His Father's face. It is blessed to feel Him ministering to our needy souls.

> "He to the needy and the faint
> His mighty aid makes known;
> And when our languid life is spent,
> Supplies it with His own."

He gives life out of His abundant fulness, He puts forth His almighty power. At times I am ready to say, "Head o'er all is Christ to me." Blessed be His Name, He came not to be ministered unto. If He did, as a condition of salvation, woe, woe were me! But oh, the heart-melting feeling of the Son of God in human flesh ministering life, healing, grace, comfort, strength, and mercy with His own gracious hands to such poor sinners; and when unbelief and

carnal reason and Satan would combine to make the soul
put all away, He shines with glorious rays upon the be-
nighted heart and speaks with sweet overcoming power. . . .
Oh, the glorious scars of which Hart speaks! what peace,
healing, and satisfaction they bring into the soul! Through
them the soul goes in and sits before the Lord; through
them the soul sees rays of divine glory; in them infinite
justice is fully satisfied, God is well pleased, the law is magnified and made honourable. They are the satisfaction of
eternal Deity, the life, healing, peace, and comfort of the
Church. I wonder not, my dear friend, at the answer the
Church gave to the question, " What is thy Beloved more
than another beloved," etc.   J. K. P.

Of the very many attacks launched against Mr. Popham,
that which was commenced in 1918 and continued for some
years, was especially virulent. In a number of letters and
pamphlets, with the aid also of other professed Strict Baptist publications, the veracity of our dear friend and the
integrity of his position in the denomination were impugned.
In this nefarious business, born of envy, the instigator en-
listed the aid of several ministers and members of churches
(many of whom proved themselves to have been misled),
publishing in all more than 100 pages of seductive argument,
misconstruction, innuendo and abuse. The Lord's servant
was at length compelled for the sake of truth to publish
one or two replies, at considerable cost of time, exercise of
mind, and money. God vindicated the truth, and eventually,
some years later, the originator of the calumnies was brought
to voluntarily acknowledge his wrong and to request forgiveness, which was given, first very graciously and unreservedly
by the chief sufferer, Mr. Popham, then by the Committee
of the " Gospel Standard " Societies who were involved. The
matter was indeed a very great anxiety to our dear friend,
and now that the heat of the controversy is gone and most
of the contestants gone into eternity and oblivion, we cannot
but admire—in calmly reviewing the documents relative
thereto—the great grace bestowed by the Lord on His servant, enabling him to act tenderly in His fear under great
vexation through long-continued public defamation. In how
many instances has the promise been manifestly verified, " I

will make them to know that I have loved thee " (Rev. iii.
9),—a promise given to Mr. Popham in his early days of
trial at Liverpool. The following reference to this painful
experience is from a letter written at that painful period:—
  " Many times have I sought the Lord about the matter.
He alone knows the fear, searching and pain I have suffered
lest I had injured the holy Word of God. Oh if the Lord
will enlighten my blind mind and move my dead heart to
seek His glory in and among the churches before I die! I
desire the good of our people and the glory of God. Poor
Zion! . . . I feel a mere vile nothing and unworthy of consideration, but since He who condescends to love, choose, and
bless worms and use them for His own glory, has sovereignly
laid His right hand on me and made some little use of me,
I desire so to live and walk as to please Him and hurt none
of His people."
  It will here be convenient to insert extracts from two
addresses given at the annual meetings of the denomination,
that readers may possess his own account of the case.

CONCERNING THE FALSE REPORT THAT HE HAD RETRACTED
  FROM THE " GOSPEL STANDARD " ARTICLES OF FAITH.

*(Extracted from addresses at the annual meetings of the
Societies.)*

  " First of all I would say, Fellow Members of the ' Gospel
Standard ' Strict Baptist Societies, I stand before you as a
member of this denomination. Legally I am a member of
this denomination. I say it for the sake of some whose minds
may have been poisoned. . . . On October 11th, 1901, as you
have heard read from the minute book of that date, I signed
with this right hand, the articles of these Societies. My
name is there. I signed the articles because I believed them,
and I believe them to-day. It will be fifty-six years ago at
the end of the approaching summer, since it pleased God to
appear to me. He made me know in a distinct manner and
in some very effectual measure what His holiness was. I
believed, and said mentally, ' Where that God is, I shall
never be.' He made me know His majesty and His glory.
I set to work to make myself better, and failed. I fled to
the Congregationalists, the most respectable body of dissen-

ters as it then appeared to me. In a providence which,
were I to relate it to you, might appear to you, as it does to
me, all but miraculous, God brought me to know the Strict
Baptists, brought me to a living hope under my never-to-be-
forgotten friend—and at a subsequent date, my pastor—Mr.
de Fraine, of Lutterworth. He afterwards put away my sins
by a distinct application of the blood of Christ, and a revelation of His infinite mercy to me. He called me, as I trust,
into the ministry. Forty-seven years ago next month I was
invited to take the pastorate of the church at Liverpool. I
mention this because of its connection with my relation to
our Societies—with one Society, as it then was. By my position in the church at Liverpool, I was brought into acquaintance with the late Mr. John Gadsby, and through that I was
placed on the original committee of the Aid Society. I
suppose I am the only person now living [1920] who was a
member of that committee. After some years of membership
I left that committee, for *purely personal reasons*. It has
been insinuated that I withdrew from subscribing to the
articles. It is absolutely false. I returned, not to articles
from which it is said I departed, but by invitation to old
associates and associations. Upon my return I signed with
my own right hand the articles of faith. By certain representations made I am and have been a most dishonourable
man. No man of the world with any sense of honour, apart
altogether from religion, would have done what it has been
reported I have done. I should have been most dishonourable
if, while pretending to support these articles, I had not
subscribed to them; I should have been going about these last
eighteen years under false pretences; should have been occupying a position for the past fifteen years with respect to
the magazines, to which I had no legal right. Blessed be
God, it is not true. I have occupied a position to which, in
the first place, I am legally entitled, and have been so all
these years. Very unworthily and feebly I have occupied it.

Now I have to ask you to excuse this obtrusion of myself
on your attention, but it is due to the denomination, it is due
to you who are assembled to know precisely the position
which I occupy. . . . I need say no more, except this: that
the dishonour which has been heaped upon me by unjust

insinuations concerns also the committee. For if they had knowingly smuggled me into the committee, to occupy the position to which I had no legal right, they with myself would have been dishonourable men. But they did their duty, passed a resolution that I should come back into the committee upon certain conditions, which conditions were complied with when I entered my name on that book. . . . This is why I stand where I do and as I do. It is not easy for me to speak of myself, but I deemed it expedient to do so in the painful circumstances in which I am placed. I hope it may please God that as a body of people we may come to a better understanding of our true position when the din of this controversy has passed away, and that good may come from Him who is ' wonderful in counsel and excellent in working '."

Only those who know the burden of ministerial care can appreciate the temptation under discouragement to discontinue. The extracts following shew somewhat of the conflict the " standard-bearer " suffered and the divine consolation he enjoyed in connection with his denominational leadership:—

" By God's mercy we, as a denomination, must abide by what is our foundation. Though I am abused, called harsh, narrow-minded, etc., the sense given of divine approval has thus far more than counterbalanced all that. . . . Many things within and without tend to weary one. Rightly you interpret my desire for liberty from my present position and its awful responsibilities. But *just now I would not seek it.*"

Tiptaft (one of the ' Seceders ') is reported to have frequently said, " If your religion does not interfere with all your life's circumstances, it will soon interfere with none." His meaning obviously being that a true and lasting religion influenced the whole of its possessor's life. The worthy minister at Brighton could not lightly change his residence; in a matter so comparatively trivial he needed God's guidance. To one whom he honoured with intimacy he wrote, " It may surprise you to hear that I have procured another house. It has long been my anxious wish, on my wife's account, to get a house with all we require on two floors. I expect we shall go in about the end of the month. It will be a wrench to

leave this dear place where so much trouble and countless
mercies have been experienced; but a kind of necessity is on
me." He moved into his last earthly residence in the spring
of 1926.

For many years, the circulation of the *Gospel Standard* has
slightly declined—a reflection of decay in spiritual appetite.
Mr. Popham, sensitive of this, delivered himself of the following observations at the annual meeting of the Societies
in April, 1922:—

"With regard to the falling off in the circulation of the
magazines, I do not know what I personally can do to alter
that (for *I* cannot alter; for I have nothing new to bring
before the people). And if the Lord spares me, and I should
hold any longer the position I occupy to-day, then I must go
on as the Lord helps me just in the old ways. What I have
said to the committee, I would say to you, to the whole
denomination represented more or less here now: that is, if
it should be thought that a change of Editor would be
beneficial to the churches, and in any proper way advance
the circulation of the magazines, and therefore the income
from them, it has but to be hinted to me, and I should at
once retire.

"I have felt sometimes the burden has been almost more
than I could carry, and have wished many times in secret
that if the Lord would allow me *with a smile* (not a frown)
to give up, and just sink back into my old position, I should
be very glad and thankful too. But if the trustees of the
magazines and the churches should think it well for me to
continue a little longer, I am willing to do it. And if the
shrinkage could be stopped and the income rise, it would be
very pleasing to me. The great thing is *edification*. The
great end of all in the churches, God's own great end, is His
glory by Christ Jesus, world without end. He has instruments, and I have some reason to think and believe that He
has made me a little useful to the churches. I hope that
God will graciously look on us. . . ."

On Wednesday, October 18th, 1922, to mark the fortieth
anniversary of Mr. Popham's pastorate at Galeed, a service
was held in the afternoon, when Mr. J. E. Hazelton preached
from Deut. ii. 7 a very appropriate sermon. In the evening

after prayer by Mr. J. Banfield (deacon), Mr. Popham gave an address. After which Mr. Banfield in the behalf of the church and congregation, presented the pastor with a cheque for £201, as a token of their regard.

CHAPTER THIRTEEN.

" With long life will I satisfy him, and shew him My salvation."

1924—1931. Preaches at settlement of Maidstone pastor— eightieth birthday recognition—sixtieth anniversary of Galeed— Trinitarian Bible Society—Sovereign Grace Union—afflictions— death of a deacon—" A Timely Call "—letters to church and congregation—suggests retirement—pastoral concern.

AFTER the death of Mr. E. Ashdown, who for many years had presided at the church meetings for the friends at Priory chapel, Maidstone, Mr. Popham accepted the invitation to render the like service. He preached there one Tuesday evening a month from 1904 till 1924, when the present pastor was appointed. During some trying periods the Brighton minister's counsel had been owned of God to preserve the church at Maidstone from disintegration; though there were some very sad occurrences, and the Lord's judgment on several opposers was solemn indeed. He retained the confidence and the love of the godly at Maidstone, which was marked by a presentation on his relinquishing the position on December 2nd, 1924. On that evening he preached from two texts: I Tim. iv. 16; Heb. xiii. 17, giving both to the newly-appointed pastor and to the church sober, wise exhortations and instructions. His labours were truly abundant, yet he sought grace and strength lest any one duty should suffer. Writing concerning this he said, " It would grieve me if through our various occupations our correspon-

dence should diminish; but I hope we may both press
through intervening crowds. Much have I lost through my
idleness and yielding to the tempter's subtle suggestions
that barrenness felt was a proper bar and reason for silence.
Some gracious corrections have been given to me; yet my
heart is slow to learn and ready to forget." The recipient
of that letter read in it the affectionate admonition of a
father in the faith.

Though he manfully struggled on in spite of frequent
illness and increasing age, very occasionally to an intimate
friend he would disclose his difficulty in sustaining his manifold labours:—

". . . I am old and know it. The meeting proved too
much for me. Exhausted, I was kept in bed from Saturday
till Tuesday, and yesterday the doctor said, 'Scrap every
engagement,' and further, 'You are not going out to-night.'
But I went (help was given to speak from John xvii. 9; a
marvellous chapter), and am no worse this morning. My
desire is to know and have power to do the will of God,
either in going out to speak in His Name, or remaining at
home. Pray, O pray for me. I am in a new path, great
physical weakness and a corresponding mental inability for
work. I cannot accuse myself of idleness, but I feel indis-
posed for work."

The occasion of Mr. Popham's eightieth birthday was
marked by his affectionate church and congregation by a gift
of £200, presented by the deacons on December 19th, 1927.
Acknowledging this on Monday evening, January 2nd, 1928,
after rehearsing some of the Lord's wonderful workings
connected with the church and his coming amongst them, the
pastor concluded by saying:—

"You have borne with me; you have been extremely kind
to me. Great changes, of course, I have seen, as you can
realize. I have practically buried all the chapel-full of
people I came to in 1882. One member of the church
remains in Brighton—dear Miss Davey, ninety-five years of
age. I hope the Lord is still with us. . . .

"What will keep the church in the right place and make
it fruitful in the knowledge of God? The answer you will

find in the gospel according to John, in Christ's words, ' I am the Vine, ye are the branches.' Only union, only sap from union flowing to the branches—individual members of a church—will make the church and the members fruitful. Nothing else will. I have warned you at times concerning the day in which we are living. The denomination to which we belong is a very small one; and there are changes coming, some have come—great changes, not for the better. But what I would say is this: Seek the sap, seek communications from the Lord, seek His blessed power in your souls. Three things will be necessary. (1) A deep conviction settled in the heart and held by faith, that only sap can make a person or a church fruitful. I hope you will have that; that it will grow with you; that the form without the power may never satisfy you. My friends, seek sap, that is, seek to ' grow in grace and in the knowledge of our Lord and Saviour, Jesus Christ '. (2) The second thing is that that faith, without which you can never be lively, may issue in many prayers. It will make you hungry for God, for the Lord Jesus, for the Spirit, for the Father. (3) And the third thing will be, that your prayers should embrace the ministry and the minister. If you have those, then there is hope that in the midst of decay and changes here and there, in the midst of a desire and design to ' make the services more attractive ' in some places by having four hymns and other things—from such things you will turn away, and you will find yourselves hankering after vital divine things.

"Perhaps I ought not to have occupied so much of your time this evening, but I think I have a desire to honour God, and to show how my being here proceeded from Him. He has honoured us together. We have not been without our sorrows; we never shall be while here, with the corruption of our nature and the causes of separation from the Lord. But let us, as enabled, offer thanks to God for His great mercies. . . . I want to thankfully acknowledge your continued goodness, kindness, and liberality towards me. When the deacons brought the amazing gift that you had placed in their hands, I *felt* it. It is a very poor and inadequate word, the best and only one I can say,—I do acknowledge, as in God's sight, your kindness. That you should have been able

and willing to put into my hands a cheque for £200 was
indeed wonderful to me. May the Lord sanctify it. May
He be graciously pleased to accept our praises."

The rule at Galeed was never to hold anniversary services,
and there has never been a "tea-meeting" there; but on
sundry occasions some special event was marked by special
services for thanksgiving. October 17th, 1928, was one of
these, when the sixtieth anniversary of the opening of the
chapel was observed by two services. In the evening Mr.
Popham preached a remarkable sermon from Isa. xliii. 15:
"I am the Lord, your Holy One, the creator of Israel, your
King." Any who attended that service expecting some
merely naturally interesting retrospect would be disappointed, but several have reason to remember the solemn
impression that sermon made upon their hearts. The awful
weight of responsibility in the ministry for which he felt
accountable to God, precluded him from trifling with the
people by merely entertaining them. In a sermon at this
time this sacred charge and care was mentioned:—

"Many an hour in the night when perhaps (and I hope)
you are fast asleep, this church is on my heart before God—
your state, whether you are exercised, whether you are seeking God, whether you are tender in your consciences, whether
you are humble, whether kept lively; and I am putting
myself always in this—'Lord, do keep us.' I have seen many
changes here, how many more I shall see, the Lord only
knows; but one change that I have often thought about, I
have not seen, and hope I may not—God has not left us, so
far as I know and can judge, to receive and walk in any
error. Now, brethren, hold fast what you have received.
It may bring much reproach upon you, but hold fast to
what belongs to a church-state."

Among Mr. Popham's many activities, for some years he
gave annually an address at the local meeting in support of
the Trinitarian Bible Society, and for a time consented to be
the local "President". In accepting this position, he said
(explaining that his age prevented him from additional
activities), "If by using my unworthy name, one copy more
of the sacred Scriptures is circulated, it will be well." One

of the addresses—a most concise definition of the Word of God—was so appreciated that it was printed in leaflet form entitled, " The Holy Bible," and about twenty thousand were circulated. Writing of this, he said: " It is an amazement to me, and if it is useful in one instance, I hope if I am allowed to know it, it will deeply humble me." Normally his addresses appeared in the Society's Quarterly Report, and it will be conceded that they considerably raised the calibre of those annual meetings. Grace was given him to seek above all things the edification of the church and the spiritual profit of the hearers. Mere platform commonplaces he abhorred.

His connection with the Sovereign Grace Union for some years had the same object: " To spread pure literature I shall give my mite, but cannot support the ' aggressive work '." Several years he preached the annual conference sermon, and once he wrote a ' paper ' on " The Covenant of Grace and the Atonement ", which (owing to his illness) was read by Mr. J. E. Hazelton, and afterwards published by the Union. He was most careful that any such activity should not interfere with his first work, his pastoral charge at Galeed.

Among several other pieces of Mr. Popham's published by the Sovereign Grace Union, were two very important pamphlets, " A Faithful Message " and " Keswick Teaching ". Both were reprints from the *Gospel Standard*, the former being the New Year's Address of 1929 and the latter a Review of the official Keswick Convention Report for 1929. Both contain most gracious handling of the truth with solemn admonition and grave warning against subtle errors. It has been insinuated that Mr. Popham exceeded his right in " interfering " with matters outside his own denomination. That he laboured unwearyingly for the defence of the truth and for the real good of the churches is manifest to all who have the cause of Christ at heart, and the fact that his treatises appealed sufficiently to the executive of the S.G.U. to incline them to republish them disposes of any charge of denominational bigotry. His chief concern was, nevertheless, the preservation of the churches from error. He wrote:

" My reason for taking notice of it " (the Keswick Report)

o

"is that for years I have heard whispers concerning some of our people leaning to Keswick; and though I believed the teaching was erroneous, yet lacking authentic information, I could not speak. Now I am in a position to warn my unknown friends, and say to them, Touch not, taste not, handle not the unclean thing of universal redemption; for it is a deep dishonour cast on the glorious Redeemer, who obtained eternal redemption, and purchased the Church with His own blood. It impugns the justice of God, of whom it is written, ' A just God and a Saviour.' Have nothing to do with the flattering, natural faith preached; it is not true to the Scripture teaching on that vital subject. Leave the so-called ' deepening of spiritual life', the consecration, the returning home of the pilgrims with the vows of God upon them. Remember that underlying all Keswick teaching is a redemption which does not redeem, a Saviour who does not save, a Lord who does not reign, except with the consent of that natural faith, which, according to Dr. Scroggie, is possessed by the avowed infidel equally with the children of God."

Neutrality, compromise, universal charity—popular though they are—he knew to be seriously deceptive. Nor were his treatises mere negatives; in denouncing error he used the spiritual weapon of the Word of God, whereby the godly were both warned and edified. Since his death the Sovereign Grace Union has produced a volume embodying four of Mr. Popham's valuable treatises, prefaced by a brief biographical sketch.

Personal affliction and affliction in the church again exercised the Lord's servant in 1928, when he wrote, after enumerating the various cases of illness: "Is this state of things Fatherly chastisement, or for some evil thing among us ? This is one of my burdens. My own case is far from satisfactory. ' They shall still bring forth fruit in old age ' is to me a solemnly trying word as I view my barrenness. John xv. tells me how I can be fruitful, but the union and the abiding in Christ are the vital points. I desire a living not a mechanical union to the true Vine. . . .

"It is a new thing for me to be considering a journey and trying to measure my strength by inches, and it is not pleasant; but as my bodily strength has much decreased, services become more and more difficult. I mean not to create an impression that I am left without help. The Lord is good. But the ministry among us is in a serious condition; my own is. The state of the churches much occupies me now. 'And the glory of the Lord went up from the midst of the city and stood upon the mountain which is on the east side of the city' (Ez. xi. 23), is a solemn word, and to me it appears to be now having a fulfilment with respect to our denomination and the people of God in the land."

In November, 1929, the church at Galeed sustained a heavy loss—much felt by the pastor—in the death of a beloved deacon, Mr. T. Lewis, a man of gracious humility and tenderness. Much afflicted, he, with his godly wife who predeceased him some years, exerted by a sober example much beneficial influence in the church. Their memory is fragrant. Three of their children are members of Galeed, each having been baptized by Mr. Popham.

Although his ministry was eminently spiritual and never intermixed with politics and other topics, Mr. Popham ever took a lively interest in the nation's weal and felt much for the rising race. As occasion required he called the denomination to united prayer, usually presiding at the representative meeting held in London. One such occasion was in December, 1929, when in response to a "Timely Call" a large assembly protested against certain modernistic utterances of highly-placed dignitaries in the religious world and solemnly re-affirmed their belief in the entirety of the Word of God. A report of this meeting appeared in February, 1930, issue of the magazine; also an account of a protest made on December 29th, 1929, at Galeed by the congregation and pastor, against the congratulatory message sent by the king to the pope. These were no mere theatrical displays, but were the result of serious exercise and concern for the glory of God in the land. He also referred in the junior magazine to similar matters, warning the young of the dangers, and pointing them to the only Source of truth and salvation.

In the autumn of 1930, Mr. Popham contracted a chill which affected his right lung, resulting in six months' illness; although not wholly out of the pulpit all that time, con-

stantly recurring pyrexia frequently kept him in bed, and
at his great age was a source of much anxiety. In the first
three months of 1931 he was almost wholly laid up, and it
was seriously wondered whether the end might not be
approaching. Several times he mentioned to the deacons the
advisability of his resigning his pastorate, to which suggestion of course they had but one answer—he was too deeply
in the hearts of the people for resignation to be entertained.
His tender concern for the good of the cause and his constant
desire for spiritual benefit and a good issue to the trial will
be observed in the letters he wrote to be read at the services,
which are here given:—

To the Church and Congregation at Galeed.

My dear Friends,—It is a great disappointment to me not
to be with you to-morrow, but clearly it is the will of God
that I shall not be. It appears that my illness is of such
a nature that, while I do not suffer pain, exertion either
mental or physical, sends up my temperature and renders
me ill, and unable for anything. This trouble, commencing
on November 24th, by a chill caught in London, keeping me
in bed for three weeks, has reduced my strength so much that
my doctor said to me on Thursday last that I must go away
for a change, and not preach again till the beginning of
April. To me this was a great blow as, though I knew I
could not now physically stand in the pulpit for many
minutes, I hoped I might be strong enough to be with you
the following week.

For you I feel much; yet very thankful that the Lord has
favoured you with the unity of the Spirit since my illness.
I have often during this time of trial thought of Paul's
beautiful words to the saints and faithful brethren in Christ
at Colosse: "For though I be absent in the flesh, yet am I
with you in spirit, joying and beholding your order, and the
stedfastness of your faith in Christ." Now may I add the
following verse, an exhortation: "As ye have therefore received Christ Jesus the Lord, so walk ye in Him" (Col. ii.
5, 6). Thus this affliction may turn to the furtherance of
the gospel (Phil. i. 12), that the gospel may extend its
gracious life, light, and power, and give the soul satisfaction,

peace, and rest. When affliction is the means which the Spirit uses for the furtherance of the gospel, then, both in the individual and in the church, God is glorified. And this is to be observed in the church in a time of affliction. If instead of scattering, there is a closer cleaving, a spirit of prayer and of union, a desire for the sanctifying power of the Spirit, a feeling after the power of truth in the reading, and a seeking the glory of God, then we may hope the affliction is not in anger, but love.

For myself, I had more favour at the beginning than in these later and more wearisome days; but my hope is fixed on the Rock. I need much of the Spirit's power in patience to possess my soul during the weeks the doctor says I must be silent. . . . Keep together, dear friends. You are always in my prayers. Pray for one another, and for good Mr. Pack who will (D.v.) be with you to-morrow evening, and for me in this trying time, that if it is the Lord's will that I may again speak among you, it may be with more of the unction of the Holy One than ever.

Your affectionate Pastor,

Brighton. Feb. 14th, 1931.   J. K. POPHAM.

He went to Milford-on-Sea on February 27th, but was confined to bed almost all the time there.

My dear Friends,—Though absent from you in the flesh, yet I am with you in spirit, and earnestly desire that you may feel the life-giving presence of the Lord, that you may so see and feel the glory of His Person as the apostle John did, as to fall at His feet as dead, even poor dead creatures, and feel the life-giving touch, and hear the divine voice saying in your hearts: "Fear not; I am the first and the last: I am He that liveth and was dead; and, behold, I am alive for evermore. Amen. And have the keys of hell and of death." The same religion be mine. There is too much to-day of our own life, not much of the death which the glorious presence of Christ begets. That experience of death [to sin, self, and the world] we know only by the love of Christ. The death coming on us when the power of sin works and prevails is too much among us and in us, and it is to be feared that that is too often taken for the other.

We speak of ourselves as poor dead creatures. Very true. But does that bring forth the merciful voice of the divine Majesty, or does it not rather leave us at an awful, and alas! a deathy distance from the Saviour, the living One, and His living, uplifting voice, even with some sort of self-satisfaction, under the power of self-deceiving? Christ's majesty and mercy join in communicating life and the courage of faith, the warmth and sweetness of humility.

Though unable to be with you, which is an affliction added to my affliction, I feel it a privilege to speak to you with paper and ink, and to say I desire that your hearts may be comforted, being knit together in love, and unto all riches of the full assurance of understanding, to the acknowledgment of the mystery of God, and of the Father, and of Christ, in Whom are hid all the treasures of wisdom and knowledge. May none of you rest short of that " full assurance of understanding ". Hunger is not eating; longing is not satisfaction. But a sense of sin, of being lost, feeling the power of unbelief, a view, though distant, will beget hunger, longing to partake of the precious Bread of Life, and to be in union with Christ, Who is life. Be ours the sense of sin, ruin, death; then a sight of the Redeemer in all His grace, love, blood, righteousness, and the application of all to us, so that we may sing:

> " O my Jesus, Thou art mine,
>   With all Thy grace and power;
> I am now, and shall be Thine
>   When time shall be no more;
> Thou revivest me by Thy death,
> Thy blood from guilt has set me free;
> My fresh springs of hope, and faith,
>   And love, are all in Thee."

By God's mercy we have arrived at this quiet place, and hope we shall feel enabled to rest. But oh, I fain would be with you, even if I could not preach to you! You are in my heart, to die and live with you. May the Spirit of God be with you, and in you, and sanctify you wholly, make this day one of the days of the Son of Man. May He grant that when you are at His table, the Holy Ghost may make known the majesty, efficacy, and all-sufficiency of the precious death

of our Lord and Saviour Jesus Christ in each believing heart.
And also pray for   Yours affectionately,
Milford-on-Sea.   Feb. 27th, 1931.   J. K. POPHAM.

My dear Friends and Fellow-Helpers, the Deacons of the
Church at Galeed . . .,—My heart is so with you to-day;
and remembering that you will meet to-morrow evening to
do the work the Holy Ghost has called you to (Acts vi.), I
feel disposed to send a word of good-will and desire for the
help of God, by whom you are enabled to hold the mystery
of the faith in a pure conscience. We can never enough
bless the Most High God for calling us to know, love, and
worship the adorable Lord and Saviour, Jesus Christ. We
were dead in trespasses and sins, walked according to the
course of this world, according to the prince of the power of
the air. But God, who is rich in mercy, when we were dead
in sins, quickened us together and raised us up together, and
gave us peace by the cross of Christ. What motive so
powerful, so rich, so sweet as the grace of God, to move us
to serve Him in His Church? To me it is denied to serve
Him in the gospel for a time, and how deep is my sin in the
ministry! In long silence, many searchings of heart have
caused me deep shame. I have been half-hearted, selfish,
proud, idle in the work of the Lord. Pray for me if you
feel able.

To-morrow evening you will be meeting. . . . The Lord
direct your hearts into the love of God, and into the patient
waiting for Christ, and grant you the wisdom needed for the
impartial distribution of the free gifts of the Church this
evening. . . . Our love to your dear households. If you feel
disposed to remember us, not only in prayer, but also by
post, we shall feel it very kind of you.
                    Your affectionate Pastor,
Milford. March 1st, 1931.   J. K. POPHAM.

To the Church and Congregation at Galeed.

My dear Friends in the Lord,—Once more I write to you
from my bed. . . . Early this morning the words of Eliphaz
came into my mind: "I would seek unto God, and unto God
would I commit my cause; which doeth great things and
unsearchable, marvellous things without number." This I

was enabled to do, with sensible submission to His divine
will. For that will is good, acceptable, and perfect. My
little faith believed it was good and perfect, and felt it was
acceptable. Throughout yesterday I felt keenly the relapse,
and wondered what it meant. Yet I was enabled to say to
the holy Majesty of heaven, I was not disputing or resisting
His will. The path of tribulation is appointed for all who
find the strait gate and narrow way. Therein faith has
plenty of work and also room for its greatest exploits; and
surely its greatest exploit is, " That ye may know that ye
have eternal life, and that ye may believe on the Name of the
Son of God " (I John v. 13); to believe on the Lord Jesus
Christ as our Redeemer, Saviour, Refuge, and Advocate,
when evil abounds and our enemies are strong; to believe in
that love which many waters cannot quench, neither floods
drown, which is unpurchasable. When the icy flood of our
unbelief chills every feeling of desire, love, adoration, and all
prayer, oh, then, to " build upon a base that nothing can remove ", but to " trust electing grace and everlasting love "!

If the Lord will, I hope to see you all soon, and to endeavour to speak what I am unable to write. May the
Lord's presence be felt in your hearts, and your faith abound,
and love move each child of God to greet each other with a
kiss of charity.

Your affectionate Pastor,

Milford. March 13th, 1931.   J. K. POPHAM.

Mr. Popham returned to Brighton early in April and was
enabled to preach a few times, but had frequent relapses.
Having a great desire, he once again visited Wiltshire and
Kent, but the reaction brought trying exhaustion and other
engagements were compulsorily cancelled. His fervent interest in the cause of Christ, of the dear flock at Galeed and
of the denomination, was however maintained, and even
during the long affliction he wrote considerably on matters
affecting the body of churches, advising, encouraging, and
warning:—

" It appears that the time has come when my labours, if I
live a little longer, must be confined to home (Galeed).
Yesterday the exhaustion was almost too much, though help

was given. Oh! 'happy is the man that hath the God of
Jacob for his help, whose hope is in the Lord his God.' A
great word was that to me more than fifty years ago, and
now I am old I believe He will not forsake me. But the
conflict is severe. Gal. v. 17 (" The flesh lusteth against the
Spirit, and the Spirit against the flesh ") is solemn but hopeful.
The first I know; the second I hope is true in me. . . . O for
more knowledge and experience of Him who is the ' brightness of His Father's glory and the express image of His
Person '. I am lean and barren. I have many times desired
grace to ' set my face to seek the Lord ', as Dan. ix. 3. So
much sin, so many particular sins, so many other matters,
and so little prayer. Also II Kings xiii. 18, 19. I seem not
to know the A.B.C. of divine methods. God's purposes
stand, but His methods are strange and I am ignorant
(James iv. 2—8), and can use for myself Hart's word, ' Lord,
instruct me, I'm a fool '."

"Ignorant of the A.B.C. of divine methods!" How such
a confession emphasizes the greatness of the loss sustained
by the removal of so deeply-taught and humbled a minister
from our midst!

CHAPTER FOURTEEN.

*" Be thou faithful unto death, and I will give thee a
crown of life."*

1932—1933. Death of two deacons—jubilee of pastorate—Mr.
Kemp's funeral—failing health—desiring to depart—illness of wife
and granddaughter—favoured in soul—continuing contention for the
faith: the God-honouring Movement—indefatigable labour—wise
counsel—serious illness of Mrs. Popham—calls denominational
prayer-meeting.

1932 was an eventful year to the beloved pastor of Galeed.
The loss by death of several members of the church, including two deacons, and the pastoral jubilee occurred

during the year. On February 3rd, Mr. A. S. Palmer died
in the Lord, and on August 19th his dear friend, Mr. J.
Banfield, fell asleep in Jesus. Of this latter bereavement
Mr. Popham wrote:—

"At midnight his prayer was answered, 'Jesus, fetch me
home.' Our loss is great. A sense of desolation is in my
heart. B. was, as you know, no common deacon. The one
word with me from the moment I heard the solemn news
was, 'Thy kingdom come; Thy will be done.' But as the
days go by I find it more and more difficult to realize my
dear, close, and most kind friend and deacon is no more.
His presence was always unobtrusive and yet pervasive. Now
I find much searching. Solomon bids us 'Consider the work
of God: for who can make that straight which He hath made
crooked?' Our beloved friend had the 'good name' Solomon commends, and truly the day of his death was better
than the day of his birth. To me it is a searching event, a
day of adversity. Had it occurred a few days earlier, the
jubilee services would have been cancelled. But the final
arrangements were made and the advertisement printed. But
O under what a cloud we shall, if spared, meet! My poor
barren sinful life, my corruptions, and backslidings are ever
before me. Present circumstances seem like so many candles
by which I am searched. Now and again a little breathing
space is given. Ps. cii. 17: 'He will regard the prayer of
the destitute,' etc., was a good word yesterday, and was my
text. . . ."

Reference in a sermon on August 28th, 1932, to the death
of Mr. Banfield, deacon. (*Text:* Rom. xiv. 9.)

"If we had been consulted as to the death of our friends,
deacons and members, this year, we should have said, 'Lord,
we cannot do without them.' And there is a hardness in
having to do without them; in this the Lord has shewn us
'hard things' and given us 'the wine of astonishment' to
drink. It is a great thing to be enabled to say, 'The will
of the Lord be done. Thy kingdom come, Thy will be done.'
I find it very difficult to realize that our beloved brother is
taken away. He has filled, if I may say so, so filled the
life of the church here; that is to say, acted as deacon and
threw himself, heart and soul, into the matters of the

church, and with gentleness and love has walked among us.
To myself he has been so much that it is very difficult to
me daily to realize that we shall have him no more with us.
And yet one can say one would not wish him back. Oh no!
he is with the revived Lord. He is one of that company of
which the apostle speaks in the Hebrews, 'The spirits of just
men made perfect.' And O fellow-believers, God can bring
you to that company, even by faith. Says Paul, By faith we
have come to this company, and see the glory and joy with
which they are satiated and filled. When you get near to
that company, the sight of what they are enjoying makes
a person so blessed say, O that I may soon be there!

'Far from a world of grief and sin,
With God eternally shut in.'

O to be brought honourably to the grave, as our brother was
brought to his, saying with his last breath, 'Lord Jesus,
fetch me home.' Perfectly conscious up to the last moment,
he had no fear of death, but triumphed over the monster;
and now, dead to us, he lives to God. O happy change! I
never thought to see the day when I should bury him."

"The time is short for us. Not only we must needs die,
but perhaps soon. My heart sinks as I think of the changes
death will ere long make at Galeed, and I would gladly not
see them. But God's will is the best. O to be ready to die!
To be able to say, 'I know whom I have believed, and am
persuaded that He is able to keep that which I have committed unto Him against that day'."

Some of his real friends feared lest he might be inflated
by the notice taken of his ministerial jubilee; others, whose
religion consists chiefly in what Philpot calls " galvanism ",
were jubilant that Galeed's pastor should at last appear to
justify their own carnal religious movements. The following
sentences, culled from letters, will effectually answer both,
and evoke admiration and gratitude for that grace which
subordinated, in his heart, every circumstance to the honour
and glory of God.

" This has brought much exercise on me. My fear is that
God will not be Alpha and Omega. How I have asked Him
not to permit us to provoke His Fatherly jealousy. What

a blight such a sin would bring on us! May the power of
God preserve us from it; may His holy fear, which seems to
include all worship, be powerful in me and all concerned. In
this matter we need Christ to be made unto us wisdom,
righteousness, sanctification, and redemption. May prayer
be given to you for us, and to us all."

It is just this secret tenderness in the fear of God and
the sense granted to him of His divine Majesty being First
and Last, that enabled him to take a calm view of that which
would intoxicate many a minister. He was deeply and continually shewn his nature, which produced that humble estimate of himself, and was accompanied with simple faith in
the merit and blood of Christ, savouring his writings and
preachings:—

"What hours I spent last night, unable to sleep, in seeking
mercy, grace, wisdom, strength for that day; I need more
prayer and sympathy than you."

After the event he wrote:—

"I am grateful to all my kind friends and their expressions of most undeserved recognition of my unprofitable life,
but I cannot publish them [referring to the Addresses pre-
sented]. . . . I was, and am, honest before God in saying I
am unworthy of the kindly notice taken of me. I never
thought I had so many friends. . . . I am weary, weary of
self, of men, of not praying, of wrong praying, of a barren
heart and a barren life in and out of the pulpit."

MR. POPHAM'S FIFTIETH YEAR AT GALEED.

The jubilee services were held on October 5th, 1932, the
Countess of Huntingdon's Chapel, North Street, being hired
for the occasion. The accommodation was fully occupied at
both services, it being computed that 1,700 people were
present. The sermons preached were printed in the denominational magazine at the request of the "Gospel Standard"
Committee. In a prologue, Mr. Popham says:—

"My heart and my ambition will be content if God is in
any measure magnified in me. What the Holy Ghost says
of David shines in my eyes, and I desire no better thing to
be said of me, in my own small measure: 'For David, after

he had served his own generation by the will of God, fell on sleep, and was laid unto his fathers, and saw corruption ' (Acts xiii. 36). When I found that the services were to be held, I said that the first hymn should be the first in Gadsby's selection: ' Great God! how infinite art Thou!' the rest were chosen by my late dear friend, Mr. Banfield. At the services the Lord was felt to be present, and the spirit of worship and reverence was very manifestly an answer to prayer." (*Gospel Standard*, 1932, page 353.)

After the afternoon service, there were two " Addresses " presented to the honoured minister, one from his dear church and congregation, and one by the " Gospel Standard " denomination; each being accompanied with a cheque. That from the church was read by Mr. I. Farncombe, deacon; and that from the denomination by Mr. G. D. Clark, the chairman of the Societies. The text of the Addresses here follows:—

Address from the Church at Galeed.

To Mr. James Kidwell Popham, Minister of the Gospel, and Pastor of the Church and Congregation worshipping at Galeed Strict Baptist Chapel, Gloucester Road, Brighton.

Our beloved Pastor, and honoured servant of the Lord Jesus Christ,—We, the favoured church and congregation over whom it has pleased the Lord to place you as overseer, desire this day to acknowledge the great goodness which He hath bestowed on us, and to give unto Him the glory due unto His Name, for His abundant mercy in maintaining you over us during the long period of fifty years, to which your pastorate has now attained.

Many now in heaven, together with many now on earth, have abundant cause to bless the great Head of the Church that it pleased Him to place you over us, a pastor after His own heart to feed us with knowledge and understanding, seeing that your ministry has been blessed of God to the quickening of their souls into divine life, to their being turned from darkness unto light, and translated from the kingdom of Satan into the kingdom of God's dear Son. Many such seals has the Lord given you to your ministry,

confirming the word with signs following, and thereby testi-
fying abundantly that it has been His work to establish you
over us.

In your ministry, you have not shunned to declare the
whole counsel of God, and have sought to know nothing
among us save Jesus Christ and Him crucified, labouring
day and night in your prayers to God for us; and the fruits
of your labours are manifest, not only in our midst, but also
up and down the land where, in the providence of God, you
have been enabled to speak in His Name. As your concern
has been that we might be established in the truth, so also
you have not ceased to oppose and warn against the errors
and heresies that have lifted up their heads.

Besides your labours in the study and in the pulpit, your
pastoral visits to those who have been in trouble or sickness
have been owned and blessed of the Lord.

The promise with which the Lord graciously started you
in your ministry at Galeed, saying, "I will help thee," He
has abundantly fulfilled; so that you may say, "By the help
of God I have continued unto this day." Times of sickness,
times of trouble, times of opposition within and without,
times of darkness and calamity in the nation, have called
for an exercise of that divine help which was surely promised, and which has been as surely afforded as occasion
required.

May we this day give glory to the Lord for these His
mercies, praying that they may be continued to us, and that
you may yet be spared to labour in our midst for some
while to come.

And now, our beloved pastor, we desire you, as an expression of our sincere affection and esteem for you, to accept of
this cheque for £175. Also we wish to present to your
beloved wife this cheque for £30, as a small token of our
appreciation of her loving care for you, and the great kindness and practical sympathy which she has ever shown to
such as have been in trouble or need amongst us. The Lord
bless you both, and continue you to each other and to the
church, if it be His will.

To God the Father, God the Son, and God the Holy

Ghost, be ascribed all honour, praise, and glory, both now and for ever. Amen.

On behalf of the church and congregation,

Yours very affectionately,

J. BANFIELD* ⎫
I. FARNCOMBE. ⎬ *Deacons.*
S. F. PAUL ⎭

ADDRESS FROM THE " GOSPEL STANDARD " COMMITTEE.

Dear Friend,—The Committee of the " Gospel Standard " Societies felt that the celebration of your Jubilee as Pastor of the church at Galeéd would be a suitable opportunity for the denomination to recognize your long services as Minister and Editor, in which capacities you have received grace to " contend earnestly for the faith once delivered to the saints ", to the edification of many.

In this we would first gratefully acknowledge the goodness and mercy of Almighty God in raising you up and endowing you with the qualifications to preach the everlasting gospel of His grace, both by voice and pen. Thanksgiving rises to the great Head of the Church from many hearts that have been favoured to receive the living truth through you as His instrument, upon whom has been bestowed gracious ability to declare with unction and faithfulness the whole counsel of God. That health and strength have been sufficiently maintained for this arduous labour through so many years is also freely acknowledged to have been of the Lord's mercy.

But, secondly, as we are enjoined in the Word of God to " give honour to whom honour is due ", and also to " esteem very highly in love " the servants of the Lord for their work's sake, your friends in this country and also in that wider sphere where your ministry by pen has extended, owe a debt to you as God's servant for so long a period of faithful and willing service.

As a small expression of their gratitude to God, and a token of their love and esteem for you as His instrument, your many friends through the denomination ask your acceptance of the accompanying cheque for £225.

It is also in their hearts fervently to desire, if God's good

* This was signed before August 19.

pleasure, that you may be spared yet a while to serve Him
a little longer in the churches on earth; and that your latter
days may be spent in much enjoyment of the presence and
favour of the Lord, and cheered by many manifestations of
His Spirit's mighty work through you in the hearts of men:
as it is our firm persuasion that, when the will of God has
been accomplished concerning you in this world, you will at
that day, through grace, receive from the Lord, the righteous
Judge, a crown of righteousness.

It gives us great pleasure to-day to mingle our praises
with those of your own church and people, while at the same
time we sympathize with you all in the very severe loss you
have lately sustained by the death of two valuable deacons.

We recognize, too, the great goodness of God in giving
to you an affectionate helpmeet in Mrs. Popham, whom we
pray God to spare to you.

Yours in the bonds of the everlasting gospel,
Signed on behalf of the Committee,
G. D. CLARK, *Chairman.*

MR. POPHAM'S REPLY.

I think you will just have to excuse me from saying much.
Surprise at what has been read and presented to me is a
poor word; I am *astonished.* The church at Galeed has done
this to my utter amazement. No hint of it had reached me.
By a side wind, I knew that the Societies intended to say a
kind word to me. But of the presentation of the cheques in
these days of stress and poverty—poverty likely to increase
in the nation, and also therefore in the churches—I do not
know how to say what I feel. I desired no such expression
of the kindly feeling of my immediate friends, and if you
will allow me, I may just say this, that by my natural disposition I like not publicity, and it has been often very
difficult for me to realize that I have been known outside
my own small church and congregation. I hope that it may
please the Lord to grant that the few days remaining to me
here may be spent in His service.

For my wife, I would thank you most warmly. Our more
immediate friends know her worth, and the care that she
takes of me, and on her behalf I know that I may say that

I do very warmly thank you for what you have said and done.

Now, kindly accept this acknowledgment. "Thank you" is a poor word, but it expresses just what I feel; that is to say, my whole heart-felt thanks I render to you. If the Lord will spare me a little longer, then I hope to use what strength He gives me, and what grace He may bestow upon me, in His service, both in our own little place, and also in the churches by the magazine. I do thank you.

THE EVENING SERVICE.

Before commencing to read at the evening service, Mr. Popham spoke as follows:—

"I deeply feel my position to-day. I thank my friends who have come from various distances to show their kindly feeling to me: from Scotland, Blackpool, Bristol, Bath, Canterbury, and many other places. I speak the truth when I say I am conscious of not deserving such a demonstration of kind feeling as the congregations to-day manifest. I ask myself, 'What have I done?' I am a plain man, and a plain, much-tried preacher, and it is difficult for me to realize that I am known outside my own small congregation, or at most perhaps occasionally thought of by the readers of the magazines which I endeavour to conduct.

"I attribute all this to God's infinite kindness to me. Those of you who take the little pamphlet placed in the pews, 'A Humble Memorial to the Lord,' and care to read it, will know how I came to the pastorate which is now fifty years old; therefore there is no need, and it is not my intention to occupy your time with any personal references beyond what I have there made. If now I may just fade away from your view, and God will kindly make Himself 'Alpha and Omega' in this service, it will be an answer to many prayers. May He grant that answer. I design, by the help of God, to put man where he ought to be,—in the dust. And so I will read the words of the Holy Ghost as recorded by Paul in the iiird chapter of his epistle to the Romans."

Mr. Popham's text on this occasion was Rom. i. 16, 17: "For I am not ashamed of the gospel of Christ," etc. The sermon appeared in the *Gospel Standard*, 1932, p. 361.

P

On the wrapper for November appeared the following acknowledgment:—

A Word of Thanks.

To all my friends who, in thought, in prayer, in presence, in gifts, in letters and telegrams, took notice of my jubilee, my warmest thanks are hereby given. It is impossible for me to thank them otherwise. It was a remarkable day to me. When the deacons of the church at Galeed first named their design to notice the event, I emphatically said, " No! take no notice of it." But when they informed me that many people from different parts of the country had expressed their intention to come to any services which might be held and that it would be unbrotherly not to provide accommodation for them, I yielded. How the event became so widely known I am not aware. The day has passed. It was an astonishment, really a revelation to me. I never knew so many people thought so kindly of me. . . . Two thousand of the " Humble Memorial to the Lord " were printed and were distributed at the services. I hope the Lord was honoured in His own gracious answer to prayer. Prayer was made, and I believe answered, that He would be " Alpha and Omega " in the services. There was remarkable quietness. The services commenced and ended with the hymns. [This refers to the unauthorized striking up of the Doxology by someone in the congregation.]

With regard to the gifts made to me. I received them in the spirit in which no doubt they were given. I am painfully aware that, in this time of drastic " cuts " in wages and salaries, and the distress of business men, some of whom I personally know are living on their capital, and others who, retired from business, find their greatly-reduced incomes barely sufficient for their needs,—to such it was difficult to give as they did. With these facts before me I am surprised at the large sums given me. The Lord knows how the poor gave and perhaps squeezed out of their " abundant poverty ", and He will not permit them to suffer. Whatever was given was without my knowledge. If in any case or cases I can show my appreciation of the love which was in the gifts, it will be my pleasure. And while the Lord continues my life, and strength to labour, my desire is to do more work in His vineyard. To all whom I serve in the gospel, I say: " Brethren, pray for me." J. K. POPHAM.

Another remarkable event in the year was the death on October 22nd, of Mr. J. Kemp, the veteran pastor of Bounds Cross chapel, Biddenden; at whose funeral on the 29th Mr. Popham officiated, when a large concourse of people gathered. A Memoir, "John Kemp of Biddenden," was published the following year.

Mr. Popham's friends began to see old age setting in upon him, although he continued active in the ministry; frequent attacks of illness now overtook him, in which his soul was much exercised and sometimes greatly favoured: " Physically my strength is decaying. I am under a sort of necessity of seriously considering whether the time has come for me to resign the pastorate. For once on the Lord's Day I am physically able. In the afternoon I begin to cough and am so exhausted as to be unfit to go to the evening service. Yesterday on getting home from chapel I was hardly able to get upstairs and into bed. I feel for the dear people, but it may be the time has come for them to be tried. . . . Galeed is not to-day what it was some few years ago, and I am very troubled about it." Early in 1933 he wrote:—

" I was taken ill on Saturday, and am in bed and must remain for a few days; a touch of pleurisy. Yesterday the line, ' And if free grace, why not for me? ' dropped into my heart. Oh the sweetness, greatness, power, and glory of grace! grace abounding over the aboundings of my sin!* I am disappointed at having—as it seems—to remain here a little longer. My soul desires to be with the Lord and without sin. I fain would know the infinite glory of Rev. vii. 17: ' For the Lamb which is in the midst of the throne shall feed them, and shall lead them unto living fountains of waters. . . .' Yet am willing to live if only the Lord will make me a little more useful."

When partially recovered from this illness, Mrs. Popham

* How often we heard our dear friend express the desire that if anything were placed on his tomb-stone, it should be the words, " Where sin abounded, grace did much more abound " (Rom. v. 20). Grace was his favourite theme.

was taken ill, also his dear granddaughter. There was also
much illness at the chapel. Under these depressing circumstances, he received a gracious help which he thus described:

" . . . My rapidly fluctuating temperature makes it uncer-
tain whether I can go to any given service, but the Lord
was good, I took both services in the evening; but the
exhaustion was painful. Only God knows my difficulty in
believing such a person can be saved. Sins *seen* and *felt* and
a legal heart, make hard work. But the other day, Rom.
v. 17, 18, ' For if by one man's offence,' etc., came into my
mind, and then to stop objections it was as if an audible
voice said in my heart: ' Is this sufficient, canst thou believe
this ? ' Instantly I said, ' Yes,' and was O so surprised, the
surprise was intense. Then I asked to be taken home where
I should no more sin. But here I am sinning, mourning,
almost forgetting the kindness of God my Saviour! The
glory to me of Jer. iii. 1—4, 13, 14, I can never describe:
' . . . yet return again to Me, saith the Lord. . . . Only
acknowledge thine iniquity . . .' etc. Often my heart is
saying, ' I will confess my transgressions unto the Lord; and
Thou forgavest the iniquity of my sin.' I think at times my
day is near its close. At times I long to be in the holy
society. Here all, even the best, is mixed, in my case
marred. Yet I trust it is true that the Lord thinketh upon
me. Luke ii. 14 was good to me the other day, and I tried
to reach the unreachable,—' glory to God in the highest.'
He inhabiteth eternity. Still we hope—yourself and all
saints—we have begun the ' lasting song '. Rev. iv. 10, 11,
and v. 8—14 is the highest redeemed men and holy angels
can ever reach."

During the illness of Mrs. Popham, October, 1933, he
wrote:—

" An astonishing sense of the Lord's love came suddenly
and overwhelmed me while anxiously watching the sufferer.
I felt and said, ' I am not fit for such a favour.' While she
was suffering I asked her how she felt, and the answer was,
' I feel Jesus is my righteousness,' and some other words I
could not distinguish. In a sense this made all easy."

This is not the place to enter upon controversial matters,
but it would be unwarrantable to withhold all reference to

the grace bestowed upon Mr. Popham in his contest for the
truth in its purity and power, for the defence of which he
was ' set '. He was no trifler, no unprincipled combatant, no
mere rancorous fault-finder, no idle carping critic, but moved
with a jealousy for the honour of God and with the highest
of purpose to defend His truth, the Lord's servant laboured
on for the good of the churches, in face of increasing infirmities of age, afflictions, bereavement; frequently wearied,
sometimes sweetly encouraged.

In his position as minister and editor of the denominational magazine, Mr. Popham was for many years called
upon to stand firmly for the sacred truths which distinguish
the *Gospel Standard* churches from other Strict Baptists;
and very ably from time to time did he "contend for the
faith once delivered unto the saints ". Attempts were made
openly and also insidiously to obliterate the distinction, and
bold claims were made by certain magazines to represent
"*all* Strict Baptists ". In our magazine, at the annual
meetings of the Societies, in his ministry, and by correspondence our dear friend defended the truth, and insisted on the
necessity of the knowledge of it in the heart, and a consequent separation from error. It will have already appeared
to the enlightened reader how Mr. Popham was by especially
clear divine teaching equipped for this honoured and yet
thankless task. So far from being self-sufficient, however,
those who knew the secret exercises of his heart were aware
of the deep anxiety this duty was to him. On one occasion
when engaged in preparing a piece for the *Standard*, he
wrote:—

"May the Lord give you and others who know Him so
as to have access to and power over the Angel, who know my
heavy duty, power to pray for me. The serious falling of
the circulation causes questions as to my resignation. Yet
it may be taken as a painful sign of the low condition of the
churches. The —— [another magazine] may, probably will,
flourish and increase. I have no use for the sentimental
platitudes they feed on and offer their readers, having too
much exercise and trouble about myself and the present state
of Zion. Many appear strangers to the awful, glorious
perfections of God, so sanctifying to the Puritans."

The year 1934 brought its quota of trial. With his wife ill and worn down by lack of sleep, the pastorate of his beloved Galeed, his ministry elsewhere, and a fresh necessity for "contending earnestly for the faith" in regard to the denominational position,—interspersed with "seals to his ministry" which, with the encouragement of Deut. x. 12, 13, "moved my disobedient stupid heart a little this morning"— thus the year opened:—

"It is pitiful to see such weakness in respect of God's glory when the time for a stand has, in the judgment of some, evidently come. The remark about 'forcing a separation' is a poor, thin subterfuge. You and I must, in an important sense, stand alone. I feel the Lord's word in Isa. iii. 1—4 is true of C. How solemn and sad is the conclusion that the Lord has left us! How then can we stand and fight the good fight of faith? In personal experience we fail without Him. So in public contention for the truth. We each need the power of Christ to be faithful. The word, 'Be thou faithful unto death,' has caused many petitions to go up to the throne of grace for power and wisdom to keep it. Occasionally Solomon's bed is before me, and the duty of the men around it, and their swords. Woe is me that I am not valiant!

"I too well know what people mean and desire in so-called 'experimental preaching'; which is, as dear Mr. Marshall said to me fifty years ago, 'killing the churches.' The people have become J. C. Philpot's 'dram drinkers'. A few words of the letter of truth will, like a small piece of gold-leaf, spread over acres of error. Hence the painful mixing—'all are equal and alike'."

To that school of religious thought which considers neutrality, comprehensiveness, and universal charity synonymous with a 'Christian spirit', the severity and virility of Mr. Popham's truth-defending criticisms were naturally unpalatable and were resented; but relished by those whose regard for the serious concerns of eternity outweighed mere humanistic considerations. Such received the benefit intended by the gracious and skilful critic: for in his severest castigations Mr. Popham aimed first at the elucidation of Truth and second at the emancipation of the misguided. Concluding a

Review, after dealing faithfully with the error, he makes the following tender appeal:—

"Suffer this word from one who would not wantonly wound you. I am acquainted with the trials, temptations, burdens, and sorrows of the ministry; and having made innumerable mistakes, and grievously failed in the work, I need much mercy and forgiveness. Let us humbly seek the things wherewith we may edify one another, and be for the glory of God in the Church by Christ Jesus."

Since that appeal appeared ineffectual, the labour of a further lengthy letter in defence of the truth was the result. Its closing paragraphs will reveal how dear our friend held truth irrespective of personal considerations:—

"You ask, 'Is the Holy Spirit quenched?' My answer is, 'Yes, and that by yourself.' Who can imagine that He was other than quenched or grieved when you poured out that turgid stream of words, when you dishonoured the simplicity of the divine Being, allotting to Him parts, *Interior*, therefore necessarily, *Exterior?* when you degraded the mighty God by dogmatically affirming He was under the power of Satan for forty days? and when by the clearest implications you allowed your hearers to conclude that 'mental conceptions' of Christ were the same thing as the Spirit's inwrought thoughts of the Lord of Life? Without doubt in all the above errors you quenched the Spirit. You claim I Cor. xiii. I do not think you manifest it in your letter, while it is not difficult to imagine you aim at making it a cloak for your sermon. But I have proved you guilty of uttering error against the Lord. God's charity rejoiceth in the truth. You regard my criticisms as 'cold, carping, hyper-criticisms of mere words with their many and varied significations'. Surely you very seriously condemn yourself in the above sentence. 'Mere words in their varied significations' in theology? that is to say, in things pertaining to the Being of God! Let your words be loose, play with them as you will when dealing with human subjects; but when Jehovah is the awful, the profoundly mysterious Subject, either absolutely considered, or in His subsistence, then always, everywhere, in every sermon, speech, letter, they should be simple, incapable of a secondary meaning. . . . I really mean this

kindly, but fear it will annoy you. However I commit it to
God."

His faithfulness, which earned the gratitude of some,
brought attacks and abuse from various quarters; but as the
honour of God was involved, His servant " endured hardness
as a good soldier of Jesus Christ ". And the Lord gave
him some very sacred encouragements in his soul and in the
church. Several young men were led to publicly confess
Christ and join the church at Galeed during the years 1933,
1934, and 1935, while several of the old saints were removed.
Reference to these changes, mercies and judgments, occurs in
an address given by him at Galeed on December 27th, 1935:

" We have had much trouble in this year; thirteen or
fourteen of our church and congregation God has removed
by death; some in the providence of God have been removed
from the town; and so there has been a solemn dealing of
God with us. Well would it be for us if enabled to humble
ourselves under the mighty Hand that has touched us, dealt
so solemnly with us. But though He has taken away so
many godly people, and during the last few years has removed four deacons from us, we are not utterly cast down,
because He has continued mercy to us in giving us other
godly deacons. Do not pass that by as a small matter, that
the church should have godly deacons. And besides which
He has graciously given us recently new members, young
men, whom may the Lord teach and bring on their way, that
nothing may be lacking to them. May He help us to look
to Him for the future."

In the spring of 1934 a northern pastor and his church
felt moved to pass a resolution re-stating their adherence to
the *Gospel Standard* principles and practices as distinct
and separate from another element which has a more general
appeal. This was sent to Mr. Popham, who so cordially
approved of the statement that he felt disposed to submit it
to a number of ministers and deacons. Together with an
explanatory word, that statement was published in the
periodical over the signatures of those approving of this
re-affirmation.

During this anxious time Mrs. Popham was taken unwell
and a slight operation became necessary, and other trials

and cares weighed heavily on our dear friend. But the zeal of the Lord maintained him when tempted to lay down his weapons. A letter written at the time evinces a prevalence of grace over nature, for the discouragements were many:—

"I omit ——, as in my judgment the good man would still advise waiting. If it came to an inevitable stand he would make it, but anxiety to please all will always make him hesitate. I hope the clean fear of God moves me. Always I have protested that no personal conflict have I with any person; but for the essential glory of God's only-begotten Son. If I knew more of that gracious Person and Saviour, much more jealous and zealous would my heart be for His glory. But my sins, corruptions, ignorance, half-heartedness, make it difficult for me to move. However, the state of things among us, W.'s policy, the confusion of numbers of our poor people, makes imperative the uplifting again of the banner given that it may be 'displayed because of the truth', and a definite stand; though the necessity, for the moment, puts the initiative on the worst,—a thing of naught. . . . O that the Spirit of God would help us, move us by the fear, love, and desire for the glory of God in the Church by Christ Jesus! Galeed causes me hours of anxious fear night and day. I fear some will not stand in the hour of temptation which shall come on all the world to try them that dwell upon the earth. Shall I? this is a solemn question with me. . . . Hope seems in my heart that my long endeavour to keep open the wide gulf between [us] is now to be supported by action, and I am thankful it has come during my life."

The additional labour and exercise connected with this endeavour, with the anxiety of his wife's increasing illness, had a somewhat serious reaction on Mr. Popham and he was incapacitated for some weeks in April, 1934, and thus prevented from attending and preaching at the annual meetings of the "Gospel Standard" Societies. A letter sent to the chairman manifests that he was far from indifferent. An extract follows:—

"Dear Brethren and Friends,—God, who worketh all things after the counsel of His own will, hath prevented me from meeting with you to-day. The loss is mine. My desire for

you is, that you may seek Him who is full of grace and
truth, even though it be as seeing Him as departing from
the city and standing upon the mountain which is on the
east side of the city (Ezek. xi. 23). And thus seeing Him,
may power be given you to lay hold of His strength—('Let
him take hold of My strength, that he may make peace with
Me; and he shall make peace with Me,' Isa. xxvii. 5,) and
prevail upon Him to return and pour upon you the spirit of
prayer, as showers, that you may spring up as willows by the
water-courses; and thus may His glory be the *first* of your
desires to-day, and the *last*. . . ."

It may be permissible to here give a few notes made of
conversations during this illness: In March he was very ill
and said, "Will it not be wonderful to die in the Lord? I
find it sweating work to get to heaven. God has been so
good to me. I have said, 'Do take me home, Lord.' But
here I am, in pain. Have asked for submission, and the
other day could say, 'Thy will be done.' Could a little understand Paul (II Cor. xii. 9): 'Most gladly therefore will I
rather glory in my infirmities, that the power of Christ may
rest upon me.'" . . . *April 23rd*. Had been very low in
mind, far off and feared he should die and be lost after all;
but added, "I do not feel that now. The Lord kindly
reproved me by the word, 'How long will it be ere ye
believe Me?' (Num. xiv. 11) as if He said, 'Is all I have
done for you nothing?' It was as if all that had been
hidden, and I, an unusual sinner, faced with my sins! But
faith in the Lord Jesus revived. And if I should die to-day
[very deliberately spoken] you can tell the friends that I die
casting myself unreservedly upon the illimitable ocean of the
merits of the dear Son of God and His atoning sacrifice. It
will make no real difference, although I should die in the
dark; what He has done will stand." The dear man did not
die in the dark, as the sequel will show; and he had some
more work of faith and labour of love and patience of hope
to be exercised withal yet.

Not until after three months' absence could the good pastor
resume his preaching at his dear Galeed. On June 24th, he
preached for the first time, from Ps. lxxxix. 19; and in the
evening from Col. iii. 11. The substance of these two ser-

mons was printed (Monthly Sermon No. 308), and though brief they are full of spiritual power.

The publication of the God-honouring Movement (*Gospel Standard*, April, 1934) was the signal for a counter-publication, misrepresentation and abuse, with veiled threats of legal action, etc. At this juncture, it was suggested to Mr. Popham by the Societies' chairman whether it might not be well to let the denomination speak for itself in the matter, and a meeting was advertised and held in London on July 13th, 1934. There voted at that meeting for the continuance of the " Gospel Standard " as a separate body of churches, 407; against 28. A full report of the meeting appears in the *Gospel Standard*, 1934, pages 257—292. Unable to be present owing to his great weakness, Mr. Popham wrote a most able statement of our position, which was read. It is believed that prayer was given and answered that day, although very soon a movement was set on foot to counteract the decision. A Declaration was issued to canvass the churches, and a few unsuspecting friends unwittingly joined with the recalcitrants. But the decision had been made, and the dissentients were at liberty to withdraw their names from the list of accredited ministers; they were not excised by the magazine trustees.

All this sad display of vacillation on the part of a few, and the attempt to drive a wedge between friends by veiling the true cause of separation from the erroneous body, caused the dear leader much pain and sorrow. But not chiefly from external matters did his sorrow arise. Discerning the innermost cause of declension he wrote:—

" The report of the meeting will be printed. It will be a mercy if God is pleased to revive in any measure His gracious work in our midst. The line was drawn; the answer to the *one* question put before all our readers in the advertisement, was answered. But the *spirit* of the separation must come from Him who gave it to Philpot and his friends. It is now said that he was jealous of the Editor of the *Gospel Herald*, hence the controversy! A fearful statement! God is not acknowledged. The day may not be far distant when men will know He is a jealous God. May He teach us to ' stand in awe and sin not ' so as to provoke Him.

. . . One consideration must be emphasized,—that the needed, the God-honouring separation supported by so decisive a vote (407 against 28), will not, *cannot make us more spiritual*. . . . The very decisive vote will make the neutrals angry and encourage all who fear God. Knowing many of both sides I anticipate the displeasure; but 'if God be for us, who can be against us?' If the concern, the prayer, the desire for a clearer, more separate walk, should issue in the return of the Holy Spirit to the men who sigh and cry for the evils of their own hearts and among us, it will be seen and felt that the meeting and the vote were for the glory of God. I believe prayer was made of many. As the lack of unction in the ministry is one cause of our lean condition, so the return of God will be known by signs following. O that there might be such a revival! . . .

" The spiritual side of the question is the most, the only important side. The whole matter is solemn and weighty, but it will be a mercy if the absence of God's glory from us is the greater part of our burden and sorrow. If that is so with any of us, the rest will I think be made plain, and we shall see the good hand of God with us. Ps. lxxx. looks to only two objects: the first (4—13) humanly-speaking hopeless, the other (17—19) full of glory—a ground for a plea, a feeling of stedfastness. The first is in my opinion our case. May the second be given to us."

Another letter (written " with continued tremor ") has this good advice:—

" Jude 3 is best: ' Contend '—not with man, but ' for the common salvation, the faith once delivered unto the saints '. Gideon, Shamgar, Samson, David, and others have come to my mind at times. One petition has been in my heart—that the Holy Ghost might so shine in the hearts of the people when assembled, that the glory of the only-begotten Son would set their souls moving, believing, loving, adoring Him, and with the psalmist, ' hating every false way '."

The dear man's tenderness of conscience was at times very touching. To an intimate friend he made the following confession:—

" I fell in with the strong assertion without a thought or prayer. Seeking the Lord should have been the first. O my folly and sin! But through God's great goodness I got a good word Lord's Day afternoon: ' Whoso keepeth the fig tree shall eat the fruit thereof: so he that waiteth on his Master shall be honoured ' (Prov. xxvii. 18). O that I could live according to it! One mercy is left us—the throne of grace. Oh may we be enabled to avail ourselves of it! I want the nourishment of the Bread of Life, an *applied* truth. More and more the awful importance is in my heart. ' Aptness to teach ' is a solemn and heavy word. I am put to shame by such a Scripture. But Ecc. xii. 10, ' The preacher sought to find out acceptable words,' etc., has been a help and encouragement to me."

Similarly on another occasion, feeling he had spoken when silence would have been wiser, he said:—

" My conscience made me sorry to have taken up what ought to have been left in the hands of God. Oh that J. K. P. were not so forward to speak, act, and live in things in which he has no right to breathe! I desire to be kept more and more in the Bible. Yesterday Jer. iii. 1; Hos. iii. 1, were again made a sweet word to me."

Such tenderness of conscience, humility, and self-abasement may be taken by self-confident spirits to be a sign of weakness, but in reality it was just there where his strength lay,— in that secret exercise before God, that clearing of himself in repentance, prayer, and faith in the blood, merit, power, righteousness, and wisdom of Christ.

The additional strain of much correspondence, editorial work, and attendant anxiety, again manifested itself by a serious development in October, 1934, and the local doctor consulted another. His state of mind at this solemn juncture is best conveyed in his own language:—

" I may with great care be saved from the shakings and go on for a long time, *or* a serious crisis may suddenly come, and the end. The doctor does not advise tying me down to inactivity, as with the activity of my mind it would be irksome and even injurious. I am now face to face with a solemn thing. It is impossible for me to express the beauty I have seen in Mary's absolute submission to the Lord. ' And Mary said, Behold the handmaid of the Lord: be it unto me according to Thy word ' (Luke i. 38). With all my

unspeakable sins and iniquities, I have fallen down on the
infinite merits of the Lord Jesus Christ, and I plead and
believe His word spoken to me many years ago, 'Where I
am, there shall also My servant be' (John xii. 26). My
heart objects my unfaithfulness, but His faithfulness answers,
goes deeper than all my lack and sin, and reaches heaven. . . .
[After naming several sad denominational matters.] Oh, but
the absence of God from us is but little felt, or if and where
felt, not much confessed. We as a poor body much need His
gracious return. It may be His will to give me rest before
the crisis comes which I believe is coming.

"My love in the Lord to R. and to yourself. You have
always been a comfort to me and I thank the Lord for you.
When I am taken, help the people here as much as you can.
You will remember your promise to bury me.

Your ever affectionate and grateful friend,

Brighton. 1934.   J. K. POPHAM."

Submission and yet a yearning for rest is evident in the
midst of increasing languor and weakness, and the many
sorrows connected with the churches, besides the serious
illness of Mrs. Popham. In a letter arranging for a denominational prayer-meeting in London which he could not
attend, he wrote:—

"If I live and can go to chapel, one service will be my
utmost. The Lord can do without me, and if He would
shine on me I would gladly go to heaven. My poor wife is
still a great invalid, she is weakness."

This meeting was called in no perfunctory manner. The
terms of the announcement drawn up by Mr. Popham are
instructive and worth recording:—

"The true Church of God has always found times of
affliction of every sort to be times of special need, whether
personal, as Job xxiii. 1—5; David, II Sam. xv. 31; or
public and general, as in the return of the captivity under
Ezra and Nehemiah; or the judgments of God on His sinful,
sinning people, Joel i., ii. 12—18; Acts iv. 23—31; xii.
3—5; xv. 1—3. In each of the above cases the need was
very pressing, and prayer was the only resource, for the men,
the people, were feeble. They were led by the Spirit of
grace and supplications to the throne of grace; there 'the

arms of their hands were made strong by the hands of the mighty God of Jacob'; He 'taught their hands to war and their fingers to fight', and they overcame sin, the world, and the devil.

"No one belonging to us can doubt that the present time is with us a time of trouble. Will the Lord bow down His ear and hear us? Will He repent, as He sees us bending before Him, confessing our sins, humbling ourselves, and pleading the blood of Christ, and putting, as enabled, our sad and evil case into the hands of the Advocate with the Father, Jesus Christ, the righteous? (I John ii. 1.) With our condition much on my mind, I wrote to the Committee and suggested a day for humiliation, confession, and prayer; and it was agreed that such a day be held. . . . The good Lord give us one heart and one way in this matter, and grant power over the Angel, and thus bring down answers of peace, or rebuke and chastening, as shall be for His glory in us as a small body."

CHAPTER FIFTEEN.

" We are troubled on every side, yet not distressed."

1934—1936. Death of Mrs. Popham—a clear denominational statement—sustained—necessity for continued contention for defence of truth—resignation of Editorship--fresh preaching engagements—*Gospel Standard* centenary—desiring to serve while life spared—pointed questions—last publication—unflagging interest in cause of truth.

AFTER nine weeks' illness of a distressing nature, the Lord took to Himself on December 17th, 1934, Mr. Popham's devoted help-meet. Through this great trial, and in the constant anxiety of the ministry and his editorial duties, the Lord supported His servant by His Word. When in November his wife's case was pronounced hopeless, Mr. Popham wrote:—

"This is a terrible blow. Ps. lxii. 8: 'Trust in Him at all times, ye people, pour out your heart before Him; God is a refuge for us,' quieted me a little. Now I need submission. My petition for her is that the Lord would shorten tribulation's days, however dreadful the removal will be to me. Isa. xliii. 2, 3, supports me: 'When thou passest through the waters, I will be with thee,' etc."

After the sad event, in the struggle against natural rebellion, grace mercifully prevailed:—

"'Desolation' is the word which sets out my sad case. I feel shattered. At times it is all but intolerable. Yesterday was a sore day till the evening, when it seemed a near approach to rebellion if not the very nature of that awful sin. I try many times in the day to thank God for His great mercy in taking my precious one to Himself; for life to her, if she had recovered, would have been weakness and pain. But O my need of unreserved submission to the 'good and acceptable and perfect will' of God is very great. To labour in prayer seems to be the life set before me. . . ."

A brief "Remembrance" of Mrs. Popham (written, under evident sanctification of the sorrow, in Mr. Popham's concise style,) appeared in the *Gospel Standard*, 1935, page 79.* With a view to show how the grace of God supported and instructed His dear servant under the most desolating bereavement, a passage from the "Remembrance" is here transcribed:—

"In the midst of this grief, I saw the truth of what has often been said, viz.: that the life of God has its seat in the heart, not the brain. On one occasion I said to her:

'Christ is the Friend of sinners,
Be that forgotten never.'

Instantly a quiet, sweet smile lighted up her face. Whenever I said a few words of prayer, she was at once quiet, and distress went from her countenance. At another time I saw her lips moving, and asked if she was trying to pray, and again she smiled her utmost. I doubt not her heaven-

* See also 1936, page 189.

born soul responded to the good news, though her natural
power was gone. It was good and sweet to me, in the
sorrowful circumstances, to witness spiritual intelligence
when nature could not speak. The thought that this painful-
sweet may one day meet a similar case, and thus be to the
praise of the glory of divine grace, moves me to record it;
though it may appear somewhat of a mystery, because the
ordinary way of the manifestations [of grace] are by faith
apprehending and the mouth confessing: 'I believed, and
therefore have spoken.' . . . In shortening tribulation's day
for my beloved wife, the Lord has made me desolate, and I
would continually submit to His most holy, wise, and good
will."

Only his most intimate friends knew *how* desolate the
bereavement rendered God's dear servant, for he did not
wear his sorrow on his arm. During the long and painfully
anxious ordeal of Mrs. Popham's affliction, Mr. Popham was
occupied with—among other things—the necessity of preparing and issuing a clear statement of the denominational
position, the re-affirmation of which in the previous July
having been made by some an occasion of schism, and misrepresentation was rife. This statement appeared in the
Gospel Standard of January, 1935, in the form of a New
Year's Address. It is a temperate statement evidently written under a solemn sense of obligation for the defence of
truth, with a view to dispel misunderstandings, and written
in love, with grief for the necessity. This effort made, under
such painful and difficult circumstances, for the maintenance
of the doctrinal and practical standing of the *Gospel
Standard* Strict Baptists, met with some abuse and considerable approval. This is referred to incidentally in a letter to
a friend:—

"It is a strength to me to know you appreciate the
Address. Writing it (after destroying one written with
labour, which was true but sharp) was singularly easy.
Several appreciations have come to me. If but my dear one
could have been here she would have very warmly entered
into them; but the Lord is wise and good in this so grievous
a dispensation, and He has not left me without help and
comfort."

Q

In some respects the last Annual Address in the magazine, January, 1935, was one of the most important he ever wrote, and one of the most difficult. It commenced: "The time has come for a plain statement of our exact position to be made. . . . On the grief it is to me to take up the case I will not dilate . . . to speak of them as opponents is a sorrow." The concluding sentence is, "May the holy Pattern set before us by the apostle Paul be with us (Phil. ii. 5)." The re-reading of that Address might be fruitful even yet in breaking down some prejudices, through the mercy of God; and therein it might be true, as in respect to his ministry we believe it is, "He, being dead, yet speaketh."

Many long years of loving valuable service to the denomination was now drawing to a close. Age, bereavement, sorrow, disappointment, his approaching end, were among the influences which brought our friend to the decision that his editorial work in connection with the two denominational magazines must cease; and accordingly he gave the trustees notice in January, 1935, and his resignation took effect in June of that year. He wrote of this to an intimate friend:—

"It is better that it should be now than that illness or death should throw on the trustees the election of a successor, as it were, in a moment. . . . Increasingly I feel unable for the work; sometimes in the night I literally shake as the next month's work stares me in the face. It is a sad pleasure to think that my work is so near an end. I have of late prayed for a love visit and then to depart and be with Christ. One service on the Lord's Day is quite enough, though I go twice, but in weariness. I desire, however, to acknowledge God's goodness. He helps me, and some appear to receive good."

His formal resignation is here subjoined:—

To the Trustees of the *Gospel Standard* and *Friendly Companion.*

Dear Friends,—Herewith I formally confirm my resignation from the Editorship of the above magazines which I verbally gave on the 11th inst., to take effect in June,—that is, the June number will be the end of my office. My age and attendant infirmities make this step necessary. My endeavour to continue till June gives you time to elect my

successor and him time to prepare the July number. A point
has been before me since my verbal resignation—that it is
better that I should do it now than struggle on until I broke
down perhaps suddenly and thus throw you into confusion.
The severance from the magazine work will be attended
with regrets. My shortcomings are before me and I confess
them before the Lord. Perhaps the Lord has made a little
use of my unworthy pen. *Among my regrets* in connection
with the work, *my endeavour to keep open the breach
between ourselves and the E.V. denomination has no place.*
I have much work in secret in confession of sin, *but that
endeavour has no place,* though a humble tender spirit may
not have been unmixed with my own spirit. To the Lord I
look for forgiveness of all the sin, defects, lack of love for
Him, humble, holy zeal for His glory, and desire for the
good and edification of His people, that have been in my
poor work. I thank Him for the honour of being spoken
and written against, and for the love, kindness and appreciation shown me by many both at home and abroad.

  Believe me, dear friends,
    Yours affectionately in the truth,
January 22nd, 1935.   J. K. POPHAM.

Although the defence of the gospel for which Mr. Popham
was 'set' (Phil. i. 17), was to him a very serious business,
yet there were occasions when his observations concerning
his critics were somewhat amusing, so true and laconic; but
he never allowed himself in jesting. On one occasion at a
meeting in committee he could not resist an opening for
facetious repartee. Of this he wrote:—

"I left the meeting guilty for the lightness I fell into.
Psalm li. is much with me, verse 10 my text last evening:
'Create in me a clean heart, O God, and renew a right spirit
within me.'"

We believe he never was known to utter an unbecoming
word when in the pulpit: gravity, solemnity, dignity ever
marked his utterances. And the influence pervaded the
chapel, as has often been remarked. Indeed, in conversation
also, he was remarkably enabled to follow Titus ii. 8:
"Sound speech which cannot be condemned;" at once an
example and a reproof to many.

In March, 1935, within three months of his great bereavement, his daughter, Miss Popham, was taken seriously ill. The man of God is *seen* in trouble. As a father he was exceedingly tender. Grace did not make him a stoic. Though largely inured to trial, grace taught him the need of constant exercise, and mercy brought the peaceable and spiritual fruit of righteousness to him:—

"It is truly a blow; but while feeling crushed it came into my mind, 'Not in anger but from His dear covenant love.' The effect was good; I could only weep tears of confession of my dreadful sins, melt before the Lord, with a strong desire now in my heart to say, 'Thy will be done.'"

Mercifully for them both, Miss Popham's affliction was brief, and she was enabled to tend her beloved father to the end of his days.

On being released from the heavy responsibility and exacting labours connected with the magazines, Mr. Popham was not idle. To the surprise of his friends, he recovered strength sufficiently to visit again and preach at several places, including Wiltshire and Lancashire, where several testimonies of real blessing on his labours were given. The Lord was very manifestly with His dear servant and his ministrations on those journeys left behind a savour of Christ. He was remarkably helped, too, in preaching the annual sermon for the "Gospel Standard" Societies in April, 1935; the text being Lam. iii. 40. By very many it was felt to be a most salutary word preached by one of ripe experience and under the weighty influence of the Spirit of truth.

As an expression of gracious humble discernment in one so well schooled, the following deserves record:—

"My own ignorance of Christ is matter for sorrow, and occasions errands to the only effectual Teacher. I see the poor churches going astray in seeking *evidences*. They are being fed on evidences. Hence much if not the whole of our present confusion. From wrong impressions of it, doctrine is not relished. Legality is one result, and sad turning away from the precept. Reflection on my own ministry is most sad to me. The word which [first] laid the ministry on my heart with some conviction, is often a grievous word and a sorrow: Isa. lii. 11, 12. My confession is that I have not been ' clean '. My heart backslidings are before me from the first till now. The retrospect is most painful, and the thought of the pulpit is often heavy to me. A comparatively young preacher, not a pastor, came to see me, and I felt I would rather tremble than walk in his unhumbled boldness."

When in August, 1935, meetings in connection with the centenary of the *Gospel Standard* magazine were held, such was Mr. Popham's affectionate interest in the cause of God and truth that although suffering from an attack of laryngitis, he travelled to London and sat on the platform during the afternoon meeting, though prevented from speaking a word. It was truly touching to witness this exertion made to openly declare his unflagging concern. The next day he addressed a letter of encouragement which, by his request, was printed in the *Gospel Standard* within the report of the meetings. His tireless solicitude and tender regard are now sorely missed. More than a touch of real pathos lies in his hopefulness regarding the return of God's glory, expressed in a letter to a friend:—

"The atmosphere of the meeting I attended—and of the whole day, from reports I had—raised hope in me that the remnant might yet be revived, and some of the younger people see the Lord's returning glory, as we who are near the end of our pilgrimage may not see. Oh it will be wonderful to see the power and glory of God among us! The degeneration which I see is most painful; our young people do not know it. What changes I have witnessed! what divine goodness have I been the recipient of!"

In October, 1935, Mr. Popham baptized personally for the last time, although several were afterwards baptized at Galeed by deputy. The number of members in the church at the beginning of his pastorate was 70, and at his death 107.

Mr. Popham's loyalty to the throne was intense and real, but to him it did not consist in excusing everything the sovereign or the government did. He owned a greater Sovereign. The following opening sentences of a sermon preached on the occasion of the death of king George V., in January, 1936, illustrates this sanctified loyalty:—

"We are here this evening under a great cloud, a great

sorrow: God has taken from us a good king. It may be that we have not fully recognized the goodness of his character and reign. We have lived quietly for some years, and he has reigned wonderfully. We have much to be thankful for in the example he has left us. It has transpired that his grandmother, the late Queen Victoria, had a promise from him that he would read the Bible every day; and that he has done so. At the jubilee last year (1935), it was mentioned that there has been a beautiful family life, that the evenings in his family were mostly spent just simply as we ourselves live. There was a pure court, purer perhaps than there has been in the past, for which we again should thank God. He appears to have won not only the respect but the love of the whole empire. He was by proclamation, on his ascension to the throne twenty-five years ago, a Protestant. It could have been wished that no word, no act, against that should have been. But when he congratulated the pope, that man of sin, it was contrary to his oath, his proclamation. This is a word concerning him for whom I personally have ever had the greatest respect, as also for his grandmother, the great Queen Victoria."

Without hardly daring to expect consent, but as a matter of affection, the committee requested Mr. Popham to consider preaching the annual sermon in April, 1936. The veteran preacher, the favoured man of God, in accepting the invitation, replied:—

" My age warns me to be careful. Specially this week I have *felt* to be the old man; it may be only the effect of the trying weather and the long dreary winter. This feeling of tiredness and indisposition to work is rather new to me. . . . After all, we are in the hands of a good God, where in our right minds we desire to be in all matters, specially those which affect the Church of God. His things are solemn and first. If I had more grace I should be more watchful of His operations in my own soul in all things. My lacks are more and more before me, specially in the ministry, and I am often much depressed and discouraged. I would be thankful that Christ is not, never will fail nor be discouraged. But we are in a black night and apparently near a world judgment. The Lord will arise and shine on

His Church, but not until the judgment falls on us and the nations. Oh to be in the chambers! Though I judge we as a small remnant are in a low condition, I am at a point as to who is the chief sinner. Our inward condition is known only to ourselves and to Him who will cause His churches to know that He it is who searches the hearts and reins; and who will give to every man according to his works. How I tremble at times at the Word of God!"

To the great surprise of all and the joy of the godly, Mr. Popham attended and addressed the afternoon meeting, and preached in the evening from Eph. iv. 4, 5—an exhortation to unity in the truth, unctuously spoken and most fitting for the last solemn message to the denomination.

The annual sermon was preached by him on twenty-seven occasions; and very remarkable discourses they were. Additionally, for many years he presided over the afternoon meeting, when his addresses were the well-weighed utterances of one feeling the great responsibility of the position he occupied. When it is considered that the mornings of those annual days were spent in attending committee meetings where in serious matters decisions were required, exacting much close sustained thought, it will be recognized that in this connection alone Mr. Popham's labours for the churches were considerable, for which he ever owned the goodness of God in strengthening and helping him. Many who were favoured to listen to his addresses and sermons at these denominational meetings returned to their various places strengthened in faith.

Never far from his mind in these later days was the approaching day of death. To it he frequently alluded. A deeply heart-stirring reference is extracted from a letter to a son in the faith:—

"I shall be glad to see you at the service if the Lord is there. May you be enabled to engage His divine Majesty to be present! Oh what death reigns when He is absent! Have you R.'s works? If not, will you accept the copy I have? I am clearing out many of my books, as my reading days are closing, and I would like my dearest friends to possess some little remembrance of me. . . . THE BOOK I desire to be more and more graciously acquainted with in the letter, spirit, and power, is the *inspired Volume*. Recently one night when awake some of the gracious testimonies the Lord has made over to me came to my mind, and I felt and said, ' I could die on these;' then the atonement came before me and I said, ' I could die on that,' and could not forbear to ask the Lord to take me to Himself without further delay."

Later he wrote:—

" A feeling possesses me at times of desiring to use my remaining strength in the best and *most solemn service the world knows,* even though my sense of coming short grows, and I am often ashamed before the best Master, of my poor service. Yesterday was a good day to me, especially in the evening. Text: Prov. viii. 34, 35. Not once in many years have I thanked the Lord for His gracious assistance as I did last night; the *rule* is I am too distressed and ashamed to do more than mourn before Him after preaching."

Yet again, the dear aged saint and minister freely expresses himself to his closest friend:—

" I can hardly believe my sermons can be of service to the churches, they are too poor. I am worn out, and truly retirement would be best for me. For a few hours I seem to pant for God, then slip down into a dark and dead state. My age naturally has dulled perception,* as it has crippled my body. I fear I shall only be a burden, if nothing worse, to the church. . . . My engagements look formidable; yet I am sure the Lord is sufficient for them, but will He be ? I feel *withered*, really *tired*. O to be kept from murmuring! What need have I of special grace, and yet seem not to have ordinary grace. Yesterday Ps. lxxxvii. 7 attracted me; it was my text this morning, but I failed, and am sorry."

He was much comforted in the midst of the desolation brought by his bereavement, to which he alluded in a sermon, April, 1936: " Earthly comforts die and are taken away; and the vacant places made by their removal cause much pain. But sometimes there comes in place thereof, the Lord Himself; then you are content, you want nothing else. You can honestly say in this comfort, ' Whom have I in heaven but

---

* This was never manifest in his ministry.

Thee?' He supplies all vacant places, and brings a little
heaven into the heart."

Being searched himself and tried, he was capable of putting close pointed questions to others. To a minister he thus
wrote:—

". . . It clearly appears that your steps were directed to
B. for a distinct purpose. Man's goings are of the Lord;
how then can a man understand his own way? Divine
purposes ripen. . . . Was it long after that first visit when
conviction of sin and condemnation came into your conscience? and then mercy, forgiveness, and liberty and, following that experience, the call to preach? All the ways of
God for and in His people and ministers have a stamp of
divinity on them. 'All Thy works praise Thee, and Thy
saints shall bless Thee.' As viewed from a distance those
works appear wonderful and produce humility, worship,
adoration, and confidence. 'Who delivered us from so great
a death, and doth deliver: in whom we trust that He will yet
deliver us.'

"Do you find the Lord with you in your own experience?
and in the ministry? We need to know something of the
hell of sin within us and the aboundings of grace over sin;
then the unction of the Holy One in the labour of the
ministry. Do your vines appear to be flourishing and the
grapes give a good smell? Do you and the people perceive
the faithful and true Witness expressing approval of your
works while reproving for some things unworthy of your
profession as the angel of the church? Oh but it is solemn
to be a minister and a pastor! I Tim. iv. 16; II Tim. ii.
15, are solemn words to me, and constant sighs and confessions does Isa. lii. 11 cause me."

Not much evidence of "dulled perception" in that!

In June, 1936, Mr. Popham was taken suddenly ill, col-
lapsing through the great heat. The doctor "came just in
time to keep me alive and work disappointment; for while
I was conscious and could pray, I was earnestly entreating
the Lord to take me to Himself, so that I should sin no
more. Now I am recovering, but very weak." The deacons
were at their minister's house at the time of his collapse, and
then retired to one of their houses where prayer was made

for him. In faith Mark xi. 24 enabled them to believe that
the valued life would be spared. The doctor's own verdict
was, "You have had a serious illness and a *miraculous*
recovery."

Submission to the Lord's will and constraint of love
evidence themselves in the following relation of this illness
and its effect through grace:—

"In the night of Wednesday at 1.30 the Lord came to me.
First, the Fountain opened for sin, etc.; and I fled to it
and was cleansed. Then I saw the Trinity, and worshipped
and praised each Person; and then Jehovah in Unity. Oh
the nearness of the Lord to me and my nearness to Him!
Then Isa. liv. came to my mind, and my weak body could
scarcely bear the weight, power, and glory of vers. 7—10:
'For a small moment . . . but with great mercies will I
gather thee,' etc. I will I may never forget this wonder to
the vilest, most polluted, corrupt creature on earth. It broke
me to pieces, melted me into the sweetest contrition and self-
abhorrence; and then I believed I should live and not die,
and ventured to say to the Lord I would gladly use every
ounce of strength I might ever have in His service, and He
seemed to accept me in that."

The following Lord's Day, to the astonishment of all, Mr.
Popham was actually in the pulpit, preaching from Ps. ii. 6,
which was preceded by a relation of his illness. (See *G.S.*,
229—236.) Within a few weeks he was again at his loved
employ, fulfilling many engagements in various parts besides
preaching at his dear Galeed. But a recurrence of illness
soon again laid him aside. He thus wrote:—

"I am again ill. Though I kept it from the people, I was
ill in the pulpit last evening. . . . I am feeble, too feeble to
move. Engagements have to be cancelled. The Lord is very
good to me. In the train coming home yesterday Eph. i. 6
fell on my soul with such sweetness I could not avoid weeping [a *most* unusual thing with him]. In regard to having
to cancel engagements, the Lord's word to David, 'It was
well that it was in thine heart,' etc., sustains my hope that
I was not wrong in desiring to do what He will not permit
me to accomplish."

After a few days' rest, we find him again fervently desiring to be engaged: " Preach I must if able to get into the pulpit. It is my best place. I am going to H. to-day and P. to-morrow, if all is well."

Again in a sermon at Galeed, September 27th, 1936:—

" . . . My days are short of course; and some of you know that in a recent illness God was so near to me that all I wanted was to die, never to sin again. But I am spared a little longer; and if spared and enabled to preach, I hope to continually try to set up before you—though feebly, inadequately—this wondrous Person, the Lord Jesus Christ, my Hope, my Life, my Eternal All; and to warn you who know Him not, that dying in your sins you will find the power and terribleness of that two-edged sword that goes out of His mouth. He will smite you with it. May He save you in His great mercy; bless the church; grant that we may still be an orderly little church, walking in the fear of the Lord, and in His ordinances blameless; comforted by the Holy Ghost."

In the autumn of 1936, Mr. Popham issued his last separate publication (except the monthly sermon), entitled, " The Form of Sound Words: the substance of five sermons from II Tim. i. 13."*

But poor dear honoured man, though richly blessed by his God, in respect to the Church on earth his last days were his worst, and being not a stoic nor a superficial optimist, he keenly felt the sad declension:—

" Surely God has forsaken us! I have a heavy loss to meet, but that is not so trying as the evidence, to say the least, of apathy. I suppose the title is enough to create a smile,—' Do we not know and possess the Form of Sound Words ? ' As editor and leader—you cannot separate the two—you can only feel discouraged and all but hopeless; your position is most trying, yet you are safe. The day is coming when you will see that your God has heard your sighing, and all the time of it had set you in safety from him that puffeth at you. Error ever finds company. You

* A notice of this truly valuable and weighty production (still obtainable from Farncombe's, price 9d.,) appeared in the *Gospel Standard*, page 393.

have a good God. He is stronger Who is in you and Whose
cause you maintain, than all that may rise against you. Very
solemn is Isa. liv. 16, 17. *Two* sides. Oh to be in verse 17:
' No weapon that is formed against thee shall prosper,' etc."
Whenever at all able he would be in the pulpit, though
frequently quite unfit. In a sermon on Lord's Day evening,
October 25th, 1936, he bore the following wonderful testimony to the support of grace:—

" When I reached home from the service this morning, I
was so exhausted, I mentally said, I shall go out no more
to-day. Instantly, powerfully, sweetly, this great word
dropped into my heart, ' My grace is sufficient for thee '
(II Cor. xii. 9). It melted me into a wonderful happiness,
and I said, ' Lord, I can go on that word.' And I am here.
He knows my physical condition, of which I do not wish to
speak, but I do want to honour Him. His goodness once
or twice this afternoon was so powerful that I could only just
bear it. A verse of a hymn often sings in my heart; I do
not sing it—it sings in my heart; it did so this afternoon:

> ' Thou shalt see My glory soon,
> When the work of grace is done;
> Partner of My throne shalt be;
> Say, poor sinner, lovest thou Me ? '

The word ' soon ' as I measure it, may not be God's measure.
He may spare me longer than I think He may. But O the
glory, the wonder of grace! and it is greater to me than to
any of you—than it can be to any of you, because of
my unusual sinfulness and sins. And I say again and
again, ' But, Lord, my life, my sinful life, my unprofitable
life!' But He will not listen to me; He just, as it were,
covers it all. The infinite merit of Jesus Christ is sufficient.
On that I live, on that I shall die. And I thought one thing
that I would say to you this evening was this: If I do not
speak much more, this is my testimony, that what I have
preached to you these many years, I am now living on. I
am supported by those precious doctrines which I have
known and preached very feebly, and I believe the day is
not very distant when I shall be with Him. . . . I am willing to bear what He has laid on, as long as grace is with
me as it has been this afternoon. I would not be without

the affliction; my present choice is that since He has sent it, I would not be without it; and if He will use me a little longer, and His will is that I should continue in this physical condition [he was in almost constant pain], what is there to fret about? what is there to murmur at? O what a beautiful word of Paul to the Romans: 'I beseech you by the mercies of God that ye present your bodies a living sacrifice, holy, acceptable unto God. . . . That ye may prove what is that good and acceptable and perfect will of God.'

"Now, brethren, I know this is the religion that will save you, if the Lord gives it you. You will never be lost if He gives you this religion; and perhaps some of you younger people, when I am taken may remember some things that I have said, and this among them, that this religion, that is to say, *the grace of Christ alone, will save you.* If you lack that, you will never be in heaven. May the Lord take us into His care, and bless the little church here. We are an aged congregation and church mostly, but may He still be with us. And when He takes me from you, may He still be with you, and hold you up, and keep you in His clean fear. O that *clean* fear! It has shined in my eyes. 'The fear of the Lord is clean.' It will keep you from sinning, and it endures for ever."

Towards the end of the year 1936 we find him suffering almost constant pain, baffling to the doctors, and ultimately pronounced incurable. This is how the news affected him:—

"Though I had a desire to die, the thought of long suffering was distressing. It does not necessarily mean that I shall have incessant pain, but attacks. Yesterday and to-day it has been acute, but a feeling that I am in God's hand has quieted me. Last evening it was so bad I could only speak for a short time. But we both have a good God. You have, I hope, many years before you of life and usefulness in the Lord's vineyard; my days may be few. The Lord heal you, if it please Him; if not, give you grace to submissively endure to the end of the trouble. The one thing I desire to live for is to preach. The Lord appears to be gracious to the people. If the King of glory pays you a love visit, He will be welcome and almost make you oblivious to your ailment."

CHAPTER SIXTEEN.

" Where I am, there shall also My servant be."

1936—1937. Eighty-ninth birthday—retrospect—illness—messages to Galeed—again occupies pulpit—dying counsel—the funeral.

His eighty-ninth birthday, December 20th, 1936, was spent quietly with his family, all being present except his son in South Africa. He was very gratified by the visit of four ministers from the Free Presbyterian Church of Scotland who were in London. His predilection for the godly Scot was proverbial:—

" On their arrival I said to them, This is to be a Scotch service. And it was throughout. I much appreciated it."

The state of Mr. Popham's mind at the end of this his last year is best ascertained in letters from which extracts are here subjoined:—

" A desire and a design to do whatsoever we do to the glory of God can only be in our hearts by the grace of God. What painful proof one has of the self-seeking, pride, arrogance, and evil of every sort! O the blessing of humility! But to be truly humble we must be *humbled;* humbling *circumstances* alone are insufficient. The ' mind that was in Christ' must be breathed into us by the good Spirit of Christ. Thus favoured, a sinner can do all to the glory of God. An old man is an old sinner. By grace, he may be also ' a little child ' and ' die an hundred years old '. O if it may be so with me! I wish there might be less and less folly emerging. . . . O that Christ would come and dwell with us all and always! My conscience bore witness against me a week ago that I was not straight with John xiv. 23, and yet the Lord Jesus came, only He did not abide. Yet I loved Him a little and my heart melted.

" When I look back upon my long life and ways I am more ashamed and fearful than I can express: ' O Lord, righteousness belongeth unto Thee, but unto us (me) shame and confusion of face.' How much we shall see of the New Year we shall enter in a few hours we know not. Added to my years is my daily affliction and pain. The future is wisely hidden from us. May we be enabled to commit our way to Him who has been so gracious to us in the past. I have now entered my ninetieth year and so must not expect to remain here much longer. ' I am a stranger on the earth: hide not Thy commandments from me.' "

The following was written to the daughter of an old pilgrim the same age with himself:—

My dear Friend,—. . . It is a mercy for me that the Lord's people can pray for me. I am pleased to hear of dear Mr. B. He, like myself, is approaching the end of this mortal race; he so runs as to obtain. The same is, I trust, my aim. Forgetting the things which are behind, he is reaching after the things which are before, and pressing toward the mark of the prize of his high calling of God in Christ Jesus. Oh what a crown of glory awaits him! what a harp! what a sight of the King in His beauty in the land which is, for the moment, very far off! As a family, how you will miss him, his counsels and love; but you will perhaps see him suffer so as to feel thankful for his everlasting release and entrance into life immortal.

Give my love to dear Mr. B. and all the family.

Yours affectionately,

Brighton. December, 1936.   J. K. POPHAM.

The year 1937 opened with weakness and pain, and yet all-sufficient grace was manifested. How unflagging was our dear friend's interest in the denomination and in the cause of truth generally, is seen in a message to the " Gospel Standard " Committee in January, and read in the evening to the friends assembled for prayer and thanksgiving for the nation's deliverance in connection with the abdication of Edward VIII. It reads:—

Dear Friends,—Unable to meet you, I write this from my bed to wish your meeting may be owned and smiled on by the Lord Jesus, that He may give the Spirit of grace and supplications; also of thanksgiving for the most wonderful deliverance to the nation and empire: a deliverance we could hardly hope for in the face of the paganism, modernism, and all the evil much prevailing. But God is great in goodness, patience and power. May conviction of personal sins, denominational sins, prevail so far as to bring sincere confessions, and faith in the Person, blood, and righteousness of Christ prevail so as to prevent despair.

Your affectionate friend,

J. K. POPHAM.

He was able with difficulty to preach on the morning of January 31st, and then took to his bed. He developed an incessant cough, which was very distressing. His constant desire was to be taken to heaven, but prayed for submission to live if it were God's will. Not until February, 1937, did the modern Mr. Valiant-for-Truth relinquish writing the monthly letters to the young people for the *Friendly Companion*. The intimation of this is so characteristic that a quotation seems fitting:—

" Please excuse my not writing the usual ' Monthly Letter '. I am too ill to continue it. Kindly tell my young friends this, to me, sad fact: I shall write no more monthly letters. They will still have my best wishes for their temporal and eternal interests. . . . I am still in the same condition of body, often longing to depart and be with Christ which will be far better. Recently one of the worst, if not the very worst, attack of pain went in the pulpit with me and continued. It is still with me but not so severe. Contradiction though it is, I want to say if I can be of any help, let me."*

This illness continued and increased, congestion of the lungs supervening. During the time he addressed frequent letters to his beloved church and congregation, evincing his tender care for them; a few extracts of which here follow:—

February 7th, 1937.—. . . Now I ask your prayers for me in this heavy trial, that I may say from my heart, " Thy will be done in earth as it is in heaven." I am in waters, rivers, fire, but do not believe I shall either be drowned or burnt. Pray that I may gain by this trading. If I am restored to you, may I come in some measure of the fulness of the blessing of the gospel. The Lord has not left me comfortless, according to His Word; He has made it good: " Because I

---

* He had heard that his correspondent was afflicted and, intrepid, made this suggestion! Truly he " Looked not on his own things but on the things of others."

live, ye shall live also." My absence from you is a trial
which I desire may be sanctified to me—you are in my heart
to die and live with you. Seek grace to be as a company
" following on to know the Lord ". " Seek the Lord and His
strength, seek His face evermore." Walk in love; mind not
high things; wait for the power of the Holy Ghost to enable
you to fear the'Lord, to reverence His holy Majesty in His
dealings with us. In all things, by all means, labour to enter
into His rest and to grow in the knowledge of Christ, in
whom dwell all the riches of mercy, grace, righteousness,
peace, and truth.

14*th*.—. . . To the communicants I would say, May the
Lord give you the divine welcome which He gave to the
Church of old: " Eat, O friends, yea, drink abundantly."
The free gospel table to which you have come is a remembrance of infinite love and suffering. Avoid the party spirit
into which the Corinthian church fell and for which it was
reproved and condemned by the Lord through His servant
Paul. If one sits down to the Table with enmity against
another, does it not come near to eating and drinking unworthily ? O brethren, avoid, flee from so grievous a sin,
and seek grace to remember Him whose glorious essential
Name is love. . . .

Note of a visit, Feb. 10*th*, 1937.—Speaking of one disaffected,
he said: It is the warp of prejudice; only the great Zerub-
babel can reduce the mountain to a plain. None need repentance and forgiveness as I, and I have prayed that the Lord
Jesus, who is exalted a Prince and a Saviour for to give
these two great blessings, will give them to me. Reviewing
my life, I thought of what Covell said, " If you want to
make thorns for your dying pillow, walk carelessly." I have
walked badly,—proudly, unthankfully, carnally, selfishly, (I
could not exhaust the long catalogue;) but—though this is
not my dying pillow; perhaps I shall preach again—I have
no thorns. I thought of Paul's word, " The Son of God who
loved me and gave Himself for me;" and I said, " But that
was for Paul, Lord." It was as if He then said, " And for
you too." I am never without pain—not always acute—but
I thought of that:

R

" His way was much rougher and darker than mine;
    Did Christ my Lord suffer, and shall I repine ? "

I am in the fire, but He is fulfilling His word to me, " When
thou passest through the waters, I will be with thee; and
through the rivers, they shall not overflow thee: when thou
walkest through the fire thou shalt not be burned; neither
shall the flame kindle upon thee." This is the will of God;
the " good will of Him that dwelt in the bush ". The Lord
only knows what Galeed has been to me—there is still a
little remnant of gracious souls left. When Mr. White (the
first pastor) was on his death-bed they sent and asked him
what the new chapel was to be named. He said, " Galeed "—
a heap of witnesses. God has made it that. It was as if
the Lord said to me the other day, " Them that honour Me
I will honour." I said, " Lord, have I been enabled in any
little measure to honour Thee in my ministry ? " It appears
to me that He is honouring me now, and a part of that
honour is that He inclines the people to attend the services
as if I were there. I cannot express how precious Christ is
to me now. I can say that every day He gives me some
token of His love.

To the Church and Congregation.

February 21st.—As we are in a common affliction we need
to be " strengthened with all might by the Spirit, according
to His glorious power, unto all patience and longsuffering
with joyfulness, giving thanks unto the Father which hath
made us meet to be partakers of the inheritance of the saints
in light." I pray God may make known to you all " what
is the riches of the glory of the mystery among the Gentiles,
which is Christ in you the Hope of glory ". And may the
services to-day be made by the Holy Ghost sanctifying to
your souls in and by Jesus Christ, giving you to know that
" ye are complete in Him ", and grant you faith that " as
ye have received Christ Jesus the Lord, so you may walk in
Him ". I beseech you to take heed to your spirit in this long
affliction. May the Lord help each of us exercised by it to
look and wait for the " peaceable fruit of righteousness ".
When it may please the Lord to restore me sufficiently to
meet with you again, we know not. Here is work for faith,

patience and submission to the Lord, whose way in this affliction, and His paths, are not known, being in the mighty waters. You are in my prayers night and day in all your services. May you who fear God be "filled with all joy and peace in believing" in our Lord Jesus Christ; and may the regenerating power of the Holy Ghost reach those who without it must die in their sins. . . .

26th.—The promise of the Holy Ghost made by the Lord Jesus is vital to the Church to the end of time. In your meeting this evening I beseech that divine Spirit to be with you; to be in each regenerated soul, and particularly lead to the throne of grace those who feel their need of mercy and grace to help. May the Spirit cause a gracious oneness in those who are silent and those who speak in prayer. I am with you in my spirit and would fain be with you in person. A pastor's heart runs after you in your private exercises, family trials, soul conflicts, and the comforts of love, the fellowship of the Spirit. May that divine Teacher lead each praying person in the meeting to pray for your afflicted pastor.

March 7th.—It is a grief that I am still unable to be with you, but the doctor thinks it will not be very long before I am able again to preach the Word of Life among you. It is a comfort to me in this long trial that you still meet at Galeed where the Lord has placed His Name. One mercy God has bestowed upon us, even the gift of gracious deacons whom I love, and in whom I have full confidence, and rejoice to see them walking as one in their sacred office. Now may the Holy Ghost be in every gracious soul to-day, making the services at Galeed spiritual, a worshipping of God Who is a Spirit, and must be worshipped in spirit and in truth. May that dear congregation at Galeed be under the sacred influence of the Holy Ghost. In that case God will be pleased and your souls enlarged in faith, in the knowledge of the Person of Him who made all things and is become Head of all things to the Church, which is His body. . . .

10th.—The divine Potter has power over the clay, and in infinite goodness to you of Galeed He is making known the

riches of His glory on the vessels of mercy which He had
afore prepared for glory. The beauty, the sovereignty of
this has shone in my heart to-day, and sweet is the hope that
the heavenly Potter has gone to prepare a place for me,
along with you. To me, the chief of sinners, it is amazing
what trouble the heavenly Potter should take to form me,
with yourselves, for His glory. He saith in Holy Scripture,
"This people have I formed for Myself, they shall shew
forth My praise." I believe that divine Scripture is being
fulfilled in you. May your service this evening have that aim
and tendency. As to my body I am as clay, and what the
Lord is about to do with me I know not. But my doctor is
bringing a 'Specialist' on Friday. In a sense I am not
anxious, because a sweet hope strengthens my faith. May
your prayers for me be ceaseless. God has bound us together
and therefore in the affliction we are one. O the loveliness
of Christ as expressed in His Word, "If any man sin, we
have an Advocate with the Father, Jesus Christ the righteous." . . .

14*th.*—Your assembling yourselves together is not only a
beautiful ancient custom; it has divine authority. We are to
consider two great ends in regard to it. *First,* the worship of
God. Earliest Scripture tells us that Job assembled himself
with his children after their birthday celebrations to worship
God. Holy Scripture forbids the neglect of assembling ourselves together. Already had the subject gained a kind of
importance by the neglect of it: "As the manner of some is"
(Heb. x. 25). The great end of public worship is to acknowledge
the eternal majesty of Jehovah as He has revealed Himself in
Christ. Your assembling yourselves therefore, brethren, is of
great spiritual importance. *Second,* it is also of importance in
regard to mutual edification, as saith the Scripture: "Let us
consider one another to provoke unto love and good works;
not forsaking the assembling of ourselves together, as the
manner of some is, but exhorting one another, and so much
the more as ye see the day approaching." . . . May dear
Galeed still be the object of His special care. Never meet
anywhere for any purpose other than the simple public
worship of God. All pictures of every sort and kind turn
your backs upon. May simple public worship such as has

ever been observed among us be continued by the grace of the Holy Ghost. May to-day's services be owned of God the Spirit in your hearts, and may your afflicted pastor not be forgotten in your prayers. Ask among other things, if the Lord will, that I may the sooner be restored to you. To all seekers of the Most High God I would say, Let us follow on to know the Lord. May He be powerfully among you to do you good spiritually and everlastingly. I desire that the mercy of God to us as a people should be recorded in two cases:

1st. Our dear fellow-member and sister, Miss W., recently experienced the Lord's goodness in preventing the destruction of her home by fire. For many years she has been confined to her bed and is therefore unknown to many. The fire was mercifully confined by the Fire Brigade to one room. 2nd. Our beloved brother and deacon, Mr. T., who was recently rendered unconscious for two hours by a ' heart attack '. Mercifully he is spared to us. By these afflictions it may be the holy will of God to sanctify us as a church and people more and more to Himself. . . .

17th.—Again you meet under clouds of divine judgment. First, the devastating floods: where were villages are now rivers. But beyond relating the terrible fact, there appears to be no sense of God's hand and judgment in the sorrowful condition of the nation. Be it given to us as a little church and congregation to acknowledge God, with searching and trying of our ways before Him. 2nd. My long affliction. The doctor still hopes that I shall again meet with you. Meanwhile let us endeavour to bow in humble confession of our sins before the divine Majesty, and, looking by humble faith to the Lord Jesus, seek a time of refreshing from the presence of the Lord. I am present with you in spirit, praying that the Holy Ghost may pervade the souls of His people, so that there may be an entrance into the Scripture which says, " There is therefore now no condemnation to them which are in Christ Jesus, who walk not after the flesh, but after the Spirit." In ourselves we are poor ignorant carnal creatures, sold under sin. But the life of Christ in the soul is mightier than indwelling sin, so that while we sorrowfully cry out, " O wretched man that I am! who shall

deliver me?" there are happy moments when we thank God
who gives us the victory through our Lord Jesus Christ. ...
While you pray for all saints according to Scripture injunction, may you remember your affectionate pastor.

21st.—Again you meet under the terrible frown and anger
of almighty God; in making farms into rivers, some villages
have to be evacuated. All is richly deserved by us, an apostate nation. In your prayers and confessions of sins, personal, collective, and national, do not omit this grievous
condition of the nation and the world. Much lawful anticipation of the coronation of our king is being entertained, but
to all thinking people the whole must be marred by the
present condition of our land. Be it given you, brethren, to
mourn over the painful evidences of Jehovah's anger against
our own apostate nation. You meet again in the Name of
the Lord Jesus to serve Him in His holy gospel. In His
great mercy He has given us three deacons beloved and walking in the spirit of love and good will. This morning there
are but two present, but by the help of the Lord they will
be sufficient for each important service.

While we cannot but feel the affliction laid on us by my
protracted illness, there is yet much cause for thankfulness
you meet as you do. Thanks be to the Most High God who
in the midst of wrath remembers mercy—mercy which
endureth for ever. Continue the usual services Lord's Days
and Wednesday evenings as proper services, to conduct which
He has given us deacons endowed with wisdom and grace.
The prayer-meetings on Friday evenings give the gracious
praying men an opportunity to pray in public for the peace
of Jerusalem; a privilege that has a blessing attached to it:
"Pray for the peace of Jerusalem; they shall prosper that
love thee." Dear brethren in the Lord, I am not without
hope of being with you in body as I am now in spirit and
affection.

O may the Lord the Spirit be poured upon each soul born
again. "Born again" includes struggling, panting, discouraged, overthrown by corruptions, temptations, serious difficulties in holy providence; but these things cannot hinder,
much less destroy, the work of grace. To all seekers I would
say, rather the Lord says, "He hath not said to the seed of

Jacob, Seek ye Me in vain." O blessed, though cast down seekers,

> "Press through the crowd
> In your foul condition;
> Struggle hard, cry aloud
> On the Good Physician."

Wait on God, wait for Him who has said, "They shall not be ashamed that wait for Me." The day will come when the troubled seekers will break forth in the joyful sound, "This is the Lord, we have waited for Him; we will rejoice and be glad in His salvation." O Christ's heart is toward them that seek Him; a blessed day is coming when each seeker shall break forth into singing, "As the apple tree among the trees of the wood, so is my Beloved among the sons. I sat down under His shadow with great delight, and His fruit was sweet to my taste" (Song ii. 3). While I thus dictate, my heart is enlarged to Christ. O if I were but with you I could tell you He is the Friend of sinners. I have found Him such. Seek Him, seek Him; though He hide Himself behind dark clouds of seemingly angry dispensations, yet His gracious word is, "Seek the Lord. Come, buy wine and milk without money and without price." O believers, all things are possible to him that believeth. You will yet see that a frowning providence brought to you intimations of His love. Why does He allure you and bring you into the wilderness? Even that you may not find your own way, and then He will graciously say, "I am the way, the truth, and the life." There is none like Christ. "He is the brightness of His Father's glory and the express image of His Person; who when He had by Himself purged our sins, sat down on the right hand of the Majesty on high." O brethren, see what a Christ you seek and love and serve! there is none like Him. "The chiefest among ten thousand." He Himself only knows Himself, as the hymn-writer says,

> "God only knows the love of God,"—

He utters this gracious word, "Blessed is the man that heareth Me, watching daily at My gates, waiting at the posts of My doors; for whoso findeth Me findeth life, and shall obtain favour of the Lord. But he that sinneth against

Me wrongeth his own soul. All they that hate Me love death " (Prov. viii. 34—36). . . . .

Now may Jesus subdue our corruptions and fill us with such knowledge of Himself as shall cause us to say, " He is the chiefest among ten thousand, and altogether lovely." I commend Him to you. He alone is worthy of commendation. I rejoice at your meetings, it cheers my heart that you meet together as if I were with you; and if it be the holy will of the Lord I hope to commend Christ among you in person as I have lamely done in the past. But all human commendation is lame and maimed. He only knows His own worth. . . . We are all poor ragged lame beggars. If we have proper shame it comes from Christ's grace to us. Nobody knows the love of God but God Himself; therefore He must shed it abroad in the heart.

Brethren and friends, I would thank God who gave me the place among you, maintains it, notwithstanding my unworthiness, and many, many shortcomings. Pray, pray for your afflicted affectionate pastor.

24th.—The faith which God gives He tries. The trial of faith He Himself says is precious; not the faith only, but the trial of it is more precious than gold, though it be tried with fire. The faith we profess to have given to us as a church and pastor is being tried, tested. Gold put in the fire is relieved of its dross; so faith put in the furnace of affliction loses none of its intrinsic worth, only its dross. Our faith is being tried. Shall we stand? Shall we hold fast to that great God whose faithfulness reacheth unto the clouds, and whose oath and promises pledge Himself to us? Let us endeavour to " hold fast the beginning of our confidence firm unto the end ", as the apostle speaks. . . . Flesh and blood dispute every inch of the way of faith, yet may we be enabled to hold fast the faithful word. Our corruptions may seem to contradict our gracious experience, may darken our sky, and contradict the promises of God to us; but let us hold fast the promises of God [by faith,] the trial of which is more precious than gold.

I pray that your service this morning may be a very gracious one; God the Father, God the Son, God the Holy Ghost presiding and being present in every living soul. . . .

April 4th.—By the mercy of God you have not forsaken the assembling of yourselves together as the manner of some was, and is to-day. May the Holy Ghost, without whose gracious teaching and inward operation there can be no acceptable service or worship, descend upon you and work mightily in you " unto all longsuffering with patience and joyfulness " in the path of tribulation. Two things I enjoin on you. 1st. Never leave out of your prayers the petition for the promised coming to you of the Holy Ghost. 2nd. Beseech Him to guide you into all truth, and to sanctify you through the truth, according to the prayer, that is, the authoritative asking, of Christ (John xvii.). All acceptable worship is by the Holy Ghost. May your services to-day be conducted by that divine Spirit who " helpeth our infirmities with groanings which cannot be uttered ", but which, though unutterable by us, are according to the will of God as recorded in Holy Scripture. Therefore I entreat now that divine Spirit to be in your services, that your prayers, confessions, thanksgivings, and praises may come up before God in the golden censer in which are the prayers of saints (Rev. viii. 3): It is a joy to me in my present captivity to know that Galeed still worships according to Scripture, and I pray that the God of all patience and comfort may fill your hearts with " all joy and peace in believing through the power of the Holy Ghost " (Rom. xv. 13). Remember that Christ condescended to say that wheresoever two or three were gathered together in His Name, there He would be. In your prayers forget not your captive pastor who lives for you, though at present unable to meet with you. The report of your meetings fills me with joy. God the Holy Ghost make your services to-day profitable. God bless the aged saints, encourage the young seekers, and pervade the services with divine influence. Let me remind you that the great and only proper Object of worship is God: " God is a Spirit, and they that worship Him must worship Him in spirit and in truth. For He seeketh such to worship Him." If the Holy Ghost sets that truth on your hearts it will purify you from carnal ideas of public worship. Public worship cannot be too simple. . . . With love from your affectionate pastor.

7th.—To the church of God worshipping at Galeed: I wish

divine peace and holy prosperity. It is worthy of attention that Christ speaks of His Church as one: "That they may be one." Here are no distinctions, as Christ Himself says to His Father, "That they may be one as We are one." And the apostle Paul says, "There is neither bond nor free, ye are all one in Christ Jesus." This blessed oneness sweeps away all natural distinctions and puts us each on the same level. Jesus Christ Himself says, "I in them, and Thou in Me, that they may be one in Us." This gracious truth received by faith shows that though there are differences in experience, there is none in the sight of a holy God, between those to whom Christ is the life, light, foundation, the way to heaven, and the truth. Thus Galeed church is one with the church at Jerusalem, at Iconium, at Lystra, at Thessalonica. May it please the Holy Ghost to bear into the heart of every member the greatness, sweetness, and blessedness of this divine truth. Here let all distinctions fall; all are one in the ever-adorable divine Head, Jesus Christ.

I pray that the service this evening may be made conducive to the edification of the body of Christ. Also may souls that cannot do without Christ be powerfully attracted to Him by the enlightening unction of the Holy Ghost. The Lord be with you all. . . .

11*th*.—To all who have obtained like precious faith with the Elect, may grace and peace fill your hearts, thus making your worship spiritual and acceptable to God. One more Lord's Day I am detained a prisoner; yet, in regard of meeting with you, a prisoner of hope. You have in your gatherings together the Word of God on your side: "Wheresoever two or three," etc. If we are enabled to trace the decrees of the Holy Trinity, faith will take us back to eternity when the Father gave His Son to men and men to His Son. That holy decree has taken effect in every quickened elect person in your midst, and is known by the term *regeneration* and *effectual calling*. O for faith to lay hold of God's eternal purposes after which He worketh all things according to the good pleasure of His own will. Thus regeneration is the direct effect of an eternal decree. It is an establishing and comforting conclusion to which may the Spirit guide you. . . . I hope our deacons may be much

helped and directly guided in their choice of sermons,* and
that therefore your services may be honouring to Jehovah.
You may conclude that your faith is the gift and work of
God in you if it leads you up into eternal realities. May
you not be left contented with time things which are but for
a moment. It is a poor religion that lives on time things.
Would that every child of God among us might be led more
and more deeply into eternal things. It is my hope that in
a short time it may please the Lord that I may be with you
in person. Among your prayers for me put this petition:
that I may be submissive to the divine will as that will is
made known in the holy wise providence of God. I am with
you in spirit; my prayers and thanksgivings are for and on
behalf of our God-given deacons that they may be led in all
their ways in their office. Above all that the promised Spirit
of Christ may create a spiritual atmosphere so that every
child of God may breathe divine health. The one thing,
embracing as it does all others, is union with Christ: Christ
formed in the heart, the Hope of glory. That is the mystery
of God from all eternity: "Christ in you the Hope of glory."
Dear brethren, seek the peace of God that passeth all understanding. It is a divine peace. Christ is our peace when
the Assyrian shall come into our land (Micah v. 5; Eph. ii.
14). What is of God in our souls must pass our natural
understanding. O that that peace might pervade your
services to-day, that each may seek his brother's wealth. In
your prayers as a church may I have a place, that if it please
God I may soon be restored to you.

14th.—. . . As Jehovah is incomprehensible to us, He has
in infinite mercy revealed Himself in Holy Scripture in the
Person and by the work, life, death, resurrection and ascension into heaven as our great High Priest, of His dear Son.
We are to worship God in Him. I trust it may please the
Holy Ghost to descend in a particular manner upon each
child of His so as to make the worship spiritual and also
profitable. All perception of divine truth is beyond mere
human understanding; therefore for our deep humbling we
are brought to feel not only our ignorance, but that we are

* The services were carried on largely by read sermons during the
pastor's long affliction.

as beasts before God (Ps. lxxiii. 22). How low must the
Holy Ghost bring each child of God to profess, out of solemn
conviction, his nothingness and utter ignorance before God!
Thus, when Christ is revealed in the soul, there is no doubt
in regard of the Head that must wear the crown. " All hail
the power of Jesus' Name " has been a sweet hymn to me in
my affliction. Brethren, let us labour not for the meat that
perisheth, but for that meat which endureth unto everlasting
life. Look, each one blest with life, for manifestations of
the Lord Jesus. Your ignorance, corruption and death will
be more and more painful in your experience; but these
painful experiences will ever be making room for the Lord
of Life and Glory in your souls. . . .

21st.—To all who fear God worshipping at Galeed: May
the Holy Ghost grant power to lay hold by precious faith of
the Person of Christ in regard to His eternal Deity, His
sacred humanity, One Person. The faith which is the gift
of God, finds its centre and circumference in Him; and all
worship which is acceptable to God goes forth to Him.
Joseph Hart says:

> " Worship God, then, in His Son;
> There He's love and there alone."

It is therefore of vital importance to cast the eye of faith,
directed by the Holy Ghost, on His adorable Person. Your
service this evening can only deserve the name of Christian,
as it has Him for its centre, circumference, and great end.
I trust it may please God the Holy Ghost to reveal Christ
in you so as to accomplish the mystery of which Paul speaks
as being the great end in the Church, " Christ in you, the
Hope of glory." If it should please the Lord to remove the
heavy hand of judgment on the nation and send soft seasonable weather so that my doctor would allow me to leave the
house and meet with you, I greatly desire it. Meanwhile,
may your prayers be for me, that in the Lord's good time
I may again meet with you. . . . I long for the day when it
may please the Lord to grant me the high privilege of
meeting with you.

April 27th.—To the church and congregation at Galeed,
where God has placed His Name and manifested His glory

in Christ by the Holy Ghost: While it pains me not to be
able to meet with you, I take advantage of the pen to write
to you concerning Him who is our hope and joy, even our
Lord Jesus Christ. I hope the day is not distant when it
may please the Lord so far to restore me as to bring me into
your midst. Meanwhile may His holy sanctifying presence,
which, wherever it is, creates a spiritual atmosphere health-
giving and strengthening to faith, be with you. Our hope
lies in Him who is Jesus, the Author and Finisher of our
faith. I trust it may please the good Spirit to quicken, as
the psalmist prayed, in His righteousness, and cause you to
escape all the snares that the enemy is sure to lay for you
when you meet (cxix. 40; lxxi. 2). As of old when the sons
of God met, Satan came also, so now there never can be an
assembly of the Lord's people, few or many, where Satan is
not found among them as the " accuser of the brethren ".
And some poor Joshua will be found trembling in his filthy
garments (Zech. iii. 3) until his divine Advocate and Friend
appears for him and in His own righteousness clothes the
trembling soul. So may it be in your midst to-day. I earnestly entreat you all to gather morning and evening, as if a
living ministry were in your midst; and that you may look
to the Lord and not to man. For it is His blessed presence
felt in the soul that makes any service profitable. I want to
draw your attention to the most solemn truth that every
service held in the divine Name is, according to Scripture,
held before the Lord. From Genesis to Revelation everything done in the Name of God is done before Him. Every
gracious service has for substance the Holy Trinity in it: the
Father, the Son who offered Himself a living sacrifice, and
the Holy Ghost who is that divine fire that lights the sacrifice. O if we might see this glorious Trinity in salvation!
The Father to whom the sacrifice was offered, the Son who
by one offering perfected them that are sanctified, and the
Holy Ghost who by His holy fire caused the Sacrifice to
ascend in divine sufficiency. For "through the eternal
Spirit" Jesus " offered Himself without spot " to God. O it
is a wondrous sight given to faith to see the holy, holy, holy
God thus concerned in saving sinners. To some of you, my
dear brethren, this salvation has been made known. Others

of you are, as I believe, seeking it. To you I would say, as it is written, "Seek, and ye shall find; knock, and it shall be opened." For you ask divine bread at His hand who will not for that bread give you a stone. Others of you, old like myself, are approaching the end. May the Holy Ghost cause that "at eventide it may be light". It is a joy to me in my enforced absence that you do not forsake the assembling of yourselves together as the manner of some of old was, and still is with some. . . .

The Eternal Son is the divinely ordained way of access to the Father by the Spirit: "For through Him we have access by one Spirit unto the Father." O it will warm your hearts if it be given you to see how the Trinity is united in your salvation! If your hearts are affected by this truth, it will sanctify you and cause you to live by faith on the Son of God. . . .

Galeed is the place in this town where Jehovah has held His court of grace and love, manifesting Himself. There may He still show His glory. O the joy of the very anticipation of once more being in your midst! Until that day comes, pray for me that my enforced absence may be—though I do not see how—for His glory who worketh all things according to the good pleasure of His will. . . .

Brethren, seek, as directed by the apostle Paul, to increase in the knowledge of God. If thus favoured you will be established in the truth and walk in the liberty wherewith Christ makes you free.

The Lord hear us for each other and sanctify our affliction to His honour. So prays,

Your affectionate afflicted Pastor.

April 28*th*, 1937.—. . . As it was the joy of John that the Elect Lady and her children whom he loved in the truth, walked in the truth (II John), may the apostolic joy be in measure the joy of your souls not only this evening in your service, but constantly by the power of the Holy Ghost in you. The truth dwelleth in you who have received it in the power of the Lord Jesus; and as you have received it, so walk in it: "As ye have received Christ Jesus the Lord, so walk ye in Him" (Col. ii. 6). Truth is a great joy to those who so receive it, and will in measure have a sanctifying effect; thus the Lord's prayer for His Church will be answered: "Sanctify them through Thy truth; Thy Word is truth" (John xvii. 17). As you so walk in the truth in love, you will stand fast. Love is "the new commandment, that, as ye have heard from the beginning, ye should walk in it" (II John 6). Hold fast to the Lord Jesus Christ, "for many deceivers are entered into the world," and we need to regard the injunction, "Look to yourselves, that we lose not those things which we have wrought" by faith, especially as regards the Person of Christ; for "whosoever transgresseth and abideth not in the doctrine of Christ, hath not God. He that abideth in the doctrine of Christ, he hath both the Father and the Son. If there come any unto you and bring not this doctrine, receive him not into your house, neither bid him God speed: for he that biddeth him God speed is partaker of his evil deeds" (7—11). The infinite importance of doctrine, especially the doctrine of Christ, can never be exaggerated. As God has placed His doctrine in the church and the godly in the congregation, so His infinite mercy has abounded. It will be a great joy to see you walking in the truth as you have received it in the power of the Holy Ghost. May the service this evening be of a spiritual, uniting, edifying nature. "And now I beseech you that ye love one another. And this is love, that we walk after His commandments" (verses 5, 6). Thus may you be edified and nourished up in the words of faith and good doctrine. Brethren, I am always with you in spirit and prayer. May we by the power of God abide in His new commandment, that we love one another.

Your affectionate Pastor.

To the great surprise of his friends, Mr. Popham preached again at Galeed, the first time being on Lord's Day morning, May 2nd, when he spoke for about half an hour from "That ye might walk worthy," etc. (Col. i. 10). He was obviously very weak, and did not venture into the pulpit, but addressed his congregation from the desk. On Lord's Day (16th) he was able, with help, to mount his pulpit and preached both morning and evening; his texts being Num. xxiii. 9, and Ps. xix. 9. He preached in the morning of the 23rd from Col. i. 19, and for the last time on May 30th from I Peter i. 2.* It was evident that, although in his element preaching the 'glorious gospel of Christ', he was soon to realize his greatest desire,—to "go in and go no more out"—to "be with Christ which is far better". He remained in bed the following week until Thursday, June 3rd, when, it being very warm, he went into the garden for a short while, conversing there with his oldest church member, Miss M. Davey, who had called, it being her 105th birthday. A few days later he was taken much worse again, with incessant pain. His almost constant prayer was to be taken home. It was to himself and to his friends a great comfort that with the help of a God-fearing nurse and a dear granddaughter, his daughter was able to tenderly care for him the remaining few days to the end. A few sayings which fell from his lips, noted down at the time, are here subjoined.

Saturday, June 12th.—3 a.m., *Nurse's notes:* I found the dear patient had revived after being practically unconscious for some hours. His face was radiant as he exclaimed, "Happy! happy! happy! O I cannot express how happy I am! Tell my dear Galeed people, with my deep, deep, deep love, my black, black, black sins, as black as the confines of hell, are *all* forgiven. Luther said, 'Seas, rivers, oceans, of black sins'; and *my* black, black sins are all washed away in the precious blood of Christ.

> 'Jesus, Lover of my soul,
> Let me to Thy bosom fly '—

O how I love Him! and now I shall soon be with Him Who has loved me from all eternity. I am dying, am I not?" I reminded him of what he had so recently felt in the lines, "Thou shalt see My glory soon," and said, "I think you will soon see His glory now." He then repeated with much feeling the whole verse:

> "Thou shalt see My glory soon,
> When the work of grace is done;
> Partner of My throne shalt be,
> Say, poor sinner, lov'st thou Me?"

adding, "I have the Lord Jesus in my heart, and O I believe I am in His heart. O death, where is thy sting? No sting

* For this his last sermon, also his first recorded sermon (1875), see pages 291 and 304.

in death; no terror for me. O Galeed, precious Galeed! Give my love to my dear, dear friends there (naming several). They have been in my heart in life and they are in my heart now. Tell them I am dying on the truths I have preached, am blessedly supported by them." His son, fearing he would too much exhaust himself, restrained him from saying more for a time. Later, when alone, he said, (referring to the early morning,) " I saw nothing, but two voices I heard distinctly. First, the voice of conviction, of my confessions of my black, black sins. Then, the voice from heaven (O how distinct was that voice!): 'I accept the confession of your black sins. I have washed them all away in the precious blood of Christ, you are freely pardoned, redeemed by the merits of My dear Son.' Dear Lord Jesus, do come quickly! Thou knowest I do love Thee and want to be with Thee. O that Thou shouldest have looked upon and loved *me*, the worst, the vilest of sinners! I thought I should never reach heaven because of my numberless sins, but He has forgiven them all. I have numbered them all to Him as far as I could reckon them; but O that great word, ' *All manner* of sin and blasphemy shall be forgiven;' that was at my beginning given to me, and my deliverance was from, ' Forasmuch as ye know that ye were not redeemed with silver and gold . . . but with the precious blood of Christ.' " At another time he burst forth with the lines:

> " Lord, I believe Thou hast prepared,
>   Unworthy though I be,
> For me a blood-bought, free reward,
>   A golden harp for me," etc.

" O happy day! happy day! but so slow in coming. Now I am dying, I am happy. How I have loved to preach the Trinity! I am now dying on the love of God, the grace of that guilt-bearing Saviour, the love of the Holy Ghost."

Later: " O to think of all my sins, all confessed, all washed away! Come, Thou blessed Lord Jesus; Thou never hadst such a sinner depending on Thy love and grace." When fragrant roses were brought, he said, " Beautiful, fragrant! But O the ' Rose of Sharon' whose fragrance perfumes heaven! And I hope by to-morrow morning to open my eyes

S

in heaven and enjoy that blessed fragrance and look upon
that blessed 'Rose of Sharon'."

Later: "'The strong men shall bow themselves' (Ecc. xii.
3); and I, a strong sinner, bow."

To his daughter: "I know you will miss me, and I cannot
thank God enough for what you have been to me; my
other loved ones will miss me; but do not mourn for me,
try to give thanks to God for taking me to Himself. I do
believe I am going to be with Him. O what a bright
prospect!"

To a friend who at his request had travelled to his bedside:
Taking him by both hands, he said, "I *am glad* you have
come. We have discussed matters, and I am sick to death
with professors; but am soon leaving all that perplexing kind
of thing [referring to disloyalty, etc.]. The end has come
rather suddenly; O happy day! 'Happy is he that hath the
God of Jacob for his help; whose hope is in the Lord his
God.' Stick to the truths you and I have believed and professed, and stick to prayer: 'I have stuck unto Thy testimonies, O Lord.'

> 'Weary of earth, myself, and sin,
>   Dear Jesus, set me free,
> And to Thy glory take me in,
>   For there I long to be.'"

The friend mentioned his long and useful labours in the
cause of Christ. The dear dying man shook his head vehe-
mently; he would have nothing of his doings. Then it was
said, "But you have lifted up the dear Redeemer?" He
quietly replied, "I have tried to."

To a deacon he repeated the first verse of the hymn,
"Rock of Ages;" and several times referred to the two lines:

> "Be of sin the double cure,
>   Cleanse me from its guilt and power."

He said, "Oh, how many times have I prayed that before
the Lord! and what emphasis I have put on that—'*double*
cure'! He *has* cleansed me from the guilt of it, and now I
am to be for ever delivered from the power of it. I'm free!
I'm free! O happy day! I did not think I was so near.

How glad I was when the doctor told me the end was near. Happy day! The sting of death is removed: ' O death, where is thy sting? O grave, where is thy victory? The sting of death is sin; and the strength of sin is the law. But thanks be to God which giveth us the victory through our Lord Jesus Christ.' I am going to see the ' Rose of Sharon and the Lily of the Valleys '. The burden of the church will fall upon you. You will come to say, The burden of the church is a heavy burden. But the Lord will be with you. He has been at Galeed and He is still at Galeed, and He will be with you. Do not forget that the church was commenced by seven men on their knees. They had not prayed before in public, but they met for prayer in each other's houses. Perhaps there is hardly another church that was commenced just like that."

Much gracious counsel and affectionate caution did the dear pastor lay before the deacons on this the last interview; which recalls a Scripture which many years before he was wont to relate as having been given him for beloved Galeed: " And the people served the Lord all the days of Joshua, and all the days of the elders that outlived Joshua, who had seen all the great works of the Lord, that He did for Israel " (Jud. ii. 7). Frequently for many years Mr. Popham would pray that he might not die " undesired " (Jehoram: II Chron. xxi. 20), and that he " might not outlive himself ". Having observed his dear friend and former pastor, Mr. de Fraine, become latterly mentally feeble, it was Mr. Popham's dread thus to live. In these particulars and many others, the Lord mercifully regarded the prayer of His dear servant, fulfilling His gracious promises to the very end: " I will make them to know that I have loved thee;" " If thou draw out thy soul to the hungry, and satisfy the afflicted soul, then shall thy light rise in obscurity, and thy darkness be as the noon day," etc.; " With long life will I satisfy him, and shew him My salvation " (Rev. iii. 9; Isa. lviii. 10, 11; Ps. xci. 16).

By a supreme effort, as it seemed, he lovingly conversed with about twenty godly friends who called on the last day of consciousness, Monday, June 14th, giving words of advice and encouragement. Here follow brief extracts:—

" You have come to see the vilest sinner die that ever

defiled God's earth, but I am going to Him through the
blood of Christ, the love of the Father, and the grace of the
Holy Spirit. He has been precious to my soul, and the
prospect of being with Him makes me happy. It has been
as if there were two voices speaking in my heart. The voice
of conviction, and I have pleaded guilty, guilty, guilty before
the Lord. That voice has not been contradicted by God; for
He is a God of truth and does not contradict what is true.
The other voice is the voice of pardon, and with that He
does comfort me; assuring me He has forgiven all my sins.
. . . Between these two voices my life can be divided.
These words (Ezek. xxxiii. 15, 16) have been very sweet to
me: If one ' walk in the statutes of life . . . none of his
sins that he hath committed shall be mentioned unto him '.
The sweetness, the savour, the comfort of that, I can never
describe; for I was enabled to lay hold of the ' statutes of
life ', which is Christ. Now I am happily dying, not without
sins and those working vilely in me, but in the belief that
not one sin shall be mentioned to me, for if Christ be for
us, who can be against us ? I am hoping to be with Him,
without sin, soon. I am continually putting my sins before
Him, but He will not listen, except to say they are forgiven.
I have asked my children to do a hard thing: to thank God
for taking me. O my dear friends, do thank God for that!
Better is the day of my death than the day of my birth!
' Blessed are the dead which die in the Lord.' I think—I am
sure—I am dying in Him. O happy prospect! I know my
people at Galeed will miss me; my family will miss me; and
you, my friends, may miss me. But do think of my happiness! I have greatly dreaded death because of my sins, but
death has lost its sting. I leap for joy in my heart at the
thought of being with Christ soon, and of being like Him!
I cannot tell you the attraction He is to me now. I have
the devil of sin in me, but I have a greater One. Do not
think I am not troubled by my sins; I am, but I am not
condemned. ' Blessed is he whose transgression is forgiven,
whose sin is covered.' "

On Tuesday morning early, unconsciousness came and continued to the end. Death released his happy soul at 3 a.m.
on Thursday, June 17th, 1937.

Thus triumphantly ended the mortal career of one whom Jehovah loved and honoured, and used for the spiritual good and salvation of many of the sons of Zion. He left the ship of the Church—not in a storm, as in the case of Dr. Owen, but what is immeasurably worse—in a treacherous calm, lulled as by a narcotic into inertia and deadened by sloth and ease. " Woe unto us, that we have sinned! The crown is fallen from our head. For this our heart is faint; for these things our eyes are ,dim. . . . Thou, O Lord, remainest for ever; Thy throne from generation to generation. Wherefore dost Thou forget us for ever, and forsake us so long time ? Turn us unto Thee, O Lord, and we shall be turned; renew our days as of old " (Lam. v. 16—21). While it behoves us thus to lament our case, it is fitting that we should render thanks to the God of all grace for the encouraging example of the victory of faith. And should it be given to us to " look in after him " and, casting afresh the anchor hope into that ever-remaining Anchorage within the veil, through grace to " follow them who through faith and patience inherit the promises ", it will be well.

On the following Lord's Day there was much evidence of the intense grief his death caused his flock at Galeed, when his friend and son in the faith, Mr. J. H. Gosden, was entrusted with the difficult task yet sacred privilege of speaking morning and evening from " Remember them which have the rule over you, who have spoken unto you the Word of God: whose faith follow . . ." (Heb. xiii. 7, 8).

The following day, Monday, June 21st, a funeral service was held in the chapel, which with the vestries was quite filled with affectionate mourners, including his oldest church member, Miss Davey, 105 years of age, who also followed the cortège to the grave. According to his expressed desire the service commenced with the hymn, " All hail the power of Jesus' Name," and ended with hymn 806 (Gadsby's):

" Christ is the Friend of sinners!
Be that forgotten never."

It was felt that a most sacred atmosphere pervaded the chapel, and that the singing of the hymns selected by the dear departed minister raised the grief-stirred hearts of the

people to the high theme with which his ministry was
imbued. To the officiating minister it was a sad, sacred
pleasure to fulfil a long-standing promise. The Address was
as follows:—

It is a very solemn yet sacred duty that falls to our lot on
this, to us, woeful day. We rejoice and we mourn. We
rejoice in that our beloved pastor is " absent from the body,
present with the Lord "; enjoying what he long had antici-
pated, struggled for, followed after,—of which he had sweet
foretastes and now has entered into the fulness of,—that
which is within the veil, the fulness of joy and the everlasting
pleasures which are at God's right hand for evermore.
Blessed soul! fully satisfied! In the midst of the throne of
God is that sacred, once-slain Lamb, Jesus Christ, Who leads
to fountains of living waters the company of His redeemed,
the " spirits of just men made perfect "; and to that company
our dear brother has now been joined. Christ has received
him, never more to go out, never more to have a night of
desertion ("there is no night there"); never more to be
tempted by the arch-enemy of God and man, Satan; never
to again know what sorrow means, what fear is, what pain
and disappointment mean, and, best of all, never again to be
touched by or tempted to that terrible thing which brought
death, namely, sin. Heaven is a holy place, and because it
is holy it is a happy place. *There* is no capability of sinning,
no disposition to sin remaining! Perfected as to his happy
spirit he is. This is beyond our thought, but John speaks of
it, saying, " It doth not yet appear what we shall be: but we
know that, when He shall appear, we shall be like Him:
for we shall see Him as He is." And that likeness is now
in the soul, the spirit, of our beloved brother, "made
perfect."

We rejoice in considering that he now rests from his
labours; not inactive, not a dead sleep, not an unconsciousness, but a blessed, eternal, tireless, holy activity of love,
worship, praise, he has now entered upon as to his soul.
Blessed soul!

We do not grudge him this; but we mourn, we have cause
to mourn our loss. It is not a little loss. Most of us here
are more or less nearly affected by the death of Mr. Popham,

and the loss is proportionate to the value of the gift that was given to the Church in our beloved friend and pastor. He was no small gift to the Church of Christ. God endowed him with gracious ability; He endowed him also with a goodly measure of grace, so that with love he served faithfully his God and the churches—this church at Galeed in particular—through many long years. His labours were abundant, not merely when he stood in this pulpit (which to him was no light thing), but before he entered it and after he left it; and by night in weeping and praying over his hearers, that they might be "presented perfect in Christ Jesus ".

His ministry was not superficial; it was not merely official, although it possessed a divine commission and authority: it was a ministry that obtained from the depth of his own soul-exercise and soul-communion with his God and Saviour. We have lost—the church here has lost a beloved under-shepherd; and we have a right to sorrow. Not indeed as those who have no hope, for we have in our hearts a sacred persuasion concerning his perfect satisfaction and happiness; and as the Lord enables us, we feel in our hearts a gracious determination to follow him as he was enabled to follow Christ. He has spoken the Word of God here. Some through him have heard God's voice with its inimitable authority: some have heard the voice of dear Mr. Popham speaking the Word of God, but have not heard God's voice. He did not fail, in his ministry, to warn the unbelievers, to warn the wicked of the wrath to come. God made him a faithful watchman on Zion's walls. For popularity he never kept back part of the price. Mere popularity we believe he never sought: that he obtained a measure of spiritual authority in the churches was due to the fact that his ministry was fraught with the unction of the Divine Spirit, so that, at times especially, not only the believers felt the unction, but the unbelievers were stilled.

The churches, the denomination, the little body to which we belong, has lost a leader, one who was given power, discernment, ability, and authority to exercise an influence for good in days of declension. He knew the strait and narrow path and he taught it. He warned against superficiality, generality, in religion; and as he did for many years conduct our two denominational magazines, *The Gospel Standard* and *The Friendly Companion,* God used him greatly in the exercise of the gifts with which He had endowed him, for His honour and the real good of immortal souls. Arduous was his work; it was never done casually, nor prayerlessly, nor easily; but it was done affectionately and faithfully in and through evil report and good report. Controversy he engaged in of necessity, not with a view to pre-eminence but out of desire, first, to guard the truth of God, to set forth warnings against the rocks and shelves of erroneous doctrine; and, secondly, he entered upon controversy for the love he had for immortal souls. He minded not the frowns, he courted not the smiles of the world.

The family also mourns a godly, affectionate, praying father. His anxiety, his tears, and his prayers for his family are known fully only to God. May God regard them and fully answer them in His own time!

The town has lost a citizen, a townsman, honourable. The country has lost a patriot; he prayed for England, he deplored the declension of many things in the religious world, and also outside, in this our beloved land. We mourn.

But while we are full of grief and weakness in consequence of the removal of a beloved brother and friend and pastor, we also desire to express and render to God thanksgiving for what he was made to us; that for many long years we were favoured with his ministry here and in the denomination. Not a few still here, many more in heaven, have cause to bless God that He spoke to their souls through the lips and pen of Mr. Popham; that through him they received words of caution, of conviction, of reproof, of direction, of instruction, and of comfort. He was made to many souls as God's mouth (Jer. xv. 19). God made him valiant for the truth. He made him tender as a nurse to seeking souls. He made him very stern in reproving sin; he minded not the frowns of men,—he sought their real good not their smiles. Not only ought we to thank God for sparing him to us for so long, but that, as the Scripture just read (Rev. xiv. 13) declares, he rests from his labours and his works follow him. May we have grace to follow his faith (" Whose faith fol-

low ") considering the end of his conversation, the goal of his
life,—" Jesus Christ the same yesterday, and to-day, and for
ever." And Jesus Christ not nominally merely, but Jesus
Christ revealed as crucified, buried, risen, and ascended
to the right hand of God. Our dear friend died in the
faith of the atonement. The precious blood of Christ by
which the Church was purchased and redeemed to God, was
the key-note of his ministry, because it was the key-
note of his own soul's experience from early life down
to the very end. On the Saturday before he entered
glory he spoke to me very sweetly about his first deliverance
from guilt and bondage under the law in his very early days,
by that Scripture: " Ye were not redeemed with corruptible
things . . . but with the precious blood of Christ." The
atonement for sin was the theme of his heart, for sin was to
him a dreadful reality, and salvation was a glorious reality.
Satisfied with a long life he was, and now God has shewn
him His great salvation.

What can we say? Words seem to mock us. The more
we feel, the less we feel able to say. He needs no commendation; he desired none. When I spoke to him last Saturday-
week about his works, he shook his head vigorously. When
I said, " You have lifted up the dear Redeemer," he said, " I
have *tried* to." And he was successful in those attempts,
by God's mercy. Christ was lifted up before the eyes of
poor sinners, who looked and lived. He was lifted up in
some of our hearts in His love, His beauty, His goodness;
and we worshipped Him.

May the Lord in infinite mercy grant that this bereavement
may be deeply sanctified to us all, bring us more earnestly
to seek after those things which our dear brother has now
fully entered upon, and which he so long and so faithfully
preached.

In the Brighton and Preston Cemetery it is estimated that
about 900 people gathered. His friend and late deacon,
Mr. Jesse Delves, pastor at Ebenezer, Clapham, offered
prayer, after the committal sentences had been said; it being
the express wish of Mr. Popham that the grave-side service
should be thus restricted.

EPILOGUE.

"What hath God wrought?"

THE great apostle Paul describes himself in II Cor. vi. 3—11, and in doing so he also delineates the features of every true minister of the gospel. In some those features may be more defined than in others, but surely they were, through grace, clearly impressed upon the subject of this memoir. One honour he earned—his death was almost unnoticed by the general religious press. "As unknown, yet well known," could emphatically be inscribed on his frontlet. There were exceptions. Reference has already been made to Sir W. R. Nicoll. The late Dr. Dinsdale Young paid a tribute in 1934:

"I worshipped not long ago in a chapel in Brighton, as plain a chapel as you could imagine, but the minister of that chapel was a pulpit genius. He has occupied that pulpit now for more than fifty years, and is as fresh as ever, although he is eighty-five years of age. He told a friend of mine that he feels stronger at eighty-five than he did at forty. That is encouraging for some of us! Yet that chapel holds one of the largest congregations in that watering-place. There are no attractions, no side-shows, but worship, Bible-teaching, prayer, and hymn-singing. It is not the outward condition of the House of the Lord. The secret is a spiritual secret. All the great saints have set store by the House of the Lord, and I am sure it is the first mark of spiritual decline when people neglect the House of the Lord."

The Rev. T. Houghton, a friend of Mr. Popham's, devoted six pages of his periodical, the *Gospel Magazine*, to a tribute to his worth; giving some interesting extracts from letters, and a note of a visit to our dear friend at Brighton, in 1931.

The Rev. H. T. Chilvers, in *Fellowship*, wrote: "There was something very vital in a ministry that could be sustained in a town like Brighton for half a century. Galeed became a Mecca not only for those whom Mr. Popham denomination-ally represented, but ministers and people of other sections of Christ's Church were frequently found in his congregation which generally crowded the chapel. The late Sir W.

Robertson Nicoll personally told me that he always took an opportunity to hear Mr. Popham. He said, ' I like him, for he knows what he believes and does not fear to speak it out.' . . . One particular Sunday I accompanied a deacon of a large London Baptist church to Galeed, and at the close of the sermon he said to me, ' If you have any religion at all that man's ministry will find it out, and if you have *none* you are made to feel it.' That was so; his ministry was heart-searching, and if it did not uplift as the gospel can, it made you feel your need of such uplifting. Mr. Popham was an autocrat in his own sphere; he would brook no interference, and his methods of church life and work were confined to very narrow circles; but his life and ministry were fraught with power from on high, and Brighton is the poorer for his translation."

Spiritual readers will be able to appreciate the fact that Mr. Popham's ministry definitely did prohibit that lightsomeness frequently miscalled worship, which Hart deprecated in his well-known lines:

" Let no false comfort lift us up
To confidence that's vain;
Nor let their faith and courage droop,
For whom the Lamb was slain."

However the above reference to " very narrow circles " and " uplift " may be interpreted, a true evaluation of the sober ministry and church life of Galeed's honoured pastor requires to embrace a consideration of the nett spiritual results. Eternity alone will fully reveal these, but there were many and are still some who may without presumption be termed " Epistles of Christ, ministered by us; known and read of all men ". That he laid bare the foundations, discouraged superficiality, and built up surely and steadily on the Rock; that his ministry was eminently a living one arising from current exercise before his God, was testified by many who experienced through him the " demonstration of the Spirit and power ".

In days when a boasted " wider sphere of usefulness " frequently betokens a dilution—to say the very least—of the spiritual content of the ministry, as well as a proportionate

increase of unspiritual activity, we may well admire that
grace which preserved Mr. Popham (naturally ambitious)
from the lure of popularity. It was said that but for grace
our beloved Philpot (still traduced) might have been a
bishop. But both scholarly J. C. P. and talented J. K. P.
equally scorned purchasing popular applause by compro-
mising the truth. As for parsonic ostentation, neither
aspired to so much as a Roman collar! A faithful
standard-bearer on Israel's battle-field, a vigilant watchman
sounding an alarm in God's holy mountain, a true labourer
in the vineyard of the Lord, "rightly dividing the Word of
truth", a wise and diligent and tender under-shepherd of the
"flock of slaughter", a "master of assemblies" fastening
goads in slothful consciences and arrows in hard hearts, a
"true yoke-fellow" in the gospel of Jesus Christ, an affectionate and loyal friend and pastor, a stalwart defender of
the "bed of Solomon",—what he was—and Mr. Popham
was all this—he was by the grace of God.

For over seventy-two of his eighty-nine years he was a
"stranger and a pilgrim" on the earth, as all our spiritual
fathers were. Of his distinct and effectual call by grace out
of the world when but seventeen years of age, the foregoing
pages give some account. Thus clearly began his religion,
in conviction of sin and the want of God and His salvation.
Relief came after many months of trouble, by the Scripture,
"All manner of sin and blasphemy shall be forgiven unto
men;" and full deliverance by the application of the words,
"Forasmuch as ye know that ye were not redeemed with corruptible things . . . but with the precious blood of Christ."
The virtue and efficacy of that sacred truth was seen throughout all his long life, and of his seventy years' ministry it
formed the key-note.

Providential trials and deliverances he experienced many,
but he ever avoided two extremes: the making of a salvation
from temporal blessings, and the unbelieving disregard of
God in His providential dealings. Out of a gracious and
solemn exercise by trials and affliction, came much fruit in
his own soul and by consequence in his ministry. He
preached not himself but Christ Jesus the Lord. Comparatively seldom did he make direct reference to his personal

things; his ministry was not so puerile as to require its
deficiencies to be covered with trifling anecdote. He knew
and he preached the terrors of the Lord in a broken law;
and he knew and preached the sacred solemn comforts of
blood-bought pardon. The Person and work of Christ was
his theme, always with insistence upon the need of the Holy
Spirit's application. The fashionable religion of 'generalities', he eschewed perforce of inward experience as well as
from a solemn sense of the value of immortal souls. How
he would warn us that "we may be as much lost in the
'generalities' of religion as lost in irreligion"! We believe
he is "pure from the blood of all men"; and now it matters
nothing to him that to be so cost him a not inconsiderable
measure of persecution from those who love to be at ease in
Zion, no less than from the world.

Broken-hearted and hungry sinners found in his ministry
a tenderness which emanated from constant personal exercise
and from the abiding power of a gracious word conveyed by the
Spirit to his soul in his first days of preaching: "If thou
draw out thy soul to the hungry, and satisfy the afflicted
soul; then shall thy light rise in obscurity." Remarking
thereon, he once said to us, "And it *was* obscurity." The
scenes at the funeral, described in the local press as 'un-
paralleled', (notwithstanding the shortness of notice and the
inconvenience of the day for distant friends,) evidenced that
a living light surrounded his memory.

His pastorate at Liverpool was fruitful in the calling by
grace of a number of persons and the deliverance of others;
many also were instructed, reproved, fed, comforted, and
blessed through him in the north. Bitter trials he had, persecution and temptation; with grief he has told of a period of
inward heart-backsliding, and with gratitude he remembered
the Lord's wonderful kindness in clearly restoring him. All
which things were reflected in his ministry. Favoured beyond
many were those who enjoyed—guilty indeed were those who
despised—our dear friend's early ministry there. His coming
to Brighton fifty-five years ago, and his fruitful ministry
and wise pastorate there, is cause for thanksgiving in the
hearts of very many godly who with him are now 'safely
landed', and in not a few who are left

"To struggle with the powers of hell
   Till Jesus bids us go."

God's kindness in the gift of such a pastor and friend for so
many years is truly great. Our accountability is in proportion.

Mr. Popham was by divine teaching and deep conviction
a Protestant. He could not, however, unite generally with
the militant Arminian Protestantism, more noisy and political
than spiritual. Nor would he allow such topics to interfere
with his pulpit-charge in preaching the gospel. On occasions,
however, he addressed especial reference to such matters,
when his language was unmistakable. Most particularly he
deplored the semi-Romanism of the Anglican church, and
was once heard to declare that if all perjured persons were
in prison there would be few if any Anglican bishops at
large to-day! He referred, of course, to the breaking of
solemn ordination vows.

He was also very jealous of the British constitution and
vigorously resented any approach to disloyalty. He held
most decided views on the relationships of life, whether
domestic, social, commercial, or political, and through grace
he set a wholesome example. As a friend he was affectionate,
patient, faithful. At least one unworthy individual who was
allowed his confidence, had also an interest in his prayers
daily.

Mr. Popham's thirty years' editorship of *The Gospel
Standard*, and for sixteen years also of *The Friendly
Companion*, was conspicuous for ability and grace. His own
contributions were valuable for their weight and unction; his
selections were made with prayer and after tasting for himself; nothing superficial or light would he admit. In controversy with error he was resolute, at times severe; but the
secret line of living unctuous truth and his love thereto, could
be detected by the godly in his severest attack on the enemy
citadel. Righteous indignation with error and fervent love
of the truth made him many enemies and some friends.
Moreover he could distinguish between the *men* and their
errors, between individuals and systems. He was neither
disarmed by "universal charity" nor blinded by prejudice.
One rather troublesome opponent he thus neatly analysed:

"I have scarcely grasped R.'s letter. It seems sincere. If it is, he is blind. If it is not, he is—to use a mild word—*sly*." Although he took great pains and (as he would say) never reached his desired standard, Mr. Popham never wrote for the sake of exercising his literary powers. His one aim was *edification*. Mention might be made of his valuable New Year Addresses, packed full with weighty terse expressions of the "main things"; his Prayer-meeting Addresses frequently published in the magazine, being usually a choice flowing commentary of some Scripture recently handled by the expositor himself in secret before God; his Book Reviews, which were frequently more of the nature of a treatise on the subject than a mere notice skimming the surface of the book; his Answers to Enquiries, compact and always conservatively Scriptural. Adverse criticism he ministered with unflinching and incisive energy, though with a really tender regard for the criticized where any evidence appeared of teachableness and humility. Violation of the truth he abhorred and scathingly exposed, especially when he saw the possibility of unsuspecting friends being beguiled. Not infrequently he was requested to write the Preface to a new publication, which he did in no slip-shod manner; manifesting his intimate acquaintance with the volume and not concealing his love for the author and the truth he commends, and often expressing his sense of the honour done to him in being allowed to attach his name thereto.

He commenced in January, 1909, to publish a sermon monthly, which is continued to the present time, the circulation extending beyond these shores; many testimonies have been given to God's blessing thereupon. The re-reading of a letter dated December 19th, 1908, in which the minister appreciates the reporting of the sermons, recalls the attendant circumstances: A certain member of the Galeed congregation who had been noting the sermons for their own use, became solemnly exercised as to whether this was or was not pleasing in the sight of the Lord, and much prayer went up for guidance. The matter was settled by Isa. xxx. 8: "Now go, write it before them in a table, note it in a book, that it may be for the time to come." At that juncture, Mr. Popham asked for the transcript. When the war plunged everything into confusion, another reporter, driven by the air raids from London with his wife and family, settled at Brighton, and patiently and skilfully reported the sermons verbatim to the last one preached by Mr. Popham. Surely the purpose of Jehovah was in this circumstantial detail!

Besides his magazine pieces and the monthly sermons, his separate publications include the following:—

1875: " Imperishable Grace."
      " Moody and Sankey's Errors," etc.

1878: " Thoughts on Regeneration."

1886: " Divine Sovereignty."

1893: " The Perfect Man and his God."

1899: " To my Church and Congregation."

1903: " A Protest." (re Christ's Impeccability.)

1906: " Preaching the Gospel."
      " The Place of Rest and Satisfaction."

1907: " Jesus Christ eternally the Same."
      " The New Theology."
      Volume of 25 Sermons. (I.)

1908: " A Word on Preaching to the Unconverted."
      " The Power of God unto Salvation."

1909: " The Riches of Assurance."
      " God's Kindness and Grace in Election."

1911: " How the Just Live."

1912: " Three-fold Mercy."

1913: " Death an Entrance into Life."

1914: " The Glory of Christ in Dying."
      " A Two-fold Bereavement."
      " The Mercy-Seat."
      " Comfort under Bereavement."

1915: " Mercy and Judgment."
      " Dead to the Law."

1916: " Remember now thy Creator."
      " Such an High Priest."

1917: "Christ All in All."

1918: "Christ's Word to Laodicea."
"An Open Letter to J. P. Wiles."
"A Demonstration." (Vindicating Mr. Hemington.)

1921: An Answer to Mr. W. (The Constitution, Doctrine, and Trusts of the Denomination.)

1923: Volume of 25 Sermons. (II.)
"The Covenant of Grace."

1929: "The Holy Bible."
"A Faithful Message."

1930: "Keswick Teaching."

1932: "A Humble Memorial to the Lord."

1936: "The Form of Sound Words."

———

The following texts and hymn-lines, so frequently heard to drop from the lips of their late highly-esteemed minister, will revive some sacred impressions upon the hearts of many of Mr. Popham's hearers:—

"If thou draw out thy soul to the hungry, and satisfy the afflicted soul; then shall thy light rise in obscurity, and thy darkness be as the noon day."—ISAIAH lviii. 10.

"I will make them to come and worship before thy feet, and to know that I have loved thee."—REV. iii. 9.

"When ye have done all those things which are commanded you, say, We are unprofitable servants."—LUKE xvii. 10.

"Where I am, there shall also My servant be."—JOHN xii. 26.

"God, who commanded the light to shine out of darkness, hath shined in our hearts, to give the light of the knowledge of the glory of God in the face of Jesus Christ."—II COR. iv. 6.

"Forasmuch as ye know that ye were not redeemed with corruptible things, . . . but with the precious blood of Christ, as of a Lamb without blemish and without spot."—I PETER i. 18, 19.

"Where sin abounded, grace did much more abound."—ROM. v. 20.

T

" All manner of sin and blasphemy shall be forgiven unto men."—MATT. xii. 31.

" Having forgiven you all trespasses."—COL. ii. 13.

" Can blood such horrid crimes atone ?
    Yes! blood so rich as Thine."—*Hart.*

" The blood of Christ, a precious blood!
    Cleanses from all sin, doubt it not,
    And reconciles the soul to God,
    From every folly, every fault."—*Hart.*

" For love of me the Son of God
    Drained every drop of vital blood;
    Long time I after idols ran,
    But now my God's a martyred Man."—*Hart.*

" He to the needy and the faint
        His mighty aid makes known;
    And, when their languid life is spent,
        Supplies it with His own."—*Hart.*

" Christ is the Friend of sinners,
        Be that forgotten never;
    A wounded soul, and not a whole,
        Becomes a true believer."—*Hart.*

" Though temptations seldom cease,
        Though frequent griefs I feel,
    Yet His Spirit whispers peace,
        And He is with me still."—*Hart.*

" Bring no money, price, or aught,
    No good deeds, nor pleasing frames;
    Mercy never can be bought:
    Grace is free, and all's the Lamb's."—*Kent.*

In conclusion, let it be emphasized that he ever recognized and we his survivors and mourners also recognize that

WHAT HE WAS HE WAS SOLELY BY THE GRACE OF GOD.

SERMONS

IMPERISHABLE GRACE.

NOTES OF MR. POPHAM'S FIRST RECORDED SERMON,
preached at Liverpool, 1875.*

"Christ is become of no effect unto you, whosoever of you are justified by the law; ye are fallen from grace."—GAL. v. 4.

THE object of the apostle in this epistle is to deliver the Galatians from the false teachings of those who were zealously affecting them, but not well; for they were leading them into Judaism—bringing them into bondage—turning them again to weak and beggarly elements—setting up the righteousness of the law in opposition to the righteousness of Christ; and thus taking them away from the simplicity which is in Christ Jesus. Now the apostle says, "Where is the blessedness ye spake of? Before your eyes Jesus Christ was evidently set forth, crucified among you, and you professed His holy Name and gospel, and spoke of blessedness, blessed hopes, blessed experiences, and blessed confidence; but I solemnly profess unto you that Christ will not profit you if you turn again to the weak and beggarly elements; if you are circumcised you are debtors to do the whole law, and your profession of Christ will be of no avail."

Now, my dear friends, I have had some solemn exercise of mind during the last few days, and a very great desire to lay before you the true exposition of these words. Paul bids Titus to shew, in doctrine, uncorruptness, gravity, and sincerity. This, by the Lord's help and teaching, I am anxious to do this morning. The Arminians conclude from this, and other passages of Scripture, that grace is destructible, that a child of God may finally, eternally perish; but, if they considered the *nature* of grace for a moment, they would never again teach such an error, but would, with Dr. Gill, believe that the falling away my text speaks of is a falling

---

* He was then about twenty-seven years of age, and had been preaching about eight years.

away from, not the *principle*, but the *profession* of the *doctrines* of grace.

In opening up these words, I shall endeavour, as the Lord may assist, to set before you the *nature* of grace in a threefold aspect: First, As it is seen in God the Father; secondly, As it is manifested by God's Eternal Son; and thirdly, As it is applied by the Holy Eternal Spirit.

First of all, I wish to state that our contention for the doctrines of grace is no contention for mere doctrinal statements, no empty war of words, but a contention and a war for eternal truths. We believe these doctrines, as revealed and applied, are the life, comfort, and hope of God's dear children; for they are the glorious outcome of the everlasting love of God's heart, of the gracious thoughts of His mind, and of the determinations of His will.

Now we will go to the subject in hand. I am, in the first place, to speak of grace as it is seen in God the Father. This grace is nothing less than His eternal love and favour to poor ruined sinners. It was given them in Christ Jesus before the world began, II Tim. i. 9.

It is opposed to salvation by works, Rom. xi. 6. The blessed fruit of it is: 1st, Election, Rom. xi. 5; 2nd, Salvation, Eph. ii. 8; 3rd, A good standing before God, Rom. v. 2; and 4th, Glory, I Peter v. 10. It is likewise called the abounding grace, nay, the much more abounding grace of God, Rom. v. 20. How very wonderfully it abounded in eternity; down towards its forlorn, wretched objects it looked, saw them without help, and the immediate fruit of it, if I may so speak, was the gift of Jesus Christ. It called into exercise the attributes of God, and made them harmonize in Jesus.

Justice forbad, on law grounds, the escape of a poor sinner from her stern inflexible grasp—pollution could not be permitted to approach eternal purity—but infinite wisdom found out a way. Everlasting love moved God's bowels towards poor sinners, and He determined to save them. Now, I believe, when the apostle tells the Ephesians they are " saved by *grace* " he includes all the actings of the wisdom, love, and will of God towards His people: " Herein is love, not that we loved God, but that He loved us, and sent His Son to be the propitiation for our sins." Jesus is made of God, " Wis-

dom, and righteousness, and sanctification, and redemption."
O what wonders love has done! The boundless grace of
God is seen in the covenant of grace. Boston very truly
observes that "as man's ruin was originally owing to the
breaking of the covenant of works, so his recovery, from the
first to the last step thereof, is owing purely to the fulfilling
(by a Surety) of the covenant of grace." "I have made a
covenant with My chosen." The Lord says this shall not be
like the first covenant, "which My covenant they brake,
saith the Lord." The blessed substance of this is: *I will, they
shall.* "I will be their God, and they shall be My people."
"I will forgive their iniquity, and I will remember their sin
no more." "I will make them willing in the day of My
power, and they shall not turn away from Me" (Psa. cx. 3;
Jer. iii. 19; xxxi. 31—34).

Now these everlasting hills can never move. The promises
of good in the first covenant depended upon the *character of
the person to whom they were made,* but the promises of the
second covenant all depend upon the *Person making them.*
The goodness of the man interested in them cannot merit
them, neither shall sin rob him of them, for they depend
upon a divine *shall* and *will,* not upon the poor, fickle will
of a creature. It is called the new and better covenant,
established upon better promises. It contains in itself pardon
for all the sins and iniquities of the election of grace, Jer.
xxxi. 34; it has a word for backsliders, Psa. lxxxix. 30—34;
and it says, "Mercy is built up for ever" (Psa. lxxxix. 1—4).

Oh! what a mercy it is to be bound up in this bundle of
life! Now, there are thousands who would tell you that
your poor souls may be interested in this grace of God the
Father, which was given you in Christ Jesus before the
world began, which bears such precious fruit as I have mentioned, which, to the astonishment of your own souls, so
wonderfully abounds, moves the bowels of God, calls into
precious exercise the attributes of God, from which sprang
the covenant of grace, with all its blessed provisions,—I say
there are thousands who would tell you you may be interested
in all this, and yet finally fall, that is, fall into hell! which
is to say that the counsel of the Lord may come to nought
like that of the heathen, that the thoughts of His heart may

perish; even though it is said that "His counsel standeth for ever, and the thoughts of His heart to all generations." To say that one may fall into hell, who is interested in the grace of God, is to say that from loving from eternity He may in time commence to hate; from having no fury towards a soul, He may commence to have indignation. It is to say that although He determined to dwell in this or that particular soul, yet the stubborn will, the unbelieving heart, of this or that person may frustrate His determination. But is the decree of God such a poor, weak thing that it cannot bring forth nor bear fruit without the consent of man's crooked, perverse will? why, it is to break this will, or to give a new one, that the decree has gone forth, Psa. cx. 3. What a mercy, my dear friends, we have not so learned the Scriptures of truth!

The Lord has promised to put away, to forgive the sins of His people, and He is not a man that He should lie; He has given grace to His people in Christ Jesus before the world began, and He is not the son of man that He should repent. His gifts are "without repentance". He calls His people to His feet, and says they shall not depart from Him, and His callings as well as His gifts are without repentance. "He is in one mind, and who can turn Him? and what His soul desireth, even that He doeth." "For whatsoever it pleased the Lord, that did He in heaven, and in earth, in the seas, and in all deep places." "What shall we then say to these things? If God be for us, who can be against us? He that spared not His own Son, but delivered Him up for us all, how shall He not with Him also freely give us all things?" Poor dear child of God, what do you say to these things? to the precious doctrine of the eternal choice, the everlasting love, and the gracious determination of His will to save you, as you have at times been sweetly made to hope? what could you do if these things were taken away? "If the foundations be destroyed, what can the righteous do?" Fall from this grace? why God must first cease to be; His Name, glory, and honour are all at stake, if I may so say, in this matter. Fall from this grace? God's choice become reprobation? His love be turned into hatred, and His determination to save you cease to exist? Of all impossibilities these are the greatest, if there are any degrees in impossibilities.

Blessed be God for that word, "He hateth putting away;" it suits some of our poor, fickle, and frequently wandering hearts. The Holy Ghost has taught some of us what Hart so well knew, and has so beautifully expressed:

> "If ever it could come to pass,
> That sheep of Christ might fall away,
> My fickle feeble soul, alas!
> Would fall a thousand times a day;
> Were not Thy love as firm as free,
> Thou soon wouldst take it, Lord, from me."

I now take up my second head, which is to speak of grace as manifested by Jesus the Eternal Son of God.

"Ye know," saith Paul, "the grace of our Lord Jesus Christ, that, though He was rich, yet for your sakes He became poor, that ye, through His poverty, might be rich." Then the grace of Jesus Christ is manifested in His incarnation, humiliation and death. But how much does this short statement contain—"He was rich," was with God, was God, and is the eternal Son of God! "Then was I by Him, as one brought up with Him, and I was daily His delight, rejoicing always before Him; *rejoicing in the habitable part of His earth, and My delights were with the sons of men.*" Truly—

> "This was compassion like a God,
> That when the Saviour knew
> The price of pardon was His blood,
> He pity ne'er withdrew."

No, for He said, "A body hast Thou prepared Me, I delight to do Thy will, O God!" But let us look more closely at this subject. The grace of Jesus Christ is seen, first, in His willingness to be the Surety for His poor sinful people. God the Father chose the people and gave them to His well-beloved Son. "Thine they were, and Thou gavest them Me" (How willing He was to have them!). . . . As the Father willed to save them, so He, the Son, willingly undertook in covenant for them, to be made under the law, that being in their law place, He might redeem them that were under the law, being made sin for us who knew no sin, that we might be made the righteousness of God in Him; all this He willingly before-time undertook to be and do for His poor ruined, helpless, sinful people.

Secondly, In His incarnation, at the eternally appointed time, He was "made of a woman, made under the law". Yes, poor, dear, sin-afflicted soul, Jesus, the Son of God, "who being in the form of God, thought it not robbery to be equal with God; but made Himself of no reputation, and took upon Him the form of a servant, and was made in the likeness of men; and being found in fashion as a man, He humbled Himself and became obedient unto death, even the death of the cross." Grace, free, sovereign, eternal grace brought Him down thus; "He was rich, yet for your sakes He became poor." The Son of God was made a little lower than the angels. What for? For the suffering of death. "Forasmuch, then, as the children are partakers of flesh and blood, He also Himself likewise took part of the same, *that* through death He might destroy him that had the power of death, that is, the devil."

Thirdly, In that He came to pay the debts His people owed and could not pay. He magnified the law and made it honourable; this was by going to the end of it for righteousness for everyone that believeth. He gave Himself a ransom for all, to be testified in due time,—"The Good Shepherd giveth His life for the sheep."

> "Well might the sun in darkness hide,
>   And shut his glories in,
> When God the mighty Maker died
>   For man, the creature's sin."

Yes, poor sinner, and it makes you hide your face too, and dissolves you in wonder, when your soul is favoured with an assurance that He died for you. Oh! the love that brought Him down with the full knowledge of what He must go through to redeem His people. "Awake, O sword, against My Shepherd, and against the Man that is My Fellow, saith the Lord of Hosts; smite the Shepherd, and the sheep shall be scattered; and I will turn Mine hand upon the little ones."

"He undertook and must go through;" and blessed be

His glorious Name for ever, He did go through, for "He Himself bare our sins in His own body on the tree." Poor sin-burdened one, was ever grace like this? how sweetly does it sound to thee at times! His active obedience, His bloody sweat, His groans, and His meritorious death, by these things He paid the debt His people owed. Poor sinner, "Paid is the mighty debt you owed, salvation is of grace." What love fills His heart! it is a flame which waters cannot quench, a treasure which money cannot purchase.

Fourthly, His intercession springs from His eternal grace or love. He gave an instance of it here: "Father, I will that they also, whom Thou hast given Me, be with Me where I am, that they may behold My glory." He ever liveth to make intercession for His blood-bought family—not for the whole world, but for those given Him by His Father. He did not pray for the whole world: "I pray not for the world, but for them which Thou hast given Me; for they are Thine." When He was here in the flesh, He did not die for it; and can we suppose His intercession more extensive than His work of redemption?

Fifthly, His love is seen in, and manifested by, the gracious promises He has made to His poor doubting saints. "Fear not, little flock, it is your Father's good pleasure to give you the kingdom." "And this is the will of Him that sent Me, that every one which seeth the Son, and believeth on Him, may have everlasting life; *and I will raise him up at the last day.*" All His gracious words, His precious sayings, and even His reproofs, flow from the love of His heart. Is, then, this the grace from which the apostle says the Galatians would or could fall? Surely he would never so detract from the honour of that glorious Person who had been so revealed in him, and of whom he knew so much, the efficacy of whose righteousness, and the stability of whose covenant he had so written of throughout this epistle! No, no, the apostle had not so learned Christ. Nay, even to these same Galatians he writes, "I have confidence in you through the Lord, that ye will be none otherwise minded." Fall from that grace, lose all interest in that grace, which prompted the dear and blessed Redeemer to become Surety for His people, which made Him delight to do the will of God, though that

will was, to Him, as Toplady says, " a will of suffering,"
which was such a mighty flame it could not be quenched by
all the waves and billows that rolled over it, which still
burns, and which makes Him feel a deeper sympathy with
His poor afflicted people, each one in his particular sorrows,
than they can feel for one another, Isa. lxiii. 9,—fall from *this*
grace ?   O, blessed be God, never, never!   Poor tempest-tossed
and not comforted, His blood could as soon lose its efficacy
as you lose your interest in it.   If any one of His people
could, how should He see of the travail of His soul and be
satisfied ?   You may feel as if your hope and your strength
had perished from the Lord; you may complain, as the
psalmist did, " As for the light of mine eyes, it also is gone
from me," but the mighty God of Jacob, even Jesus, stands at
the right hand of the poor to save him, and the light of Israel
will again and again shine upon your soul, for it is not
quenched.   Blessed be God, even Jehovah Jesus, His grace
is sufficient to bring every one of His many sons to glory,
and when they are all there with Him, He will say, " Behold,
here am I, and the children which God hath given Me."

I will now speak of grace in its third aspect, according to
my plan, which is: Grace as it is applied by the Holy
Eternal Spirit.   He is called the Spirit of grace for, I think,
two very obvious reasons.   First, because He is the God of
grace, equally so with the Father and the Son; what grace
the Father and the Son have, that the Eternal Spirit has.
Is it the will of the Father and the Son to save poor sinners
by grace ? so it is the will of the Eternal Spirit also.   Since
He is God, what God wills to do, it is the Holy Ghost willing.   There is but one will, one flame of love, one glorious
determination in the eternal and ever-blessed Trinity; therefore, the Holy Ghost is the God of grace.   Secondly, He is
the Spirit of grace because His work in the soul is a gracious
work.   He dispenses and applies grace, takes it out of the
fulness which is in Jesus, and puts it into earthen vessels,
dividing to every man severally as He will.   His work is
called " the grace of God ".   " The hand of the Lord " was
with those who preached Jesus at Antioch, and a " great
number believed and turned to the Lord "; then when Bar-
nabas came to see the Christians there he " saw the grace of

God, and was glad." Now "no man can say that Jesus is
the Lord, but by the Holy Ghost." But these people at
Antioch had believed in Jesus, therefore they so believed by
the precious work of the Holy Ghost in their hearts. Barna-
bas saw this grace of God; His teaching, His work in creating faith in them, and revealing Jesus to them; this was
the grace of God which he saw.

His blessed work goes by several names in the Scriptures,
and, as the Lord may help me, I will attempt to set forth
His grace, by taking a view of His work under those several
names.

Then, first, it is a creation: " Created in Christ Jesus." The
Maker of the world alone is able to make a Christian, to call
into being and exercise feelings, desires, love, and dispositions
*which did not, could not, by any human possibility, exist in
the breast of a sinner.* " If any man be in Christ Jesus, he
is a new creature,"—something that he was not before. That
power and that voice which said, " Let there be light, and
there was light," must say, Let there be convictions, spiritual convictions of sin, honest, humble confessions of it; let
there be light and life, let there be desires, prayers, entreaties
for mercy; let there be hungerings and thirstings after righteousness; let there be pantings after God, even a dear
Redeemer; after salvation, the pardon of sin, and deliverance
from the pit of corruption. The Lord, I repeat, must say,
" Let there be these things in the soul," before ever they can
be. Now, my friends, you have these feelings and desires in
your souls, and precious indeed they are, they are created by
the Holy Ghost. Taught by Him, are you not constrained
most sweetly to put off concerning the former conversation
the old man, which is corrupt according to the deceitful
lusts ? How bitter is the old way, the former conversation how
distasteful! How you desire to enter into that word, " Old
things are passed away, and, behold, all things are become
new!" This is the desire of every living soul, and to " put
on the new man, which after God is *created* in righteousness
and true holiness." This same truth of creation work is set
forth in Isaiah xliii. 21, " This people have I *formed* for
Myself; they shall shew forth My praise;" and again in
Psa. c.: " Know ye that the Lord He is God: it is He that

hath made us, and not we ourselves; we are His people, and
the sheep of His pasture." Ah, my brethren, whence is all
this? Here is the answer, "By the *grace* of God I am what
I am." "By the grace of God I am made a sensible sinner,
a needy and helpless sinner, and though in myself a wretched
sinner, yet by the grace of God I am not a despairing, but a
hoping sinner; by the grace of God I desire to love, cleave
to, and be found in the Lord Jesus." Yes, poor soul, what
you are in all these respects, you are by the grace of God;
it is He that hath made you, and not you yourself. He has
wrought all our good works in us. If it were put to us, as
it was to the disciples, by the dear Redeemer, "Will ye also
go away?" what do we think and hope would be our answer?
Do you, poor tried soul, feel as if you must exclaim, "O, but
my need of Him is so great, my poverty of soul so deep, my
sin and guilt so heavy; and I hope I have at times had such
glimpses of Him as have taken my heart away, and have
raised within me such a hope in His precious Name and
blood; that He is all my desire, either in heaven or earth"?
These feelings are the creation of the Eternal Spirit in thy
soul.

Secondly, His marvellous work is called being "born
again". As the election of grace are predestinated unto the
adoption of children by Jesus Christ, this precious new birth
is the unfolding of that decree. How many of God's dear
sons are tried about this matter!

> "We pray to be new born,
>   Yet know not what we mean;
> We think it something very great,
>   Something that's undiscovered yet."

But when the blessed Spirit comes as the Spirit of adoption
they then cry, "Abba, Father." What I wish to observe in
this place is that, at the new birth, eternal relationship is
manifested. In eternal union with Jesus, the soul now has
life from the fountain imparted unto it. At the implantation
of this new life the sinner is passive; the will has nothing to
do with it; it is wholly of God, John i. 13; iii. 5—8; it is
with the Word of truth the soul is new-begotten, James i. 18;
it is an incorruptible seed that is implanted in the soul,

I Peter i. 23. This incorruptible seed *remaineth* in those who are blessed with such an inestimable treasure, and they cannot sin, because they are born of God, I John iii. 9. When the Holy Ghost breathes life into a soul, how that soul begins to breathe, without knowing it at first, after God! "Thus saith the Lord God unto these bones, Behold, I will cause breath to enter into you, and ye shall live." This done, what a moving there is among the bones, and how quickly is the imparted life made manifest! "Then said He unto me, Son of man, these bones are the whole house of Israel; behold *they say*, Our bones are dried, and our hope is lost; we are cut off for our parts."

Thirdly, This work of grace, carried on by the Holy Ghost, is called a gift. "A new heart also will I give you, and a new spirit will I put within you, and I will take away the stony heart out of your flesh, and I will give you a heart of flesh." "I will give them a heart to know Me, that I am the Lord; and they shall be My people, and I will be their God." "And I will give them one heart, and one way, that they may fear Me for ever." This is elsewhere denominated a good and honest heart, which distinguished the only true hearer of the gospel from the numerous spurious hearers, in the parable of the sower. O precious gift! it is a heart of flesh in which the Spirit of the living God writes the truth, love, and fear of God, in which is written the secret of the Lord; it is a heart to know the Lord, and this knowledge is eternal life, John xvii. 3, and is the only true ground of a sinner's glorying here, Jer. ix. 24. It is one heart; all the saints have the same God-fearing, truth-loving heart; it is a good and honest heart, bringing forth honest, godly fruits; it is not a stout unfeeling heart—for all such are far from righteousness—it is a broken heart, a contrite heart, trembling at God's word, and the highly-favoured possessor of it wants no tenant but God Himself, "O when wilt Thou come unto me?"

There are many other things said about His precious work of grace which I cannot enter into particularly now. I will just glance at a few. Having taught a poor sinner his own inability to pray aright, how mercifully does He make intercession for him with groanings which cannot be

uttered; first showing sin, He follows that revelation by
another, even a revelation of Jesus; cutting down all fleshly
hopes, and rejecting all carnal confidences, He forms Christ
in the heart, the hope of glory, and reveals a dear Saviour
as the confidence of all the ends of the earth; making the
poor soul feel his estrangement from God, and cutting away
from him all his Arminian claims upon the mercy and favour
of God, He comes as the blessed Spirit of adoption, con-
straining the soul to cry, " Abba, Father!" an utterance this
he thought he never should, never dare take into his lips;
bringing the soul into bondage under the law, He, at the set
time, comes as the Spirit of liberty, for where the Spirit of
the Lord is, there is liberty; removing the veil, and revealing
the Son, who said, " And if the Son shall make you free, ye
shall be free indeed." He brings sweet liberty indeed, liberty
from the law of Moses, and from the curse of the law; and,
lastly, He is said to be in His people " a well of water
springing up into everlasting life " (John iv. 14; vii. 38, 39).

This, then, is the grace of the Holy Ghost, His gracious
work in the heart of a sinner. Had the apostle this grace
in view when he said to the Galatians they were fallen from
grace if they were circumcised? I know numbers would
unhesitatingly answer, " Yes," but it is because they know
not the Scriptures, nor the power of God. It is probable
that many will deny that I have given a Scriptural view of
grace. Let them accomplish two things, then I will give
way to their objection at once; let them, first, overthrow
this view *by* Scripture, and secondly, set before us another
view *from* Scripture; but in the meantime, by the help of
the Lord, we will abide by what He Himself, as we hope and
believe, has taught us. To say a sinner may fall from this
grace is simply to say that a creation work may of itself go
into nothing, that feelings which were called into being by
the Spirit can of themselves cease to exist. " But," one may
object, " in speaking thus you destroy the will of man entirely." Though this is not a question of the will at all, yet
I would observe that the objector would himself (by maintaining the possibility of falling) destroy the will of a sinner
who has been quickened by the Holy Ghost, for if ever a
will was exercised by a sinner it is in salvation matters; if

this soul could perish, violence would indeed be done to his will. Bent towards the Lord by all his poverty of soul and all the desire of his renewed will, what violence indeed would be done to this will if the devil should be permitted to drive the poor sinner into hell! To say that this grace may perish is to say that a life breathed into the soul may die away, and that the eternal decree, which brought forth so sweetly, may yet fail and be barren. What an awful impeachment it is of the honour and glory of the Holy Ghost, for it says He forsakes the works of His own hands, is careless of those He has manifested so much love to as to quicken them; nay, more and worse, that He gives desires He will never gratify, a thirst He will never quench, an appetite He will never appease; that He puts in the heart a prayer for pardon and salvation which shall not be answered! But His work is a gift, the gift of a new heart. What becomes of this? Is it taken away again? Then God would repent of His gifts, which is contrary to Scripture; it is a pure seed, incorruptible, undying, and *it remaineth* in the soul. "But," one may say, "may not Satan touch and defile this seed?" I answer, the Scriptures say not. "We know that whosoever is born of God sinneth not; but he that is begotten of God keepeth himself, and that wicked one toucheth him not" (I John v. 18). I am not, my dear friends, preaching the non-backsliding doctrine, no, no; God forbid that I should be so misunderstood by anyone. The covenant which holds fast every favourite of heaven, has a rod for each backsliding child, Psa. lxxxix. 30—32, as I observed before.

Now, my dear friends, I believe this is the true grace of God which I have, though in a very feeble way, testified unto you; I doubt not there is a confirming testimony in your own hearts. What debtors are we to grace, free grace, and must ever be. What a lovely theme it is! How it warms and cheers the heart of a sinner deep in debt, with naught to pay, to be frankly forgiven! How suitable is this free, sovereign grace to the various needs of the Lord's people; what precious words of grace drop into the heart to uphold, guide, and comfort! For the hungry there is a word, " Blessed are ye that hunger now, for ye shall be filled;" and oh, poor thirsty ones, there is a good word for you, " I will pour water

upon him that is thirsty; and floods upon the dry ground."
Grace is not suited to nor needed by the rich, the whole, the
Pharisee; but to them that have need of healing it is most
desirable. It suits the lame, for it says he shall leap; the
dumb, for it declares he shall sing; while to those who are
in graves, a gracious God says, " O My people, I will bring
you up out of your graves." To every tempted one a most
gracious Saviour says, " My grace is sufficient for thee." Are
you sinking under a burden ? there is a word of grace,
" Underneath are the everlasting arms;" let but the Holy
Ghost send that word into your heart, what a sufficient word
you will find it. The grace of the Eternal God is a three-
fold cord which cannot be broken: the grace of God the
Father, the grace of God the Son, and the grace of God the
Eternal Spirit. Happy, thrice happy, is the man who is
interested in it, for though he may fall from the present
sense and *feeling* of it, yet from the wonderful principle, the
precious fruit and the mighty work of it in the soul, never!
The Lord add His blessing. Amen.

THE SUBSTANCE OF MR. POPHAM'S LAST SERMON,

preached Lord's Day Morning, May 30th, 1937.*

" Elect according to the foreknowledge of God the Father,
through sanctification of the Spirit, unto obedience and sprinkling
of the blood of Jesus Christ: Grace unto you and peace be
multiplied."—I PETER i. 2.

" ELECT." How old is election ? Have we any hint of it in
early Scripture ? Yes, we have not only a hint but a distinct
declaration of it in Gen. iii. 15. " The Seed of the woman "—
Christ, the Head of the election of grace—" shall bruise thy
head, and thou shalt bruise His heel "—the elected Church,

* With much difficulty our late dear friend, assisted by two deacons,
reached the pulpit. He entered heaven seventeen days later.

chosen in Christ before the foundation of the world. That is the beginning of [the declaration of] election. It is a Divine doctrine, an amazing doctrine. "Elect." Why were any of us called by grace when we were dead in trespasses and sins? Why did the Holy Ghost kindle that life in our souls that will never die? The word "elect" explains it. Two women grinding in a mill, one is taken, the other left. Two men labouring in a field, one is taken, the other left. Those of you who have a hope that you are the one taken, the grinder and the labourer, will never be able to bless God enough for the distinction that He made when He called you and left the other. "Elect": Two living together, one taken, the other left. Think of it! What was there in us to give the Creator delight? Nothing. Why did He say concerning one in a family, "Go to that family and separate him from his father, his mother, his brethren, and his sisters"? Some families are wonderfully favoured, others not so. But wherever there is a call, it explains this one beautiful word, terrible to the Arminian world,—"elect." And although Arminianism flourishes, and will flourish to the end, the truth will remain. "Elect." "Chosen." Go to that village and call a few people, gather them together according to the Scripture, "Where two or three are gathered together in My Name, there am I in the midst of them." What sent John Vinall* from Lewes to Brighton every Lord's Day evening? What sent His servant John Grace to West Street? What caused seven men to begin by prayer and supplication in their houses, this cause now here at Galeed?†

---

* Mr. Vinall preached at Jireh Chapel, Lewes, on Sabbath mornings, and for some years at Providence Chapel, Church Street, Brighton, in the evening. His ministry was blest to many, but his opposition to believers' baptism and other peculiar views he latterly held caused a measure of coolness between himself and Mr. Grace, which resulted in the latter leaving Church Street where he had preached on Lord's Day mornings. Mr. Grace's friends took for him The Tabernacle, West Street, Brighton, where his pastorate commenced in April, 1847, continuing to his death in 1865. He was greatly owned of God.

† "Galeed"—the scene of our late dear friend's fifty-five years labour—was opened on the 15th of October, 1868.

"In 1867, a few people could not profit by a ministry which succeeded a minister [John Grace] by whom they had been fed with the finest of the wheat. Among them were seven men who came to be known as 'Number Seven'. These, in particular, found no meat to relieve their souls. They suffered and were exercised. Never having taken

U

The only word that will explain all to the glory of God is that word, " elect."

Then you may have a very solemn question, " Am I one? Did God think of me for good? did He lay His hand on me? " Why would the Lord do that? The only thing to explain it is that it pleased Him. Seventy disciples were sent abroad to preach; and when they returned and told the Lord of their successes in following His word according to their commission, He told them not to rejoice in their successes, but to rejoice that their names were written in heaven. To have your name written in heaven is to be elected, to be chosen in Christ, to be one with Him, part of Himself. When God created Eve out of Adam, he said, " This is now bone of my bones, and flesh of my flesh." And those who are born again are " members of Christ's body, of His flesh and of His bones " (Eph. v. 30; I Cor. xii. 27), of one Spirit with Him, one life, one nature, one heaven. Oh, think of it! " Elect according to the foreknowledge of God the Father "; that is to say, according to His eternal purpose, according to the time—if one may use that word, " time "—when He decreed that there should be a bride for His Son, and that His Son should say, " This is now bone of My bones, and flesh of My flesh." This is the Church, the bride of Christ, the ever pure bride of Christ. When therefore you read this discriminating, this wonderful word " elect ", go to Genesis and you will see the origin of it. Notwithstanding Adam (not deceived) broke the law, God had said, " There shall be a bride of the seed of the woman,— the Church of Christ."

Look, then, at this blessed word " elect ". If it troubles

part in public worship, they were perplexed. They had no plans, no ideas to work out, no determination to do this or that, no thought of attempting to gather a congregation. Not one of them had ever prayed in public, though they were known to, and loved by, their former minister. In their perplexity, sorrow, and loneliness, it came into the mind of one of them to suggest a meeting for prayer in one of their houses. This was done. At that meeting, on the seven men was poured out the Holy Ghost in a remarkable degree. This led to a second meeting, in another of their houses, when the same gracious experience was granted; and for seven weeks in succession prayer was made, according to the will of God, Rom. viii. 26; Jude 20. *Thus was the cause and interest of Christ now worshipping at Galeed, commenced."* —J. K. Popham in *A humble Memorial to the Lord, 1932.*

you, bow before God and ask Him to make it plain to you. If the enemy comes to bruise you by telling you that you are not elected, God help you to go to the Lord Jesus and ask Him to bruise Satan's head in you by assuring you that you belong to Christ. Every conquest that Christ has in you is the bruising of Satan's head. Every pain, every temptation, every sore assault, every stirring up of your native corruption within you is just that, a bruising of Christ's heel. But the day will come when there will be no more bruising of Christ's heel in the saints but a bruising of Satan under their feet, when they hope—O sweet hope! I would not part with my hope for the world, that I am going to be with Christ.

"Elect"? Generally, of course, election is the choice of one person or thing, implying the rejection or reprobation of another person or thing. Election and reprobation are correlative terms, the one implies the other. "Ah, then," says the enemy to an elect sinner, "you are not chosen, you are not one of the elect;" and he puts you to it, "*Prove* that you are." You say, "I cannot prove it." Yet you may be able to prove it. Why do you hate what you used to love? Why do you follow now what once you fled from? Why do you want Christ, of Whom if not to Whom you said, "Depart from me, for I desire not the knowledge of Thy ways"? We owe all that to this blessed word taking effect on us, "Elect" according to God's eternal foreknowledge of us. O brethren, we cannot bless God enough for election and for any comfortable evidence that we are elected. Any sweet whisper of the Spirit, any bright inshining of Christ, any comfortable persuasion by the Spirit that we belong to Christ, that we are believers in Christ, that we are fellow-heirs with Christ,—it is all wrapt up in this sweet word, "elect." Let me refer you again to Gen. iii. 15, "the Seed of the woman": God's eternal Son sent into the world to lay down His life for sin, to suffer shame and grief and sorrow and death; and guilt in all that, guilt in all that. On earth the Saviour was His Father's *righteous* servant, but in all His righteousness there was this sin imputed to Him. Oh,

"Why was I made to hear His voice
And enter while there's room?

> While thousands make a wretched choice,
> And rather starve than come."

" Elect." Is anything more abhorrent to religious men to-day
than this doctrine ? Arminianism, why, the land, the world,
is full of it. Ah, the Dutchman sowed dreadful seed when
he sowed his Arminianism, but he was not the first to do it;
it was done when Adam (undeceived) made the woeful choice
to take the forbidden fruit.

" Elect according to the foreknowledge of God the Father."
And now the means: " Through sanctification of the Spirit."
Sanctification may frighten some of you. O the terror the
word has been to me! Sanctification, where will you find it ?
If you find it rightly, you will find it in Christ. If you find
it rightly, you will find that He gives you the Holy Ghost.
Where else would you go for sanctification ? In vain would
you look for it elsewhere than in the Spirit, the Holy Ghost,
" Whom," says Christ, " I will send unto you from the
Father." O look for sanctification in the start of it, in the
carrying of it, in the completion of it, look for it by the
Holy Ghost. I have looked for it till the word " sanctification " has terrified me, because I knew it was not in myself.
I have looked there in vain; I have trembled because of my
indwelling sin. But to find Christ my holiness, my sanctification, and to find that occasionally there come gracious
operations on my soul, I have loved Him for giving me the
Spirit; and I have loved the Spirit for His work. Some of
you can say just the same; and it all comes to this, you are
elected people, according to the eternal purpose of God the
Father, through sanctification of the Spirit.

" Unto obedience and sprinkling of the blood of Jesus
Christ." What is this obedience ? It is receiving Christ
crucified for your life, your holiness, and all that you can
need. This sprinkling is the sensible forgiveness of sins; not
only the hope that one day you will be pardoned, but a *sense*
of pardon, a feeling in your soul that you are forgiven. This
is heaven on earth. " O," some may say, " shall we ever know
it ? " Are you " following on " to know it ? are you crying
to God to tell you that it is so ? are you dissatisfied with
every evidence that is short of this one blessed thing, this

holy persuasion? Ah, when you get this holy persuasion, then you have got the sprinkling, it is on your conscience as if the Lord is saying, "When your sins are sought for, they shall not be found. I have pardoned you, I have cast behind My back all your sins into the depths of the sea." What! You look for them and they cannot be found. "I have cast them behind My back into the depths of the sea." "O, but I see them." God be thanked that you do. Woe be to the man who does not see his sins, who does not feel them. I have daily conflict with sin and other things, but I would not be without that. "Lord, here I am, a poor vile sinner. I hope I have some evidence that my soul lies solemnly flat before Thee, looking unto Christ." And the day comes when you say, "Why, I am clean!

'I'm clean, just God, I'm clean!'"

O what a night that was to me in my spiritual youth, when it came into my soul, "Forasmuch as ye know that ye were not redeemed with corruptible things, as silver and gold, from your vain conversation received by tradition from your fathers, *but with the precious blood of Christ.*" I think I have told you before, that on that blessed night I said, as I laid my head on my pillow, "Now it would be as easy for me to die as it is to lay my head upon this pillow." O the blood of sprinkling! Do you know it? Are you panting for it? are you lying at His footstool? are you assuring Him that it is all you need to cleanse you, all you are desiring, even His precious blood on your conscience? Well, I would say to you, Go on in that way, follow on till you know the Lord. Then will you know the Lord if you follow on to know Him: His going forth is prepared as the morning, and His coming to you will be the fulfilment of that word, "At evening time it shall be light,"—light in your soul, light in your conscience, light in your understanding; and you will then say, "Now know I that the Lord saveth His anointed" (Hos. vi. 3; Zech. xiv. 7; Psa. xx. 6). O happy man, happy soul, that gets this one thing, the sprinkling of the blood of Jesus Christ!

Now Peter, having thus saluted the elect of God in Christ, wishes them grace: "Grace unto you, and peace, be multiplied." They already had grace, but he wishes them more grace, as he writes in another place, " But grow in grace, and in the knowledge of our Lord and Saviour Jesus Christ." To grow in grace is to have grace on grace, as John speaks, " Of His fulness "—of life and goodness and mercy and grace—" have all we received, and grace for grace," grace on grace, grace added to grace. Faith has the addition of hope; hope has the addition of glory set before it. Hope in Christ forbids despair, hope in Christ tells you to look for the end; it says, " For now is our salvation nearer than when we believed." How near God may not tell you. I keep asking Him, not to tell me exactly how near, but to take me to Himself. I say again and again, " Lord, I am nearly ninety years old, do take me home." And I think sometimes it will not be long before He does; I hope not.

" Grace unto you and peace be multiplied." What is this peace ? " The peace of God which passeth all understanding " keeping your hearts and minds through Christ Jesus, that is the peace. You say, " I cannot understand it." Of course you cannot. What you can understand belongs to your nature, but what passes your understanding is God's, God's gift. " Peace be to you." Jesus spoke that; and when He speaks it, it is effectual, blessedly effectual. I say to you, my brethren, " Grace and peace be unto you." We are a little church, and we may become smaller. " Galeed " has had God's presence, and I believe still has, and will have for a time. But this " peace of God which passeth all understanding ", I cannot understand how He should have brought this into my soul; and you may say the same. Why does He do it ? Because He will, because of His love. Each one possessing this peace will say, " I have not much of it." But Christ is full of it. He is " the Son of peace ". All we have to do is set before us in the word, " Then shall we know if we follow on to know the Lord. His going forth is prepared as the morning." " Grace unto you, and peace, be multiplied." O blessed peace! In your troubles may this peace grow in you; in your temptations may this peace overcome in you; when you are bruised by Satan, may this peace come to you, so that you may say, " Bless God for peace, peace with God." You are not at war with Him, but at war with hell and at peace with God. You may then say, "I will lay me down in peace and sleep; for Thou, Lord, only makest me dwell in safety." What a wonderful thing it is to put your head on your pillow sometimes, and say, "It is well with me," and to feel, "Now if God were to come and take me, I should be in heaven." I believe some of you could say it at times, that you humbly believe you will be in heaven when you die; and when your mortal frame goes into dust and earth, then you will have peace without interruption. Now may the Lord bless you. I have spoken in a good deal of physical weakness, but that does not matter; I know I have spoken the truth, the blessed truth; and one day I shall be in heaven, having the peace of God.

The Lord be with you, my brethren. Dear Galeed, God bless you and give you to understand the glory of election. And if you want to see the beginning of it, follow the advice I gave you at the beginning: Go to Gen. iii. 15, and there you will find the beginning of this peace: "It"—the Seed of the woman—"shall bruise thy head, and thou shalt bruise His heel." You will get many a bruise, but Satan will get more. He may bruise you a good bit, but Christ will bruise his hellish head, until there is no more bruising in store for you. May the Lord bless His truth and do you all the good you need, and convert the dead. Every true conversion is an awful bruising of Satan's head, and is the beginning of the end of sin and death in regard of that converted person. God began to bruise Satan's vile head in you at conversion; and every conquest of grace, every sweet coming of the Holy Ghost to you, every manifestation of Christ in you is just that,—the bruising of the serpent. We do not know the terrible bruising that the apostle Paul had when he had the "messenger of Satan", and constantly was afflicted. But some of us have a little anticipation of his great anticipation, "O wretched man that I am! who shall deliver me from the body of this death? Here I am pursued, forsaken, bruised, and I am a wretch. O wretched man that I am! I thank God,"—have not some of you done so? "I thank God through Jesus Christ our Lord. So then with the mind I myself serve the law of God; but with the flesh the law of sin."

Brethren, be thankful for election. Do not say it is a doctrine too high for you. Though it be a doctrine having its Divine beginning in Christ, it is not too high for a living soul; it is not too high for one who says, "Give me Christ, or else I die." O when we get that blessed Jesus in the arms of our faith, we are ready to fly away. That is how I feel; and I do long to go and be with Him sometimes. May the Lord bless you. Look at election. Election, what is it ? The choice of one person, implying the rejection or reprobation of another. And if you are panting to know your own election of God, my advice to you is, Go on, follow on, press your case.

> " Urge thy claim through all unfitness,
>   Sue it out, spurning doubt;
>   The Holy Ghost's thy witness."   Amen.

LETTERS

I.

Three Letters to a Brother.

My dear H.,—Two points in your letter please me very much, and raise a little hope in my mind concerning you; they are contained in your quotations from Mr. Hart. You feel that the case he came into—viz., not whether he *would,* but whether he *might* be a Christian—is exactly your own. Thus far you are in the right way. By this experience, so mortifying to your proud heart, you will be forced to acknowledge that salvation is, must be, of grace, and grace alone. Thus God humbles all whom He teaches and will save. So far from producing despair, this solemn teaching begets a feeling that there may be hope even for the vilest and weakest. To be sure it produces self-despair, and cuts off our proud boasting, which it is intended to do. It will be one of the lessons the Lord will most deeply imbed in your heart, that salvation is of the Lord; and one means of doing this will be by giving you some painful experience of your own helplessness, and of the fact that it is not whether *you* will, but whether He, so glorious in holiness, so fearful in praises, will. And O how certain I am that as you grow in this necessary knowledge, your own heart, full of unbelief, pride, hypocrisy, and blasphemy, will be muttering and peeping, and uttering its free-will and creature-power error against the Lord! It will mutter its impudent and impious rebellion against sovereign grace, against God being all in salvation, and the sinner only a passive receiver. It will peep for some way of escape out of this mortifying weakness, will peep for helpers, and even enter into covenant with death and make a league with hell, rather than submit to God. It will utter its error against God, saying election, salvation by grace, must be wrong, because they leave no room for human power and merit. But God will be alone exalted in salvation; and your mercy will be to humble yourself under His mighty Hand, fall down flat before Him, and own your baseness, weakness, hardness, pride, distance, unlikeness, and ruin. In due time He exalts all who thus

abase themselves; He fills the hungry with good things and
satisfies the longing soul.

The next point is,—you feel it is not whether you will
believe, but whether the Lord will give you true repentance.
Well, can you at times ask Him for that great gift? Do you
feel sometimes as if you could go as a poor, hard-hearted,
ruined sinner, and ask the Lord to grant you repentance and
remission? Jesus is exalted to give both. You feel hard-
hearted, unbelieving; may you have a heart to fall before
God and confess the worst to Him. Remember Christ came
to seek and to save that which was lost. He "receiveth
sinners and eateth with them". One thing you will feel will
be this: you cannot, dare not seek God in your distressful
case; you must [first] wash away some of your sin, subdue
some crying evil of your heart; but the gospel way is,—" I
will take away the heart of stone. I will cleanse you," etc.
When you feel your heart hardening itself,—as it will do
sometimes more than others,—try, as well as you can, to pray,
to confess your sins, and ask for a broken heart. Your weakness is not against you; your feeling that it is not whether
you will believe, but whether the Lord will give you faith,
is not a barrier set up between Himself and your poor soul;
if God be teaching you, it is one of His kind methods of
bringing you near. Seek clear work; fear losing your trouble
in a wrong way.

The Lord in His great mercy teach you, humble you under
His mighty hand, give you true faith and deep repentance,
seal pardon on your heart, and pour a spirit of prayer upon
you.   With much love,

1885.   J. K. P.

II.

My dear H.,—It rejoices me to find that you are so sorely
exercised in your mind; that you *feel* your hardness and need
of true repentance and free forgiveness. A good man said,
" The beginning of my salvation is the knowledge of my sin."
No misery felt, no solemn convictions, no sense of deep and
entire ruin, then no cry for mercy, no feeling that *God must
do all the work.* "The Lord killeth, and maketh alive; He
bringeth down to the grave, and bringeth up. The Lord

maketh poor, and maketh rich; He bringeth low, and lifteth up. He raiseth up the poor out of the dust, and lifteth up the beggar from the dunghill, to set them among princes, and to make them inherit the throne of glory; for the pillars of the earth are the Lord's, and He hath set the world upon them" (I Sam. ii. 6—8).

Misery for sin, emptiness felt, hardness of heart confessed, strong desires at times for repentance, faith and love, and for a revelation of Jesus, are as much the work of the Spirit as the sealing of pardon on the conscience and the assuring witness that one is a child of God. Your present state is not a new thing under the sun. When Isaiah saw the glory of the Lord, he became a man of unclean lips. As Daniel, Peter, and John saw the Lord they felt undone and dead. There can be no spiritual knowledge of ourselves as vile, undone sinners apart from Divine teaching—Divine shining upon our polluted hearts. The filth of the back slums of London might be a thousandfold more than it is, yet no man could see it without the sun's rays; and thus it is with respect to our filthy nature: we see it not until the Light of Life shines upon it. Then, as that Light more and more shines, we sink lower and lower under the weight of guilt and a sense of our desperate case. We are commanded to love the Lord with all our heart; but we *feel* only a heart teeming with enmity, and full of blasphemy against God. O what a solemn case! How well I remember the wormwood and the gall. This is a case for sovereign mercy flowing through the dear Redeemer's blood. The Lord will bring down your heart with labour until you find none to help, then will He show Himself strong on your behalf. What you want is a free, full, and everlasting gospel; not *yea, nay,* but yea and amen, to the glory of God (II Cor. i. 19, 20). The dear Lord of peace draw near and give you peace. . . .

J. K. P.

III.

My dear H.,—Though I cannot answer your letter as fully as I could wish, yet I feel I must send a few words. It is a good thing that you feel your old foundation " discovered to the neck ", and that you now find that true which you used to be annoyed at hearing from me. One of the worst evils is the delusion which thousands are living in,—believing themselves Christians, while they know neither their own wretched state, nor Jesus Christ as the good, *the only* Physician. Better never call Christ your Saviour than claim Him before the hand of His power has been laid on you in a work of grace. "Many will say, Lord, Lord; then will I profess unto them, I never knew you, depart from Me, ye workers of iniquity." "The Lord knoweth them that are His;" and He in His own time, way, and measure, teaches them the saving knowledge of Himself. "They shall all know Me, from the least of them unto the greatest."

You now appear to have some knowledge of yourself as a sinner. This is terrible to you; you feel hard, dark, and far off from God, without gleams of hope in His mercy; your heart remains hard, and discovers its enmity and filth. You will be the subject of many strange feelings. Sometimes your heart will be so full of wrath and so desperate in its misery, that you will even feel—it may be somewhat indistinct, though it was not in my own case—you could dare God to damn you; this will be followed by great dread and horror on your spirit, but no contrition. Divine justice strikes awe into our hearts, but does not beget love. Perhaps soon afterwards you may realize a sweet melting away of this most desperate hardness and wrath, and a little drawing near to God, and almost a sensation of love to Him. Now the first is the work of the law; the latter, the operation of the Spirit of Christ. The one turns you into yourself, presses upon you the deepest sense of your misery and ruin; demands perfect obedience, and shows you how impossible that obedience is; forbids sin, and shows its awful wages; discovers it, and makes the soul sensible of the power of lust. "Thou shalt not covet," as applied, shows us what thieves we are; though we have never touched a pin belonging to another person. This is *good*, though painful work. It prepares for the coming of the gospel, for the secret and sacred touches, motions, operations, and revelations of the Spirit. For these, look and pray; for they melt, raise up faith, hope and love, and beget repentance. Beg that you may not lose your burden in any but the right way—the forgiveness of sins. A wound only slightly healed will break out again, and be worse than before. Only the sovereign Balm of Gilead can rightly heal a rightly wounded conscience. Though you will wince under the searching teachings of God, they will end well. Don't seek for man's opinion or testimony; pray to be made right by God. True religion much consists of intercommunications between God and the quickened soul. Seek a religion, *private* in its origin, maintenance and increase; but *public* in its fruits. J. K. P.

IV.

To One Tempted.

My dear Friend in the Lord,—I have two letters from you to answer. Both of them are written within and without, with lamentation and mourning and woe. But I will venture to say that all this is infinitely better than the laughter of fools. I am not shaken in regard to your state before God by all you say against yourself. That it is sad and grievous to be in such a state of feeling I know. But the day is coming when God shall with infinite power rebuke this cruel enemy of His sovereignty and your peace. You cannot, *He can and will.* I am not going to contradict you in the things you say about your hardness of heart, but I will try to tell you of the remedy. All that is bad is too true of us. But one thing more is also true—there is a God of all grace. Yes, that God about whom and whose goodness our wicked infidelity has so powerfully, so distressingly worked, is able and will deliver you from all iniquity, receive you graciously, love you freely. You may put this away, you may think and say I am deceived, but I shall maintain my ground against yourself on behalf of yourself. An enemy, knowing well the depravity of nature, has sown this seed and, alas, how quickly and with strength has it grown. Too well do I know this. But when once more the Lord returns with mercies, what self-loathing, confession, wonder, weeping, and silence you will be filled with! You have not yet got to the end of the "many times". "Yea, many a time forgave He their iniquity and destroyed them not. Yea, many a time turned He away His anger, and did not stir up all His wrath." Do not keep silence, but write again soon; "Speaking may relieve thee." I feel so much for your brother in his sad loss, and pray the Lord may support him and make the affliction a great blessing.

Give my love to your dear father, to Mrs. T. and Mr. and Mrs. J. L. You all come in sometimes when I try to pray. The Lord bless you and that abundantly. Christ is the Fountain of Life and the living streams flowing from Him into your heart will swallow up your sad death.

We are all well and unite in love to you and your household. Believe me,

Yours in the best bonds,

Brighton. 1886.   J. K. POPHAM.

V.

To the same.

My dear Friend in tribulation,—It is not my intention "to reprove words, and the speeches of one that is desperate, which are as wind", but when you say, "The Bible contradicts itself—it says, 'cleanseth from all sin,' and yet says there is an unpardonable sin; what is true?" I will answer, "The words of the Lord are pure words; as silver tried in a furnace of earth, purified seven times." "Thy Word is very pure." The crook is in your own mind, and urged by your adversary the devil. Never give up what you are doing—crying for mercy. The Lord "shall deliver the needy when he crieth, the poor also, and him that hath no helper. He shall spare the poor and needy, and shall save the souls of the needy. He shall redeem their soul from deceit and violence, and precious shall their blood be in His sight." Your case will not be improved by anyone arguing it over with you, but by the Lord bringing you to *reason* with HIM. "Come now, and let us reason together, saith the Lord; though your sins be as scarlet, they shall be as white as snow; though they be red like crimson, they shall be as wool." You believe that you and the devil are good friends. You know not what you say. He curses and blasphemes and hates God, His people, His Word, His House, His holiness, the meekness and gentleness of Christ, the Person, blood, merits, righteousness, death, resurrection and intercession of the Redeemer. Do you mean you are friendly with him in all this satanic wickedness? that you could join him—walk in Balaam's wicked spirit of cursing God's people—be content to be shut out from God and live in the hard, blaspheming pride of despair—never to pray, never to hope, never to love? You know not what you say, your words are as wind. Neither God nor good men will listen to them. Dear, dear friend, cry on, hard as you feel, full of all manner of sin as you feel, a habitation of every unclean bird as you feel, guilty as you feel, sinking as you are, desperate as you are, dark, far off, unfeeling, unrepenting as you feel, hopeless, sentenced to death by God and conscience, as you now judge —cry on, shew to the Lord your misery and fall, as you can, on the stone which is laid for a foundation, a foundation not for goodness nor good people, but desperately wicked sinners. There is power in the blood of Christ—all you need is the powerful application of it by the Spirit. The Lord be gracious unto you at the voice of your cry. I am continually begging for you.

Now I beg you will try to tell Mrs. T. about yourself. Don't bottle this sorrow up. Remember how low she sank, how bitter was her cup. Tell her all, let the worst out, who can tell what may be the result of your so speaking. At least she will sympathize, and pray for you.

Thank you very much for your letter. I hope never by word or act to give ground for saying I do not think so highly of you. I will not repeat how fully our hearts are with you. May wisdom be given me to walk as I ought. . . . I am going to H. this afternoon. I need wisdom not only for the pulpit but also for the parlour.

Do write again soon. Accept our united love and deepest sympathy, and   Believe me,

Yours sincerely in hope,

Brighton. 1887.   J. K. POPHAM.

VI.

My dear Friend,—I hope the Lord may help, bless, and teach you; and bring your heart to that only rest for weary people—Christ Jesus. He is the " fenced place"; as the prophet speaks, " I will stand upon my watch, and set me upon the tower (*fenced place*, margin), and will watch to see what He will say unto me, and what I shall answer when I am reproved " (Hab. ii. 1). In my sorrow here—dear Mr. Marshall's illness—how instructed my poor heart has been by the above word. I was made to perceive that Christ was the Tower, and that in Him my sinful soul could hear reproof, and answer in His blood and thus live. O what a rest this—together with Isa. ix. 10 (producing fear), Rom. xii. 1, 2, and Psa. xxvii. 1—has been in this dark and painful dispensation! The Lord has talked with me of judgment, but in mercy, and the sorrow which worketh death has been taken away. My heart has had nothing to say against my deeply loved and valued friend being taken away, but getting to such a spot was heavy work. But the Holy Ghost did not leave off moving upon my heart until God's will was good, acceptable, and perfect in my judgment, and to my heart. Then did my soul find rest. Then I learned that Christ's yoke is easy, and His burden light. The way to it was by a " living sacrifice ". O, that word *living!* no dead uncared-for thing, but a living, moving, powerful will. O, the ups and downs! now yes, and then no; again, " Take him, Lord, he is Thine;" then, " I cannot bear to part with him; I cannot give him up!" Thus was I pulled to pieces for several days. How kindly and sweetly did the Lord allure me to the point. He said in David, " The Lord is the strength of my life," and this won and overcame, by its unspeakable greatness and sweetness, my afflicted and fearing spirit. His divine will became my choice, my delight. He took me up; I closed in with Him, and found enough in Him to fill my soul, still my fears, guide my feet, defend my head, teach my heart, cleanse my conscience, support my faith, and bring me through all the trials, sorrows and difficulties of this suffering state. I knew not till his life seemed to be ebbing out, how very dear my beloved friend is to me; and when I saw I might no more converse with him, no more be permitted to have his wise counsel, his godly, tender watchfulness over my house, no more hear him pray, I cannot tell you how deep the cut was, how heavy the blow; but now my heart, without loving dear Mr. M. one atom less, has found rest in Him Who is " the same yesterday, and to-day, and for ever ".

This is a selfish letter. I wanted to ask about your own case, and thought not to set out my own. I hope your heart may get some views of that lovely, gracious, all-sufficient Saviour, Who went a suffering, rugged way to glory. What a fire of Divine wrath kindled upon Him, that the soft flames of eternal love might warm the cold and sleepy hearts of His redeemed! He wept that they might rejoice. O, how a sight of Him puts the heart out of conceit with itself, and puts the world in its right place, beneath His feet! Give Him no rest till He establish your heart with grace. May we hear His voice, feel His power, view His person, follow in His footsteps, bear His cross, eat His flesh, drink His blood, have on His robe, and at last fall asleep in Him.

Yours in hope,

Brighton. Feb. 5th, 1887. J. K. POPHAM.

VII.

My dear Friend,—Your kind letter and enclosure came safely. . . . During the last fifteen years what fears, unbelief, and dismay have I felt, and how have I murmured under their power; but what goodness, mercy, faithfulness, and wisdom has my most gracious Lord displayed in His dealings with me. How great is His goodness against my baseness. I used to think I could never doubt, murmur, and rebel, as the Israelites did, if only I saw the hand of God in delivering me, but now I know that between that God-forgetting nation and myself there is no difference in respect of sin and guilt. How forgetful, fretful, rebellious, and insincere towards the Lord is my nature. " Who can bring a clean thing out of an unclean? not one." No patch will do; no scraping and re-washing; no removing of leprous bricks, and putting in new clean ones. " The whole head is sick, and the whole heart faint. From the sole of the foot even unto the head there is no soundness in it; but wounds and bruises and putrefying sores " (Isa. i. 5, 6). Thus our throat is an open sepulchre; with our tongues we have used deceit. How deeply ashamed have I felt the last day or two. How have the evils of my heart broken open to my astonished view. Sunday night I rejoiced in God my Saviour;

V

Monday night I found all manner of evil working. Trouble comes, and how weak we are. A cross lies at our door, and we sink at the sight; some gourd is withered, and we grow angry, not considering Whose Hand withered it. But anger rests in the bosom of a fool. So I have found it. There is no relief until a spirit of confession comes. This I have found also this week. And there is no hope but in the Saviour's blood and righteousness.

> " Deeds of righteousness I've none,
> No, not one good work to plead."

O, how vile have I felt myself at times! and yet I have also felt that I could not cease seeking mercy; and on Tuesday especially I felt I could not live without a Throne of grace. We are only Christians as God the Spirit makes us in soul feeling. Paul knew a man in Christ. Here is a Christian. Yet Paul had a thorn in the flesh, the messenger to buffet him; and this messenger of Satan had something in Paul to work upon, ground in which to cast his hellish seed, sin to draw forth, carnality to strengthen, and a body of sin and death to tie as a millstone around his weary, aching neck. The clean man is the man of Christ—the new creature; the unclean is the old man; they live in the same house, but how different their pursuits! What different tastes, desires, atmospheres and ends, do they seek!

I do hope the Lord will shine upon your soul, and deliver you out of your darkness. For this I have many times, since I have known you, prayed. The remedy lies in the blood and righteousness of Christ. Its effectual application is the Holy Spirit's work. What crook will not God's great salvation make straight; what stone will it not melt; what shadow of death will it not turn into the morning; all bars, separation, guilt, wrath, lack of repentance, inability to cease from sinful self, pride, terror, and every evil, the dear Son of God will, and He only can, remove. None could have a worse case than mine, no heart could be harder, yet His precious mercy I—O wonder of grace!—have not missed. If the Lord the Spirit would graciously help you to make your calling and election sure; to come as a poor, lost, utterly ruined sinner, to the dear fountain of the Saviour's blood, it would be such a help and comfort. Yes, and I believe He will. Then what pleasantness you will find in Wisdom's ways, what indescribable sweetness in the Person of Christ. Well, though the Lord tarry, wait for Him. One day is with Him as a thousand years, and a thousand years as one day. " Be constant though weak."

. . . Wishing you the richest favours a good, covenant God has to bestow in and through Jesus Christ,

I remain, yours sincerely in hope,

1887.   J. K. POPHAM.

VIII.

My dear Friend,—. . . It is an amazing mercy to have a discerning eye in respect of the Spirit's motions, teachings, ways, and admonitions in the heart. Now He wounds, opens up some hitherto undiscovered sin, shows some unthought-of danger, some unsuspected piece of deceit or hypocrisy, by which the soul is sorely cast down and cast into a searching, testing, weighing frame, being fearful of walking in some false liberty or strength. Then that blessed Spirit opens to faith's view the throne of grace and the only way, hope, life, beauty, and strength, even the Person and work of Christ. Now a word falls on the heart as a divine caution, then a sweet and suitable promise gives a lift to faith and hope, and again love is powerfully drawn forth. Diversities of operations, but it is the same God which worketh all in all. It is wonderful to be a subject of those operations; they are saving, they lead the soul into the knowledge of the Son of God, they seal it unto the day of redemption, and they glorify the Spirit, the Son, and the Father.

I could never follow people in their judgment about Spurgeon. The little that seemed right was so counteracted by the much that (as judged by the Scriptures) was undoubtedly wrong, that I always felt I must not praise him on spiritual grounds, but leave him to the just judgment of God.

With Christian love to you and yours who fear or desire to fear God.

Yours in the truth,

February, 1892.   J. K. POPHAM.

IX.

My dear Friend,—. . . I do feel for you in the sad and bitter trial which has befallen you, and in my petitions I beg that a way may be made for your escape. No new thing has happened unto you. But this is your trial. We may comfort others in their sorrows, but when we are touched ourselves we find how weak we are. Yet the Scriptures are written for our learning, that we through patience and comfort of them may have hope. May the Lord open them to your understanding in those parts which meet your troubled case, and speak them to you. He supports where He will not deliver (I Cor. x. 13). It is wonderful to escape despair when we cannot run from troubles which are of a kind to plunge us into it. What a mercy it is that the throne of grace is not blocked up and shut up against you! With one hand God broke up Job, with the other He held him up in life, and *when he was vile*, turned his captivity.

May you and your husband and his dear aged godly mother, have a gracious silence wrought in your spirits. A view of second causes will only produce more and more sorrow which will work death. The prophet's place was good and safe (Hab. ii. 1). Micah got the best of it (vii. 9). The good man was not far out when he wrote:

" To Thee every blessing we owe
Above what the fiends have in hell."

You may be ready to say to me, " If you were in our case you would know." Yes, and I should feel all you do, and more that is bad most likely. But how good I have found a wrought silence (Hab. ii. 20). How Prov. xvi. 20 has in some of my things spoken to me, bidding me call upon the Lord, my sins confess. Who knows if He will return and leave a blessing behind Him, open rivers in high places and fountains in the midst of the valleys; make the wilderness a pool of water and the dry land springs of water ? The Lord has begun to shew you His greatness, and who knows but this most grievous and bitter temporal destruction may bring both temporal and spiritual good ? He is a God which doeth great things and unsearchable, marvellous things without number (Job v. 9). All resurrections come—can only come—out of deaths. The death of the daughter brought this word from the Fountain of Life, " Be not afraid; only believe." I pray your death may bring some good, though seemingly trying word. Now if you look to the earth you can see only "trouble and darkness and dimness of anguish"; but if a great light shone (Isa. viii. 22; ix. 1, 2), then in the trial you would sanctify the Lord of Hosts. You know it is no uncommon thing for living cries, promises, hopes, appearances, beginnings, divine approaches, all to have sad darkness and deaths befall them. But O when the life of all good things comes again, all deaths must give way. Nothing can hinder Christ's holy mighty approach (John xi. 14, 15). No corruption, no stone, no unbelief, no time can affect Life's power over death.

May this be your experience in soul and in circumstances at this sad juncture. May the Lord appear for you, help, sustain, and teach you, give you to hear this rod and who hath appointed it. While He is silent to the multitude, may He graciously privately turn to you and say, " Blessed be ye poor, for yours is the kingdom of heaven."

Thank you for writing to me. Many petitions in early days went from my heart that the Lord would make me a true sympathizing friend to His poor afflicted people—the only way I could hope to help them.

With love and sympathy to you all,

Yours very truly,

Brighton. 1892. J. K. POPHAM.

X.

My dear Friend,—Much as I feel for you in your keen outward trial, I cannot but feel that you are the gainer by it. The Lord has indeed stayed His rough wind in the day of the east wind. Now you have bright clouds and grass in the fields (Zech. x. 1). May this rich mercy continue to you and your dear wife. God is His own interpreter, and in His own time you may admire that very thing which now, under the humbling power of grace, you can commit to and submissively leave in His all-wise, all-powerful hands. In many cases the Lord seems determined to have our confidence before He will give us any account of or reason for His dealings with us.

> "Then trust Me and fear not, thy life is secure;
> My wisdom is perfect, supreme is My power."

It is as if He said, "What is that to thee? follow thou Me." And when the Spirit indulges the soul with some vision of the Divine wisdom, love, tenderness, faithfulness and power, how enabled one feels to leave all, resign all, asking no questions, holding no reservations.

You are in good hands and need no man to tell you so sweetly believed and felt a truth. The cup, its size, every ingredient, every drop, you are willing to take, accept and drink. Thus sweetly do you prove that a man's life consisteth not in the abundance of the things which he possesseth, but in doing the will of God from the heart. But with this sweet resignation in your heart and confidence in your God, how watchful will be the faith you possess to see when and which way the Lord, your God and Friend, will work that deliverance you believe He will command for you. One may accommodate to such a case that gracious word,—"Looking for and hasting unto the coming of the day of God." What the Lord teacheth faith to expect, He will surely give. But when? In His own time: "We shall reap in *due* time."

I meant no answer to your letter in my sermon. I can understand how unsuited to your happy spirit any preaching on Egyptian bondage would be. Poor dear soul, I would add no bitters; rejoice and sing now the Lord has given you His bread and wine and oil. I am sure with all you have enough work for your now lively faith. May I never add burdens where and when God has removed them.

Though I am often weary of myself and even of the sound of my own voice, I feel, "Woe is me if I preach not the gospel." I am more depressed and tried than I can tell at my unprofitable ministry, and often wonder how the Lord bears with me.

May Divine goodness, love, wisdom and power still appear to your faith as engaged in your case. May you still be enabled to obey the word, "Love your enemies." Pray for

me, if you can. My friends see *some* of my poverty; only
some.   . . . Yours in the best bonds,
November, 1893.   J. K. POPHAM.

XI.

My very dear Friend,—Your letter came to hand this
morning and I thank you for it. It was very welcome. I
like its tone; I know how you have obtained the knowledge
and experience about which you write,—not as school boys
learn that two and two make four, but in and out, up and
down, through fire and water, lifting up and casting down,
sorrow and joy, heaviness for a season, manifold temptations,—by these you have lived, learned, lost and gained. " O
Lord, by these things men live, and in all these things is
the life of my spirit." A desperately wicked heart, full of
all manner of evil, is no small part of my sorrowful path;
by its powerful workings I learn in some measure how low I
am lost, how unwilling to part with evil for good, with self
for God, with sin for holiness, with the pleasures of sin for
a season for eternal blessedness. O how free and invincible
must be the grace which overturns my plans, overcomes my
heart, and makes me willing to be saved by grace!

I am very glad you had such a good feeling in hearing
dear Mr. T. I hope the influence spread generally. The
subject is one which, as opened up by the Spirit, is life to
submission, death to rebellion. The sacrifice by the Lord
Jesus of His own will in the Garden is to me a subject I
desire to enter into by the Holy Ghost for my instruction,
comfort and establishment. It was doubtless a vicarious
sacrifice; but it is also an example. This must be the way
for His followers: " Thy will, not mine, be done." We are
appointed to afflictions. Rebellion in us rises against God
who has appointed them. What a merciful help, gentle
rebuke, is a view of an obedient, submissive Lord Jesus,
offering up His own will when a suffering cup was put into
His hands! " The cup which My Father hath given Me,
shall I not drink it ? "

I have been very much engaged amongst my old friends.
Last night I was speaking at Wigston. This evening I
speak here (Lutterworth), and to-morrow evening I go to

Attleborough, and after the service to Leicester on a short
visit to Mr. Hazlerigg. I shall be not a little pleased to
return to my friends in the Lord's own time.

I have had a letter from our mutual friend, Mr. B. H.,
telling me of the Lord's mercy to his dear wife and himself.
May every needed good be upon that family.

. . . Yours in the Lord,

Lutterworth. 1894.   J. K. POPHAM.

XII.

To one under earthly disappointment.

My dear Friend and Sister,—. . . Your case is not often
out of my mind. I have wondered much about it and asked
many times, but I still wonder. The Lord has many different dispensations, but none without a reason and an *end*. If
this trying dispensation has not been opened to you, and has
not yet its end, I hope it will ere long. Some instruction
on some point is to be attained. This seems to be clear to
my mind. I don't want the matter to pass without mercy.
It would be a good finish if it ended in new hearing, but
would that convey instruction? It might; I hope it would.
I have felt—and still do—much more about it than has
been manifested. I hope I may hear if it has anything to
say to me; and that the Lord may open your ear to discipline in the matter. Thus a painful silence would be turned
to prosperity. In everything we need free mercy. The
psalmist's petition suits me well: "Cause me to know the
way wherein I should walk; for I lift up my soul unto Thee."
An answer to it would meet every case. It seemed made out
to me to-day that the way wherein I am to walk in all
paths, trials, and exercises, is by faith. But who can give
faith? The only life worth living, and the only walk which
truly honours God, is His own life, and the believing walk
in His own power. But here our very helplessness is so
made out to us that we must own our need of divine power—
the power of Christ's resurrection. After that power the
Lord makes us seek at times. By the seeking we learn
something of the sweetness there is in waiting for Him. He
sparkles in the eyes. His Person is alone excellent. God

was in Christ. His work is honourable and glorious; He magnified the law and made it honourable. And the blessed Spirit makes all this known; Jesus is the chiefest among ten thousand, and altogether lovely. I hope a measure of this mercy may be given you during your absence from us. In truth all else becomes as empty as a bubble to one who pants for the living God. Dissatisfaction is felt in all created good. "When shall I come and appear before God?" Oh, may the Spirit cause us to behold His righteousness, the robe which fits and makes meet for the marriage supper of the Lamb—the soul's last and highest aim. The Word says they are blessed who hunger for this righteousness, and, then filled, they are called to the endless feast. You will one day enter into the joy of your Lord, and no longer crave that love whose lack is so bitter to your affectionate nature. Even here when you taste that the Lord is gracious you can let all other loves go, and sing, "The lines are fallen unto me in pleasant places, yea, I have a goodly heritage." You possess a rich, an Almighty Friend, a good God, a Brother born for all your adversity. You possess, also, marks of your adoption into God's family, of your heirship with Jesus Christ, in being dealt with, chastened, reproved, brought down. I can perceive how full of affliction one of your best words is for you (II Cor. iv. 10, 11). You cannot bear about the dying of the Lord Jesus without dying in some respects yourself, and you cannot die without pain, at least the pain of a strong repugnance to the death involved in God's word *to* you and His work *in* you. "In due time we shall reap if we faint not." . . . The Lord bless you.

Yours affectionately in Him,

Brighton. 1898. J. K. POPHAM.

XIII.

My dear Friends,—It has been in my heart to write to you ever since I left home, but many things have hindered. I often feel to be under a very solemn dispensation, and that God's hand is heavy upon me; and though at times mercy has softened my heart and made my prospects good, I have many fears. It is sweet to hope all that heaven has good, but this hope is often in company with tribulation.

You and your dear husband know the path of heavy conflict, fear, darkness, distance, and temptation. It is a dangerous path. Despair and presumption line each side of it as so many deep and loathsome pits and snares of death. The everlasting safety of the saints is not seldom shut out from their view; while fears of missing that

> "Prize such numbers never seek,
> Such numbers seek in vain,"

fears of mistaking the narrow way and the strait gate, fears of procuring more stripes, of displeasing the Lord, fill the mind.

Thus moving forward is difficult, standing still impossible. Out of this perplexity there is but one way—the prayer of faith. And such a prayer is a pure gift of rich grace, goes up and enters the ear of the Lord in His holy temple through the blood of Christ. "Whatsoever ye shall ask the Father in My Name, He will give it you."

I hope that both you and Mr. L. may find your souls under the power of the Spirit giving you faith to struggle on in the difficult path, faith that has one aim above all else, —a manifestation of the Son of God, a purging away of guilt, and a receiving of the Spirit of adoption. This blessing carries so much with it. It fills the soul with peace, hope, confidence, humility, and godly sorrow.

In a measure, submission has been given and maintained in my heart during this heavy and sorrowful time. But I often fear no sweet 'afterwards' will fall to my lot; and also I think with sadness of the disappointment my friends may experience on my return, if I am as barren and unprofitable as ever. Pray for me if you can. . . . I hope you and your circle are well and that the favour of God may fill your hearts with life and peace.

I am well in health and my throat is much better. The specialist saw it last Wednesday and was very pleased with it.   With love to you both in the Lord, . . .

Chippenham. 1900.   J. K. POPHAM.

XIV.

My very dear Friend and Sister in the narrow and dangerous path of tribulation,—Your letter was a most welcome

surprise to me; but in thinking that this, my heavy affliction, has wrought so well in me, you have made a great
mistake. One of my present trials is the sad lack of
gracious effect, and this lack occasions much fear in respect
of my return to the pulpit, for I cannot avoid thinking of
the disappointment the godly, the well-exercised and discerning among the people will feel when they perceive that I
have gained little, if anything, by my painful trading.
Yes, and more: this comes upon my mind,—will the Lord
speak about me as He spoke of His vineyard by Isaiah in
the fifth chapter, verses 1 to 6? Or as Paul wrote to the
Hebrews, sixth chapter and eighth verse? Thus in leaving
my pulpit for a time, I had grievous sorrow, and now the
thought of returning to it fills me with painful apprehension.
Is this Satan's work to distract and take my mind away from
Him from whom my fruit is found, and in whom, of whom,
and by whom all my sufficiency for the ministry is? Who
but those who prove them can conceive the depths of Satan?
He sought to swallow me up when I was first laid aside;
now he tries to fill me with despondency on the ground of
my leanness.

O my dear friend, you will not be overcome; the Lord will
perfect that which concerneth you. I know your chief concern is to be right with God; but what struggles has the
devil had with your quickened soul! How earnestly and
long has he striven to rend you from God, to drive you to
despair, to distract you in prayer, to fill you with confusion,
and drown you in sorrow! But that word has taken effect
without even your knowing it, at times, "Hitherto shalt thou
go, and no further; and here shall thy proud waves be
stayed." It concerns you to come honourably through your
trials, and as that ever-blessed end can only be accomplished
by the power of God *in* you, He has promised in His Word
that "sin shall not have dominion over you, for ye are not
under the law, but under grace". How often have you
proved this! When you have said, "My foot slippeth," then
the Lord's mercy has held you up; then you have found
that *He* was in the place of trial, of sore affliction, though
you had not thought of it,—proved that in the seven-times-
heated furnace, the furnace which has burned up the flesh

and fleshly wisdom, but has not in the least injured faith,
hope, love. Your concern about *answers*, I understand.
" Continue in prayer, and watch in the same with thanksgiving," is a solemn word, and a much-needed one by such
poor, sleepy people.

When I heard of the special prayer-meeting of last week,
I felt unworthy, and humbled, and glad. *Now* I am much
wondering about the answer. I seem a little on my watch,
at times. O if only an answer of peace may be given, and
that I, an unworthy labourer, may be " restored the sooner ".
To-day I have been thinking of Hezekiah's case. But the
way to heaven lies through an enemy's country, and this
enemy refuses to allow us to pass. Deep and dangerous
because hidden, snares line the narrow and opposed way.
" Hold Thou me up, and I shall be safe." Only the omnipotent tender arms of our Lord and Saviour Jesus Christ can
bear us up; only the Lord, who walked through the dark
land Himself, can guide us safely past all the snares of
death. You have been guided, carried past many deadly
things; you will, in the same most merciful manner, get past
all that yet remain. But O the heaven that awaits you!
The Lord Jesus to receive and present you! The mansion
to house you safely, and for ever! O the visions of God
which are eternally to ravish and fill your ransomed, justified, and sanctified soul! Look up, dear and afflicted saint!
Your struggles are severe and prolonged; the end, the blissful end of them all, for ever and ever, is sure. What a
company you will join! What a song you will sing! What
a God you will know, love, serve, and glorify! I am sure
no other company, no other song, no other service, no other
end will satisfy you; and I am with you in spirit in this last
aim and end. O to be one day in Rev. vii. 9—17! . . .

Yours affectionately,

Chippenham. Nov., 1900.   J. K. Popham.

XV.

Dear Mrs. S.,—Thank you for writing me so full an
account of yourself. I like what you have written. The
Lord has wrought for and in you. It is a mercy to be the

subject of a clear work,—to have not only convictions, but pardon sealed on the conscience,—to not only be ruined but saved,—cut off as dead and reconciled in the body of Jesus through death. It is a solemn thing to be a sinner; we shall never know much of the infinite evil of sin; it is seen most as it broke the guiltless, tender, loving heart of the Saviour; and we hate it most when His bleeding love is felt in our hearts.

I am truly glad it has pleased the Lord ever to speak by me to you. He sends by whom He will send. Thus He gets all the honour. It is good to be taught and enabled to wait on Him and look for His promise, accounting Him faithful; to take shame to ourselves and honour Him in full confession of our sin and unworthiness. The painful lessons we are set we learn slowly, but mercifully the Lord is determined we *shall* learn them, and so does not spare the rod for our foolish crying. How His faithfulness is seen and valued! What an honour it is to be corrected and chastened! "If ye endure chastening God dealeth with you as with sons." This mercy you know. And no doubt when grace is in exercise you desire to walk according to His most gracious dealings with you. But how often corruptions may arise from the awful root of a depraved nature and blast every gracious godly desire! Thus there still is room for free mercy, fresh manifestations of love, pardon, and peace by the blood of the cross.

And now after so many mercies, you perhaps begin more to look to the end and meditate on the approaching day of your death. It is so with myself. O if we may but have the guidance, unction, life and power of the Spirit in us! With what tender caution we should then move in the path of peace, with lively hope for our cheerful companion. It is said of Abraham that "he looked for a city which hath foundations, whose builder and maker is God."

Often may we see the Builder and His glorious work!

With many thanks for your letter, and Christian love,

Yours sincerely,

August, 1905.   J. K. POPHAM.

XVI.

My dear M.,—. . . The Lord has been stronger than you and has prevailed. For this you will need eternity to praise Him. Your manifested, expressed enmity to Him I too well know. I felt the same before I was the age at which you felt it. But God, Who is rich in mercy for His great love wherewith He loved you, even when you were dead in sin, quickened you together with Christ. Your bitter experience with respect to your idol taught you how jealous God is. He will brook no rival. "Thou shalt have no other gods before Me," is a truth stamped—engraved—deeply in every heart in which He will dwell. How solemn and awful is that divine sovereignty which ruled, held, guided you, which permitted that "one act of folly" which shattered the idol but spared and mercifully dealt with the idolater! The Lord girded you even then, though you knew Him not. He allowed you to weary yourself in the fire, for vanity and death. It is by such means He teaches His people how madly bent on their own destruction they are, and what tribulation is necessary to separate them from the chaff of their folly. And under the workings of sin how they sink; the burden of guilt, the reflections on a mis-spent life, on the wickednesses done, the temptations to despair, the two-edged sword of some Scriptures piercing the soul, all make life hang in doubt, and well-nigh intolerable. Thus are sinners prepared for the coming of Christ to them, for the removal of their sins, the rebuking of the enemy, the pouring in of the oil of the gospel to heal all the wounds made by the sword. How wonderful to you was justification, the crown of God's lovingkindness and tender mercies! The day in which all this was done is a day much to be remembered by you. And if the way is opened for you to utter the memory of His goodness among us at Galeed it will be an additional joy to me, and I believe many would joy and rejoice with you for all the great mercy the Lord has showed you. . . .   Yours affectionately,

August, 1907.   J. K. POPHAM.

XVII.

Advice in a family trial.

My dear M.,—A. came up to see me and told me your present family sorrow, and in reply to a question on the point, said I was at liberty to write to you. But I am rather in the position of one struck dumb and only my love and sympathy for you make me endeavour to say a word.

The good Lord enable you to accept as from Him what can only be painfully bitter and sorrowful. I think my heart lays hold of your position, and my sympathy goes out intensely to you and all. But, M., you now need more of the power of Christ's resurrection than you may ever have dreamed of needing. Paul has a mighty word, amazingly bitter to the flesh: " And they that are Christ's have crucified the flesh with the affections and lusts " (Gal. v. 24). Now, whatever the "old man " may crave, the Spirit disallows. May power be given you to bow, bow between two burdens— the body of this death, and the burden of a providence too painful and distasteful to speak of.

In bowing down you will find rest. The cup which may not pass away except by drinking it, is not such as Christ drank up for you. Watch against hardness of heart against God for permitting, against a creature for occasioning such a trouble. While you argue against the *inexpediency* do not dispute the *right*. Think, too, that possibly the wisdom of God may be seen yet in what now may appear only unwisdom in man. God give you to believe in Rom. viii. 28. Beware of M. whom *you* love and seek the interest and peace of M. whom *God* loves. Hating your own life may now be harder than you ever expected.

Am I hard and untender, unsympathetic, in writing thus? I think not, according to my sense of things and my feeling for you. Only I desire good for you and victory of grace in you. Remember Him who endured the cross and despised all the shame for you; and so exhort the rest. To me it is sorrowful as if something has been done to me. Please do not think you must answer this. I would not give you the pain of an answer. But I want you to know how my heart is with you all. Yours affectionately,

Brighton. February, 1913. J. K. POPHAM.

XVIII.

To a new church member.

My dear Friend,—I am sorry to have left your letter so long unanswered; please excuse my apparent lack of pleasure at hearing from you. I do thank you for writing. You have great cause for thankfulness for " the tender mercy of our God " which, as the " dayspring from on high, hath visited you." May He often appear to you and join Himself to you whenever you walk with a sad heart. Such visits will make your heart burn within you and cause you to see Himself . again. Yes, even though you may have thought Him gone for ever, and felt of course all your hopes were buried. Oh, Christ is the only Person to be concerned to know! for if we know Him we know the Father also, and believe the Holy Ghost, They being in Him. In the little church of which you are a member, seek to walk humbly and tenderly. Avoid a party spirit. Seek the good of all your fellow-members. Consider Paul's words in Ephesians (iv. 16) respecting the Church and her union and completeness with and in Christ. " From whom the whole body fitly joined together and compacted by that which every joint supplieth, according to the effectual working in the measure of every part, maketh increase of the body unto the edifying of itself in love." The working of your faith upon Christ will make you a fruitful member and thus you will be ministering, invisibly, unconsciously, to the other living members. You have fallen on evil times. Wait on God for instruction in the nature of a gospel church, and above all aim at His glory in the church; for that is His ultimate in all His works, Eph. iii. 20, 21.

I trust you will see His glory in your family.

Yours in the gospel,

Brighton.   1914.   J. K. POPHAM.

XIX.

Fatherly Instruction to one recently entered the Ministry.

My beloved J.,—You will, I believe, be able to excuse my long silence and seeming forgetfulness. My life is a busy one, and often when an hour or two is at my disposal, I am so weary both physically and mentally, I have not enough energy to attempt anything. It is good for me that a willing mind is accepted of God. He is gracious. What a great gift is faith by which we hold fast to Him, even when we feel unable to do so. The language of a sigh is, "To whom shall we go?" It is a special favour to be weaned from, to hate self, though hard to flesh and blood. But we must die. "Ye are dead, and your life is hid with Christ in God." The path which the Father shewed to His Son, Jesus Christ, lay through death. And however we shrink from it, that is the path the same most gracious God will show to us. Paul went this way: "I am crucified with Christ; nevertheless I live; yet not I, but Christ liveth in me, and the life which I now live in the flesh, I live by the faith of the Son of God, who loved me and gave Himself for me" (Gal. ii. 20). Faith approves of this way, and when by occasions the soul gets a "good supply of the Spirit of Christ" and some bright inshining, some enlargement, then running the way of God's commandments is pleasant.

In your present life you need much grace, but not more than a *full* Christ can give, not more than a *willing* Christ will give, not more than an *ever-present* Christ does give; present, if not always perceived. "Lo, I am with you alway, even unto the end of the world." He will be with you in a double sense. For your own salvation, sanctification, enlargement in knowledge, in experience of justification, of His own most mysterious, wonderful, glorious Person, and of His Word. Then for the great and solemn work to which He has ordained and called you. You will find in this work the truth of Luther's words,—"Temptation, meditation, and prayer make a minister." O it is heavy! Yet it is blessed beyond all words. You may often be in bondage, but will prove that "the Word of God is not bound". You will grow in a trying sense of insufficiency, but that will be to make room for a sweet experience that your sufficiency is of God. You may sometimes think you were almost a lunatic to have ever entertained a single thought of being a minister of the gospel, then you will have a discovery of the glory of God in choosing the foolish, the weak, the base things, "yea, and things which are not, to bring to nought things that are" (I Cor. i. 27, 28).

W

May you be made more anxious to preach the gospel than
to preach sermons. May a single eye be given you, that your
whole body may be full of light (Matt. vi. 22). There is no
occupation so honourable as that of the ministry. There is
no height so giddy, so precipitous, as the pulpit. "Study to
shew thyself *approved unto God*, a workman that needeth
not to be ashamed, rightly dividing the Word of truth"
(II Tim. ii. 15). This is an arduous matter, very difficult.
Aim at testimonies from God in your own soul. If you live
on anything short you will die. Preach Christ; warn every
man, that you may present every man perfect in Christ Jesus.
So to preach, you will have to shew the state of men *out* of
Christ, and contend for a *revelation* of Christ; and this will
arouse the enmity of mere professors. But in all your godly
labour you will have profit; profit in these things: The smile
of God in your conscience, souls for your hire, seals to your
ministry. O rich man!

You are not forgotten at dear Galeed, nor in secret, nor by
Your affectionate pastor,

May, 1918.   J. K. POPHAM.

XX.

Concerning a Call to the Ministry.

My dear Friend,—. . . The subject-matter of your letter
is of vast importance and in the lack of knowledge of your
exercises, and of whether or not you have received any call
from the Holy Ghost, and *inward* leading preceding the
circumstances you relate, I do not feel in a position to offer
an opinion. But though I cannot offer an opinion—and if
I could it likely enough would be of no importance—I may
express my wishes for you.

i. I wish that the awful weight and importance of the
ministry may be ever more and more pressing on your heart.
To speak in the ineffable Name of God, to attempt to
express the sublime mysteries of the gospel; of the Person of
Christ; of the origin, reasons and ends of His Priesthood; of
His Priestly action in His whole course and on the cross;
to set forth the Covenants—law and grace—their several
works in the conscience; to speak the thing that is right of

God the Father, His relation to His Son, His election of His Son and the ends of that, His receiving of His poor people and making them His children, and *how* He effects the mighty change in them, and walks among them; to preach the Holy Ghost, His divine Person, His essential names, His work in and on Christ,—this is the most vital and important part of the work of the ministry, and calls for much unction of the Holy One and reading, and studying to show oneself a workman that needeth not to be ashamed, rightly dividing the word of truth. After that comes the insistence on the invincible work of grace in the elect. And for this what experience is needed and what sanity, sobriety, strictness, discrimination between natural and revealed religion, what life, light, and power from the Spirit, what understanding in the love of God, the liberty of the gospel, the purging of the conscience by the blood of Christ, and the sanctification of the Spirit! Then the opening of the *nature* and *ends* of the precepts, admonitions, and warnings of the gospel will have a proper place and proportion in a true ministry. I wish you may have wisdom to so preach.

ii. I wish your eye may be on God, His glory first of all. Isaiah was commanded to say, " All flesh is grass," etc., and that all should see the glory of the Lord. May flesh never have more importance in your ministerial eyes than the importance God gives it. Ministers must give an account to God of their ministry.

iii. I wish you may ever be clothed with humility. Painfully some know that God resisteth the proud. Also beware of the mean and vain spirit of jealousy. Perhaps no men are more liable to it than ministers, and certainly no men have less reason for it.

iv. I wish you, if called to preach, much success in the work. Souls for your hire and seals to your ministry will be a high honour. This honour comes from God; ministers plant and water, but God gives the increase.

v. I wish you may finish your course as a child of God, and as a minister, with joy.

These are some of my wishes for you. God be pleased to hear prayer for you. I am old in the solemn work, and am

now looking forward to my end.   Oh that I may reach it
honourably!   Believe me,
                        Yours in the gospel,
July, 1919.   J. K. POPHAM.

XXI.

To one newly settled in a pastorate.

Dear Mr. C.,—. . . I am not surprised at your perturba-
tion, but the word on which you are going portends disturbing circumstances. You will need to be fenced with iron.
One thing I fear for you,—the unwise adulation of some.
Too well do I know the usual result. But the Lord will
not leave you without means of help. A tender jealous
regard for His glory in the church, a labour among and for
the people in word and good doctrine, firm impartiality, a
jealousy over your own spirit, and a keeping your heart with
all diligence, will be amongst your greatest mercies. " I love
them that love Me " is a great word, and John xiv. 21—23.
" Who is sufficient for these things ? "
    The Lord looks on empty places, and weak things, and
finds in them room for Himself. But being *nothing* is harder
than being *something*.   With every good wish,
                        Yours affectionately,
April, 1927.   J. K. POPHAM.

XXII.

*To one who wavered concerning the Eternal Sonship of
    Christ.*

Dear Mr. B.,—. . . For myself I am deeply grieved about
the matter, and it has given me many errands to the throne
of grace. For it touches the glory of Christ in His relationship in the Godhead, and, by reflection, the Church of God.
Everything relating to Christ is of immense importance,
especially His Person. . . . In regard to the doctrine of the
adorable Trinity, the greatest attainment in this mystery is
to believe that God IS: " For there are Three that bear
record in heaven, the Father, the Word, and the Holy Ghost:
and these Three are One." Their separate subsistence is as
great a mystery as their Oneness. All disputes about Christ

have had their origin in attempts to *understand* Him. I noticed that in your letter you deprecated any attempt to understand His Sonship, yet you fell into the error of denying Eternal Generation on the ground of reasoning. Naturally, of course, a son is posterior to his father; therefore, thus starting, the next step was easy.

May I draw your attention to two facts? (1) The Scripture says that Jesus Christ is the Son of God. In what sense He is the Son of God has been disputed ever since His sojourn in this errant world. If guided by holy inerrant Scripture, we believe Him to be the Son of the Father in His Divine Person, the only-begotten (*monogenes*) Son, that is to say, the Eternal Son. Being a son, generation is an essential fact therein. If it took place in time, the Son *began* TO BE, and Arius was right; but if filiation was eternal, generation is eternal. "The only-begotten Son" is not a humanly-invented term, it is the Word of the Holy Ghost.

Whether *generation* is used or *sonship*, each has the same meaning, each essentiates the other. Neither philologically nor theologically, can the two terms be divided. Thus, to to believe the one is to hold the other; to deny the one is to reject the other. I observed that you deprecated the use of terms other than those of Scripture in speaking of the mystery of Christ's Sonship. Of course, this will not hold water, for when you say you believe in the Eternal Sonship of Christ, you use a term not to be found in the Bible; you express the profound truth, but in a humanly-devised term.

Here I would draw your attention to a second point. (2) Historical Christianity proves that subtle error made the coining of terms necessary, and we ought to be thankful that God raised up men to meet and combat and overthrow the heresies which arose in the early days of the life of the Church. We are deeply indebted to Him for Athanasius and many others. On so deeply interesting a subject as Historical Christianity I need not enter further, for we have full information in *Systematic Theology*, Hodge; *Historical Theology*, Cunningham; *Church History*, Milner. These authors show that the Holy Ghost powerfully enabled the

noble confessors of Christ to coin such terms as we have in
Athanasius and others.

Thus the Spirit of Christ gave to them, and through them
to us, the suitable terms " Eternal Sonship " and " Eternal
Generation " to set forth the sublime, heavenly doctrine of
Christ's relationship in the Godhead. Here I will give you
what I think is one of the most wonderful, true definitions
of the awful, blessed mystery under consideration: " Of all
the effects of the Divine excellencies, the constitution of the
Person of Christ as the foundation of the new creation, as
' the mystery of godliness ', was the most ineffable and
glorious. I speak not of the Divine Person absolutely, for
His distinct Personality and subsistence was by an internal
and eternal act of the Divine Being in the Person of the
Father, or eternal generation—which is essential to the Divine
Essence—whereby nothing anew was outwardly wrought or did
exist. He was not, He is not, *in that sense,* the effect of the
Divine wisdom and power of God, but the essential Wisdom
and Power of God Himself " (Owen, Vol. I., page 45). How
my soul has adored the Eternal Three! Christ is the Eternal
Son of God by Eternal Generation. While I live, the
memory of the revelation given to me, after long conflict
about the matter, in and by John i. 18, will be sweet, and
when I have read *Church History,* Gill, Philpot and others
on the subject, Eternal Generation has been beautiful, profound, glorious to me, and I have worshipped Him who is
thus the Son of God. It is the truth, which was as I hope
and believe, thus made known to me, which moves me to
contend for it, and my hope is that I may through the
mediation of Christ and the grace and Spirit of Christ, be
kept firm unto the end. If by the same mediation and grace
of the Spirit you are led to seek the Lord in this matter, my
hope is that you will perceive that you have, by a subtle,
unwarrantable distinction, put asunder what is essentially,
eternally one. The Lord alone, at whose merciful hand I
have sought this blessing for you, knows the joy it will be to
me to hear that the light of truth, in this vital particular,
has shined into your heart and understanding.

May I exhort you to leave reasoning about the subject ?
I know you deprecated it in your letter, yet you fell into the

error, denying what you could not understand. No man, no angel, will ever see into the Being of God. He, in Christ, is believed on in the world. Oh, to be under the most heavenly teaching Bunyan describes in his Pilgrim: "And first they shewed him the records of the greatest antiquity in which, as I remember in my dream, they shewed him the pedigree of the Lord of the Hill, that He was the Son of the Ancient of Days, and came by an Eternal Generation." Would that I might each day get a sight of Him in that particular, and in all other particulars which, equally with that, are necessary to salvation. How it would cause me to love Him!

With every good wish,

Believe me, yours sincerely,

Brighton. 1929. J. K. POPHAM.

XXIII.

My dear kind, too kind, Mr. and Mrs. W.,—. . . I was painfully straitened last evening, and sorry you had a lost journey. I am indeed unworthy to open my mouth in the name of the Lord. It is a wonder of condescension that I am allowed to stand among the saints. But O how far from us is the Prince of life! He is kind enough to show me my sins, whispering them in my ear; and they explain to me my barrenness in His service. This morning I am pained that I am so carnal, sold under sin, and that I injure His people who go to hear good news and find a straitened sinner stammering not half the truth, and scarcely mentioning the glory of Christ. O cleave to Owen and other Puritans! they preach the gospel, they open the unsearchable riches of Christ. We to-day scarcely bring Him into the pulpit. My naming Him is too, too feeble; who can see Him by my preaching? O that I could get such a sight of Him as would enlarge my heart and open my mouth! I know He is infinitely above the highest praise of men, but a minister of the gospel should speak worthily, however inadequately, of Him.

Your matters in the church are with me. Would that the King of glory would magnify Himself in your midst!

Mrs. Popham unites with me in most hearty thanks to you, and love. Your affectionate friend,

July, 1929. J. K. POPHAM.

XXIV.

My dear Mrs. W.,—It was good to read that you had been enabled to submit to the will of God in your deep sorrow, and had received some help in hearing. The Lord honours the faith He gives, and is good to the soul that waits on Him. He weighs the path of the just, not according to the believer's apprehension of his own weakness, but according to His own riches in glory by Christ Jesus. According to this tune you must say, " What hath God wrought ? "

I am writing a word with respect to your attendance at your church meeting to-morrow evening. The higher, that is, the nearer to the Scripture your view of the Church of God is, the more fervent will be your desire that the part of it of which you are a member may answer to the Word of God. . . . May the Spirit set and keep your eyes on two of His purposes in having visible churches in the world: i. *The mutual edification of the members.* Christ is the Head, " from whom the whole body fitly joined together and compacted by that which every joint supplieth, according to the effectual working in the measure of every part, maketh increase of the body unto the edifying of itself in love." Be it your endeavour to supply something to your fellow-members, that they may be partakers of your grace. ii. *The glory of God*, the most ultimate end of His good pleasure in this world and in the world of glory to come. May His glory be your aim. But a great pain will attend the above, Phil. ii. 21. Still, " Pray for the peace of Jerusalem: they shall prosper that love thee." *They* shall prosper even if Jerusalem goes into captivity. . . .

Yours sincerely,

January, 1929. J. K. POPHAM.

XXV.

My dear Friend,—Forgive me for not answering your letter earlier. The truth is it got under a pile of papers and I forgot it. One point in your letter I want to notice.

When I said that Miss M. had got the best, it was not in my intention to excuse her faults. I really only meant that she was favoured more than some who had spoken against her. That, so far, is the end of the case which has caused some of the friends real trouble. You wonder, apart from the above case, " which get the best, those who fall into sin and backsliding, and get a powerful sense of forgiveness, or those who walk in the tender fear of God, and whose cry often is, ' O give me, Lord, the tender heart that trembles at the approach of sin,' also, ' Let not any iniquity have dominion over me.' " While the former may occasionally receive clearer views and deeper sense of the aboundings of sovereign grace than the latter, yet it seems to me that being kept from wilful, persistent backsliding is the better of the two. I do not, alas, speak thus out of the merciful experience of it, but it is my judgment. And I think the Scripture shows it, I Peter iv. 3. While the sins and irregularities of the Corinthian church made way for extraordinary outflowings of grace, the gracious consistency of the Colossian church was the more commendable, ch. i. 4; ii. 5.

I thank God for you as a member of the church, and wish I could say the same of all. May the Lord keep you firm unto the end. A sense of weakness is good, a feeling of our dreadfully sinful nature is wholesome. How needful is the keeping grace of Christ! God bless you.

Your affectionate pastor,

August, 1930.   J. K. POPHAM.

XXVI.

To a Young Minister.

Dear Mr. H.,—Reflection on the question of your being able to refer questions of theology to a theologian has made me feel disposed to write to you on the subject, and perhaps also branch out to another matter.

I believe you desire to be right with God and that you would fain be a good minister of Jesus Christ. Now it strikes me that discussing the nice point which you named to me, is neither for your edification nor likely to convince the people with whom you contend. It would be better, in my opinion, to leave the technicality of the doctrines of grace or justification as being the starting point of difference between the church of Rome and the Reformation, and go at once to the matter of faith as set out in Eph. ii. 8. Is faith the gift of God? Has He given you (your opponents) that precious gift? Press that. If you still think you ought to be equipped you will find all you need in Cunningham's *Historical Theology*, his *Theology of the Reformation*, and Hodge's *Systematic Theology*. *But you will do better spending your time on your knees and with your Bible.* Seek to grow in grace and in the knowledge of our Lord and Saviour Jesus Christ, and the anointing which alone can make you useful to sinners of mankind. Your soul thus will be as a watered garden and your preaching full of authority.

This brings me to the branching out into another matter. I judge you are connected with various bodies by being on committees. I have had a little experience of this kind of thing; and knowing painfully the effect on my soul, I beg of you to withdraw from them all. Let your profession and the pulpit fill your time, heart, thought, reading and prayer. "The fruit of the righteous is a tree of life, and he that winneth souls is wise,"—not he that winneth a theological argument. The power of the Spirit is needed to give wise words, I Cor. i. 19—28; ii. 1, 2.

Please excuse the liberty I have taken in writing thus freely. You have been kind enough to call and I appreciate it; the result is this letter. With all good wishes,

Believe me,

Yours in the truth,

April, 1931.   J. K. POPHAM.

XXVII.

Dear Friend,—The [question] "If the affliction be part of His covenant of grace," can be sweetly answered by the Surety of that covenant. The way of the just is uprightness: "Thou, most upright, dost weigh the path of the just." Yet His own path is in the sea, in the mighty waters, His footsteps are not known. He will be trusted. He is *infinitely* worthy of trust. He, however, draws with cords of a man, with bands of love. As the Spirit of Christ is *in* you and shows you more and more your own sin and sins, the more you will be prepared for the manifestation of Christ He is sent to give you. Then you will increasingly feel the need of clear work and separation from the flesh, of denying *self*, of taking up the cross laid on you, of *enduring* chastening, which is neither despising nor fainting under it. Also you will see the love which is in the strokes of jealousy. How I have thanked the Lord for His jealousy, wondering that He could be jealous with regard to such a worm!

When next you come to B. be sure to come to 10, that I may be filled with your company.

Our warmest wishes for you both.

Yours in the truth,

June, 1932. J. K. POPHAM.

XXVIII.

To a Minister.

My dear Friend,—. . . We all much need God in Christ, and the Holy Ghost, in order that we may be reconciled to God from time to time, and *feel* the power of the gift of repentance toward God and faith toward our Lord Jesus Christ. What a religion! How honouring to the divine Giver, how humbling and sanctifying to the sinner! Your feeling of sorrow over poor preaching is not only yours. After a poor attempt last Lord's Day to express a little—to look an inch, so to put it, into Eph. iii. 8, I felt a grief and shame at my failure. In the vestry after the evening service one of the deacons said to me, "You can't say you have not preached a good sermon." My reply was honest,—"I can say I have preached a poor sermon, but not a poor gospel." Then Owen's word came to me: "Though I cannot preach a good sermon I can preach a good gospel;" and I was comforted. Go on, my friend, soak every sermon in good doctrine and gracious experience. As enabled, tread heavily on the monster, self, in the pulpit; and lift the Lord of glory as high as your faith can. . . .

Thank you for the cutting of ——. The editor has never, in my judgment, manifested a clear knowledge of the truth. He appears to be on the down-grade, and who can stop him ? Only God. Never expect justice where Arminianism has the sway; no, not overmuch courtesy. I think you will have to separate yourself from some with whom and for whom you have laboured. The Lord help you. On the Lord's side you must bear His reproach. But O the favour, the mercy, the honour! "Choosing rather to suffer affliction with the people of God," is a great word. Great grace is needed for such a choice, and great will be the reward. But though shame is not pleasant, yet the Holy Ghost can enable you to bind it on you as an ornament and rejoice that you are counted worthy not only to believe in His Name, but also to suffer for His sake.

It would be a wonder of grace and sovereignty if the glory of God should ever again shine on " that moribund place " at——. I should be very sorry to form an opinion of Mr. —— by any movement he makes, but I would rather stand in your place in the adverse opinion of some there, than in the favourable opinion of others.

I am returning the verses; the only criticism I venture to make is on the line, " We'll meet our loved ones face to face." It seems an assumption of the state of the redeemed in heaven. I prefer I John iii. 2. To assume mutual recognition of relatives, as such, has always appeared to lack Scriptural warrant. . . .

Your visits are always appreciated. Please renew them whenever you can. If I were more spiritual you would possibly profit. A life-long fear that I should hurt the Lord's people by my intercourse with them has sent me to the throne of grace at times. Painfully do I confess that " I am carnal, sold under sin ". Also I realize that the Lord is not with the churches now as formerly. Life divine being low in us, for the most part, there is little ministering grace to each other, little receiving of grace and truth from Christ, and therefore a lack of *experience* of Eph. iv. 16. My own confession is, " My leanness, my leanness." What then can a neighbour joint receive from me ?

God bless you and help you to pray for me.

I repeat your kind words, " With love from both to both."

Yours affectionately in the truth,

Brighton. 1933.   J. K. POPHAM.

XXIX.

Dear Mr. S.,—. . . Your trouble about yourself is no strange sound or experience to me. The power of indwelling sin and the little restraining grace, except as to outward falling, is a sore trial to me. And when evidences are darkened and one sees not one's signs—the enemy having "broken down the carved work with axes and hammers"— it is difficult to hold fast. Faith is needed to keep the narrow way, and few companions are found. In this evil and dark day it appears to be especially the case. You may reap with joy from this sowing in tears. Christ is the more needed as we grow worse and weaker, and as faith is given a sight of Him He is the more precious, and in the midst of many tossings faith is enabled to say, "My heart is fixed, O God, my heart is fixed; I will sing and give praise." A minister's trials are used for the instruction, the strengthening, the faith of his hearers, the establishment of them, and the glory of God.

If the minister is more and more searched, he searches more deeply his people, shakes them off all natural religion, and lays the foundation for them, as the Spirit has laid it in the Scripture. The professor rebels; the honest child of God may often wince, but he cleaves to the searching, the digging, the pulling down and plucking up; and when the building and planting and exaltation of Christ come, then the minister and hearers rejoice together. I hope you may find this at M.

Much bitterness is one result of the meeting; a clearer separation may be another, but not yet I fear. We are too mixed. Only the Spirit can separate the chaff from the wheat. I am receiving abusive letters, anonymous. These do not trouble me. It is *my own case*. How I need the Lord to come and clear my soul! The committee is accused of evil. Blindness is the evil state of the accusers; they do not see the real weakness and faults of the people they hate. The men of Sodom could not find the door of Lot's house. The Lord be with you.

Yours in the truth,

Brighton. Sept., 1934. J. K. POPHAM.

XXX.

Encouraging Counsel for a Minister.

My very dear J.,—Please think no more of the incident. If one I esteemed less than yourself had been in your place it would not have touched me. I think God has in a small measure enabled me to be content with Himself—this does not make you less in my heart. Your griefs I share as far as possible. You cannot possibly speak according to Holy Scripture without giving offence. The bitter experience is not unknown to others. You have been helped, supported, comforted. The silence, probably studied, of erstwhile friends, and innuendo, one is too well acquainted with. In all it is but the path of tribulation. Being a target for malicious arrows of such as delight to wound was my experience, and I can and do sympathise. The heavenly direction I got may be given to you: " Answer him not a word." " God is a very present help in trouble," and though all the earth (to be destroyed) rise up, boil, rage, tumult, and threaten destruction, it will not prevail. Christ who conquered for you once will *in* you conquer too. I doubt not all will turn for the furtherance of the gospel in and by you. The Lord never sent forth a labourer and the enemy of Christ remained quiet. Ministers to-day must follow the apostles in some measure. A man's enemies will be of his own house. Jeremiah's own relations were against him and sought his hurt. Lift up thy head, endure hardness as a good soldier of Jesus Christ. Being about Solomon's bed you must hold a sword. Christ's dear friends must defend His honour regardless of consequences. A complete armour is provided. Let thy courage wax the bolder as your foes increase. If you were on the side of the easy worldly professor you would win his applause. Your Divine Master said, " My kingdom is not of this world." Therefore the world, even though it put on the garb of religion, must hate you. It hated the Lord before it hated His disciples. Heb. xii. speaks of war in which we have not yet resisted unto blood striving against sin, either in self or in others. Gird on, dear soldier of Jesus Christ, your divinely-provided armour, patch up no inglorious peace. Better that men, yea, professors, should say,

Away with such a fellow, than declare he is a good compromiser.

The people opposed and hated Jeremiah, but he must go on declaring God's purpose. That appears to be our proper course. All results have to be left with Jehovah. May we observe the stern but encouraging word of God to Jeremiah (i. 17). . . .

The Lord has not run all our minds into one mould. Peter and John and Paul were men of God, and chosen instruments, but they naturally differed much. In regard to ——, in my view he is sound in heart and in judgment. It has cost him much to stand (his name is anathema with the " ——ites "). He has not been pulled to pieces as some, but has been much blessed to some; stand by him, although you could not walk with him in some things. . . .

Brighton. 1935.   J. K. POPHAM.

XXXI.

Dear Mr. G.,—Thank you for your letter. The path of tribulation needs and has shoes of iron and brass; you have been favoured to receive and wear them. But it is a path in which there is much fear, trembling at the Word of God, and crying for mercy, teaching, forgiveness and love.

Hart's word which you quote is a very precious one to me:

> " Rare virtues now these herbs contain,
> The Saviour sucked out all their bane;
> My mouth with them if conscience cram,
> I'll eat with them the Paschal Lamb."

It is a blessed hope that the Lord of life sucked out all the *curse* of affliction and conviction of sin, so that they are turned into a wholesome food to be eaten with the Bread of Life.

I well remember preaching at Zion, Trowbridge, from Ps. lxxii. 17. It was a special time to one at least. The blessing is needed continually. Yesterday's manna would not keep for to-day's meal. Special blessings are in most cases rare, but daily nourishment is necessary for health and strength. The good Lord be with you.

Yours in the truth,

June, 1935.   J. K. POPHAM.

XXXII.

My dear ——, . . . Even my desolation does not, cannot move me to pray. Weak and poor and sinful, my heart is broken, and occasionally the empty house is all but unbearable; but now and again I am enabled to thank God for taking my dear wife to Himself, and submit to His righteous and good will. I never was poorer nor more unfit for the pulpit than now. A real feeling of the poverty of my preachments—vapouring—makes me blush at times. I said this morning, "Lord, make me a Christian." Col. iii. 16 wounded me and yet filled me with a desire to obey. I am increasingly poor in all that pertains to the gospel. In D.'s case the Lord honoured me by speaking the quickening word in him, and what He has done will stand. Cannot the Master choose and use instruments as and when He will? It has deeply humbled and instructed me. Surely in using me He exemplifies I Cor. i. 27, 28. To stain the pride of all human glory He hath chosen the foolish things of the world to confound the wise . . . the things which are not, to bring to nought things that are. It is astonishing to me that the Most High God should humble Himself to behold such a sinner and make a little use of me in His Church.

Concerning the conclusion of Dr. A.'s sermon, it is but a little stronger way of expounding the "free offer" of most Scotch ministers and the Puritans. B— "offered" the gospel and asked his hearers why they did not come and accept. Rutherford's letters will furnish you with many examples of the same thing in substance. It is contrary to Scripture and sounds very ill coming from one who has the free grace and distinguishing love of God in his heart, and the *principle* of sovereign grace in his judgment, and the covenant ordered in all things and sure. . . .

Yours affectionately,

1935.   J. K. POPHAM.